DEMON FROM AFAR 4

KAORI YUKI

Translation: Camellia Nieh † Lettering: Lys Blakeslee

This book is a work of fiction. Names, characters, places, and incidents are the product of the author's imagination or are used fictitiously. Any resemblance to actual events, locales, or persons, living or dead, is coincidental.

IIKI NO KI
© 2012 Kaori Yuki. All rights reserved.
First published in Japan in 2012 by Kodansha Ltd., Tokyo. Publication rights for this English language edition arranged through Kodansha Ltd., Tokyo.

Translation © 2015 by Hachette Book Group, Inc.

All rights reserved. In accordance with the U.S. Copyright Act of 1976, the scanning, uploading, and electronic sharing of any part of this book without the permission of the publisher is unlawful piracy and theft of the author's intellectual property. If you would like to use material from the book (other than for review purposes), prior written permission must be obtained by contacting the publisher at permissions@hbgusa.com. Thank you for your support of the author's rights.

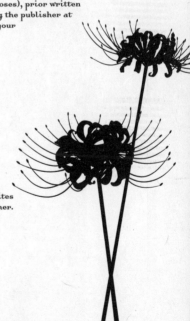

Yen Press
Hachette Book Group
1290 Avenue of the Americas
New York, NY 10104

www.HachetteBookGroup.com
www.YenPress.com

Yen Press is an imprint of Hachette Book Group, Inc. The Yen Press name and logo are trademarks of Hachette Book Group, Inc.

The publisher is not responsible for websites (or their content) not owned by the publisher.

First Yen Press Edition: September 2015

ISBN: 978-0-316-34576-7

10 9 8 7 6 5 4 3 2 1

BVG

Printed in the United States of America

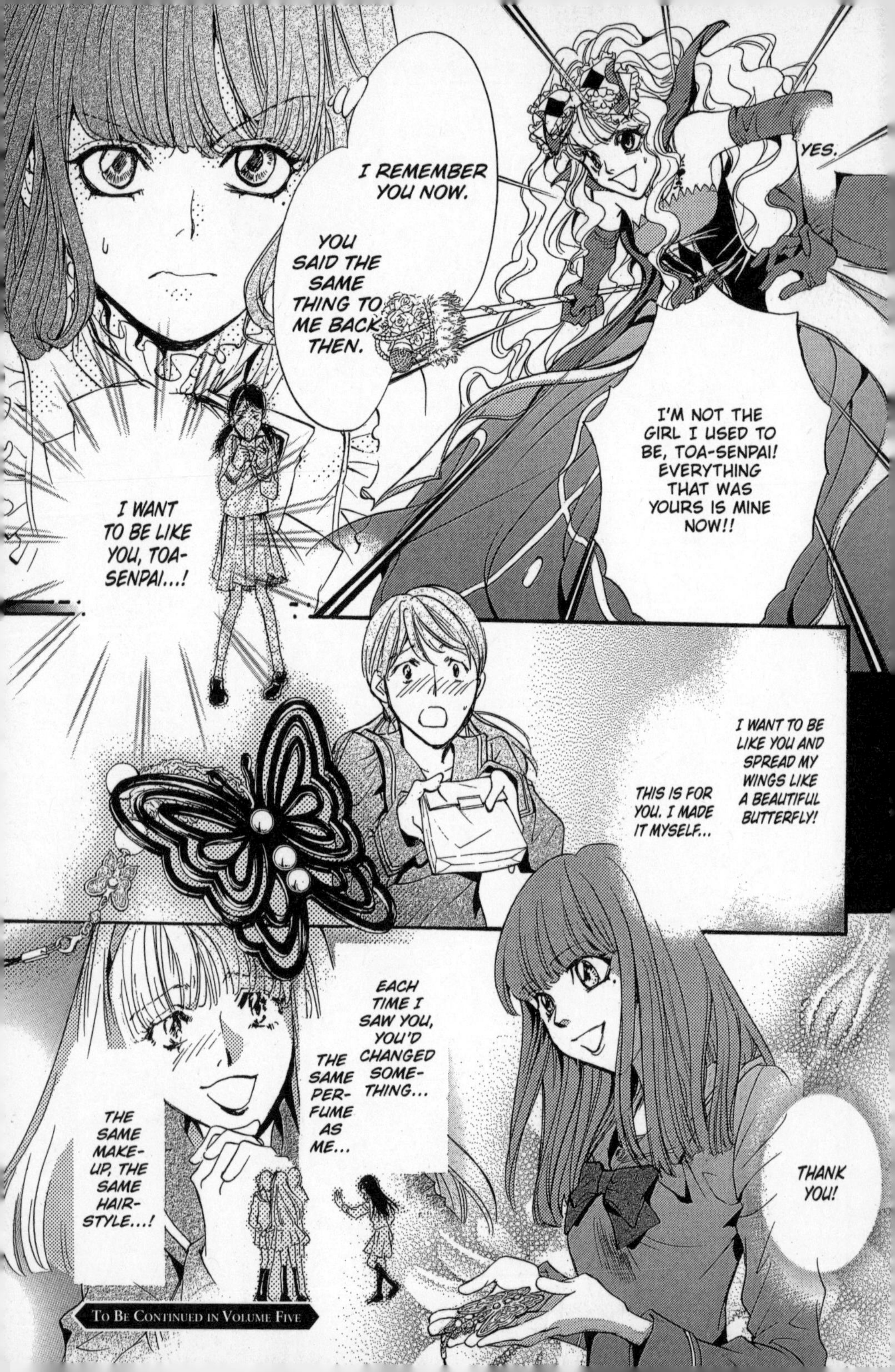
YES.
I REMEMBER YOU NOW.
YOU SAID THE SAME THING TO ME BACK THEN.
I'M NOT THE GIRL I USED TO BE, TOA-SENPAI! EVERYTHING THAT WAS YOURS IS MINE NOW!!
I WANT TO BE LIKE YOU, TOA-SENPAI...!
I WANT TO BE LIKE YOU AND SPREAD MY WINGS LIKE A BEAUTIFUL BUTTERFLY!
THIS IS FOR YOU. I MADE IT MYSELF...
THANK YOU!
EACH TIME I SAW YOU, YOU'D CHANGED SOME-THING...
THE SAME PER-FUME AS ME...
THE SAME MAKE-UP, THE SAME HAIR-STYLE...!
To Be Continued in Volume Five

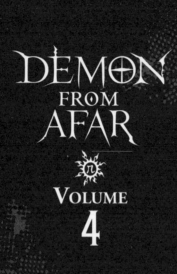

DEMON
FROM
AFAR

VOLUME
4

KAORI YUKI

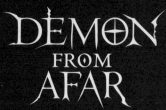

DEMON FROM AFAR

Characters and Story

Imperial Capital Arc

In an era of splendor and romanticism, Sorath, bearer of a mysterious symbol on the palm of his hand, loses three of his closest friends—Garan, Kiyora, and Noella—on Walpurgis Night at Baron Kamichika's estate. Sorath seeks revenge on the Baron, the instigator of the entire disaster, with the help of his servant, Leice.

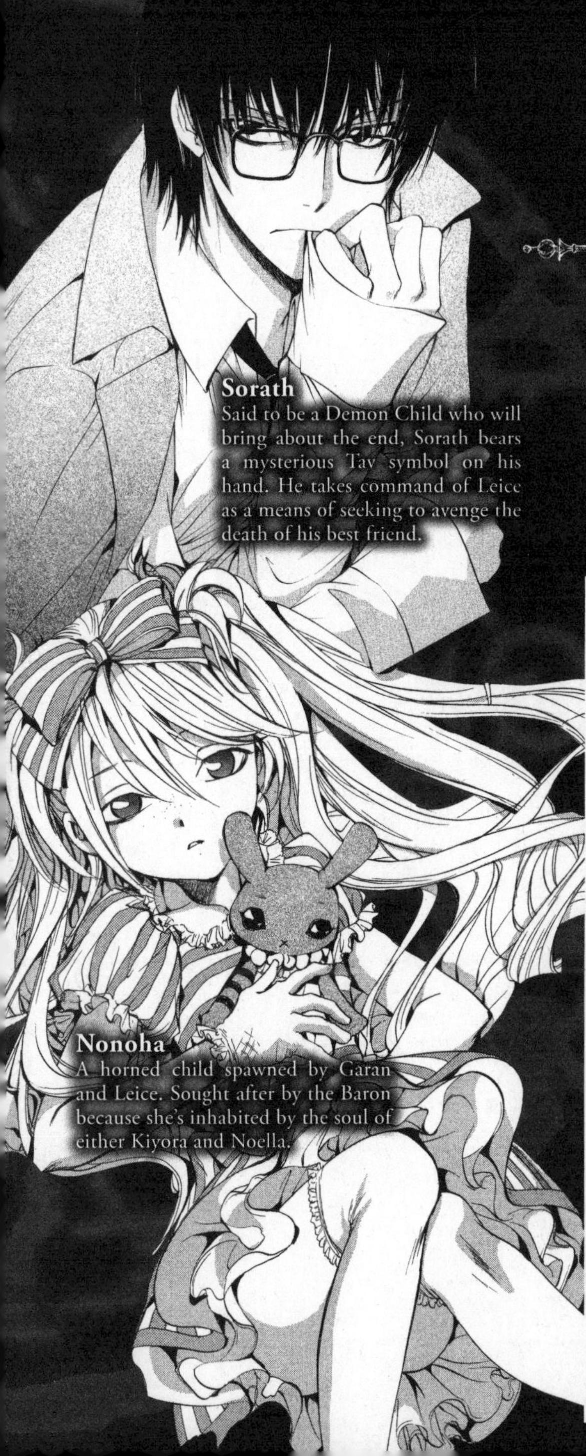

Sorath
Said to be a Demon Child who will bring about the end, Sorath bears a mysterious Tav symbol on his hand. He takes command of Leice as a means of seeking to avenge the death of his best friend.

Nonoha
A horned child spawned by Garan and Leice. Sought after by the Baron because she's inhabited by the soul of either Kiyora and Noella.

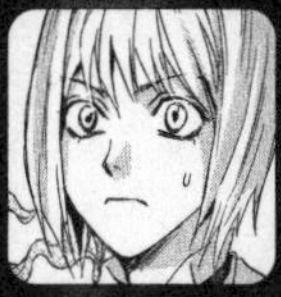

Garan
Baron Kamichika's son and Sorath's best friend; died on the night of the ceremony.

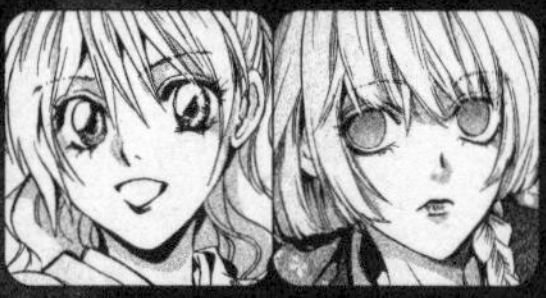

Kiyora/Noella
Mikos who lead the ceremony. Two Yin and Yang souls that inhabited the same body. Whereabouts currently unknown.

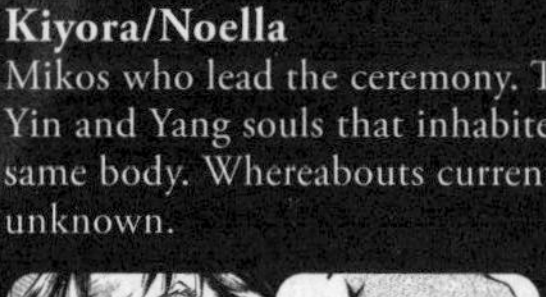

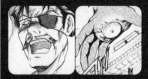

Baron Kamichika/ Lord of Great Terror
Root of everything; mastermind of Walpurgis Night.

Modern Day Arc

Pursued by the Baron's minions, Sorath flees through time to the present day with Nonoha, daughter of the deceased Garan. But even then, the Baron's demon servants continue to attack. In the center of the melee looms the shadow of Etsurou, CEO of a popular Web TV company...

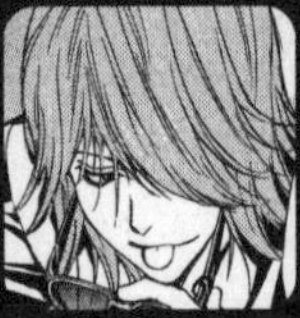

Etsurou
CEO of a popular Web TV company; seems somehow connected to the Baron...!?

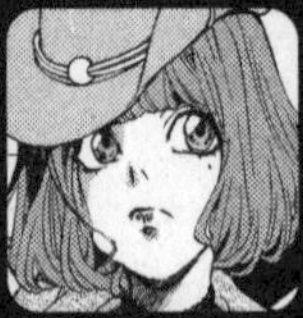

Toa Nakanohi
Popular Web TV star, feels destined to be with Etsurou.

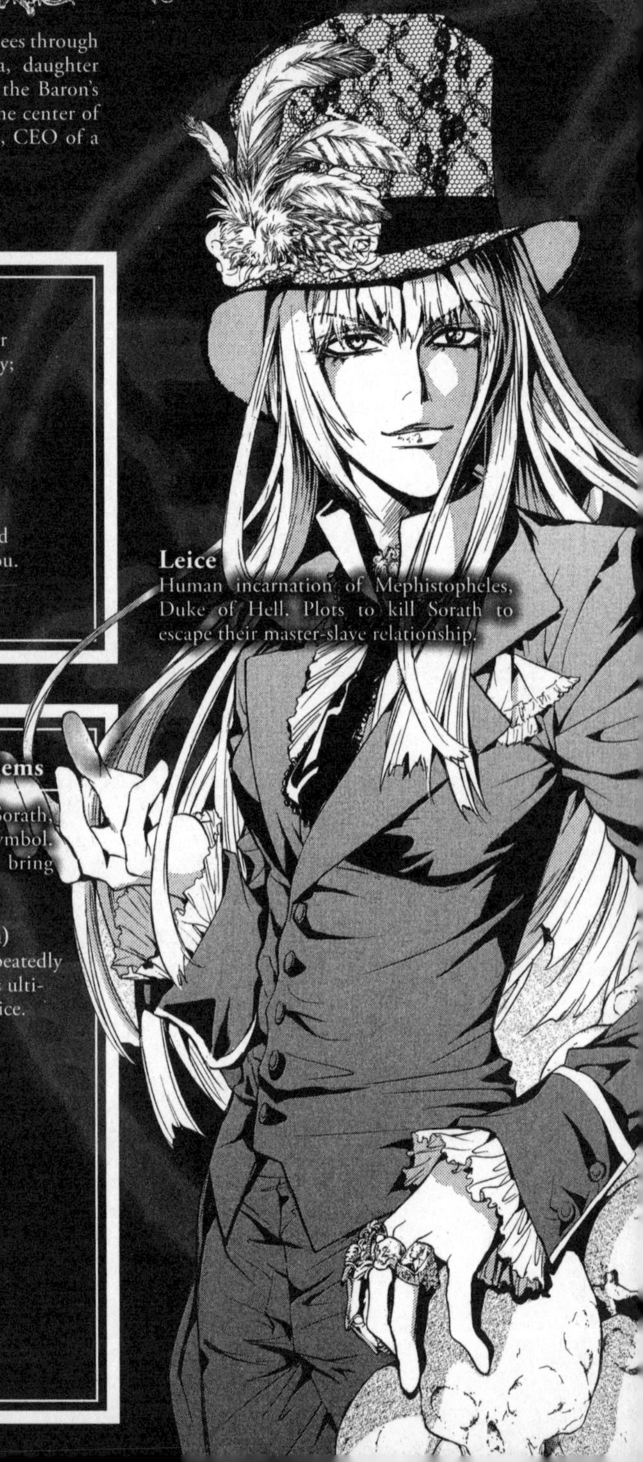

Leice
Human incarnation of Mephistopheles, Duke of Hell. Plots to kill Sorath to escape their master-slave relationship.

Characters with hand emblems

Entities who have separated from Sorath, their master who bears the Tav symbol. They watch over Sorath, who will bring the end to the world.

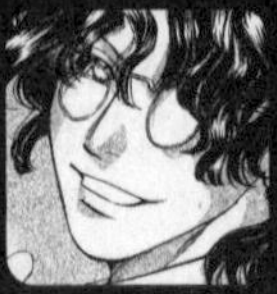

Sakaki (Samech)
Rescues Sorath repeatedly from danger but is ultimately slain by Leice.

?

Resh
Identity unclear

?

Vav
Identity unclear

Modern Day Arc
Chapter 8

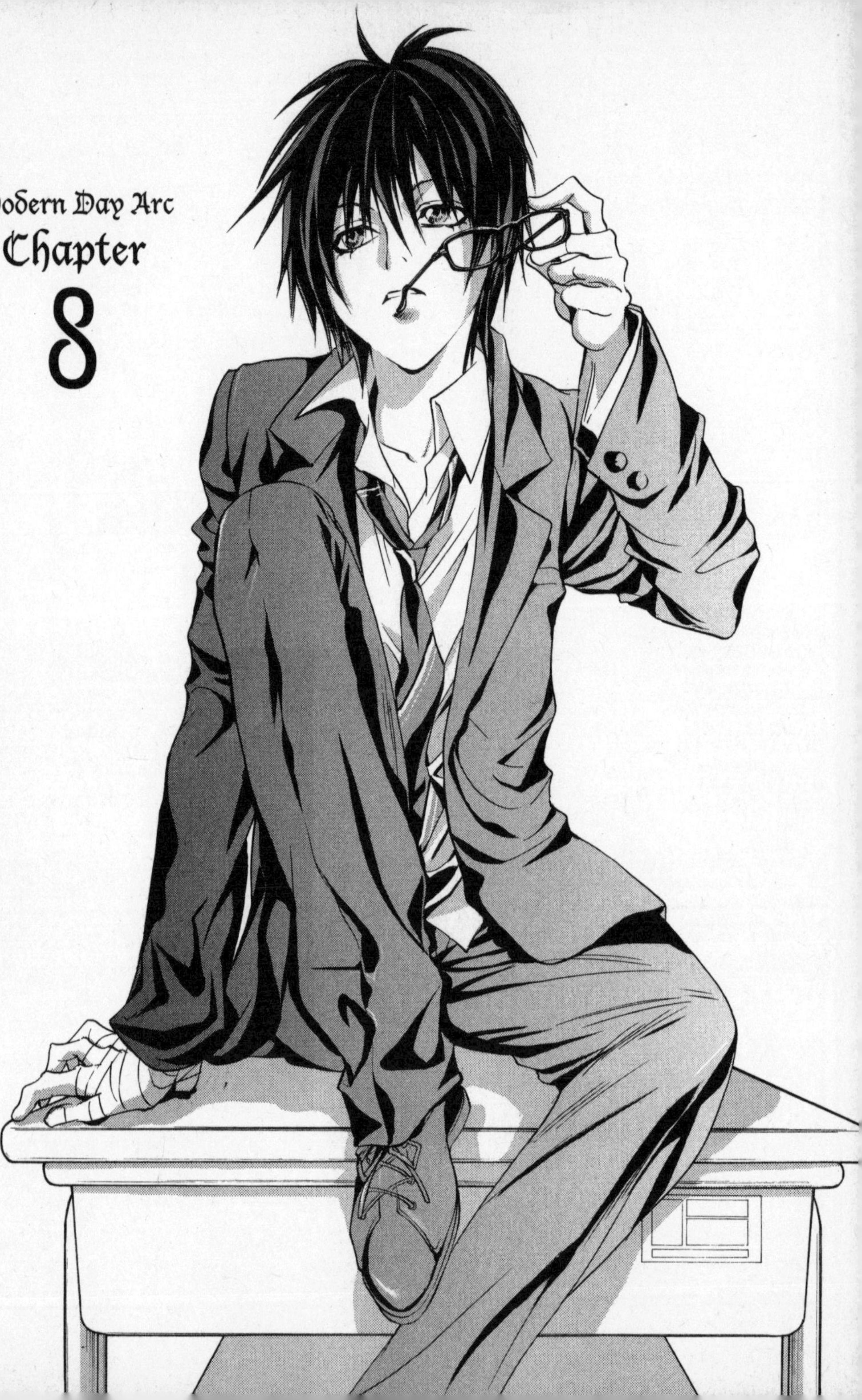

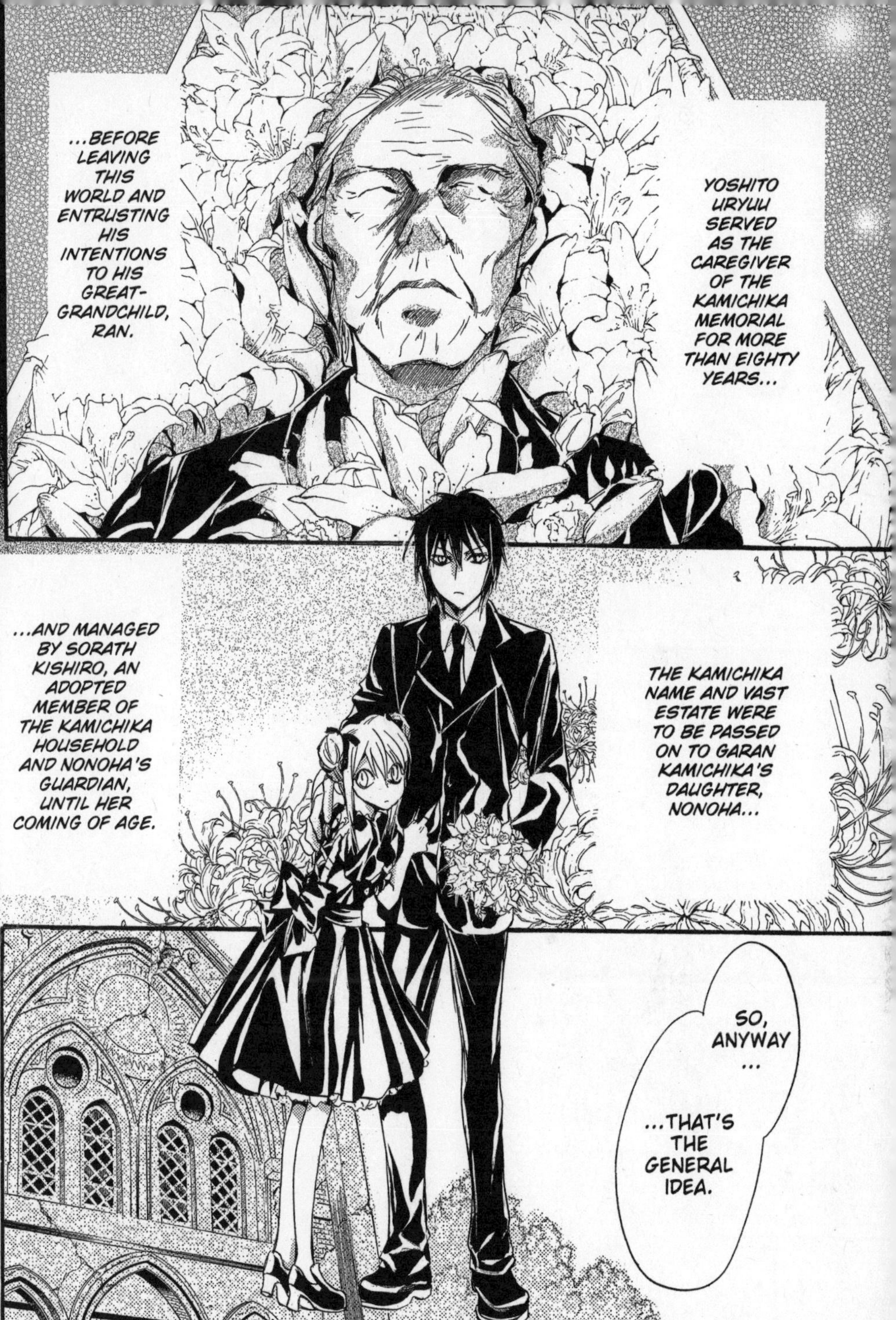
YOSHITO URYUU SERVED AS THE CAREGIVER OF THE KAMICHIKA MEMORIAL FOR MORE THAN EIGHTY YEARS...
...BEFORE LEAVING THIS WORLD AND ENTRUSTING HIS INTENTIONS TO HIS GREAT-GRANDCHILD, RAN.
THE KAMICHIKA NAME AND VAST ESTATE WERE TO BE PASSED ON TO GARAN KAMICHIKA'S DAUGHTER, NONOHA...
...AND MANAGED BY SORATH KISHIRO, AN ADOPTED MEMBER OF THE KAMICHIKA HOUSEHOLD AND NONOHA'S GUARDIAN, UNTIL HER COMING OF AGE.
SO, ANYWAY ...
...THAT'S THE GENERAL IDEA.

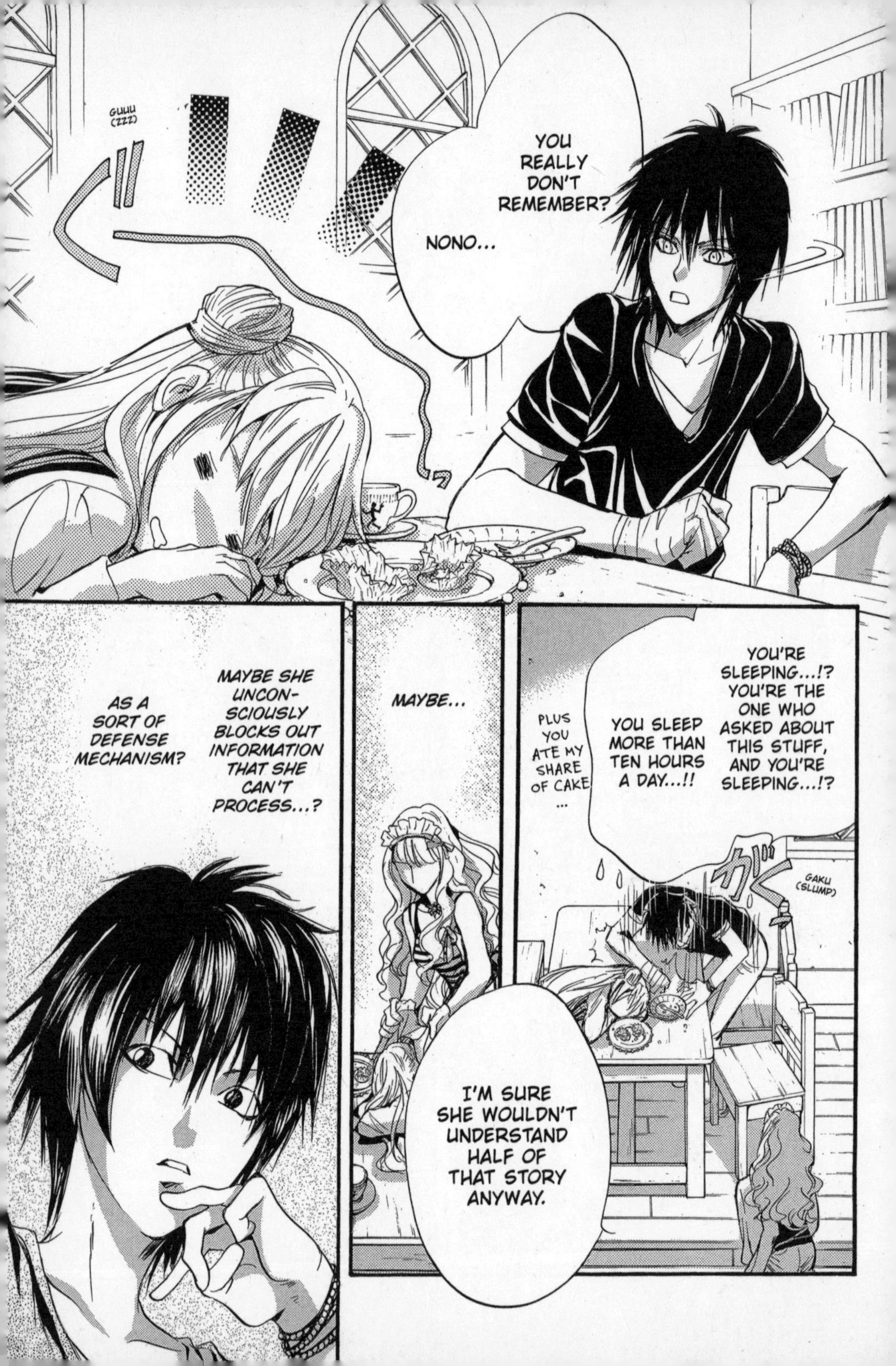

YOU REALLY DON'T REMEMBER?
NONO...
GUUU (ZZZ)
YOU'RE SLEEPING...!? YOU'RE THE ONE WHO ASKED ABOUT THIS STUFF, AND YOU'RE SLEEPING...!?
YOU SLEEP MORE THAN TEN HOURS A DAY...!!
PLUS YOU ATE MY SHARE OF CAKE ...
GAKU (SLUMP)
MAYBE...
I'M SURE SHE WOULDN'T UNDERSTAND HALF OF THAT STORY ANYWAY.
MAYBE SHE UNCON-SCIOUSLY BLOCKS OUT INFORMATION THAT SHE CAN'T PROCESS...?
AS A SORT OF DEFENSE MECHANISM?

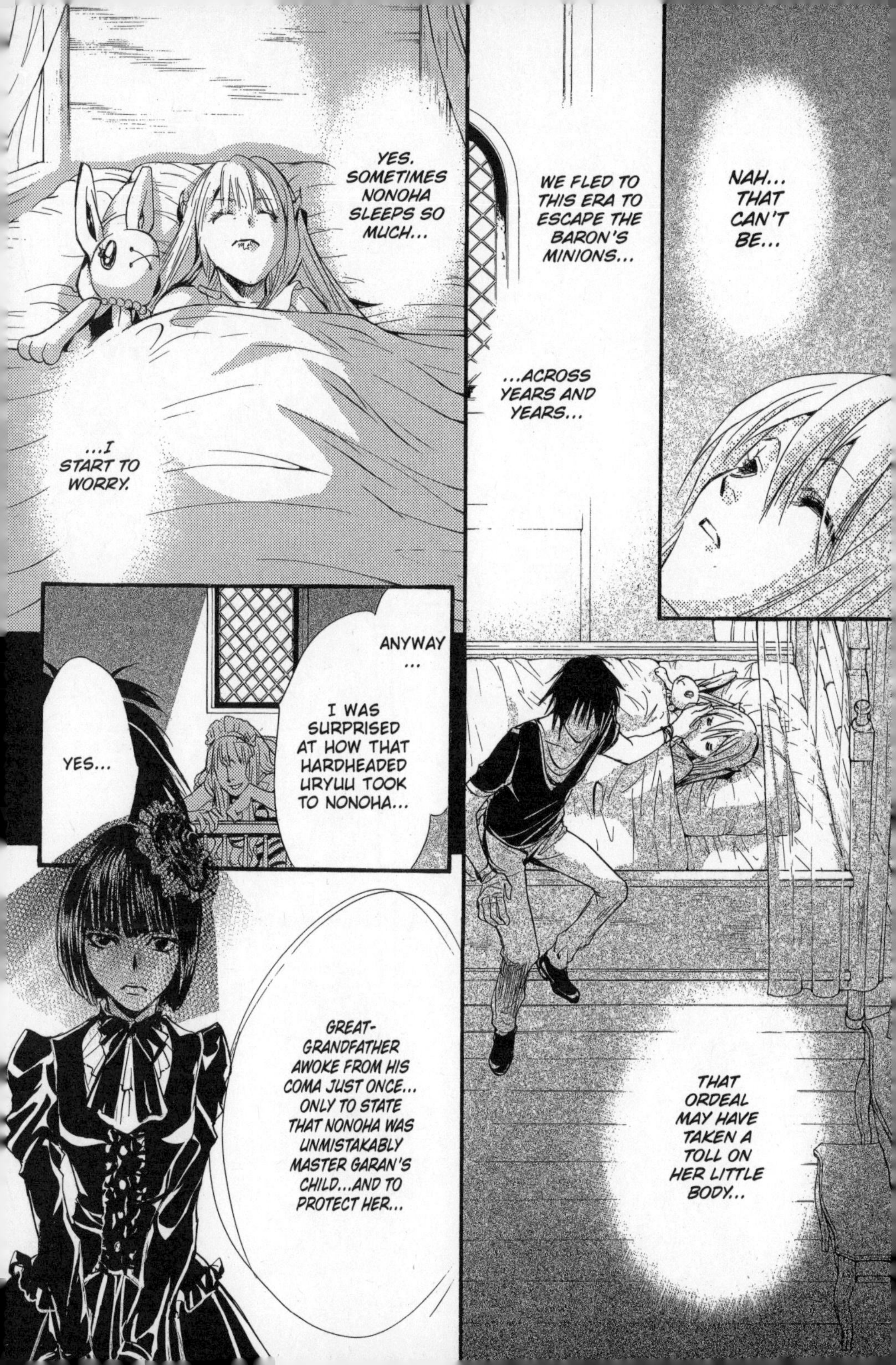
NAH... THAT CAN'T BE...
WE FLED TO THIS ERA TO ESCAPE THE BARON'S MINIONS...
...ACROSS YEARS AND YEARS...
YES. SOMETIMES NONOHA SLEEPS SO MUCH...
...I START TO WORRY.
THAT ORDEAL MAY HAVE TAKEN A TOLL ON HER LITTLE BODY...
ANYWAY...
I WAS SURPRISED AT HOW THAT HARDHEADED URYUU TOOK TO NONOHA...
YES...
GREAT-GRANDFATHER AWOKE FROM HIS COMA JUST ONCE... ONLY TO STATE THAT NONOHA WAS UNMISTAKABLY MASTER GARAN'S CHILD...AND TO PROTECT HER...

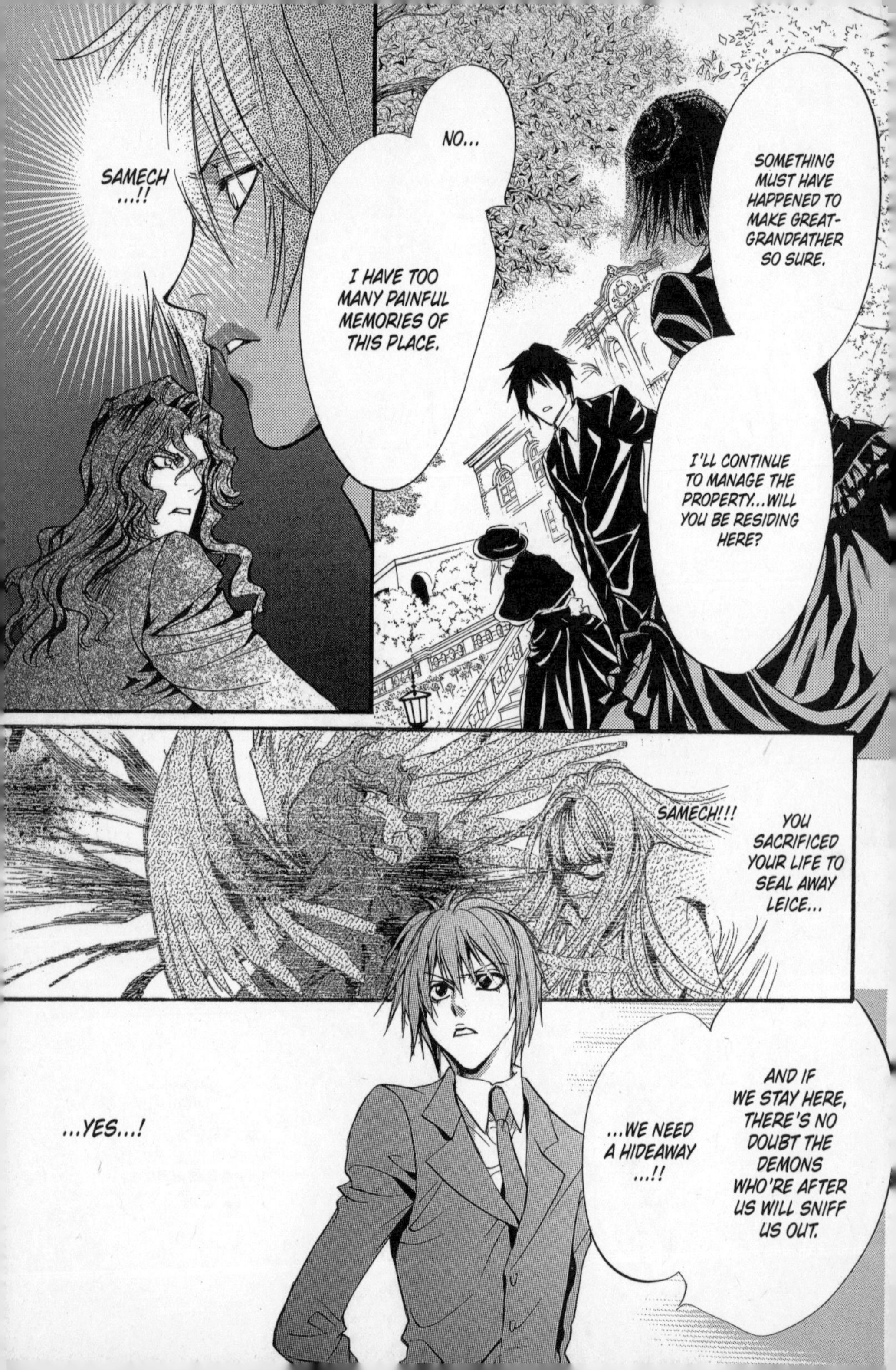
SOMETHING MUST HAVE HAPPENED TO MAKE GREAT-GRANDFATHER SO SURE.
I'LL CONTINUE TO MANAGE THE PROPERTY...WILL YOU BE RESIDING HERE?
NO...
I HAVE TOO MANY PAINFUL MEMORIES OF THIS PLACE.
SAMECH ...!!
YOU SACRIFICED YOUR LIFE TO SEAL AWAY LEICE...
SAMECH!!!
AND IF WE STAY HERE, THERE'S NO DOUBT THE DEMONS WHO'RE AFTER US WILL SNIFF US OUT.
...WE NEED A HIDEAWAY ...!!
...YES...!

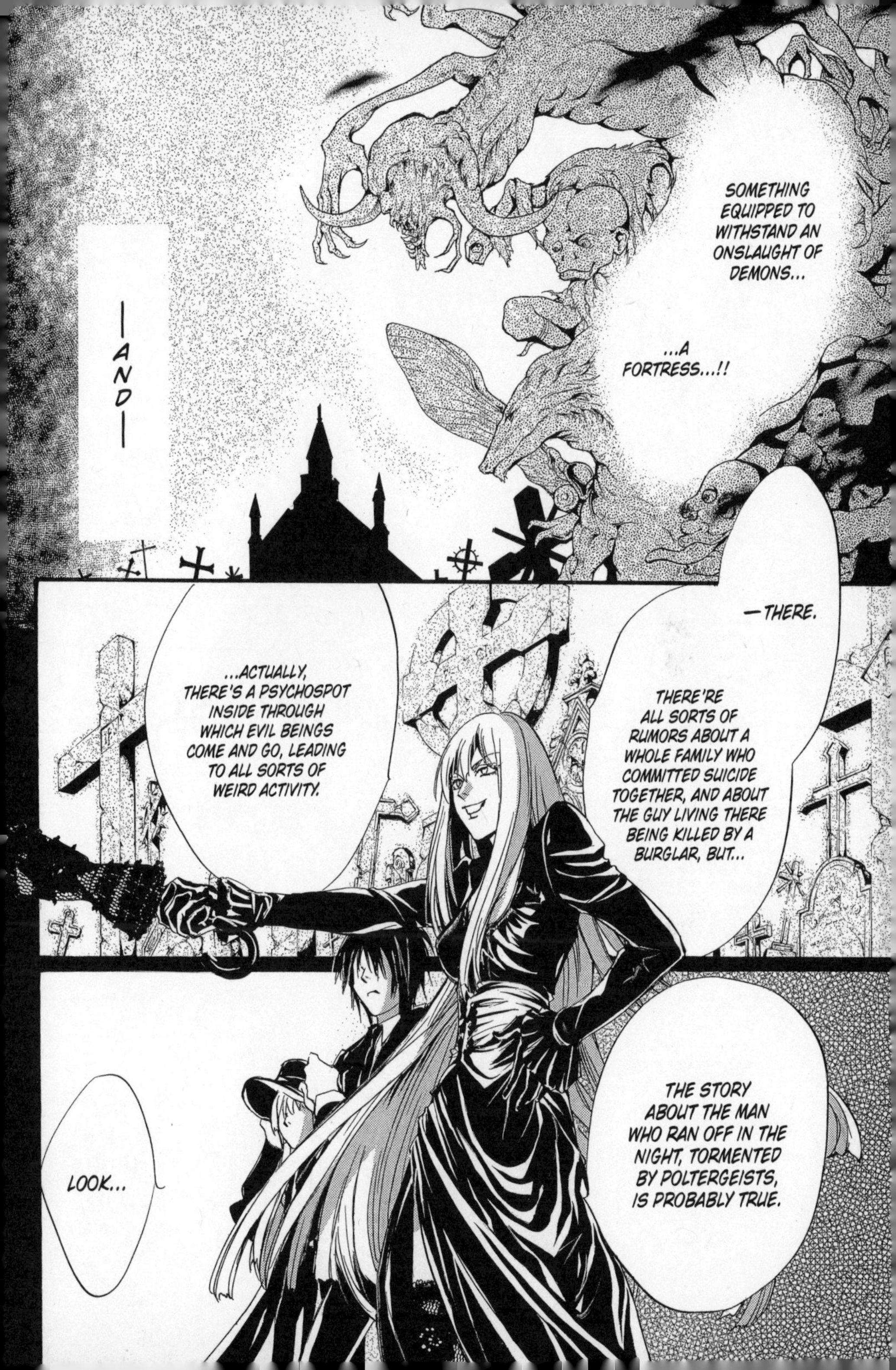
SOMETHING EQUIPPED TO WITHSTAND AN ONSLAUGHT OF DEMONS...
...A FORTRESS...!!
—AND—
—THERE.
THERE'RE ALL SORTS OF RUMORS ABOUT A WHOLE FAMILY WHO COMMITTED SUICIDE TOGETHER, AND ABOUT THE GUY LIVING THERE BEING KILLED BY A BURGLAR, BUT...
...ACTUALLY, THERE'S A PSYCHOSPOT INSIDE THROUGH WHICH EVIL BEINGS COME AND GO, LEADING TO ALL SORTS OF WEIRD ACTIVITY.
THE STORY ABOUT THE MAN WHO RAN OFF IN THE NIGHT, TORMENTED BY POLTERGEISTS, IS PROBABLY TRUE.
LOOK...

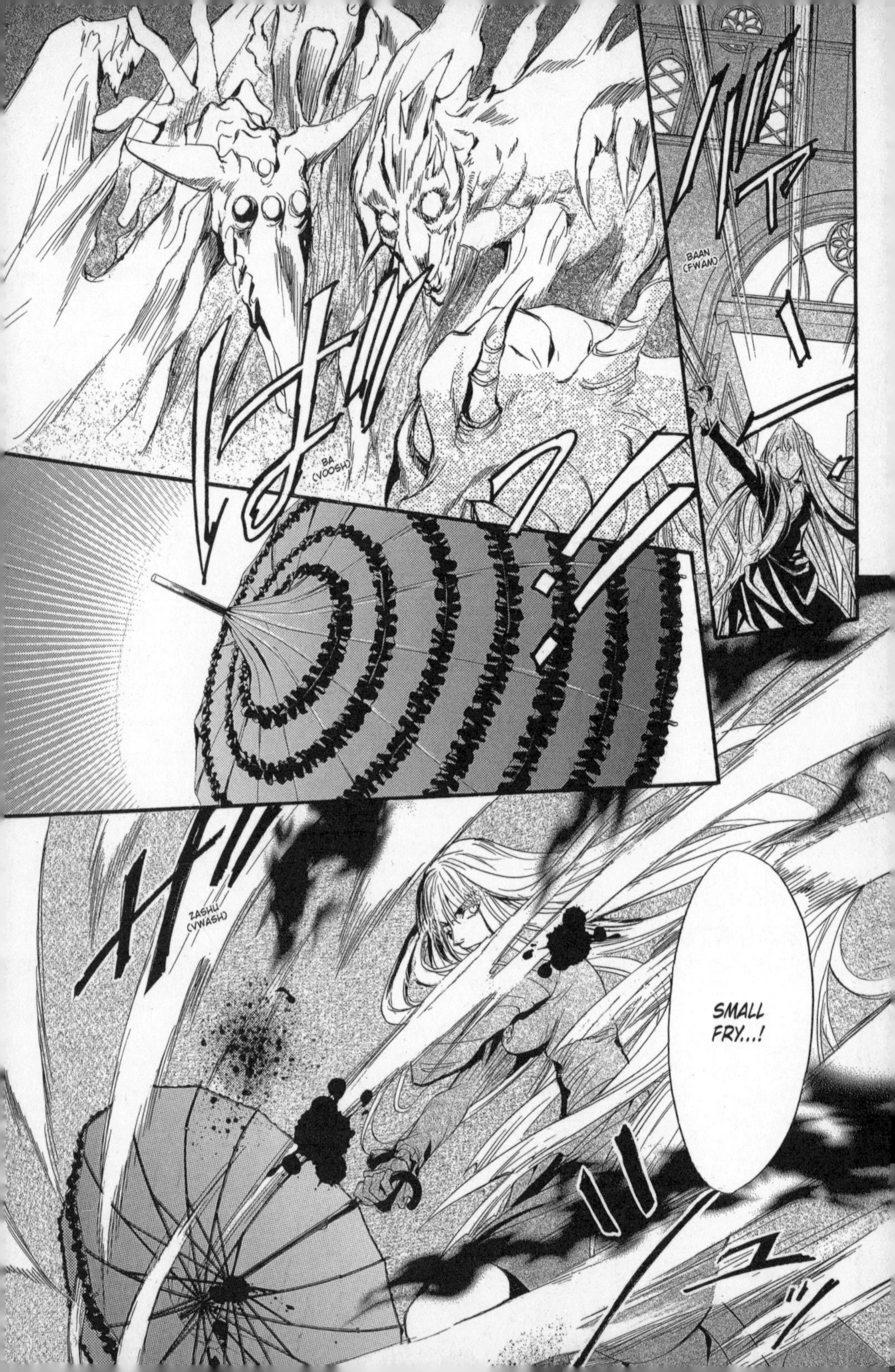
BAAN (FWAM)
BA (VOOSH)
SMALL FRY...!
ZASHU (VWASH)

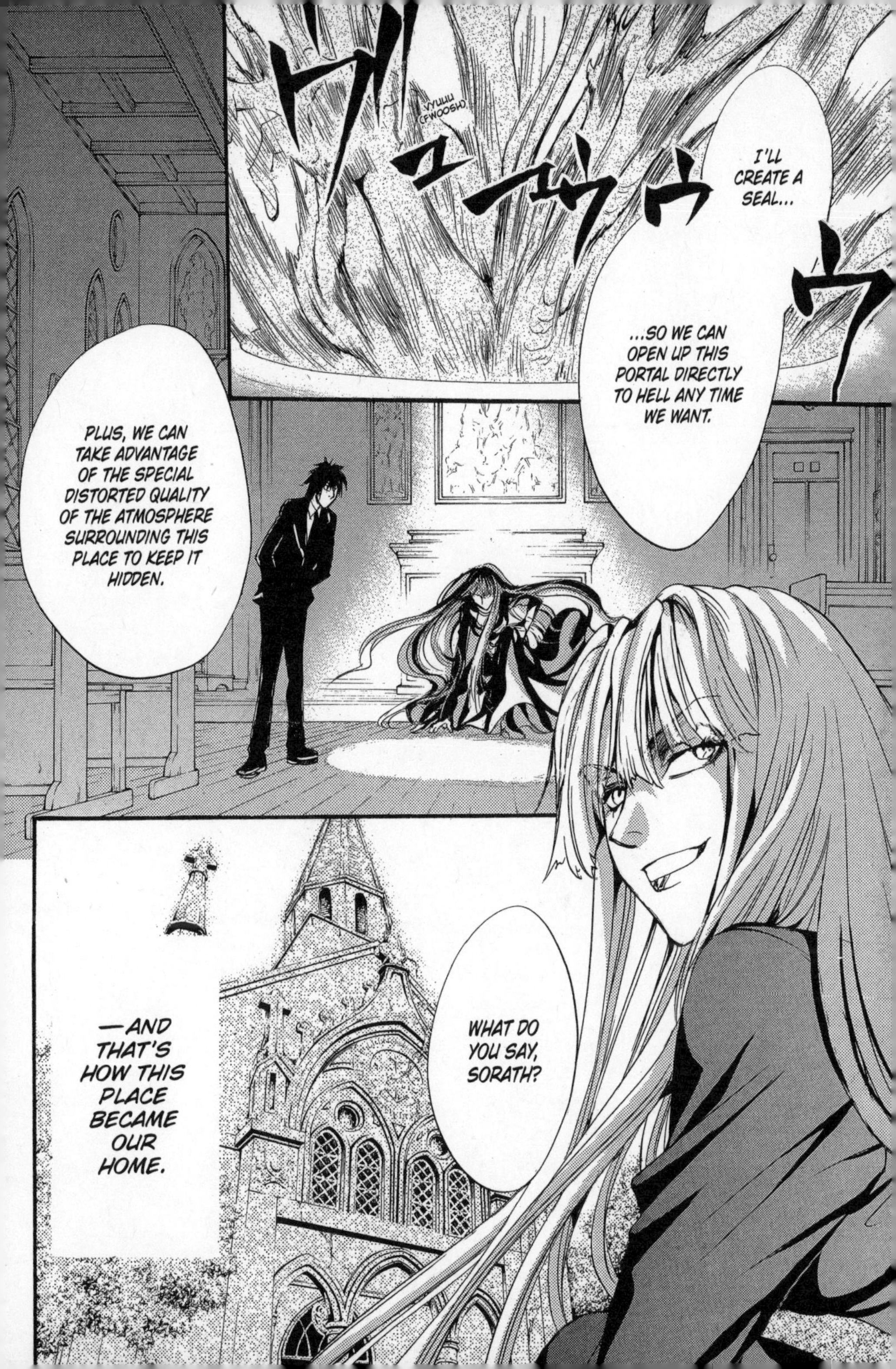
ヴュウウウ
VYUUU (FWOOSH)
I'LL CREATE A SEAL...
...SO WE CAN OPEN UP THIS PORTAL DIRECTLY TO HELL ANY TIME WE WANT.
PLUS, WE CAN TAKE ADVANTAGE OF THE SPECIAL DISTORTED QUALITY OF THE ATMOSPHERE SURROUNDING THIS PLACE TO KEEP IT HIDDEN.
WHAT DO YOU SAY, SORATH?
—AND THAT'S HOW THIS PLACE BECAME OUR HOME.

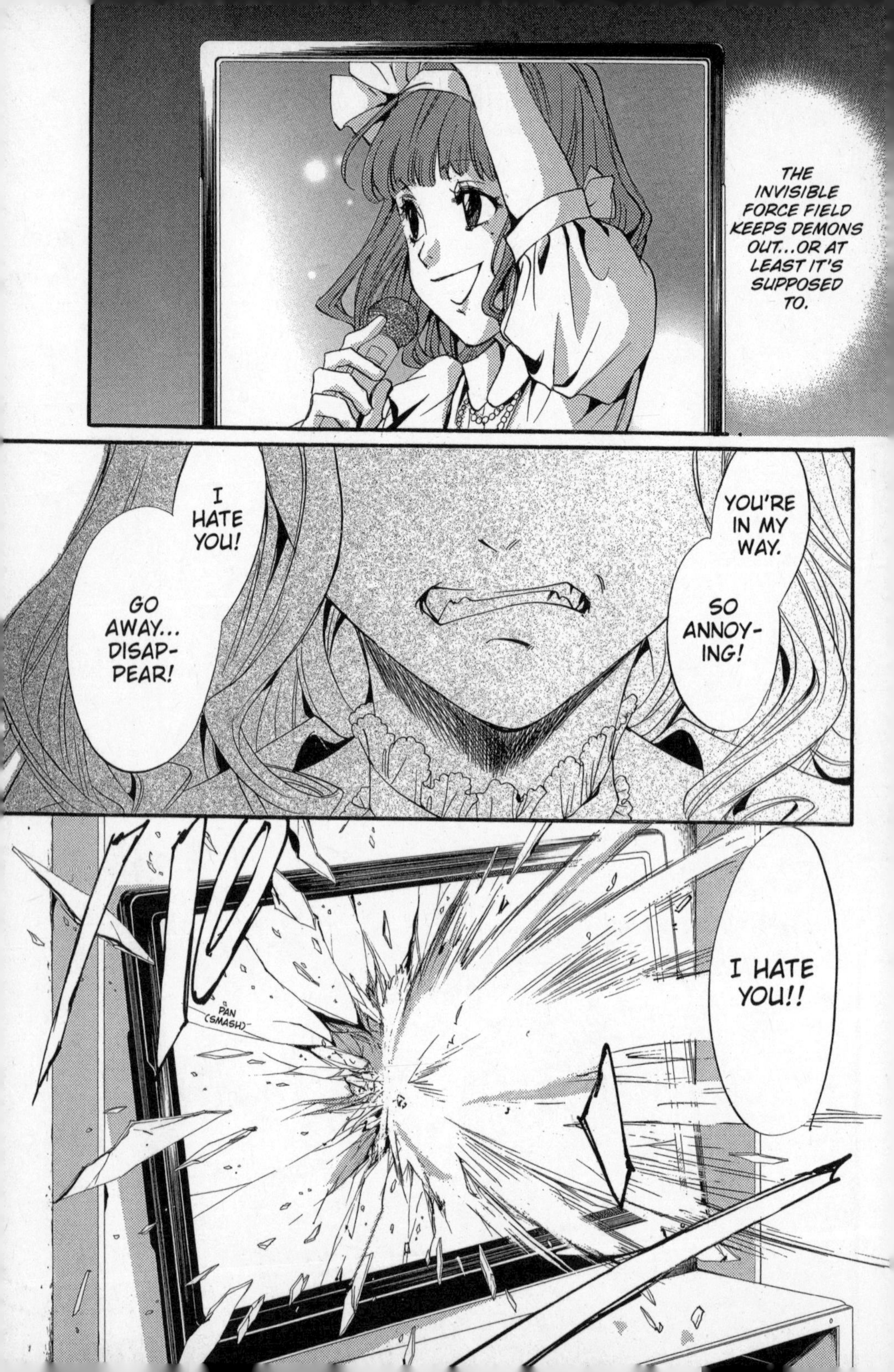
THE INVISIBLE FORCE FIELD KEEPS DEMONS OUT...OR AT LEAST IT'S SUPPOSED TO.
YOU'RE IN MY WAY.
SO ANNOY-ING!
I HATE YOU!
GO AWAY... DISAP-PEAR!
I HATE YOU!!
PAN (SMASH)

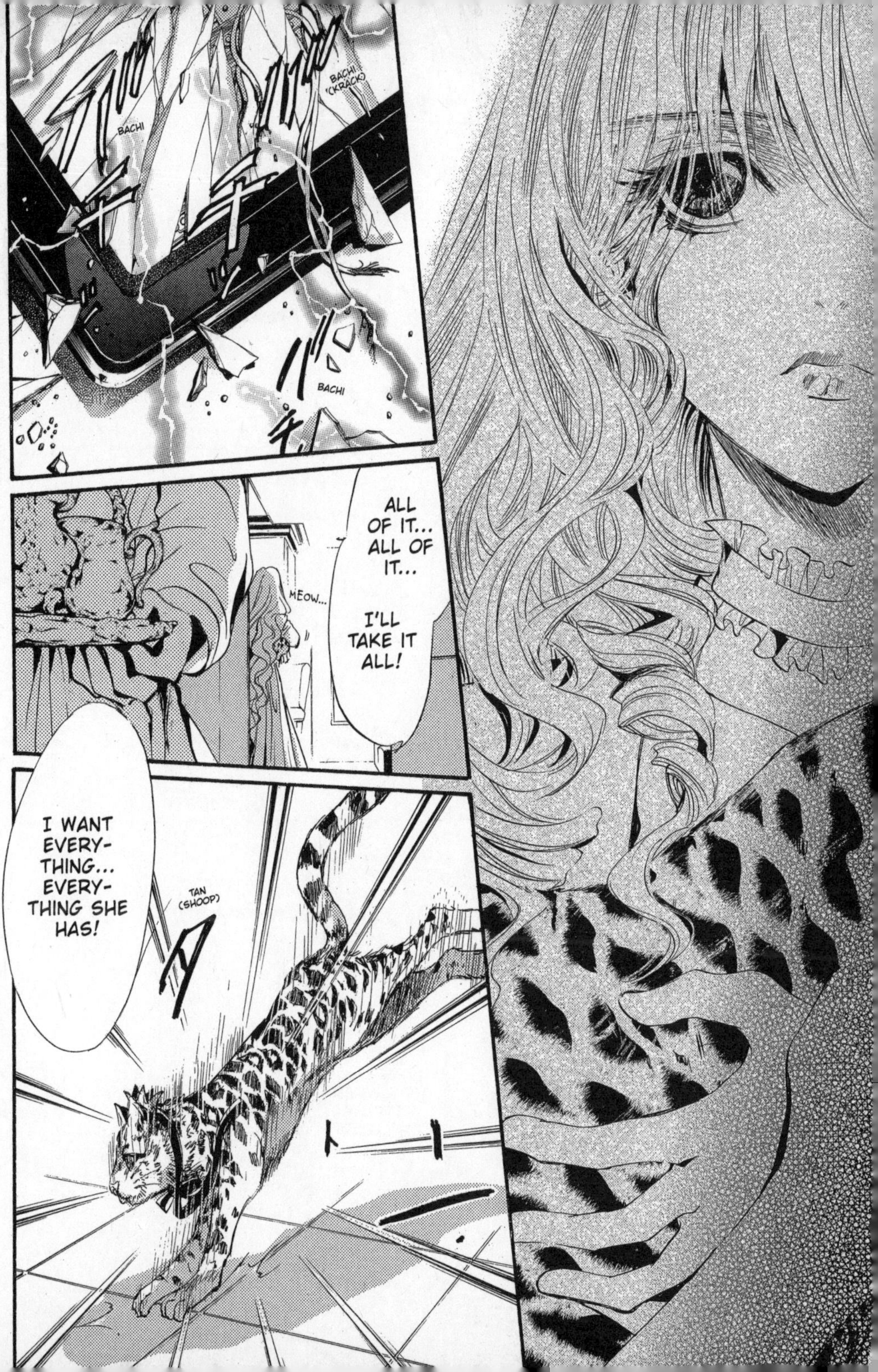
BACHI (KRACK)
BACHI
BACHI
ALL OF IT... ALL OF IT... I'LL TAKE IT ALL!
MEOW...
I WANT EVERYTHING... EVERYTHING SHE HAS!
TAN (SHOOP)

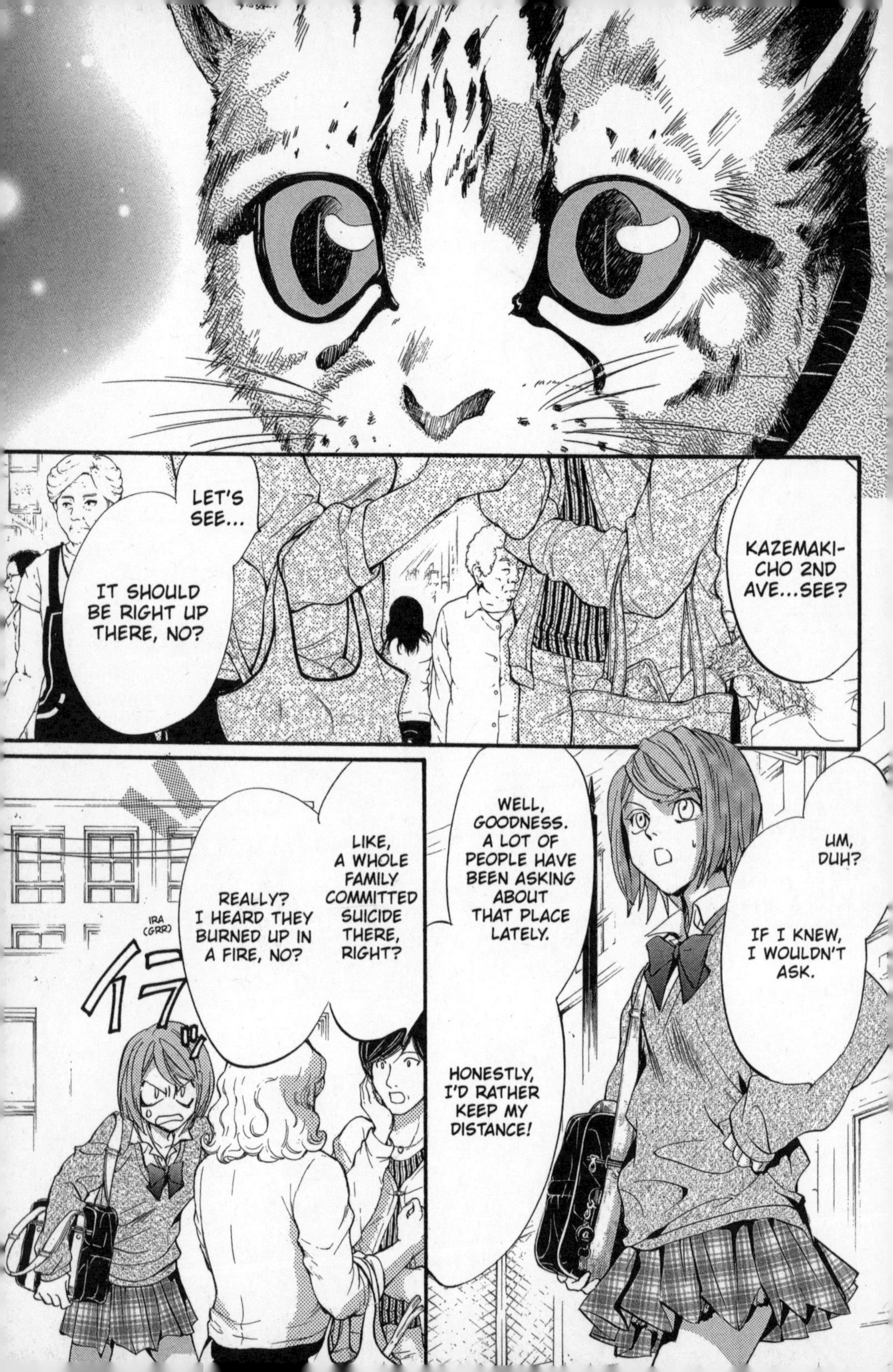
KAZEMAKI-CHO 2ND AVE...SEE?
LET'S SEE...
IT SHOULD BE RIGHT UP THERE, NO?
UM, DUH?
IF I KNEW, I WOULDN'T ASK.
WELL, GOODNESS. A LOT OF PEOPLE HAVE BEEN ASKING ABOUT THAT PLACE LATELY.
HONESTLY, I'D RATHER KEEP MY DISTANCE!
LIKE, A WHOLE FAMILY COMMITTED SUICIDE THERE, RIGHT?
REALLY? I HEARD THEY BURNED UP IN A FIRE, NO?
IRA (GRR)

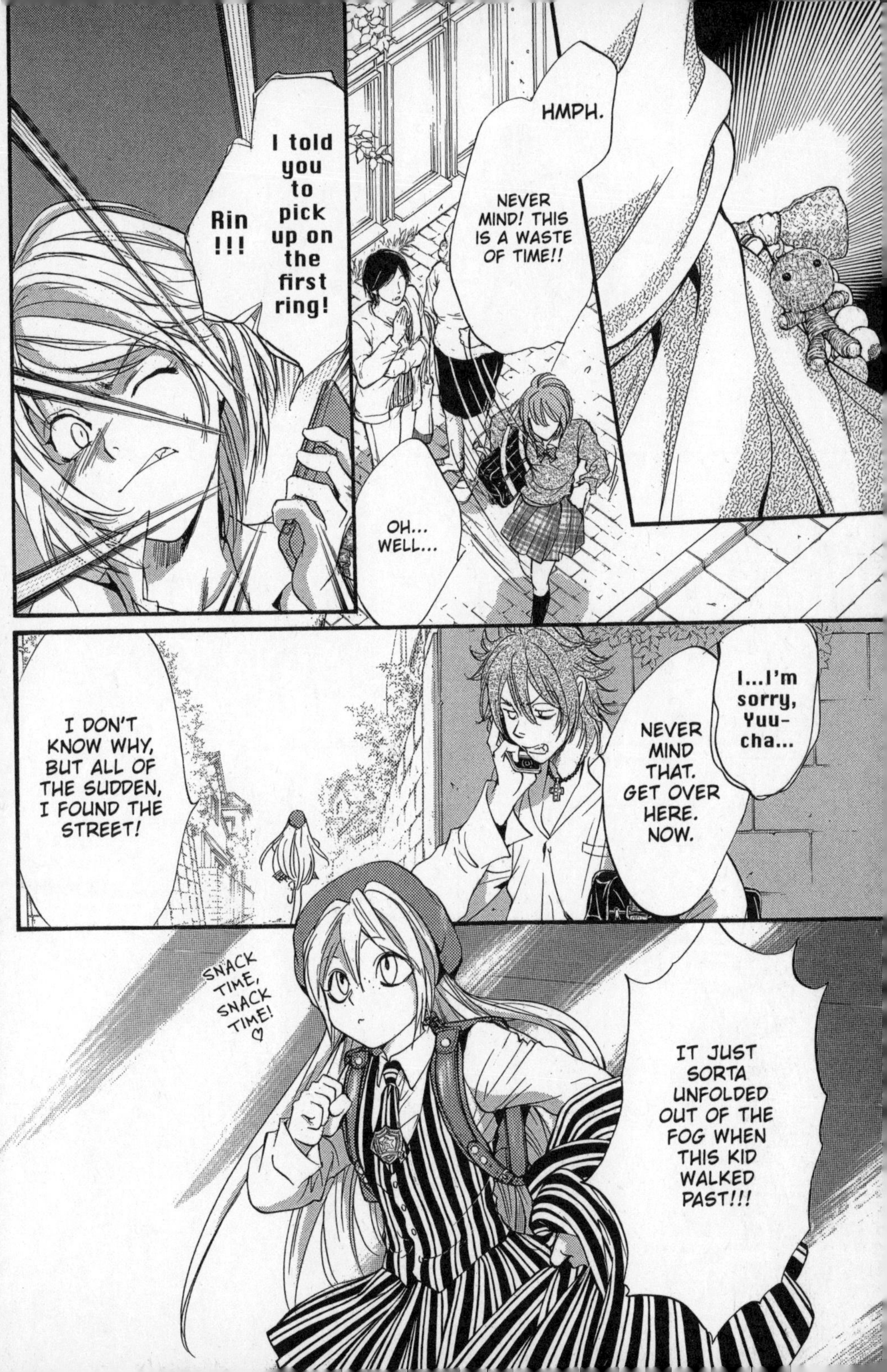
HMPH.
NEVER MIND! THIS IS A WASTE OF TIME!!
OH... WELL...
I told you to pick up on the first ring!
Rin !!!
I...I'm sorry, Yuu-cha...
NEVER MIND THAT. GET OVER HERE. NOW.
I DON'T KNOW WHY, BUT ALL OF THE SUDDEN, I FOUND THE STREET!
IT JUST SORTA UNFOLDED OUT OF THE FOG WHEN THIS KID WALKED PAST!!!
SNACK TIME, SNACK TIME! ♡

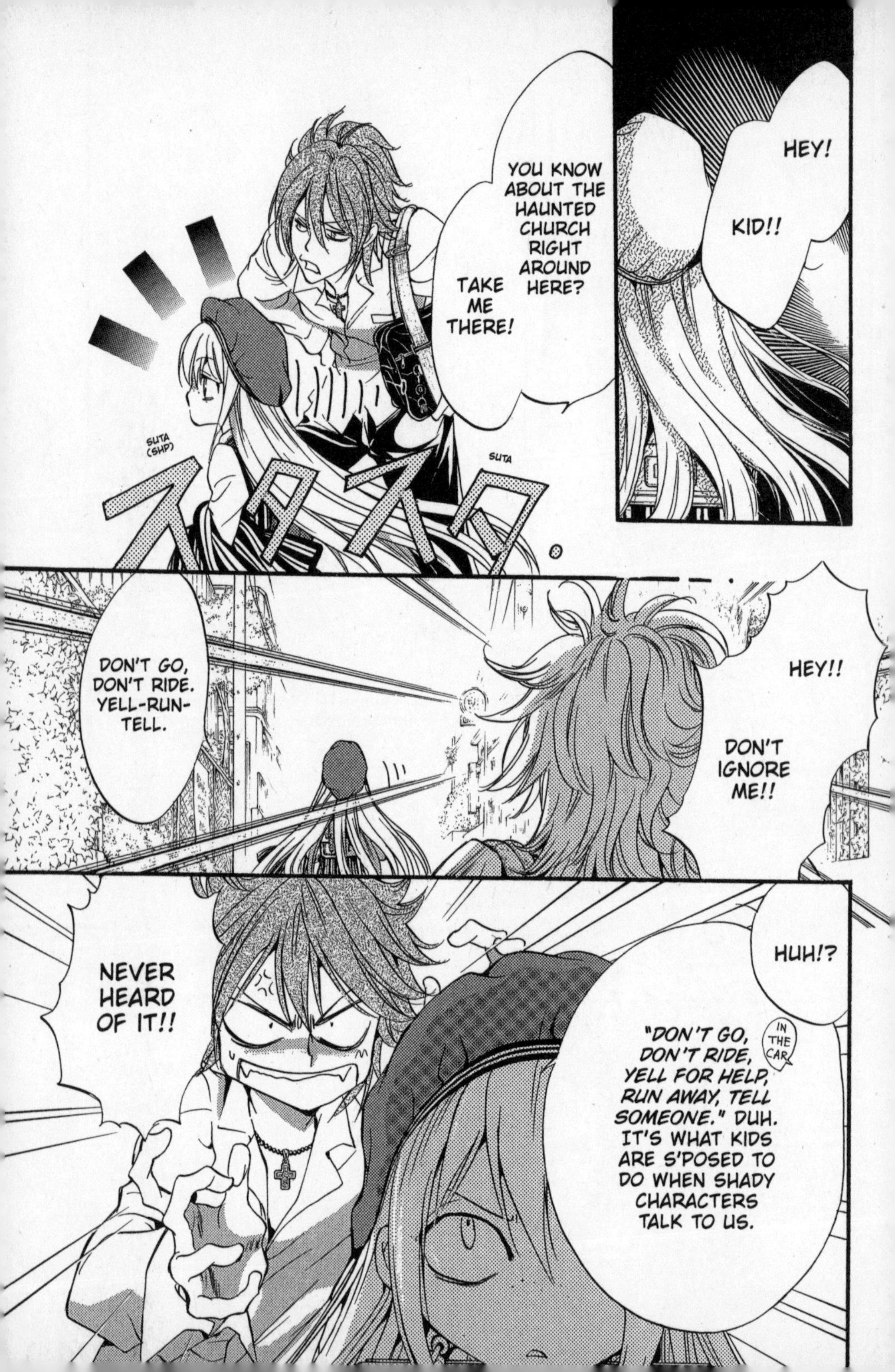
HEY!
KID!!
YOU KNOW ABOUT THE HAUNTED CHURCH RIGHT AROUND HERE?
TAKE ME THERE!
スタスタ
SUTA (SHP)
SUTA
HEY!!
DON'T IGNORE ME!!
DON'T GO, DON'T RIDE. YELL-RUN-TELL.
HUH!?
"DON'T GO, DON'T RIDE, YELL FOR HELP, RUN AWAY, TELL SOMEONE." DUH. IT'S WHAT KIDS ARE S'POSED TO DO WHEN SHADY CHARACTERS TALK TO US.
IN THE CAR
NEVER HEARD OF IT!!

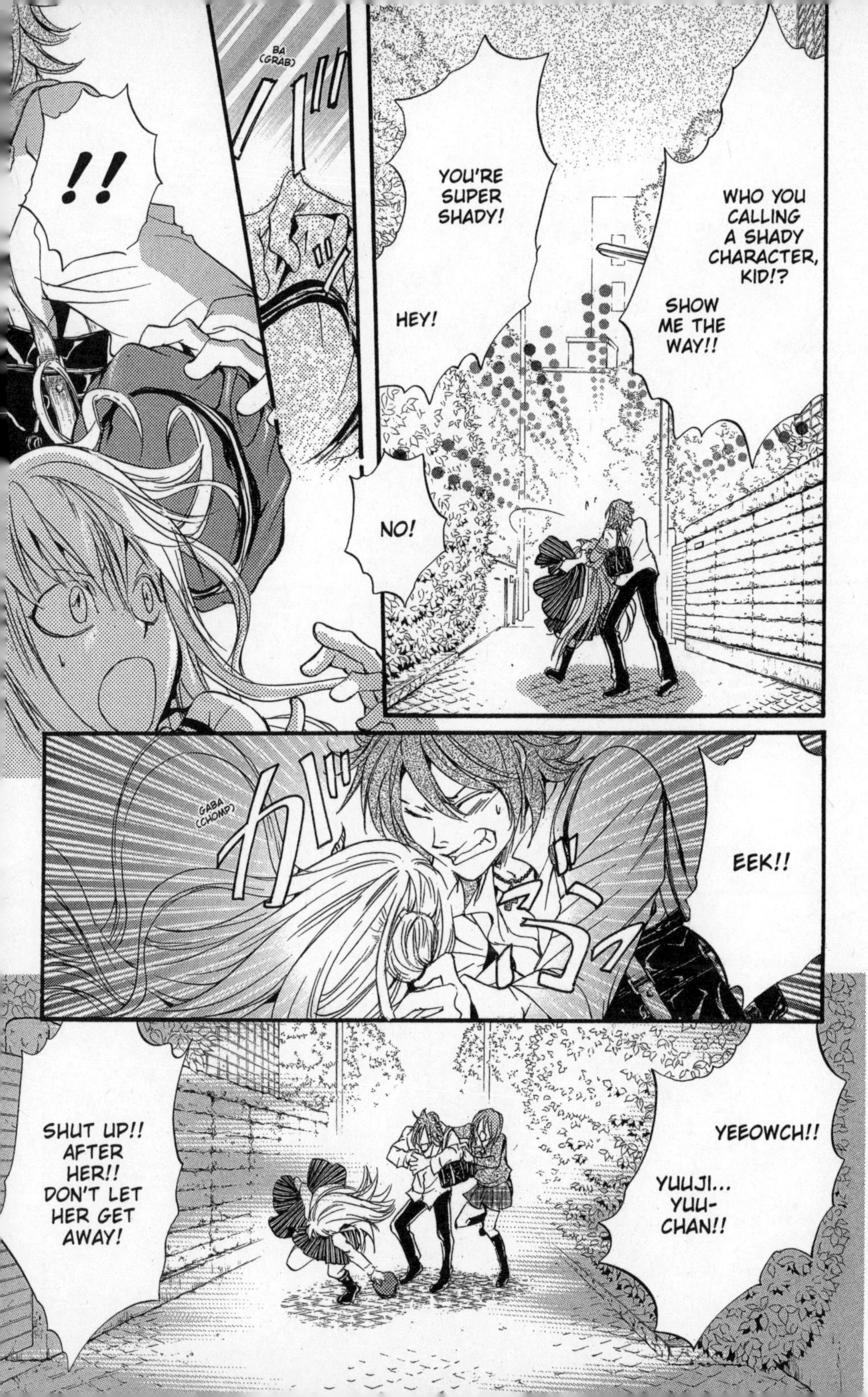
WHO YOU CALLING A SHADY CHARACTER, KID!?
SHOW ME THE WAY!!
YOU'RE SUPER SHADY!
HEY!
NO!
BA (GRAB)
!!
EEK!!
GABA (CHOMP)
YEEOWCH!!
YUUJI... YUU-CHAN!!
SHUT UP!! AFTER HER!! DON'T LET HER GET AWAY!

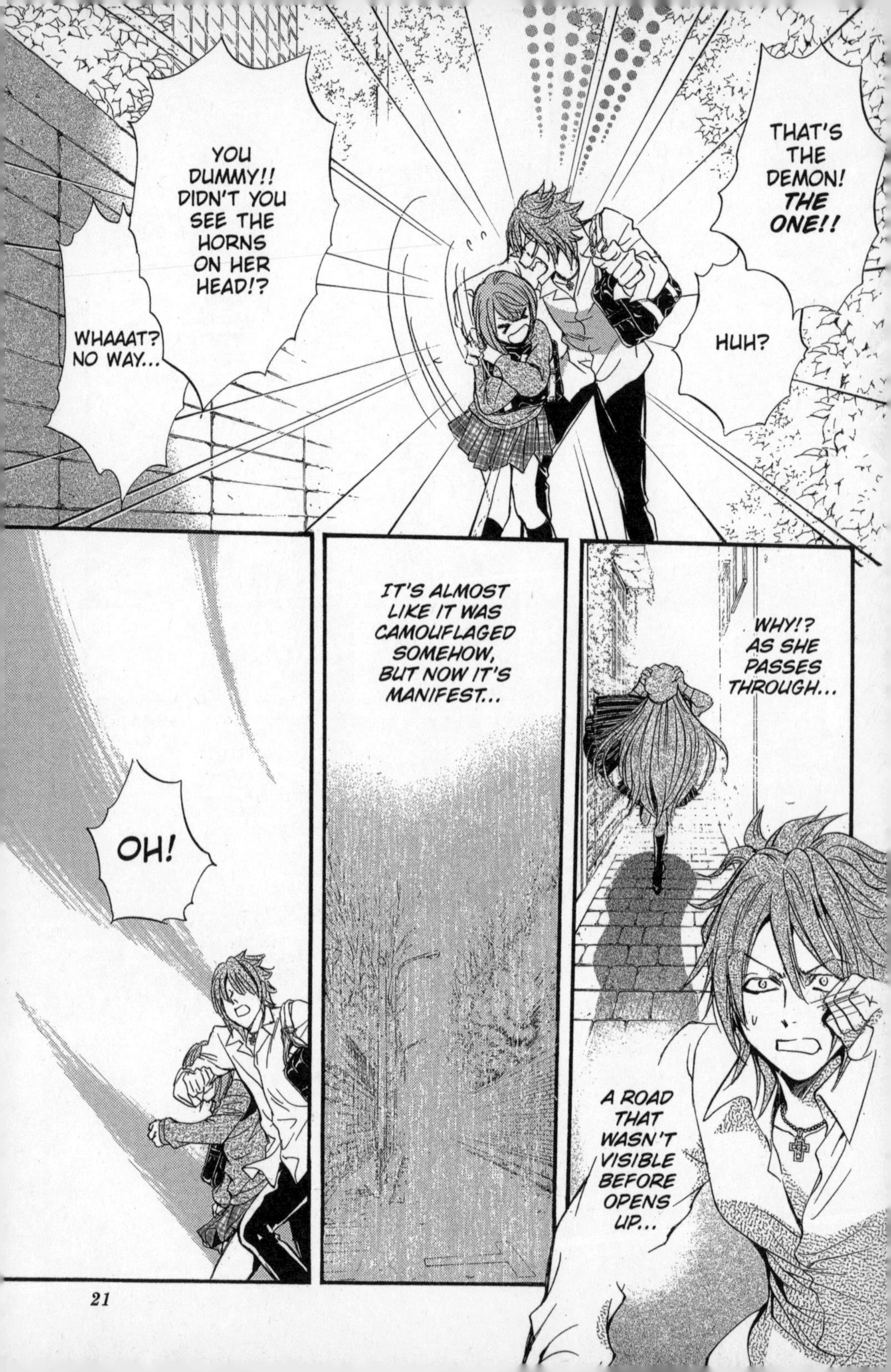
THAT'S THE DEMON! *THE ONE!!*
HUH?
YOU DUMMY!! DIDN'T YOU SEE THE HORNS ON HER HEAD!?
WHAAAT? NO WAY...
WHY!? AS SHE PASSES THROUGH...
A ROAD THAT WASN'T VISIBLE BEFORE OPENS UP...
IT'S ALMOST LIKE IT WAS CAMOUFLAGED SOMEHOW, BUT NOW IT'S MANIFEST...
OH!

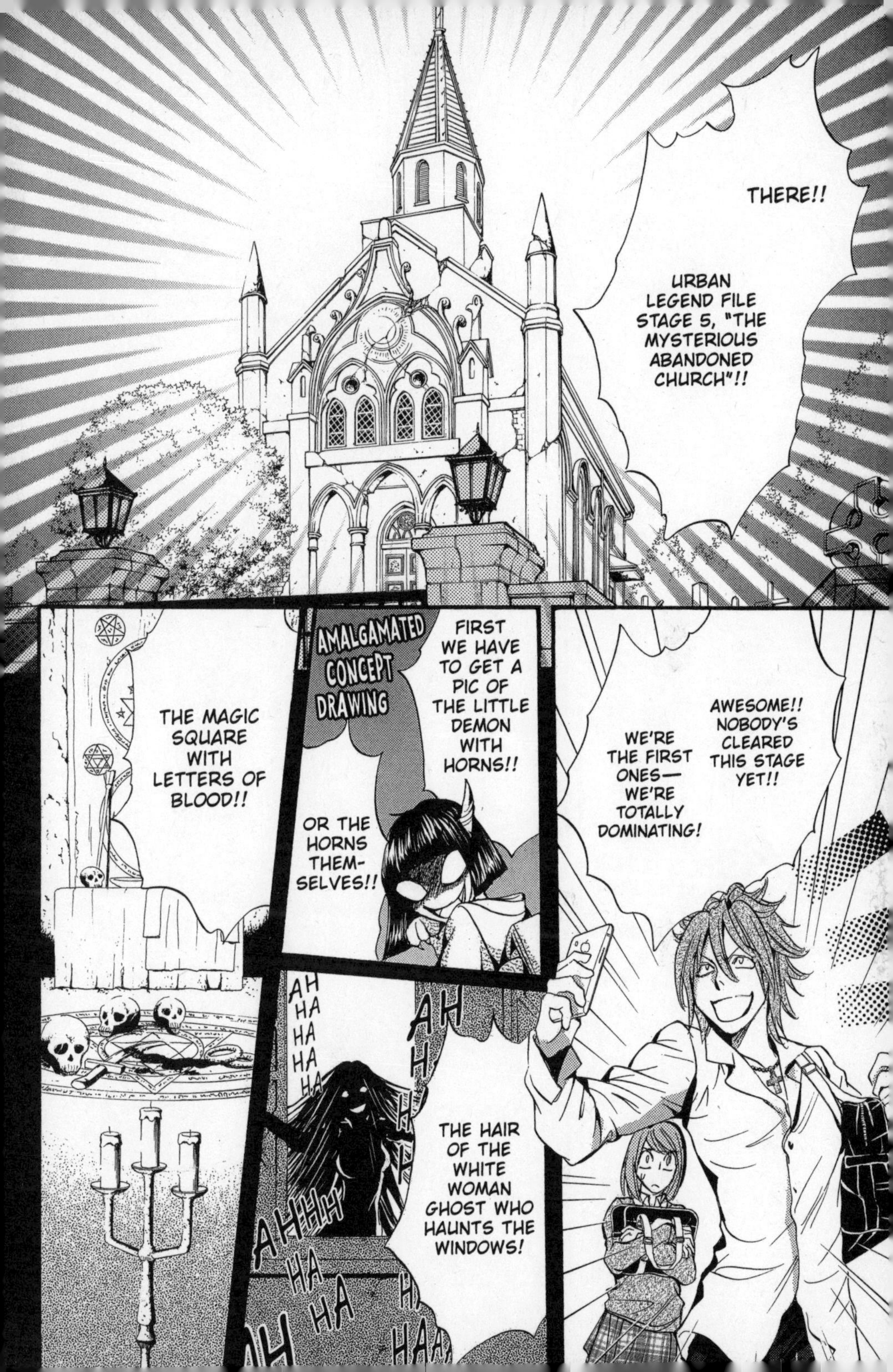
THERE!!
URBAN LEGEND FILE STAGE 5, "THE MYSTERIOUS ABANDONED CHURCH"!!
AWESOME!! NOBODY'S CLEARED THIS STAGE YET!!
WE'RE THE FIRST ONES— WE'RE TOTALLY DOMINATING!
AMALGAMATED CONCEPT DRAWING
FIRST WE HAVE TO GET A PIC OF THE LITTLE DEMON WITH HORNS!!
OR THE HORNS THEM-SELVES!!
AHHAHAHAHAHA
AH
AHHHH
THE HAIR OF THE WHITE WOMAN GHOST WHO HAUNTS THE WINDOWS!
HA HA AH HA
THE MAGIC SQUARE WITH LETTERS OF BLOOD!!

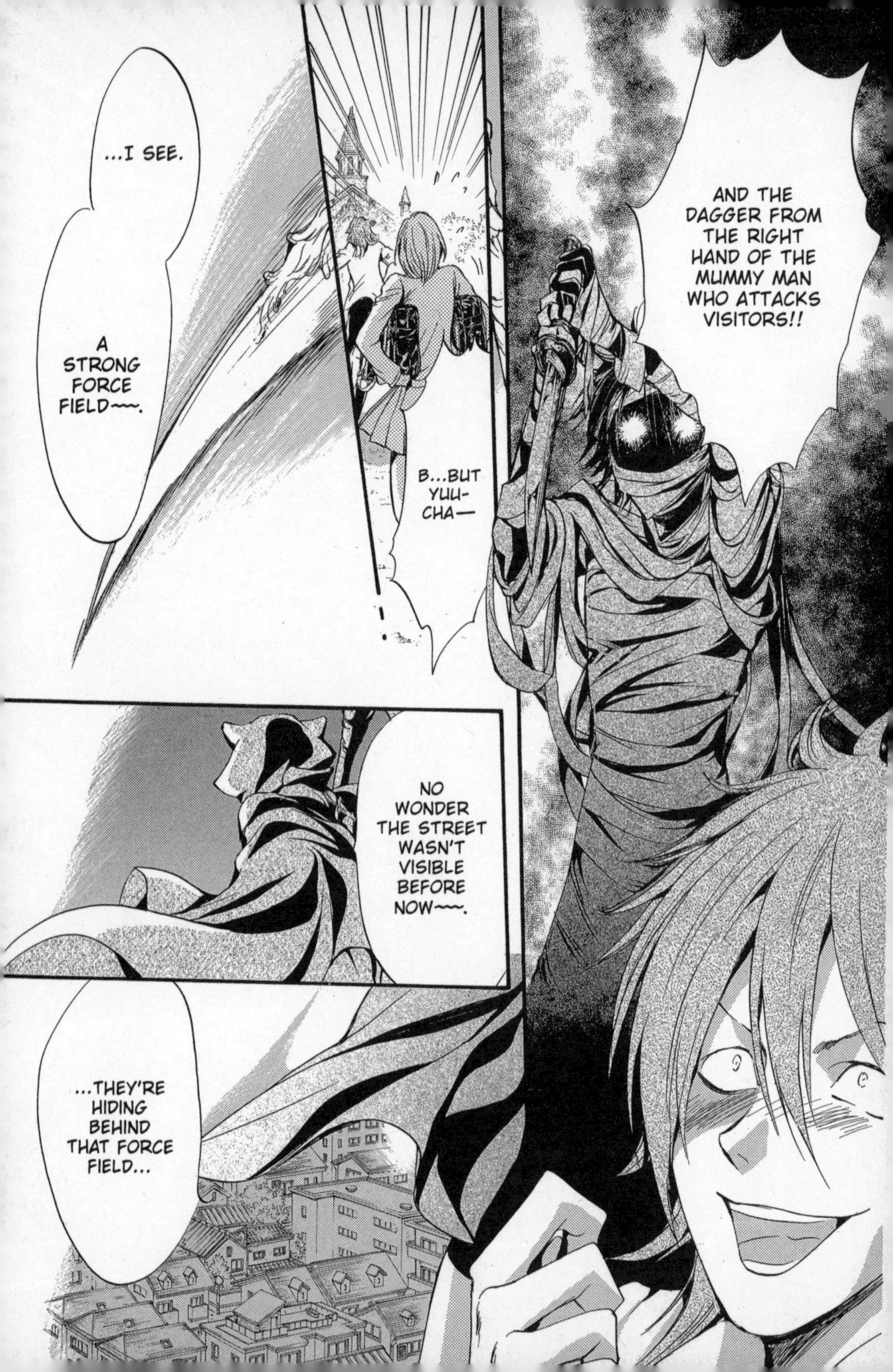
AND THE DAGGER FROM THE RIGHT HAND OF THE MUMMY MAN WHO ATTACKS VISITORS!!
...I SEE.
A STRONG FORCE FIELD~~.
B...BUT YUU-CHA—
NO WONDER THE STREET WASN'T VISIBLE BEFORE NOW~~.
...THEY'RE HIDING BEHIND THAT FORCE FIELD...

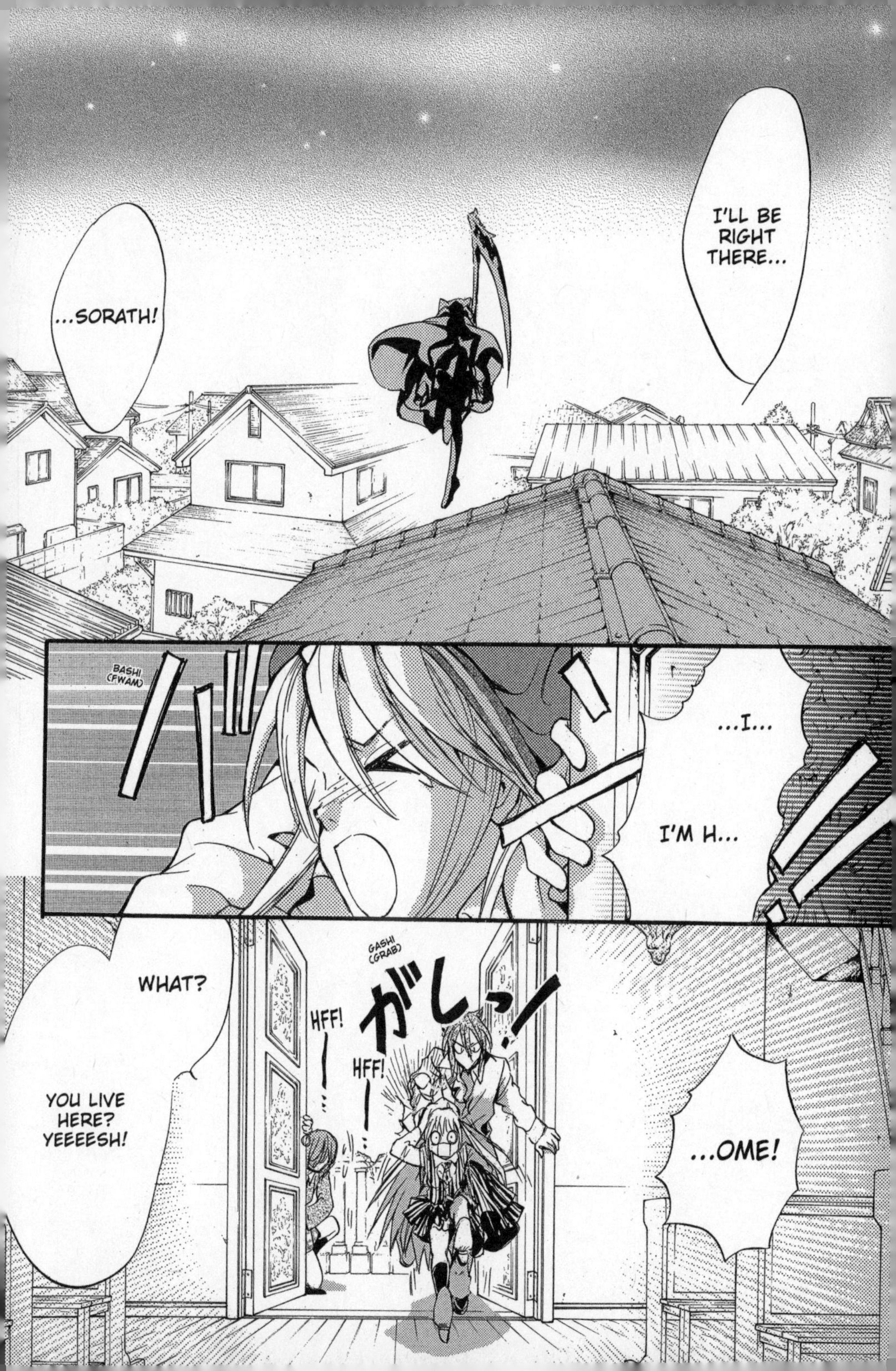
I'LL BE RIGHT THERE...
...SORATH!
...I...
I'M H...
BASHI (F'WAM)
...OME!
GASHI (GRAB)
がしっ!
HFF!
HFF!
WHAT?
YOU LIVE HERE? YEEEESH!

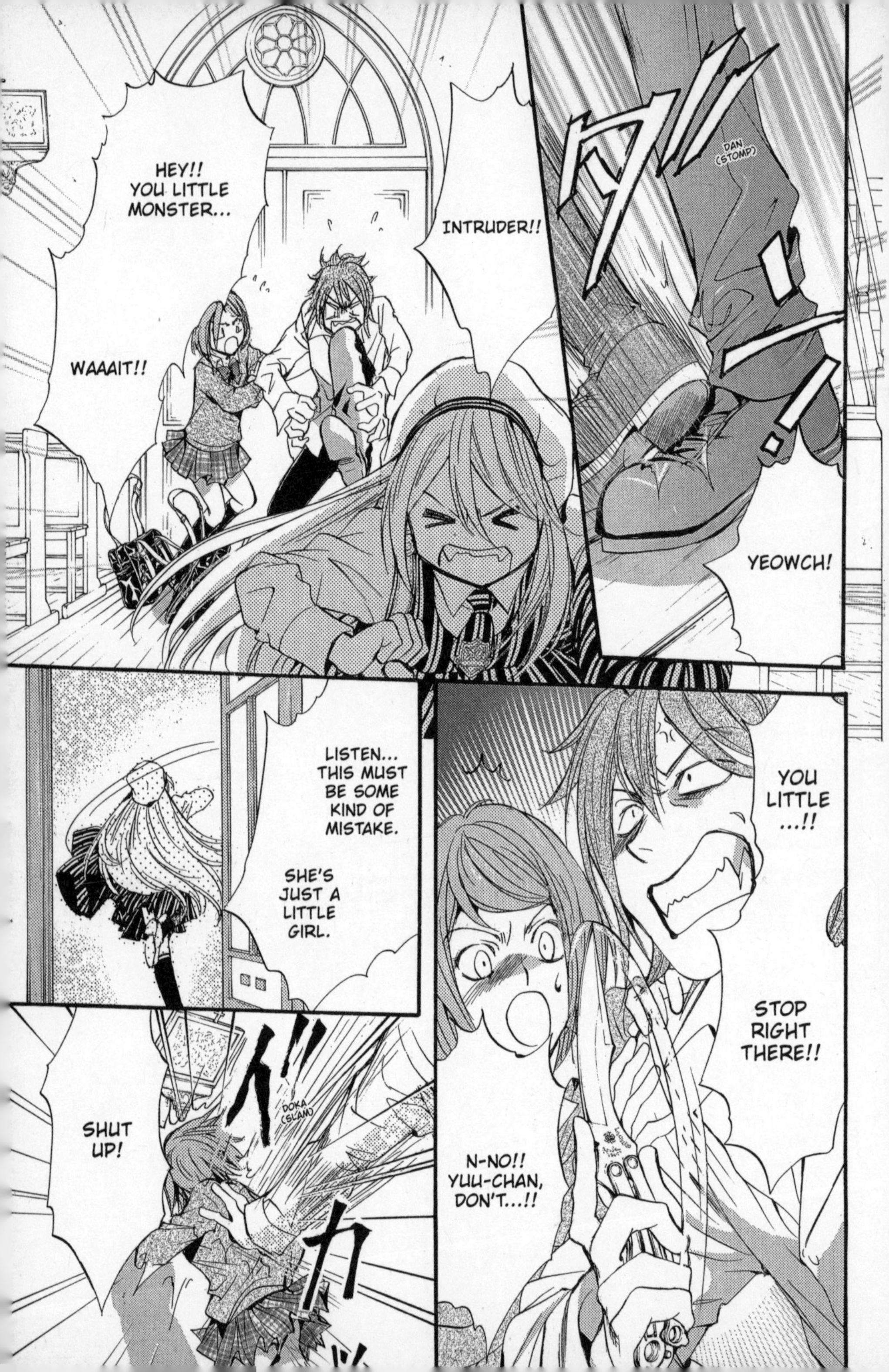
DAN (STOMP)
YEOWCH!
INTRUDER!!
HEY!! YOU LITTLE MONSTER...
WAAAIT!!
YOU LITTLE ...!!
STOP RIGHT THERE!!
N-NO!! YUU-CHAN, DON'T...!!
LISTEN... THIS MUST BE SOME KIND OF MISTAKE.
SHE'S JUST A LITTLE GIRL.
DOKA (SLAM)
SHUT UP!

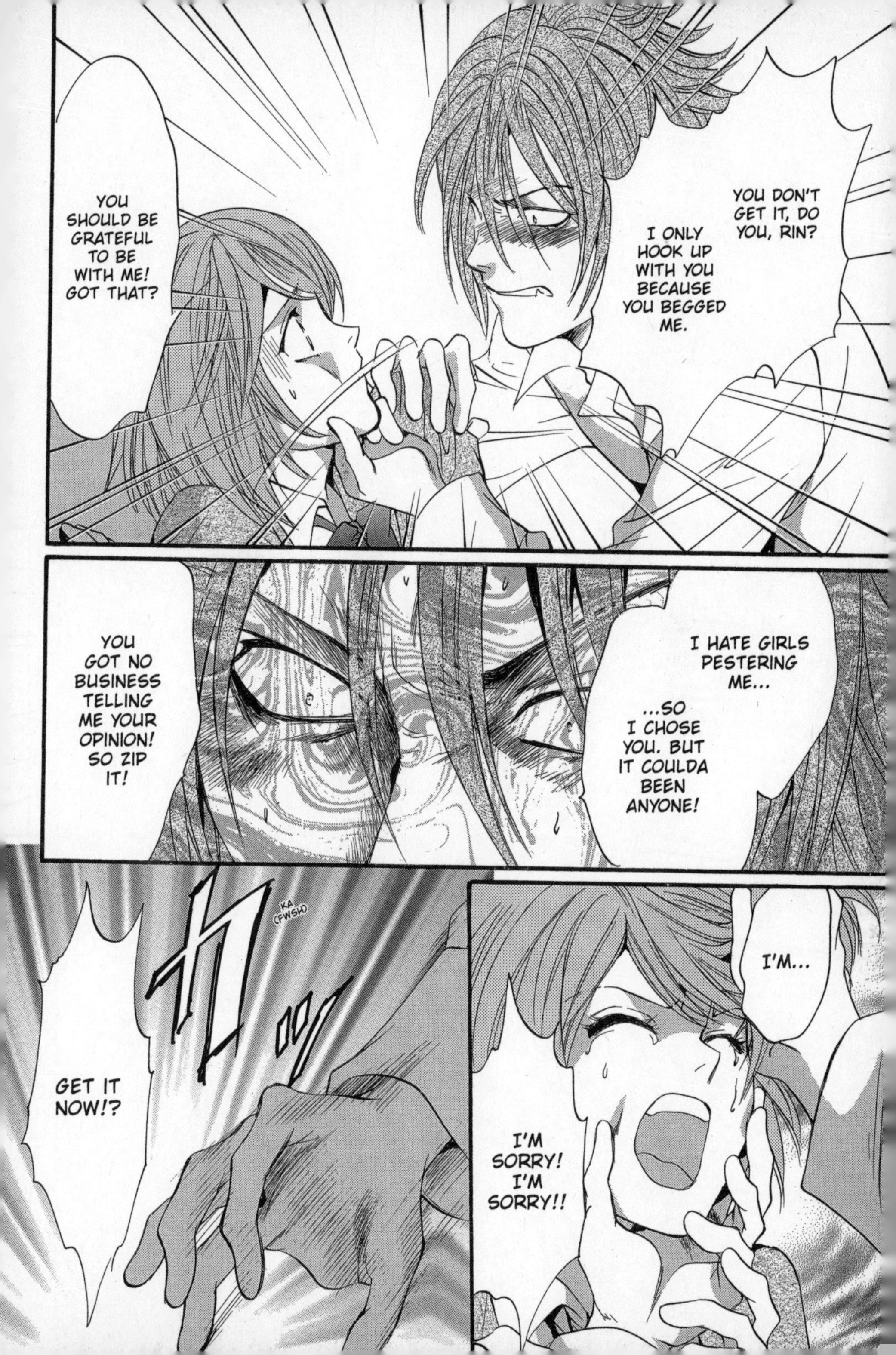
YOU DON'T GET IT, DO YOU, RIN?
I ONLY HOOK UP WITH YOU BECAUSE YOU BEGGED ME.
YOU SHOULD BE GRATEFUL TO BE WITH ME! GOT THAT?
I HATE GIRLS PESTERING ME...
...SO I CHOSE YOU. BUT IT COULDA BEEN ANYONE!
YOU GOT NO BUSINESS TELLING ME YOUR OPINION! SO ZIP IT!
I'M...
I'M SORRY! I'M SORRY!!
KA (FWSH)
GET IT NOW!?

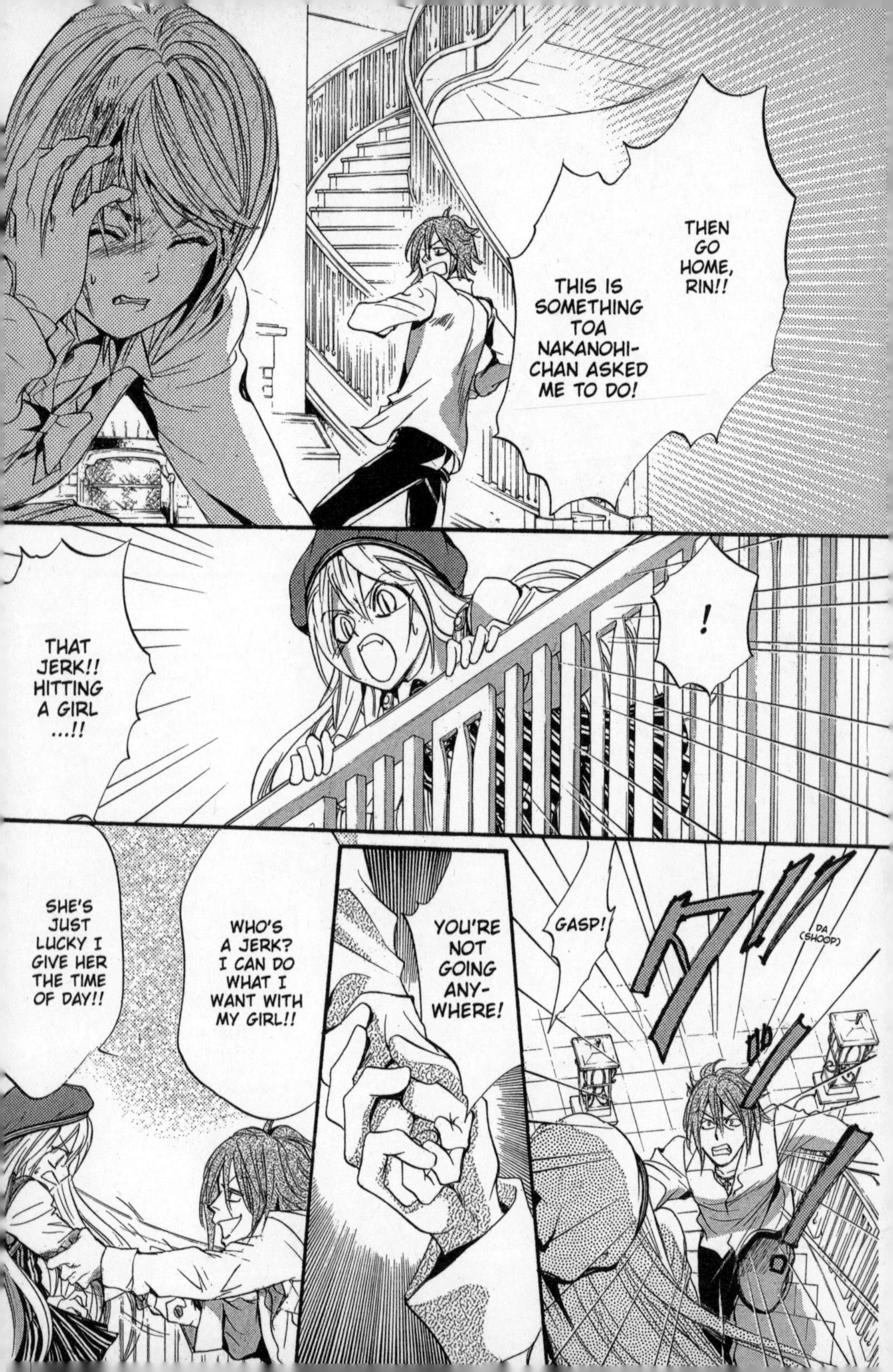
THEN GO HOME, RIN!!
THIS IS SOMETHING TOA NAKANOHI-CHAN ASKED ME TO DO!
!
THAT JERK!! HITTING A GIRL ...!!
DA (SHOOP)
GASP!
YOU'RE NOT GOING ANY-WHERE!
WHO'S A JERK? I CAN DO WHAT I WANT WITH MY GIRL!!
SHE'S JUST LUCKY I GIVE HER THE TIME OF DAY!!

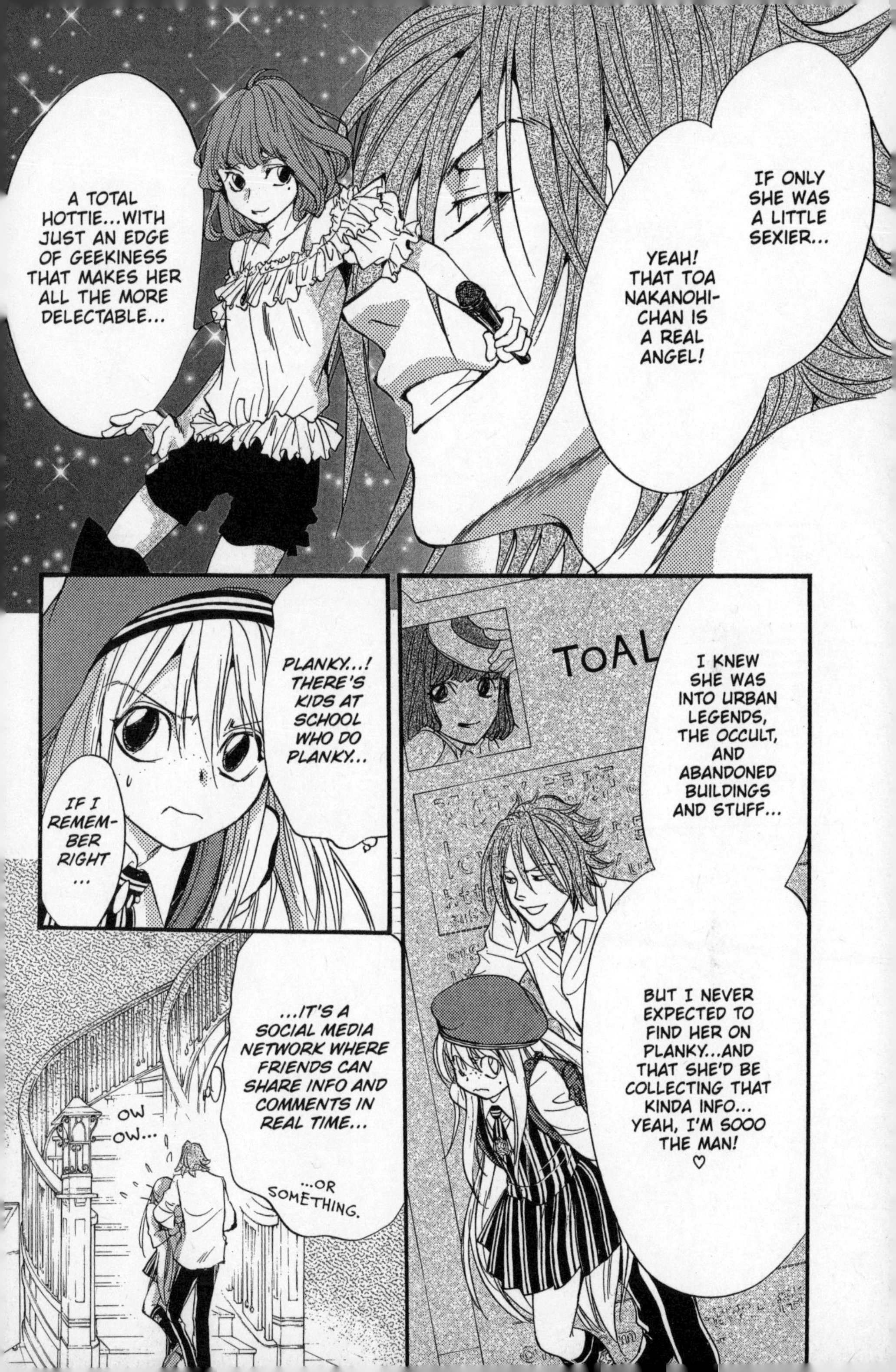
IF ONLY SHE WAS A LITTLE SEXIER...
YEAH! THAT TOA NAKANOHI-CHAN IS A REAL ANGEL!
A TOTAL HOTTIE...WITH JUST AN EDGE OF GEEKINESS THAT MAKES HER ALL THE MORE DELECTABLE...
TOAL
I KNEW SHE WAS INTO URBAN LEGENDS, THE OCCULT, AND ABANDONED BUILDINGS AND STUFF...
BUT I NEVER EXPECTED TO FIND HER ON PLANKY...AND THAT SHE'D BE COLLECTING THAT KINDA INFO... YEAH, I'M SOOO THE MAN! ♡
PLANKY...! THERE'S KIDS AT SCHOOL WHO DO PLANKY...
IF I REMEMBER RIGHT...
...IT'S A SOCIAL MEDIA NETWORK WHERE FRIENDS CAN SHARE INFO AND COMMENTS IN REAL TIME...
...OR SOMETHING.
OW OW...

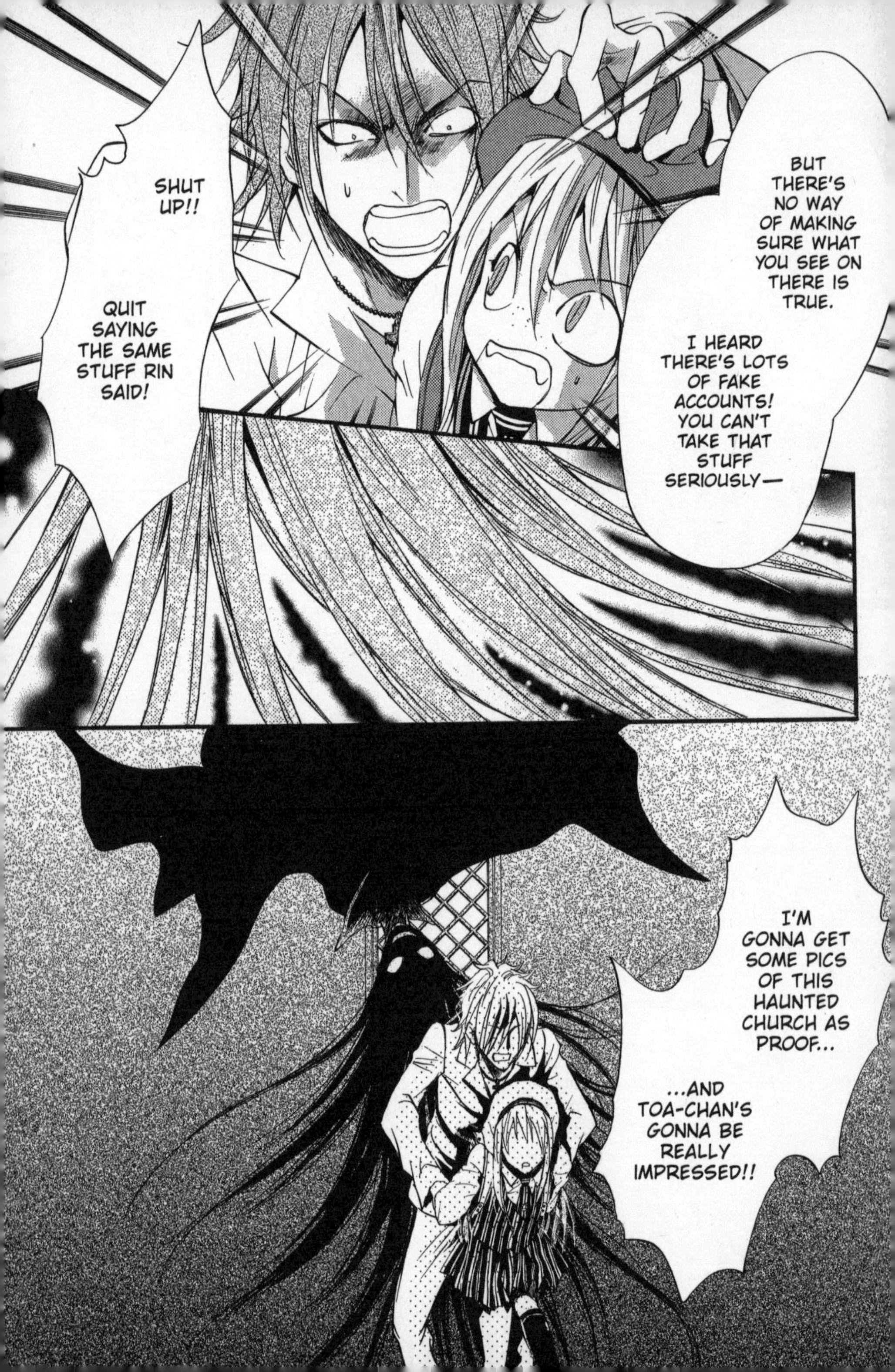
BUT THERE'S NO WAY OF MAKING SURE WHAT YOU SEE ON THERE IS TRUE.
I HEARD THERE'S LOTS OF FAKE ACCOUNTS! YOU CAN'T TAKE THAT STUFF SERIOUSLY—
SHUT UP!!
QUIT SAYING THE SAME STUFF RIN SAID!
I'M GONNA GET SOME PICS OF THIS HAUNTED CHURCH AS PROOF...
...AND TOA-CHAN'S GONNA BE REALLY IMPRESSED!!

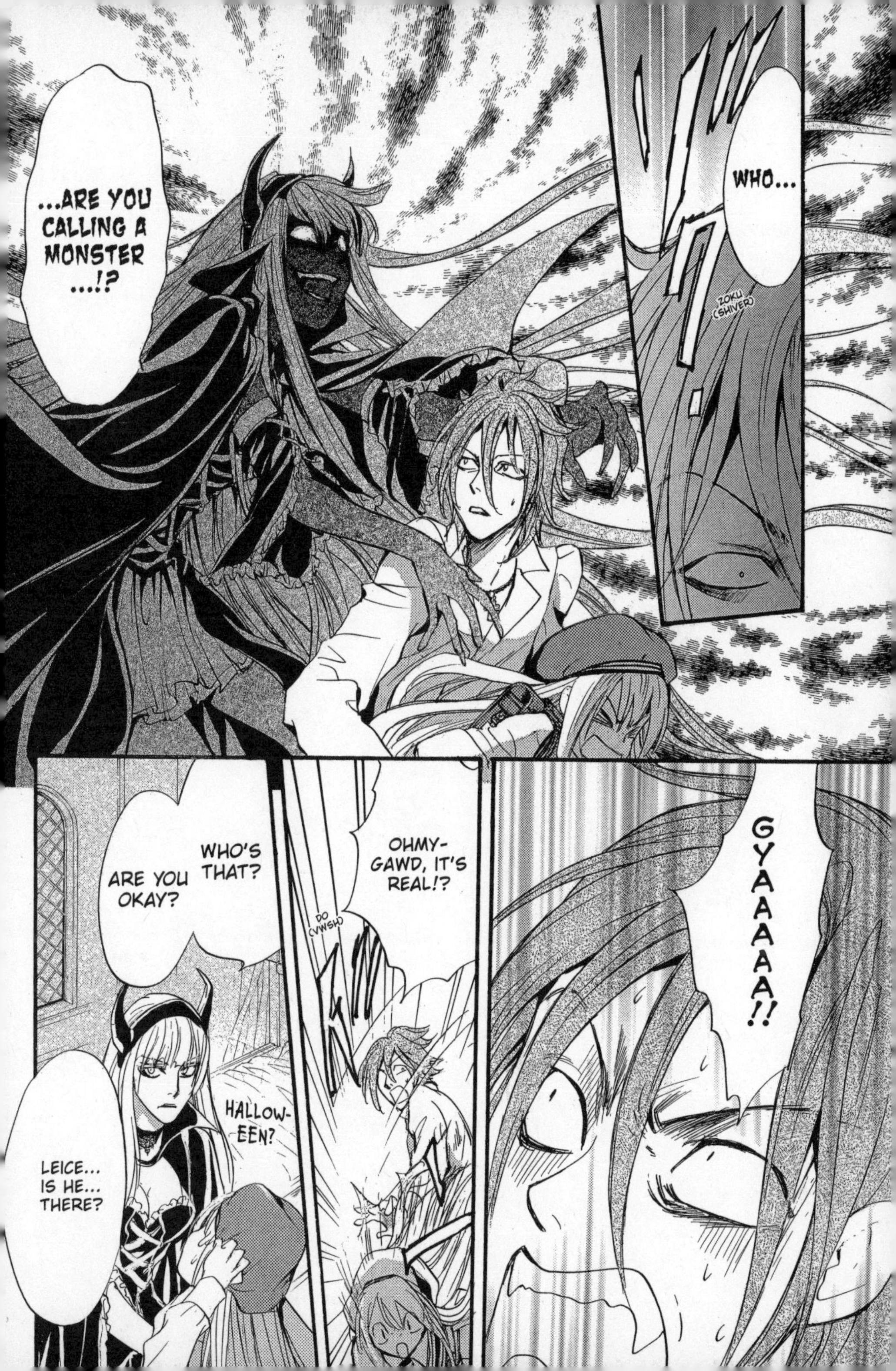
WHO...
ZOKU (SHIVER)
...ARE YOU CALLING A MONSTER ...!?
GYAAAAA!!
OHMY-GAWD, IT'S REAL!?
DO (VWSH)
WHO'S THAT?
ARE YOU OKAY?
HALLOW-EEN?
LEICE... IS HE... THERE?

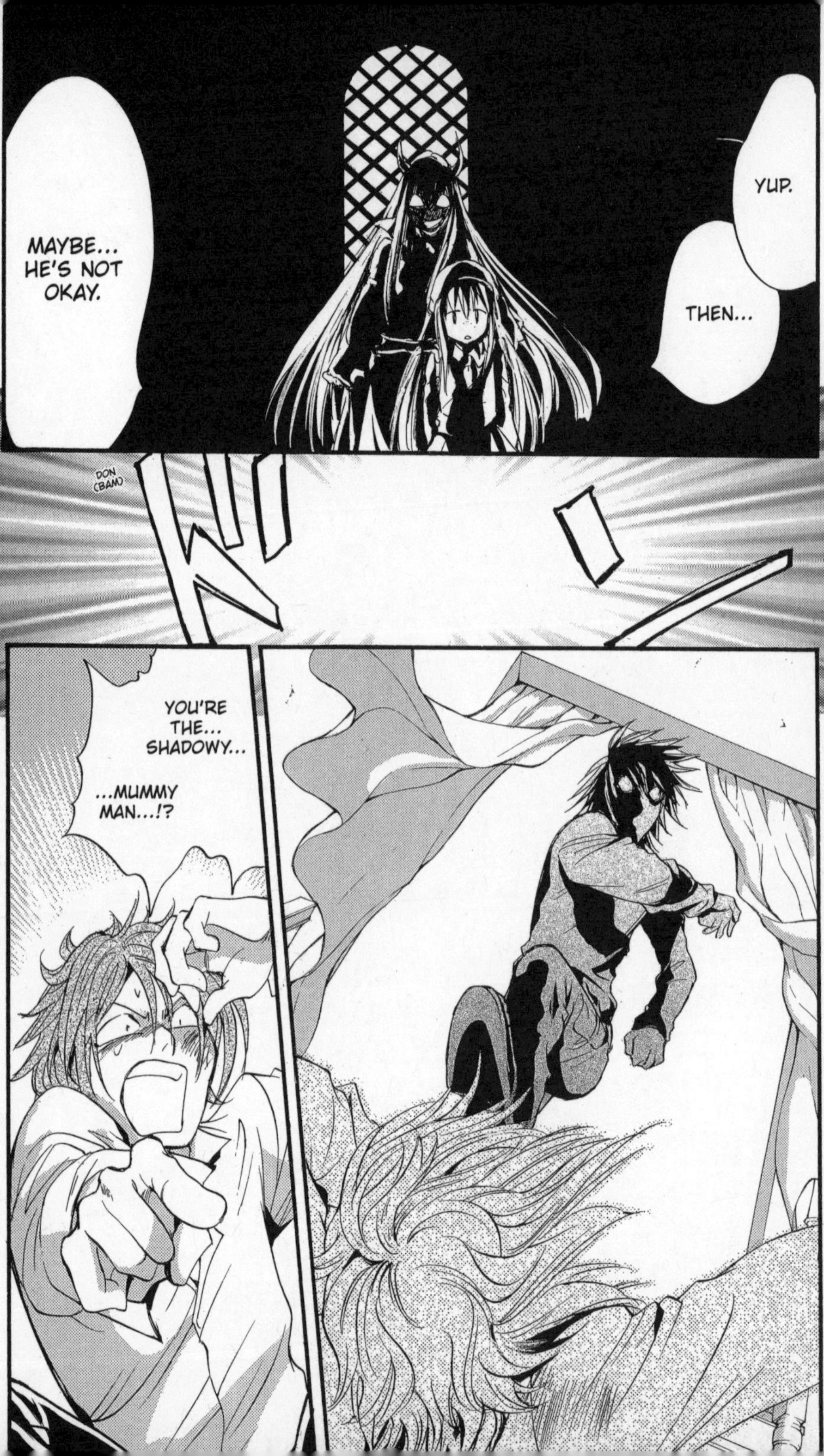
YUP.
THEN...
MAYBE... HE'S NOT OKAY.
DON (BAM)
YOU'RE THE... SHADOWY...
...MUMMY MAN...!?

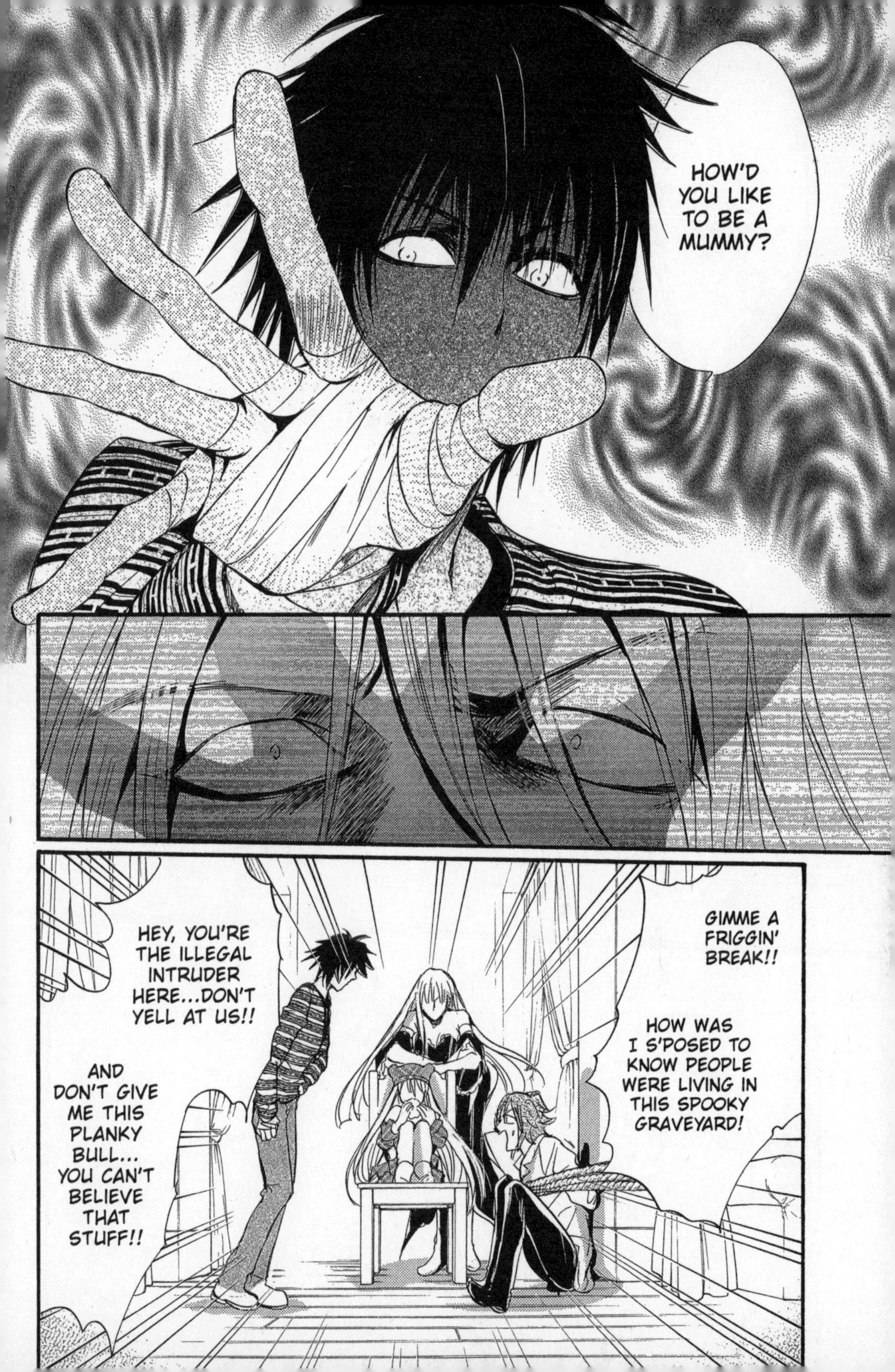
HOW'D YOU LIKE TO BE A MUMMY?
GIMME A FRIGGIN' BREAK!!
HOW WAS I S'POSED TO KNOW PEOPLE WERE LIVING IN THIS SPOOKY GRAVEYARD!
HEY, YOU'RE THE ILLEGAL INTRUDER HERE...DON'T YELL AT US!!
AND DON'T GIVE ME THIS PLANKY BULL... YOU CAN'T BELIEVE THAT STUFF!!

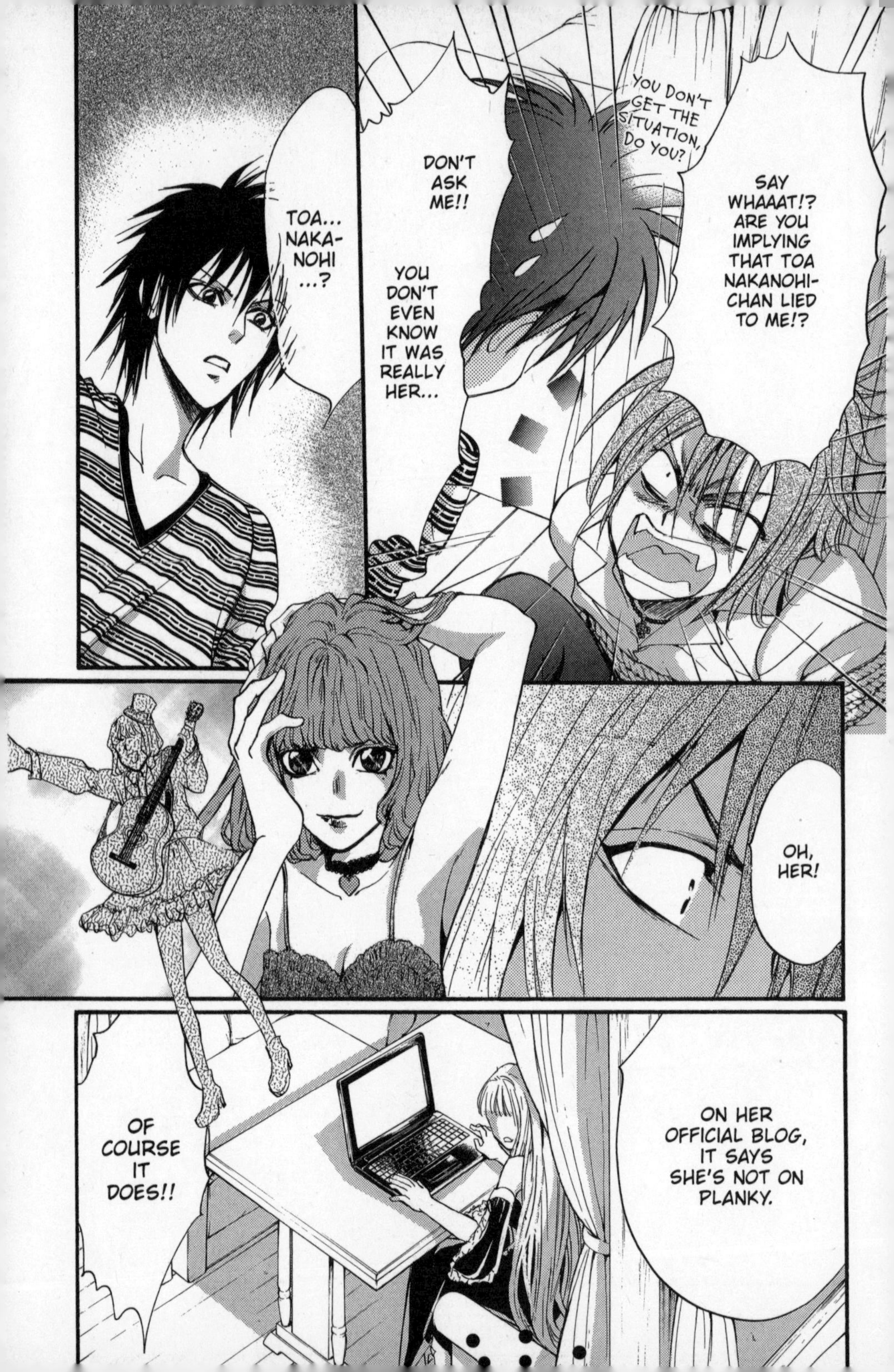
SAY WHAAAT!? ARE YOU IMPLYING THAT TOA NAKANOHI-CHAN LIED TO ME!?
YOU DON'T GET THE SITUATION, DO YOU?
DON'T ASK ME!!
YOU DON'T EVEN KNOW IT WAS REALLY HER...
TOA... NAKANOHI ...?
OH, HER!
ON HER OFFICIAL BLOG, IT SAYS SHE'S NOT ON PLANKY.
OF COURSE IT DOES!!

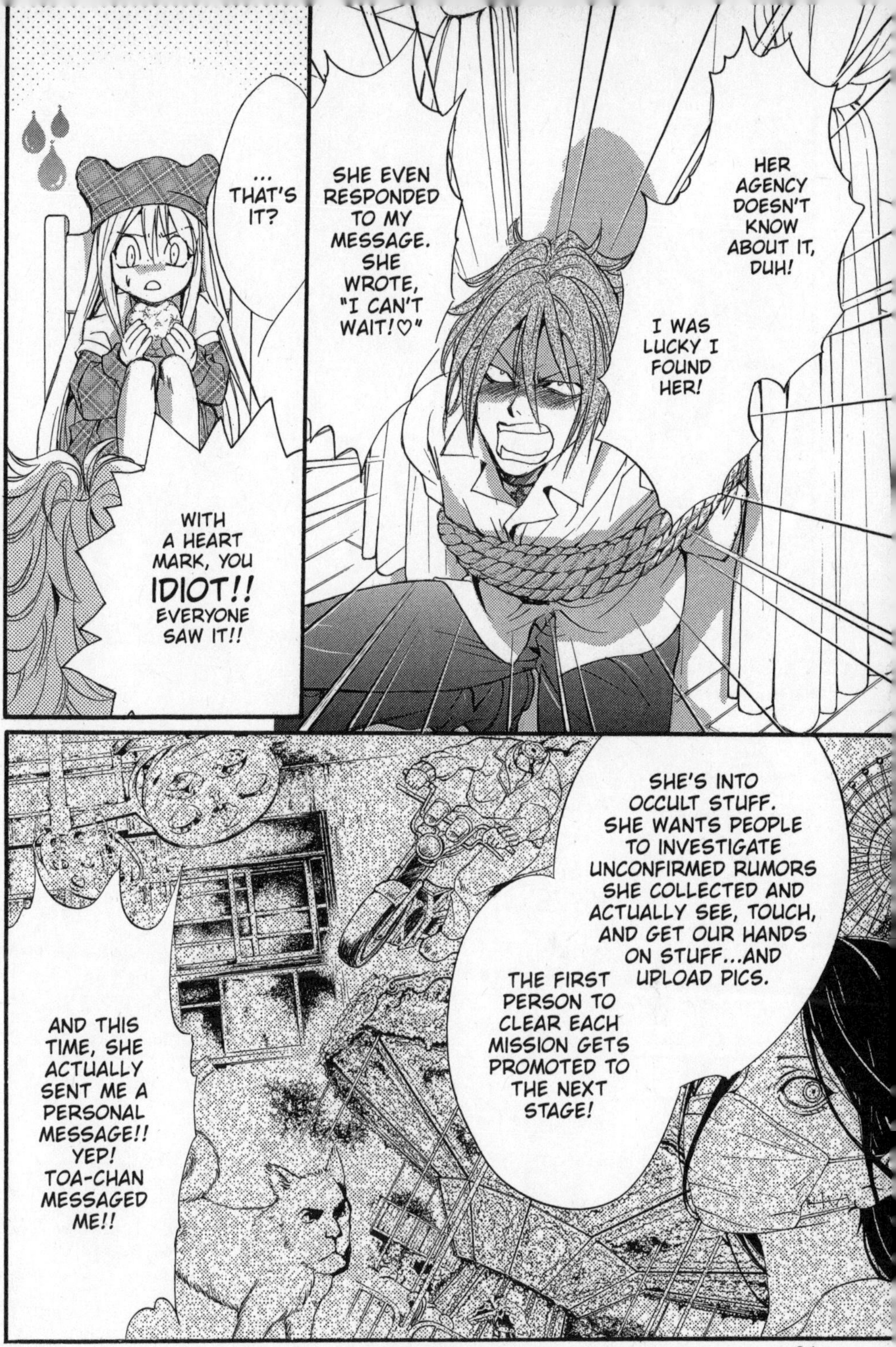
HER AGENCY DOESN'T KNOW ABOUT IT, DUH!
I WAS LUCKY I FOUND HER!
SHE EVEN RESPONDED TO MY MESSAGE. SHE WROTE, "I CAN'T WAIT!♡"
... THAT'S IT?
WITH A HEART MARK, YOU IDIOT!! EVERYONE SAW IT!!
SHE'S INTO OCCULT STUFF. SHE WANTS PEOPLE TO INVESTIGATE UNCONFIRMED RUMORS SHE COLLECTED AND ACTUALLY SEE, TOUCH, AND GET OUR HANDS ON STUFF...AND UPLOAD PICS.
THE FIRST PERSON TO CLEAR EACH MISSION GETS PROMOTED TO THE NEXT STAGE!
AND THIS TIME, SHE ACTUALLY SENT ME A PERSONAL MESSAGE!! YEP! TOA-CHAN MESSAGED ME!!

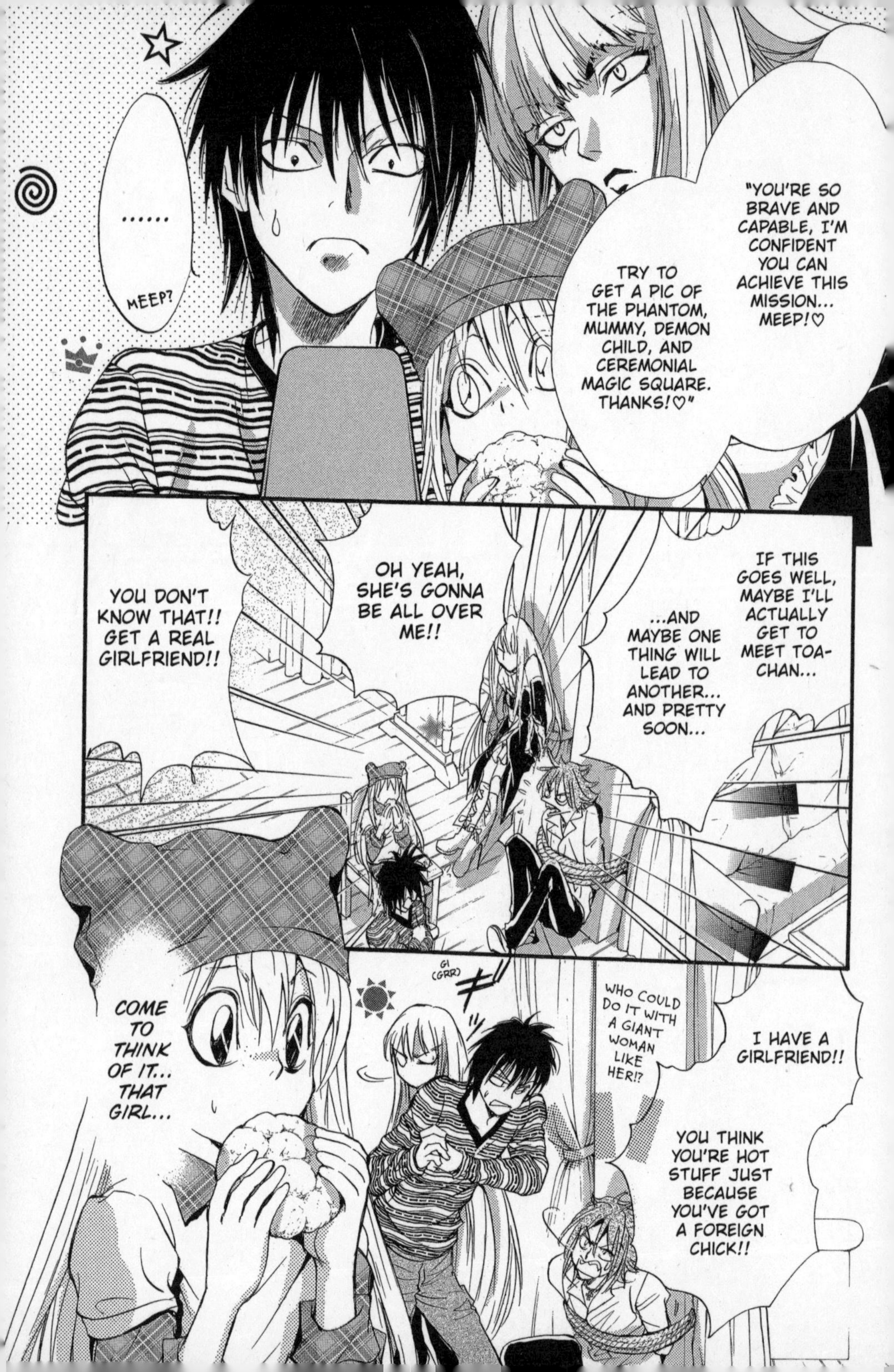
"YOU'RE SO BRAVE AND CAPABLE, I'M CONFIDENT YOU CAN ACHIEVE THIS MISSION... MEEP!♡
TRY TO GET A PIC OF THE PHANTOM, MUMMY, DEMON CHILD, AND CEREMONIAL MAGIC SQUARE. THANKS!♡"
......
MEEP?
IF THIS GOES WELL, MAYBE I'LL ACTUALLY GET TO MEET TOA-CHAN...
...AND MAYBE ONE THING WILL LEAD TO ANOTHER... AND PRETTY SOON...
OH YEAH, SHE'S GONNA BE ALL OVER ME!!
YOU DON'T KNOW THAT!! GET A REAL GIRLFRIEND!!
I HAVE A GIRLFRIEND!!
WHO COULD DO IT WITH A GIANT WOMAN LIKE HER!?
GI (GRR)
YOU THINK YOU'RE HOT STUFF JUST BECAUSE YOU'VE GOT A FOREIGN CHICK!!
COME TO THINK OF IT... THAT GIRL...

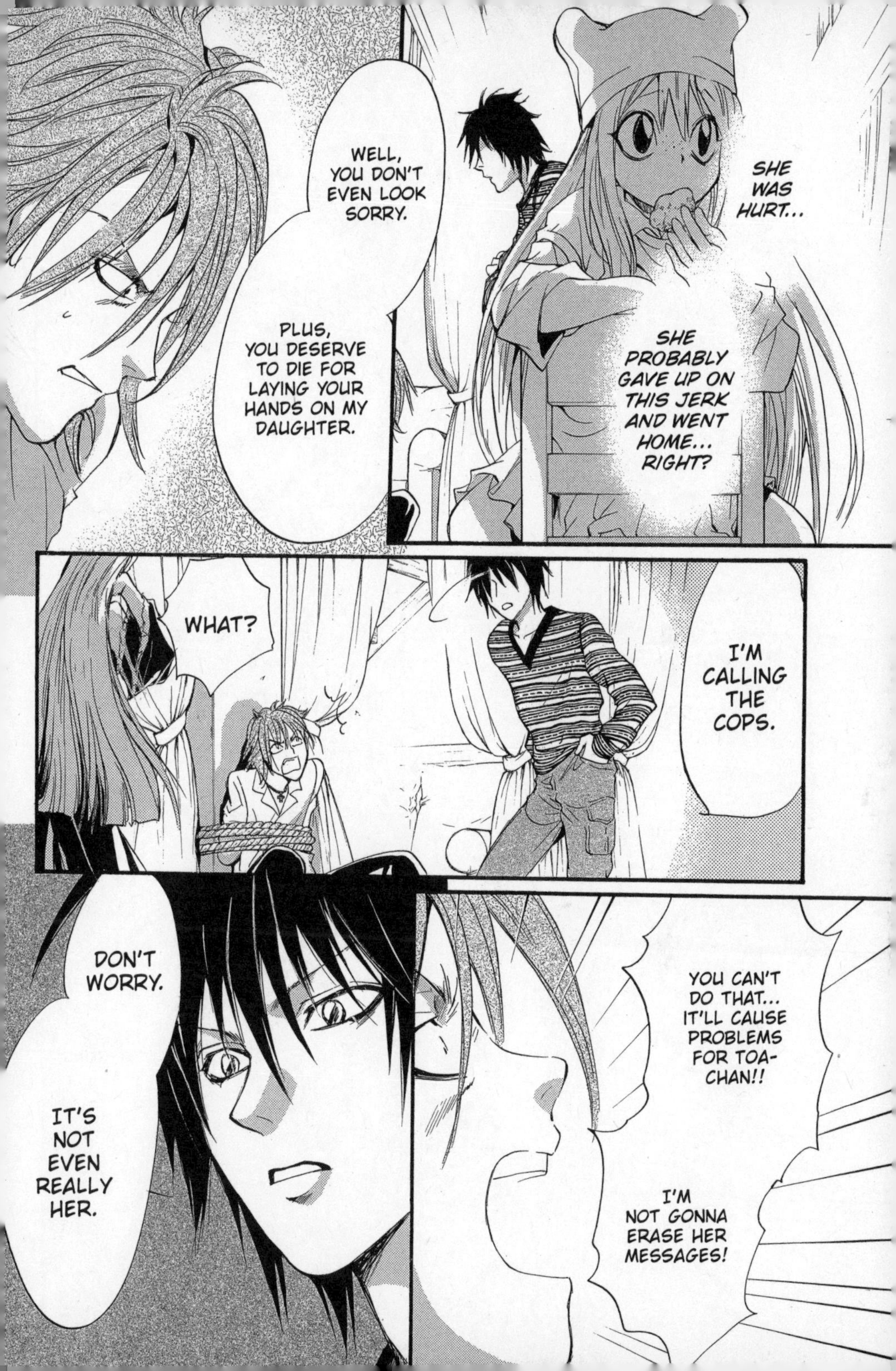
SHE WAS HURT...
SHE PROBABLY GAVE UP ON THIS JERK AND WENT HOME... RIGHT?
WELL, YOU DON'T EVEN LOOK SORRY.
PLUS, YOU DESERVE TO DIE FOR LAYING YOUR HANDS ON MY DAUGHTER.
I'M CALLING THE COPS.
WHAT?
YOU CAN'T DO THAT... IT'LL CAUSE PROBLEMS FOR TOA-CHAN!!
I'M NOT GONNA ERASE HER MESSAGES!
DON'T WORRY.
IT'S NOT EVEN REALLY HER.

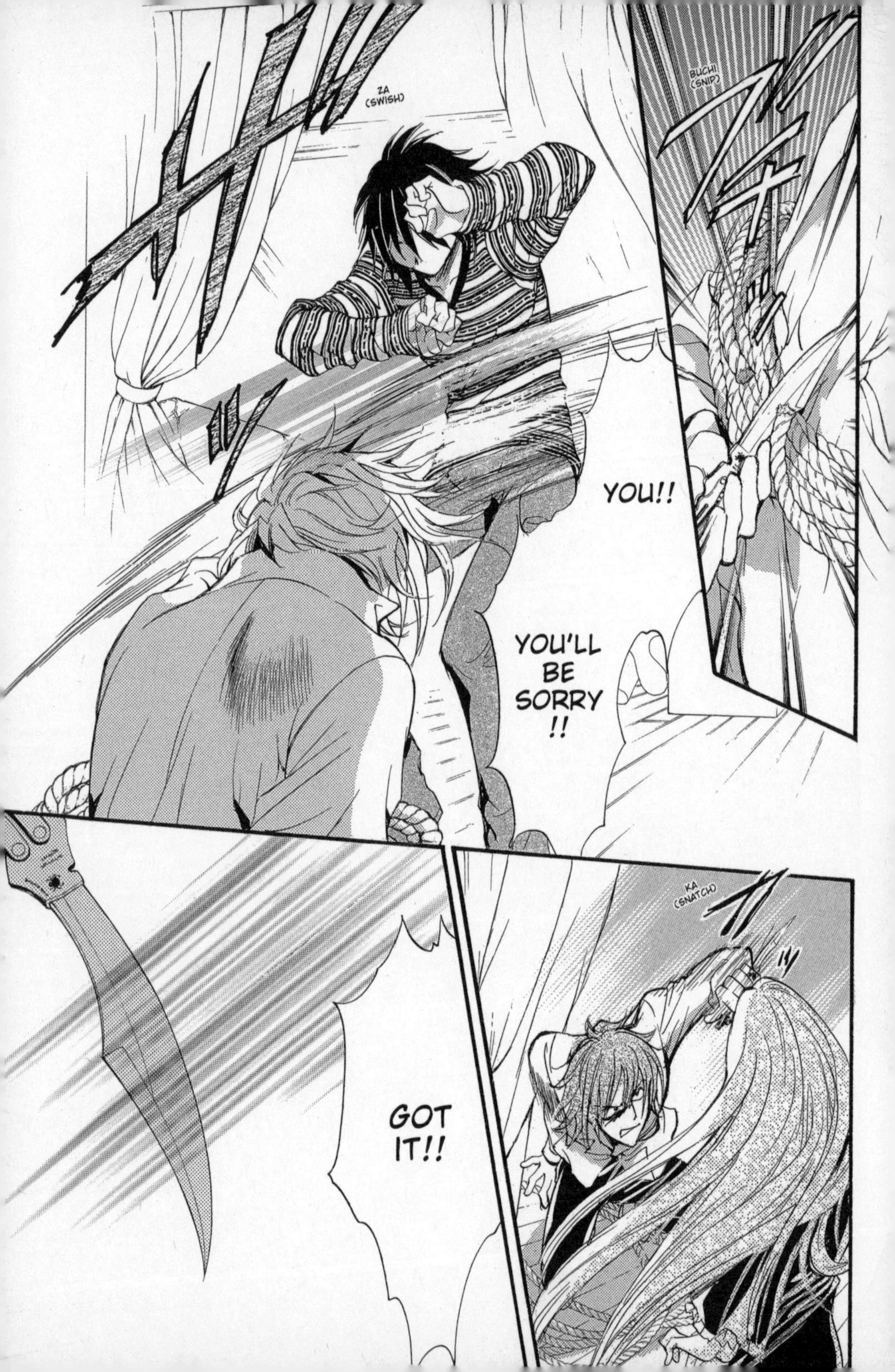
BUCHI (SNIP)
YOU!!
YOU'LL BE SORRY!!
ZA (SWISH)
KA (SNATCH)
GOT IT!!

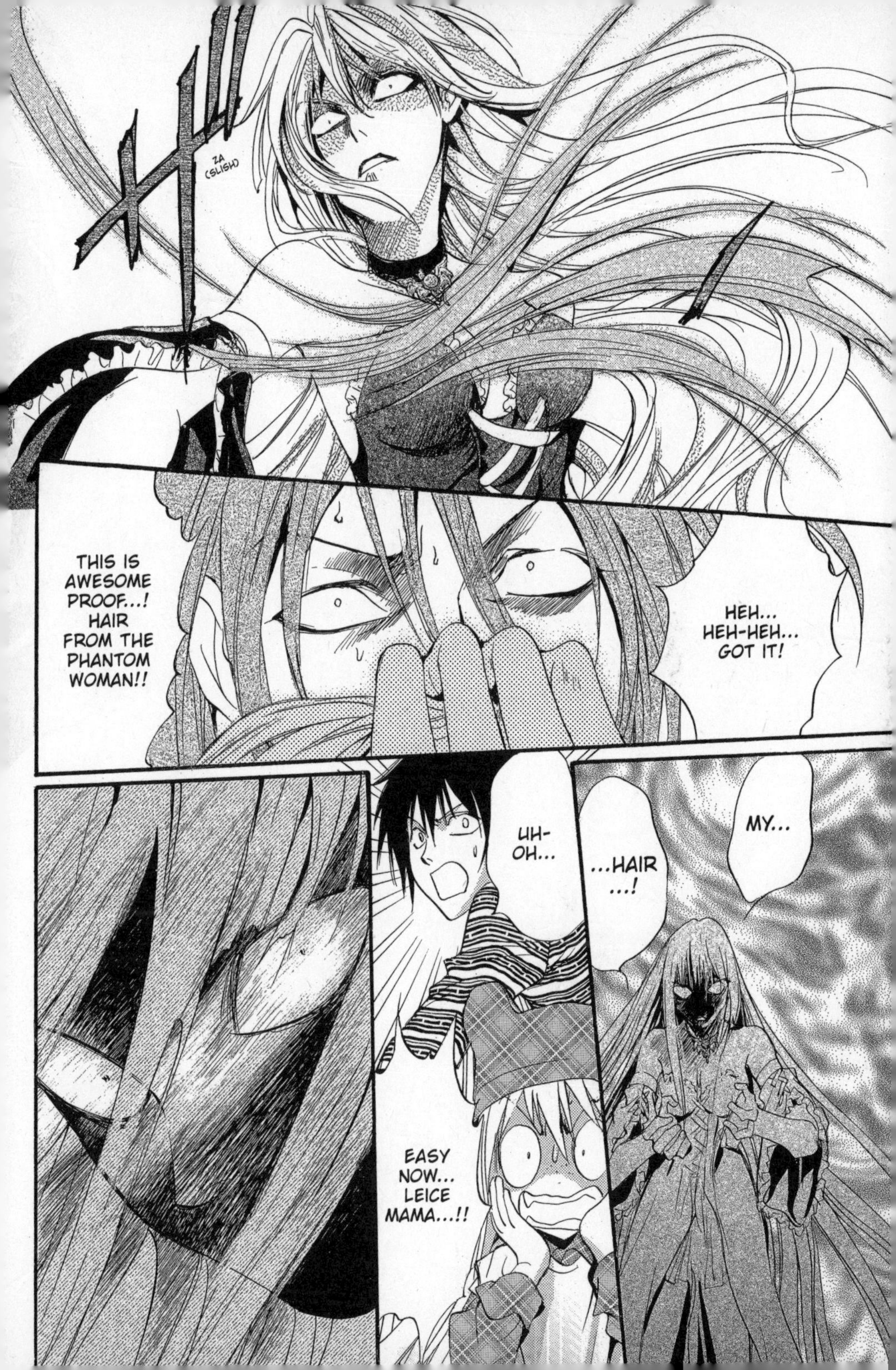
ZA (SLISH)
HEH... HEH-HEH... GOT IT!
THIS IS AWESOME PROOF...! HAIR FROM THE PHANTOM WOMAN!!
MY...
...HAIR ...!
UH-OH...
EASY NOW... LEICE MAMA...!!

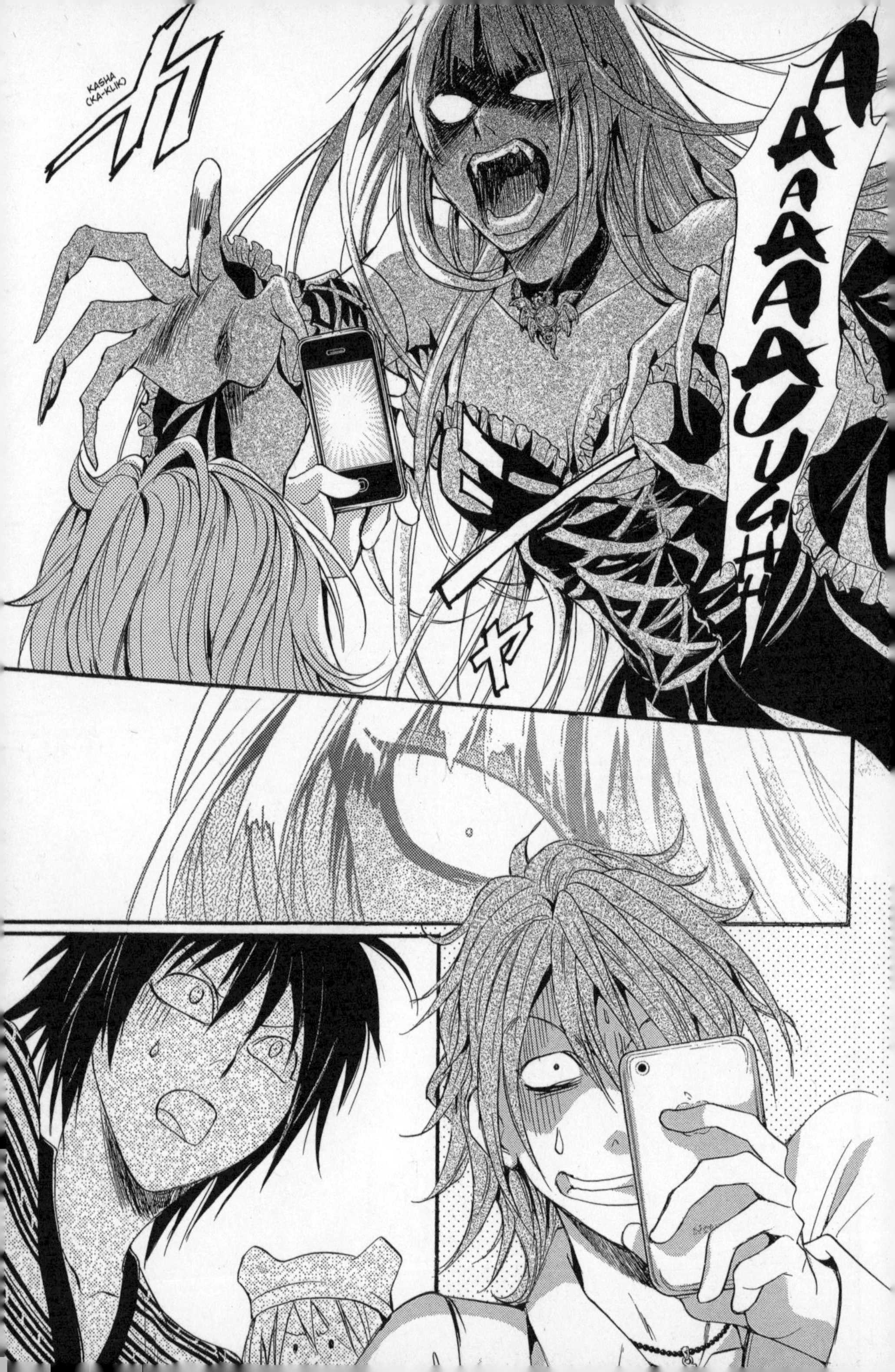
AAAAAAUUGH
KASHA (KA-KLIK)

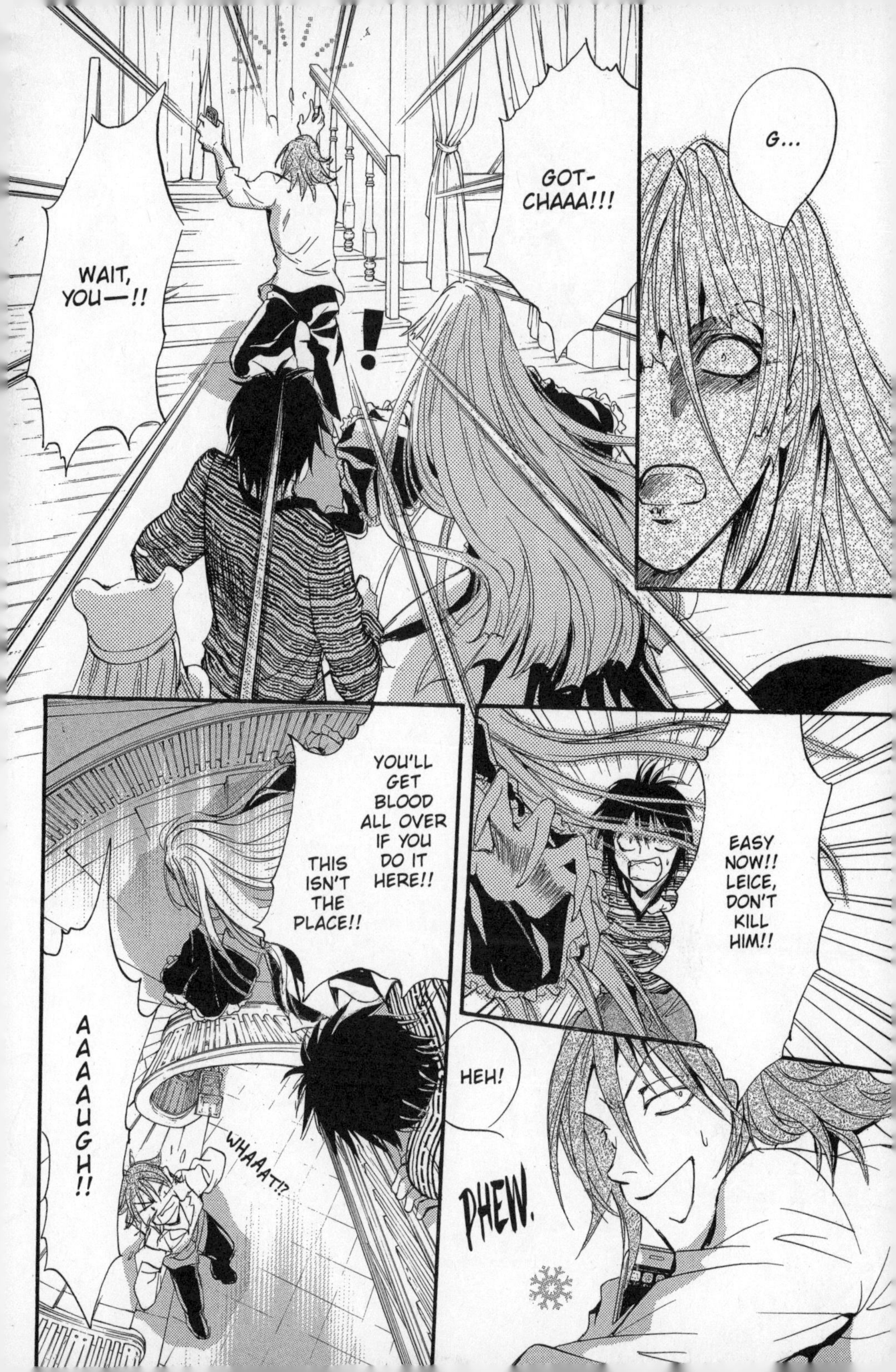
G...
GOT-CHAAA!!!
WAIT, YOU—!!
!
EASY NOW!! LEICE, DON'T KILL HIM!!
HEH!
PHEW.
YOU'LL GET BLOOD ALL OVER IF YOU DO IT HERE!!
THIS ISN'T THE PLACE!!
WHAAAT!?
AAAAAUGH!!

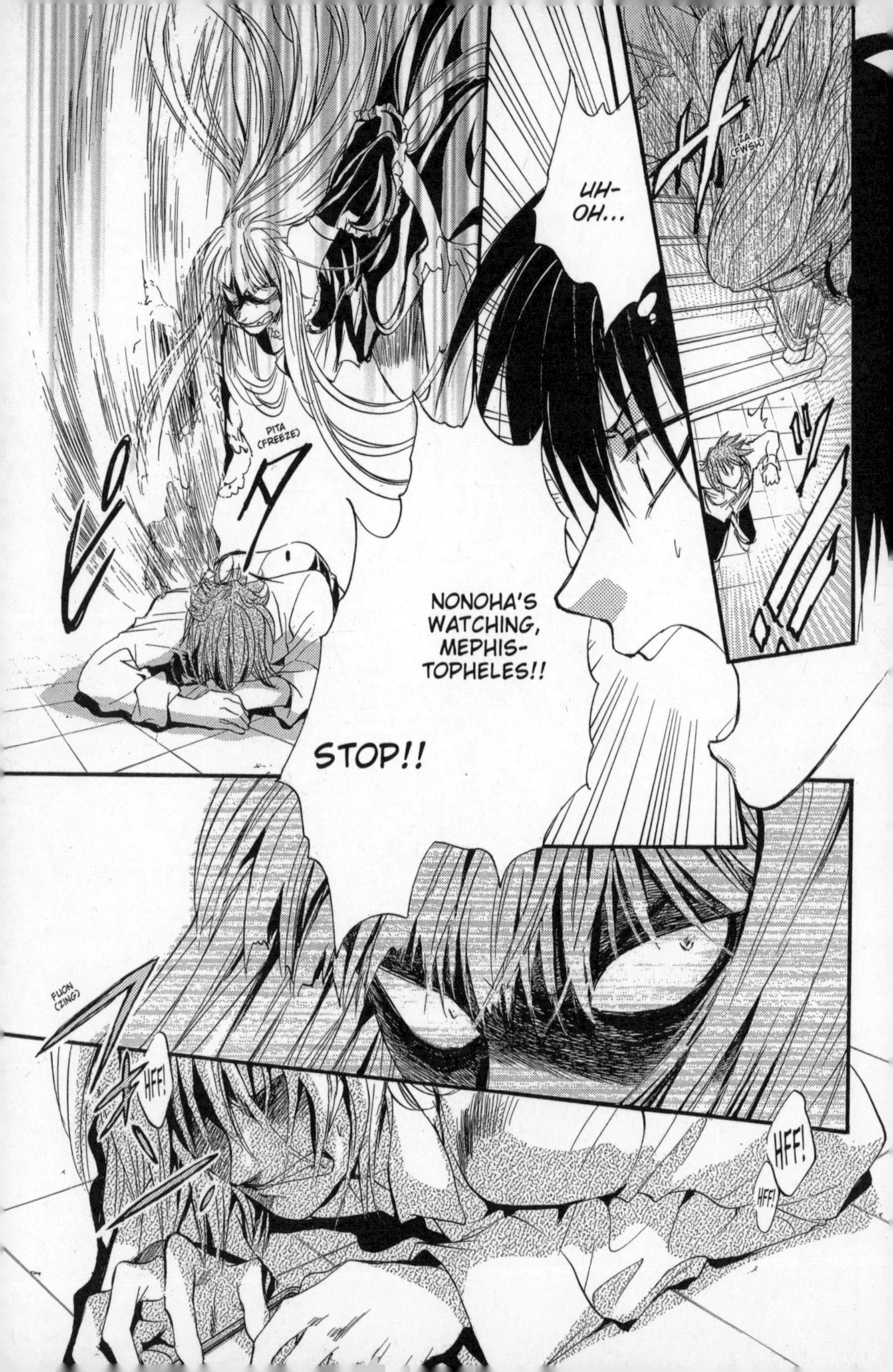
ZA (FWSH)
UH-OH...
NONOHA'S WATCHING, MEPHISTOPHELES!!
STOP!!
PITA (FREEZE)
FUON (ZING)
HFF!
HFF!
HFF!

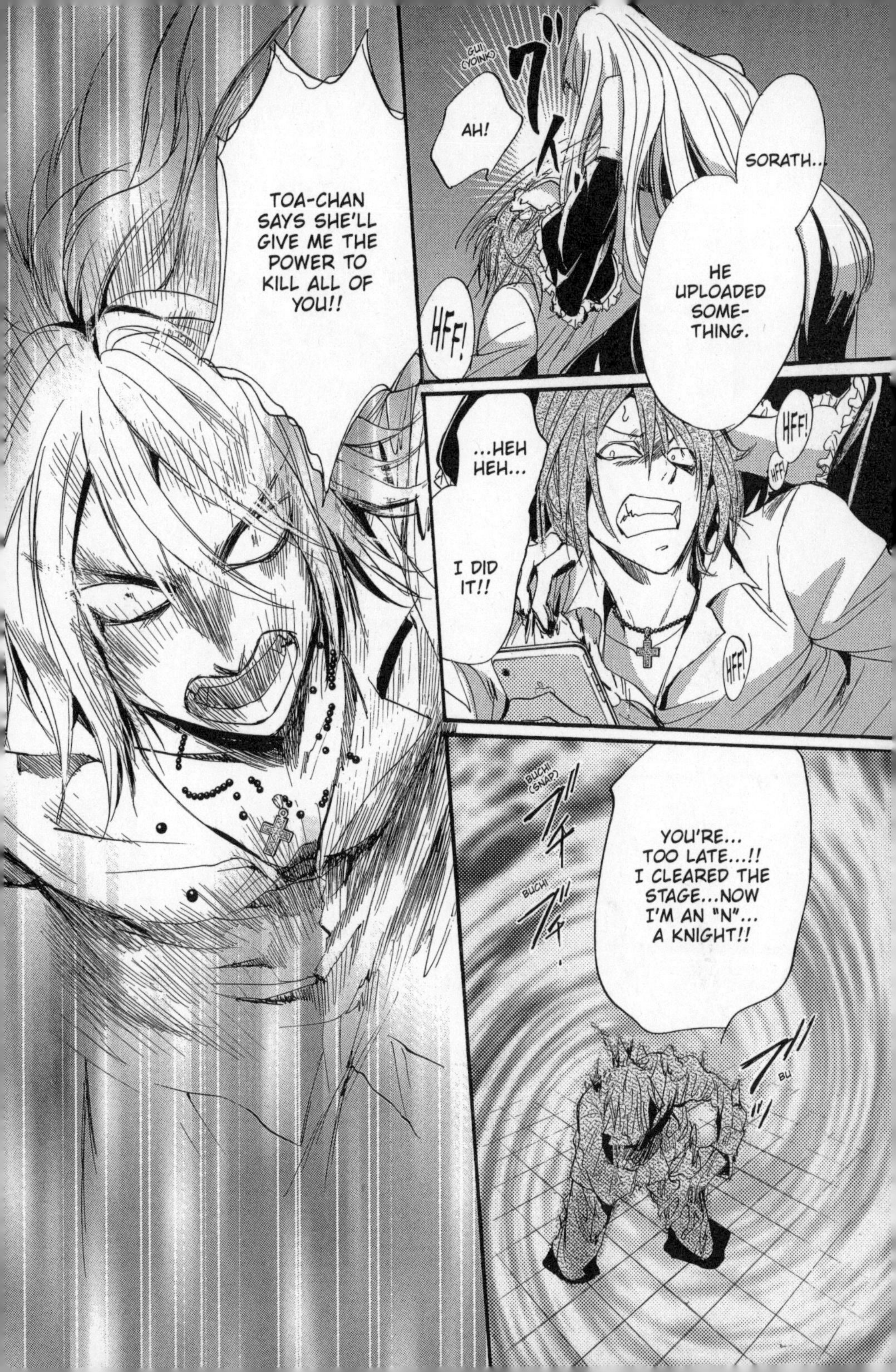
SORATH...
HE UPLOADED SOMETHING.
GUI (YOINK)
AH!
HFF!
HFF!
HFF!
HFF!
...HEH HEH...
I DID IT!!
BUCHI (SNAP)
BUCHI
YOU'RE... TOO LATE...!! I CLEARED THE STAGE...NOW I'M AN "N"... A KNIGHT!!
BU
TOA-CHAN SAYS SHE'LL GIVE ME THE POWER TO KILL ALL OF YOU!!

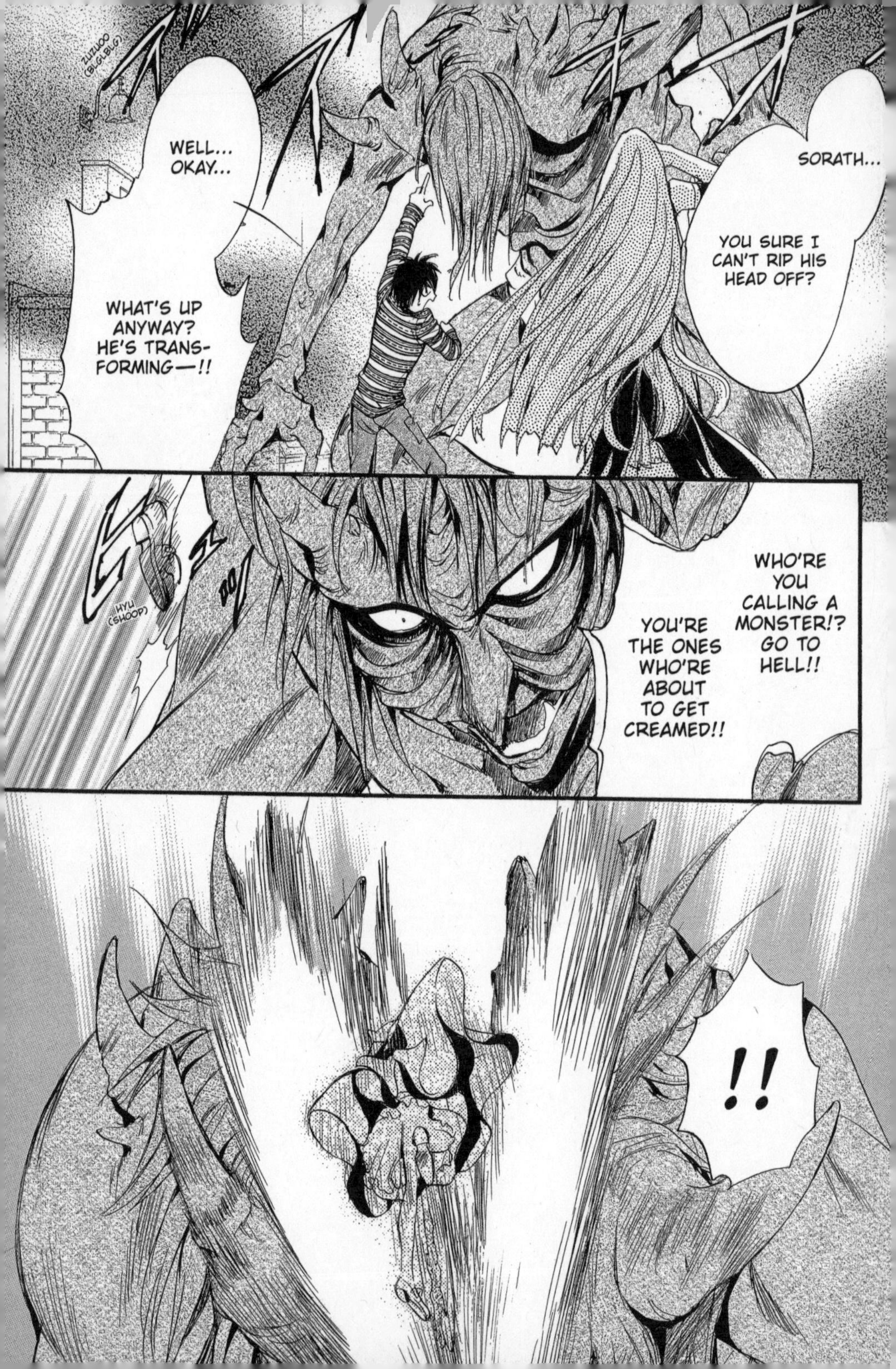
SORATH...
YOU SURE I CAN'T RIP HIS HEAD OFF?
WELL... OKAY...
WHAT'S UP ANYWAY? HE'S TRANS-FORMING—!!
ZUZUOO (BLGLBLG)
WHO'RE YOU CALLING A MONSTER!? GO TO HELL!!
YOU'RE THE ONES WHO'RE ABOUT TO GET CREAMED!!
HYU (SHOOP)
!!

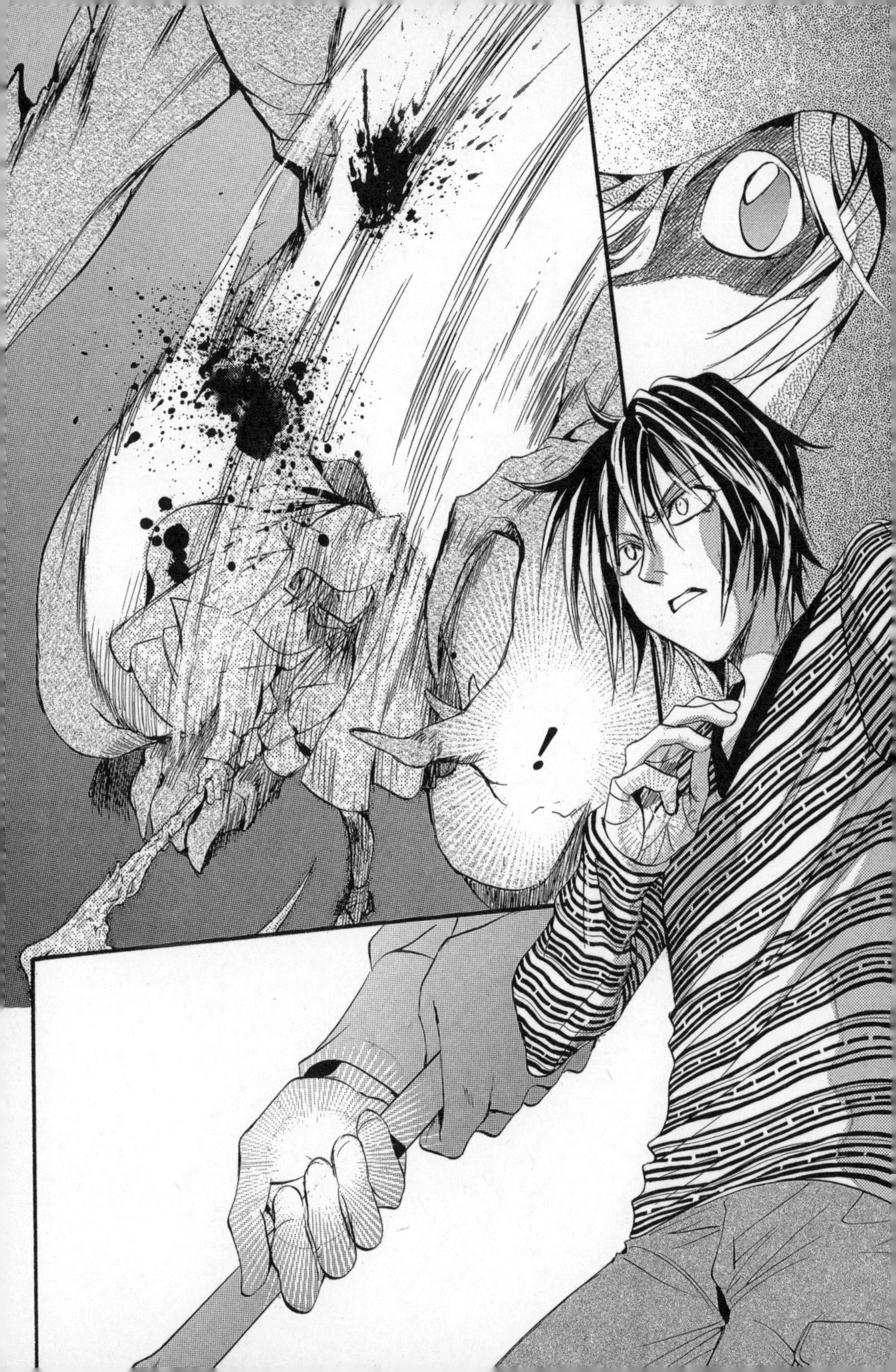
!

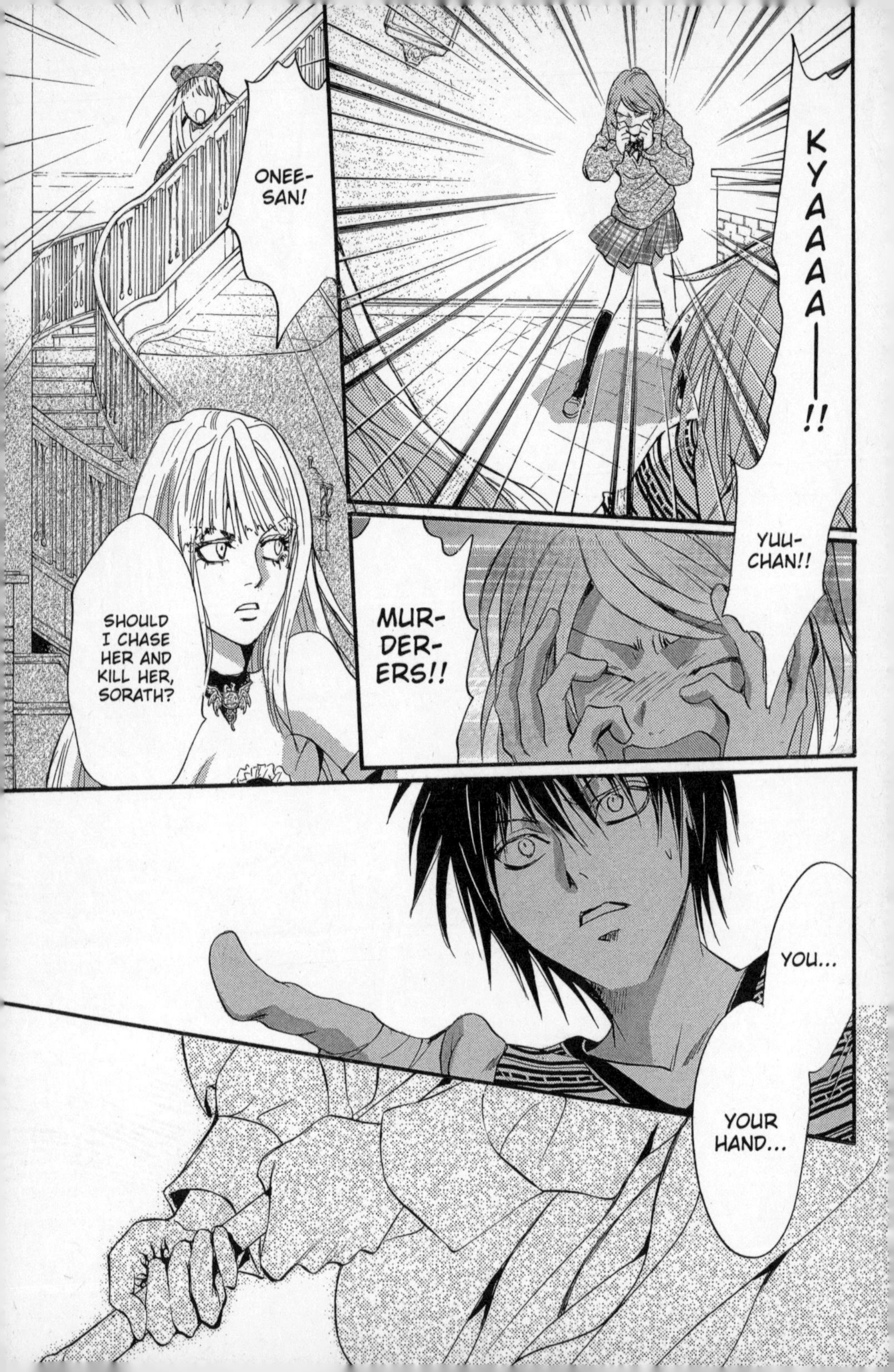
KYAAAA—!!
YUU-CHAN!!
MUR-DER-ERS!!
ONEE-SAN!
SHOULD I CHASE HER AND KILL HER, SORATH?
YOU...
YOUR HAND...

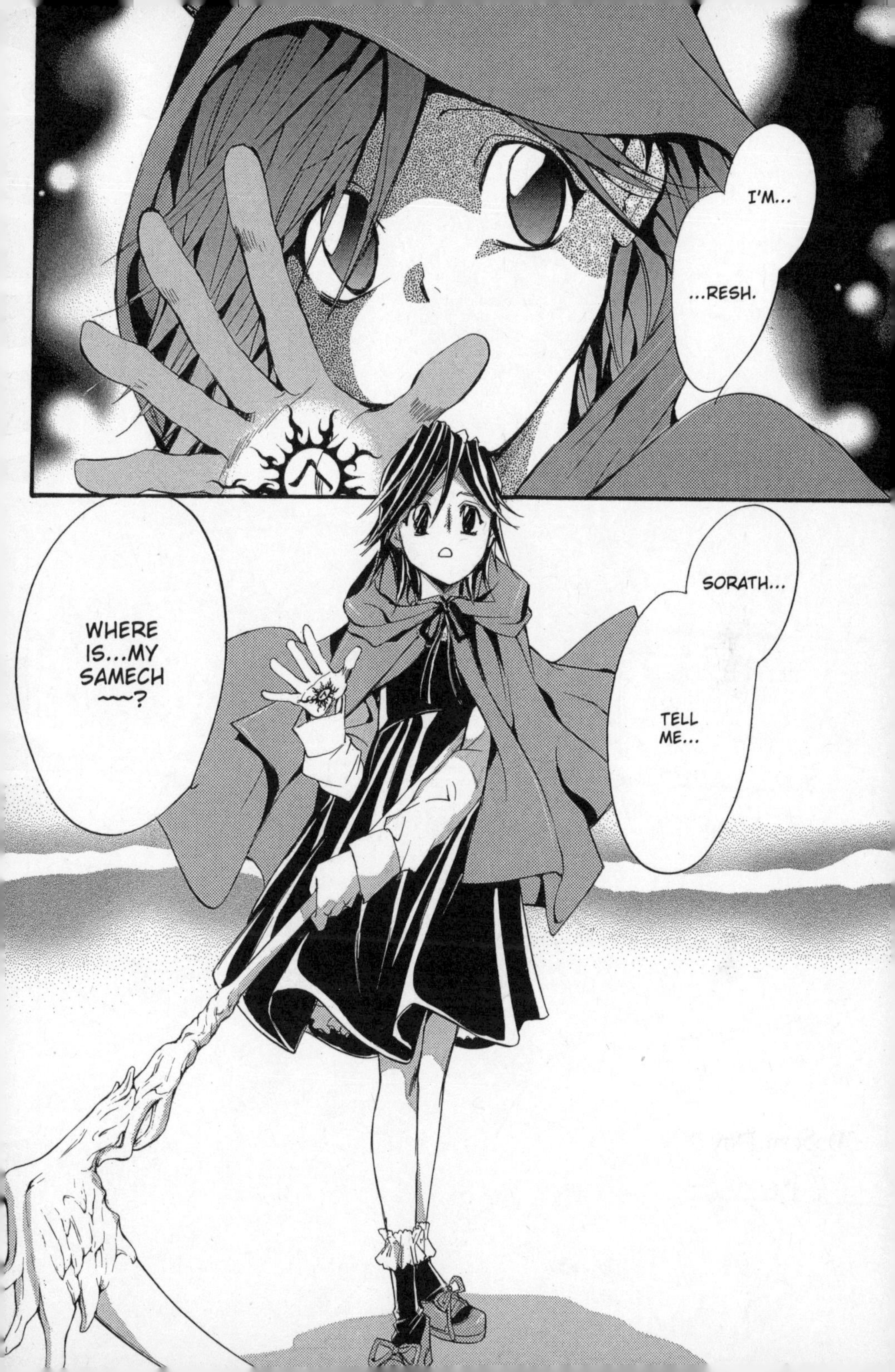
I'M...
...RESH.
SORATH...
TELL ME...
WHERE IS...MY SAMECH ~~~?

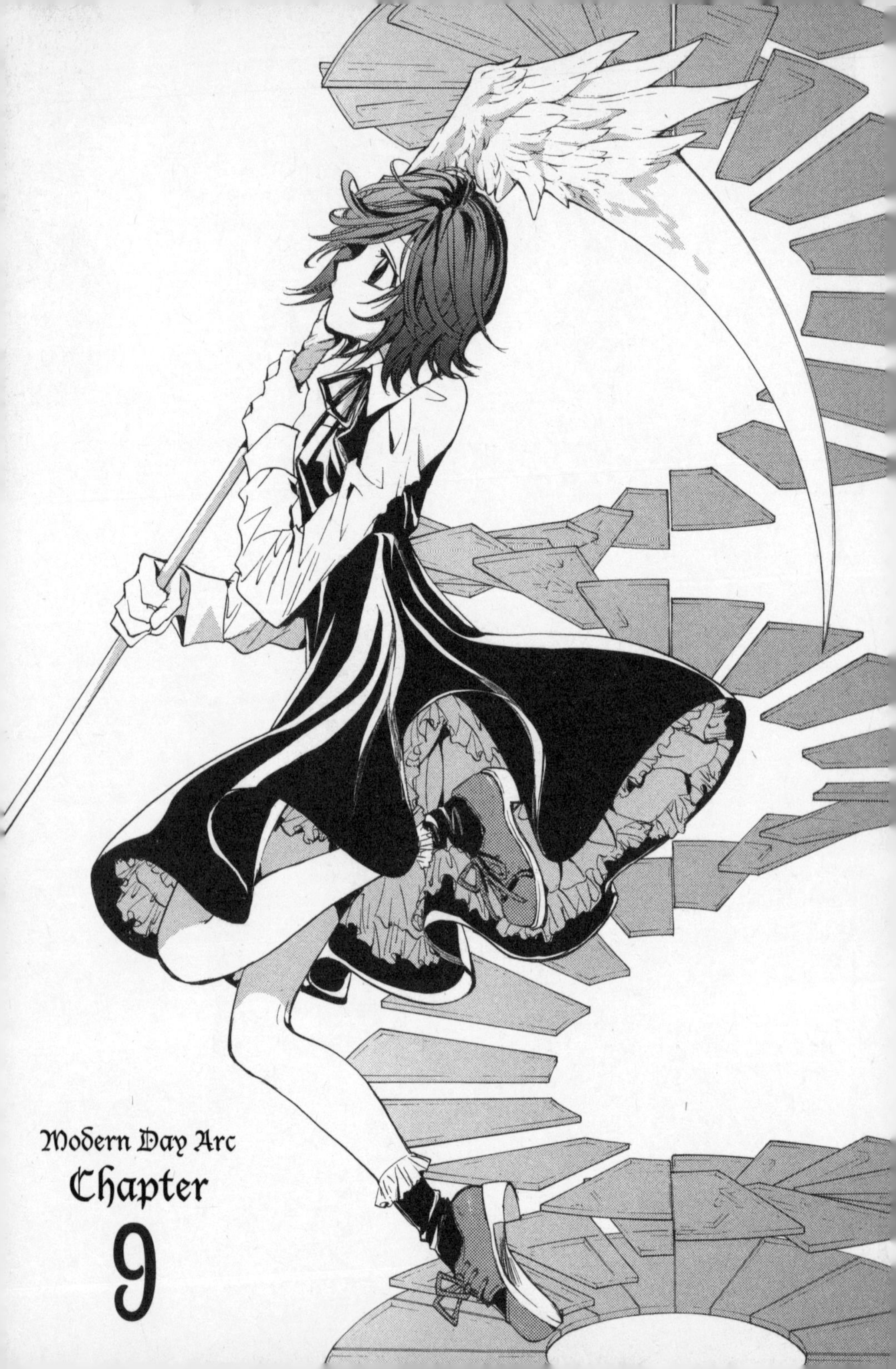

Modern Day Arc

Chapter 9

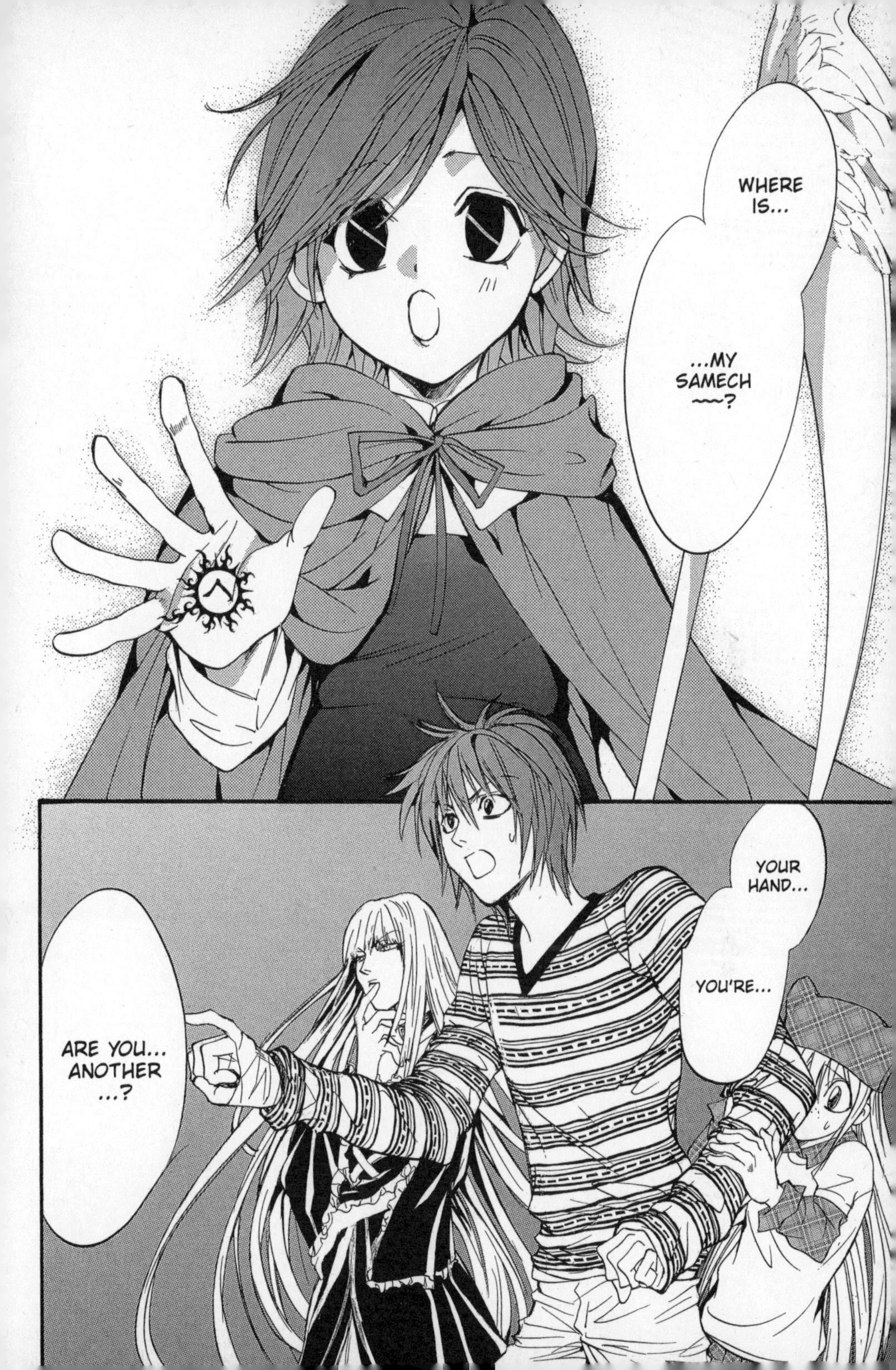
WHERE IS...
...MY SAMECH ~~~?
YOUR HAND...
YOU'RE...
ARE YOU... ANOTHER ...?

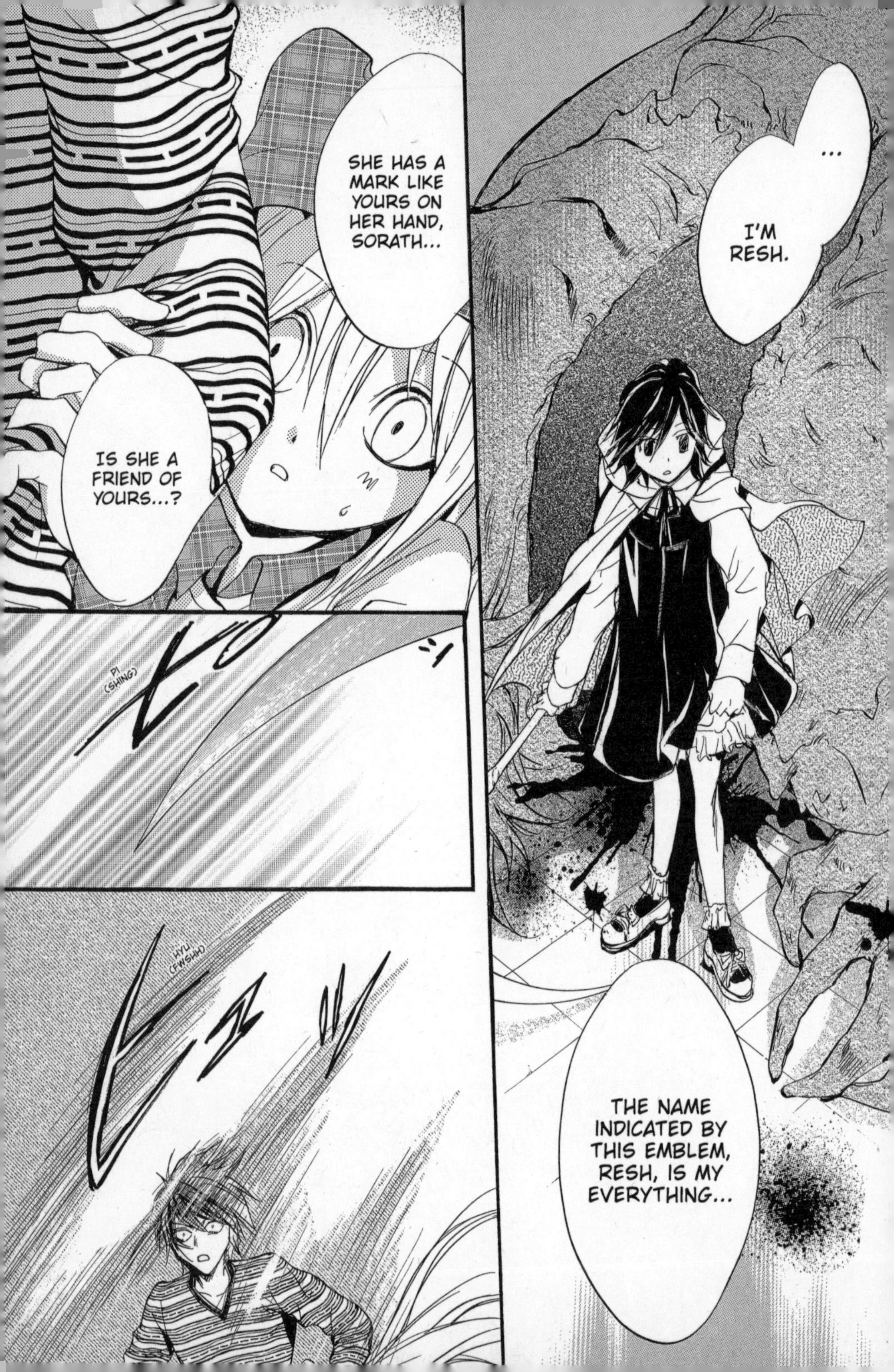
...
I'M RESH.
THE NAME INDICATED BY THIS EMBLEM, RESH, IS MY EVERYTHING...
SHE HAS A MARK LIKE YOURS ON HER HAND, SORATH...
IS SHE A FRIEND OF YOURS...?
PI (SHING)
HYU (FWSHH)

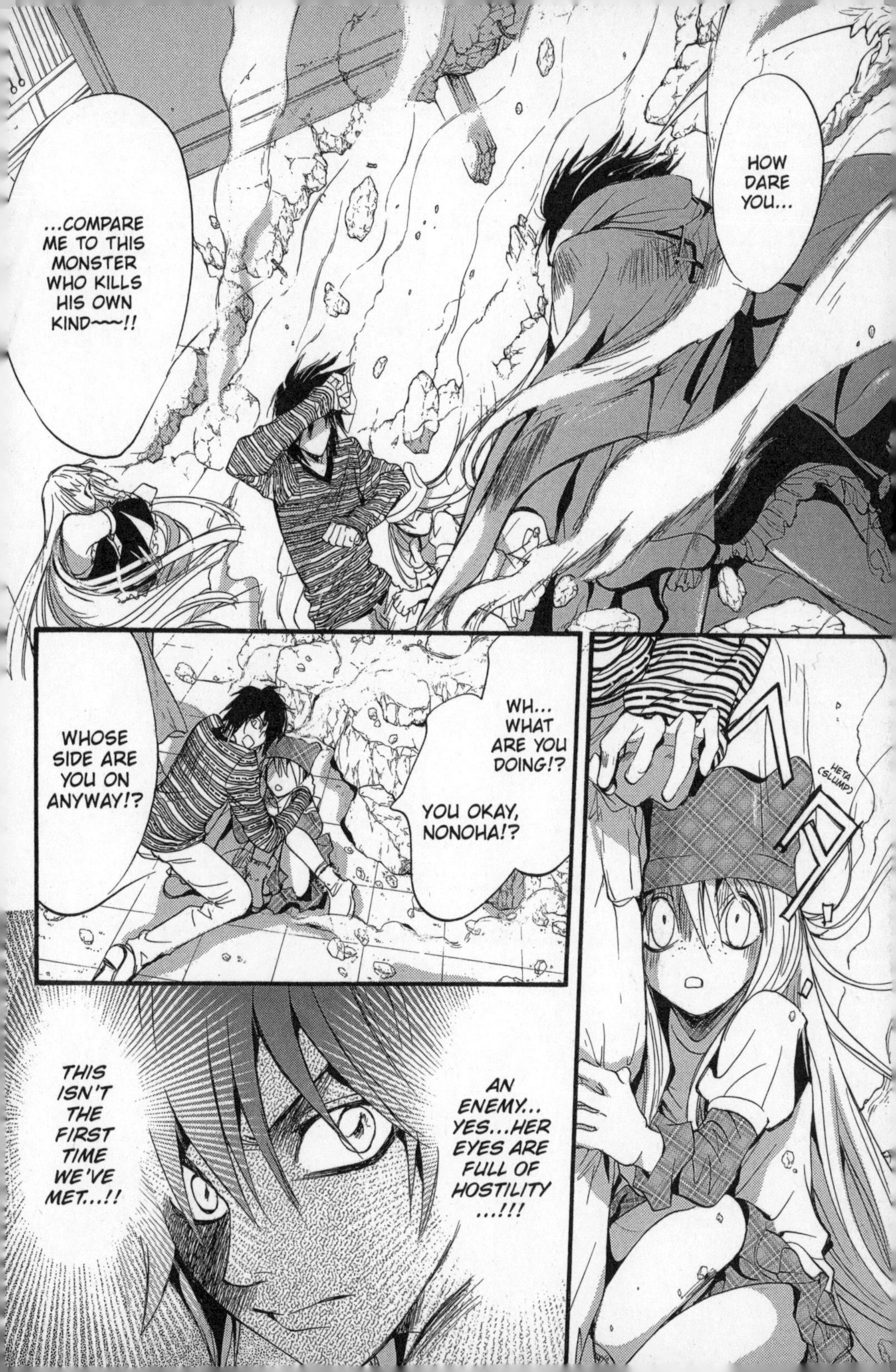
HOW DARE YOU...
...COMPARE ME TO THIS MONSTER WHO KILLS HIS OWN KIND~~~!!
HETA (SLUMP)
WH... WHAT ARE YOU DOING!?
YOU OKAY, NONOHA!?
WHOSE SIDE ARE YOU ON ANYWAY!?
AN ENEMY... YES...HER EYES ARE FULL OF HOSTILITY ...!!!
THIS ISN'T THE FIRST TIME WE'VE MET...!!

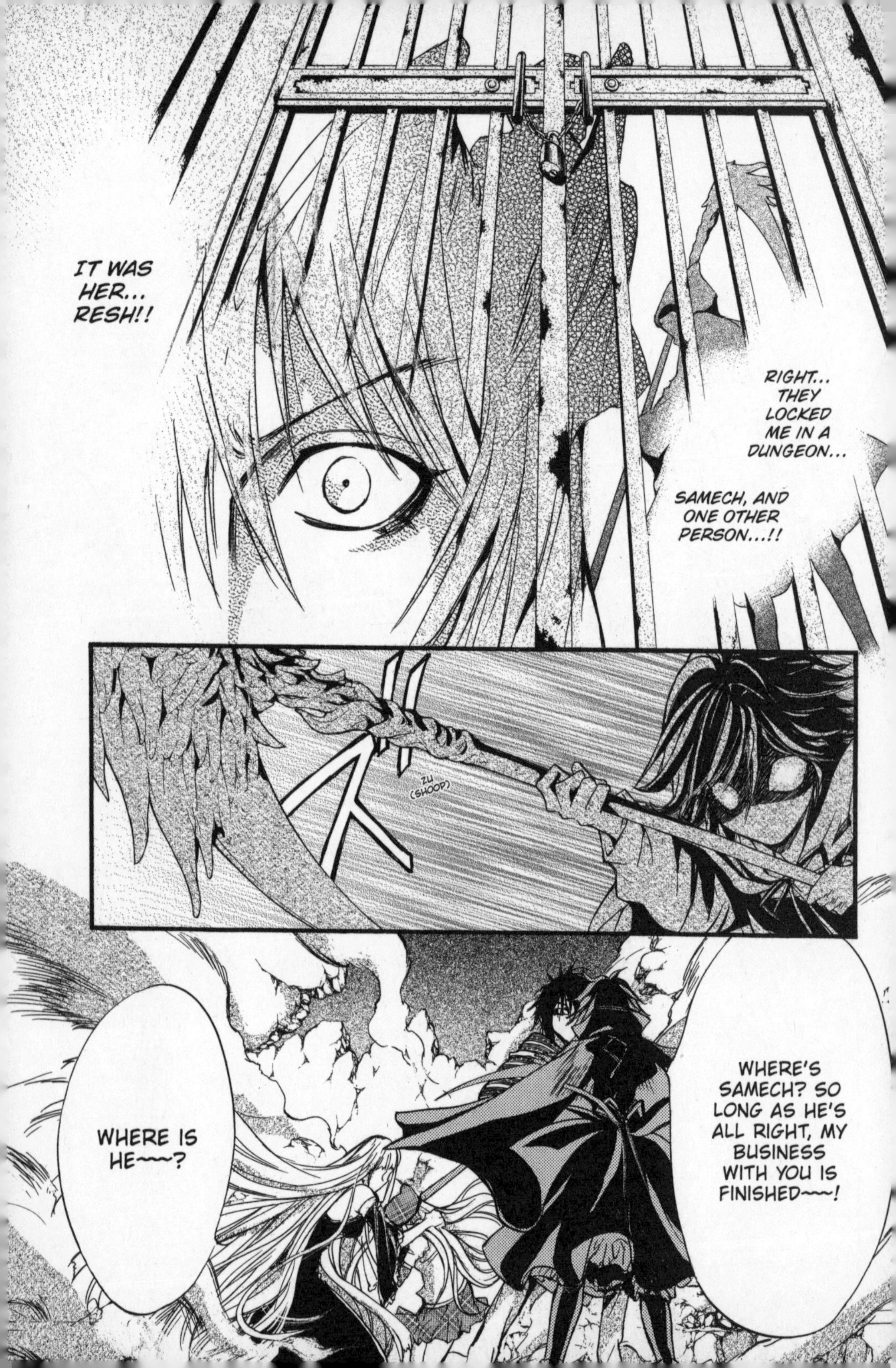
RIGHT... THEY LOCKED ME IN A DUNGEON...
SAMECH, AND ONE OTHER PERSON...!!
IT WAS HER... RESH!!
ZU (SHOOP)
WHERE'S SAMECH? SO LONG AS HE'S ALL RIGHT, MY BUSINESS WITH YOU IS FINISHED~~~!
WHERE IS HE~~~?

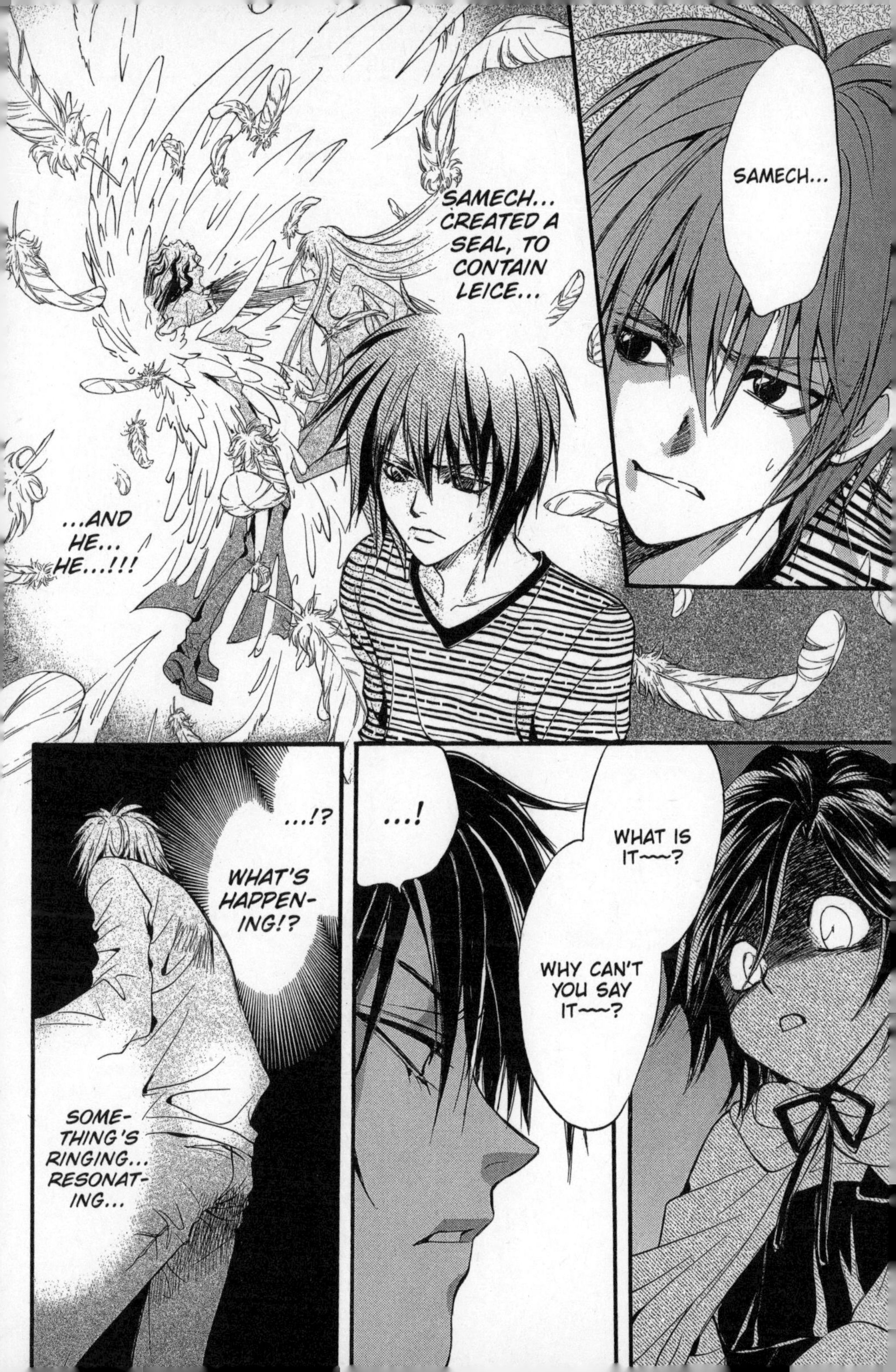
SAMECH...
SAMECH... CREATED A SEAL, TO CONTAIN LEICE...
...AND HE... HE...!!!
WHAT IS IT~~~?
WHY CAN'T YOU SAY IT~~~?
...!
...!?
WHAT'S HAPPENING!?
SOMETHING'S RINGING... RESONATING...

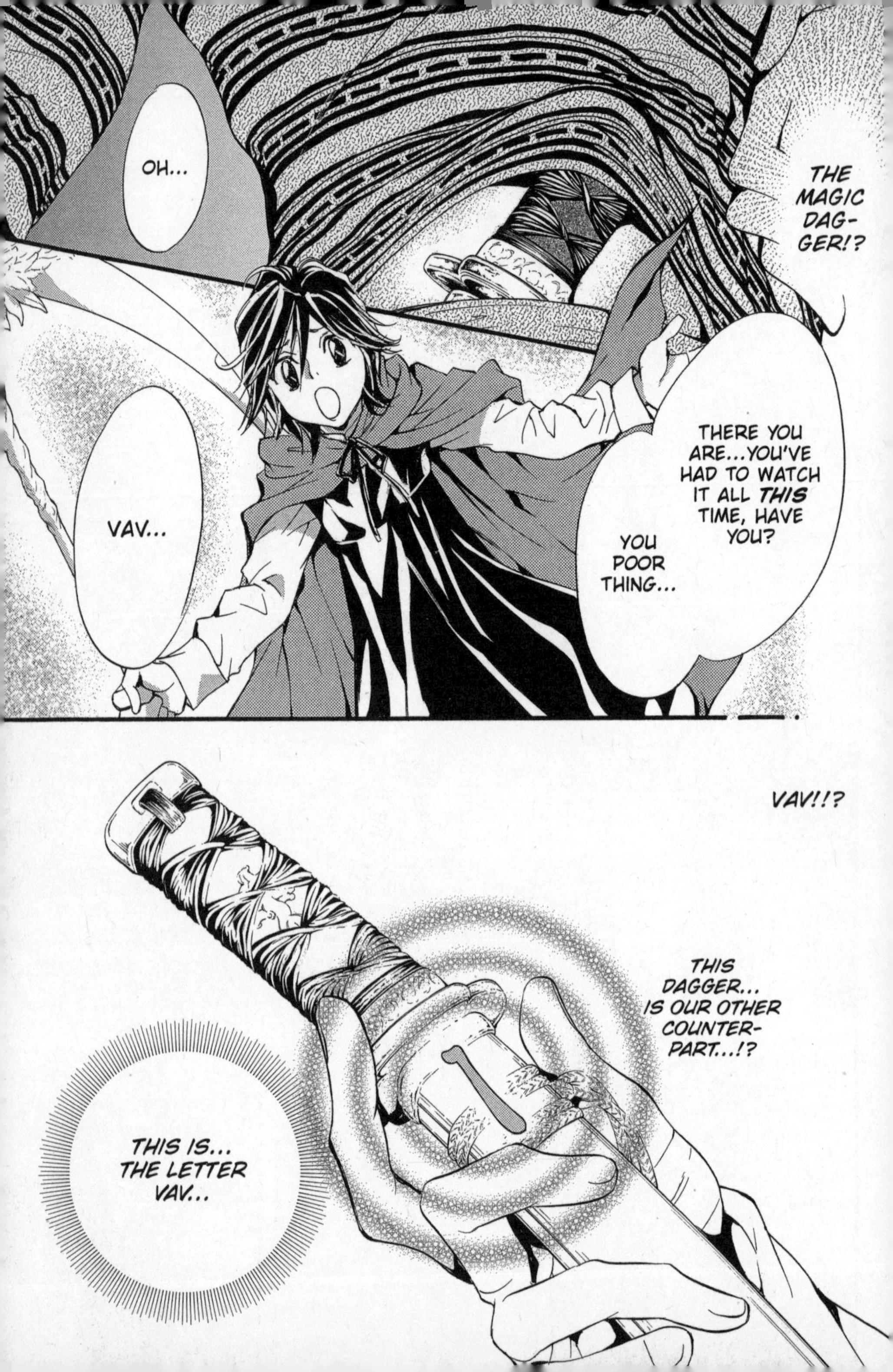
THE MAGIC DAG-GER!?
THERE YOU ARE...YOU'VE HAD TO WATCH IT ALL *THIS* TIME, HAVE YOU?
YOU POOR THING...
OH...
VAV...
VAV!!?
THIS DAGGER... IS OUR OTHER COUNTER-PART...!?
THIS IS... THE LETTER VAV...

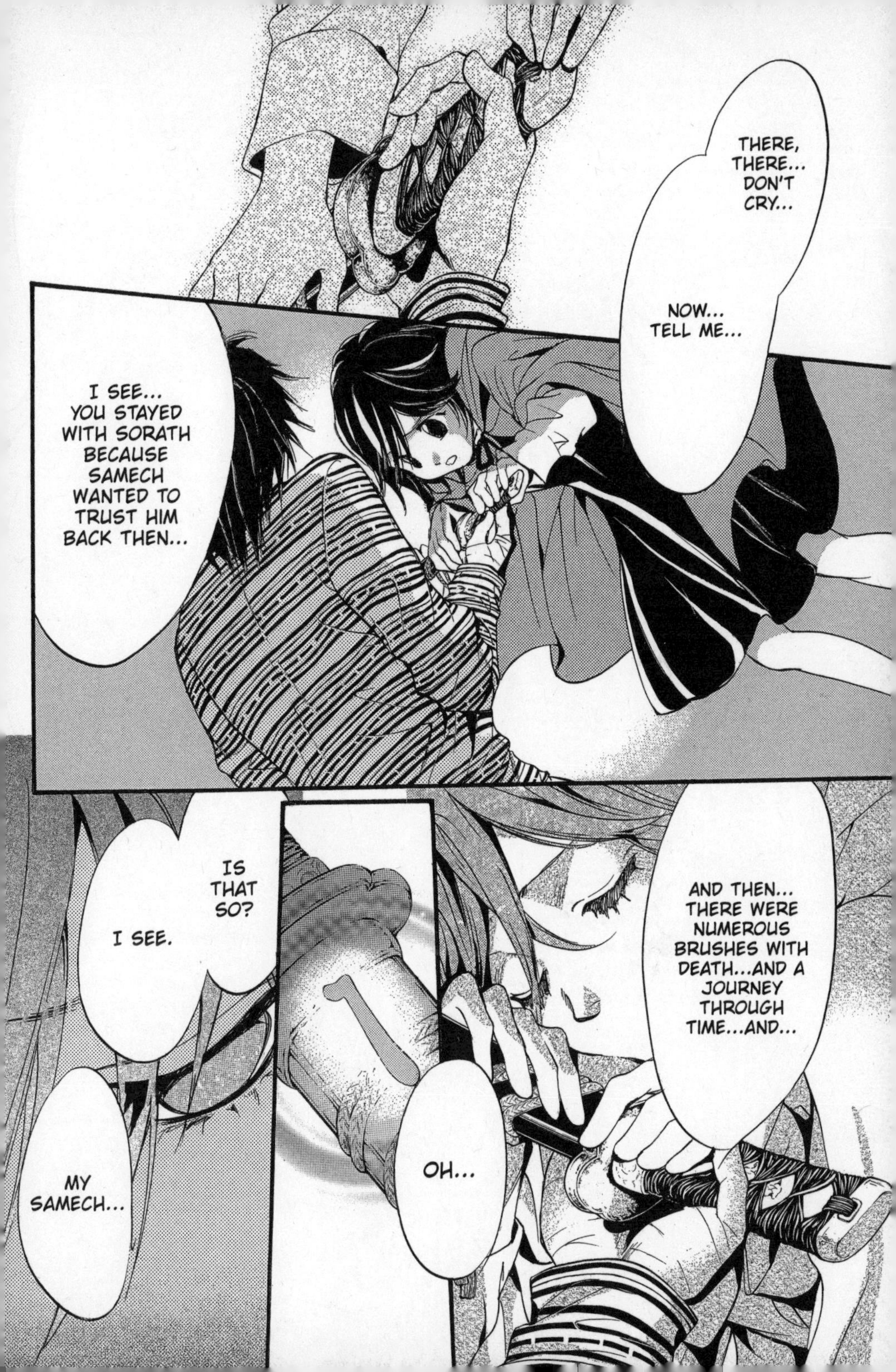
THERE, THERE... DON'T CRY...
NOW... TELL ME...
I SEE... YOU STAYED WITH SORATH BECAUSE SAMECH WANTED TO TRUST HIM BACK THEN...
AND THEN... THERE WERE NUMEROUS BRUSHES WITH DEATH...AND A JOURNEY THROUGH TIME...AND...
OH...
IS THAT SO?
I SEE.
MY SAMECH...

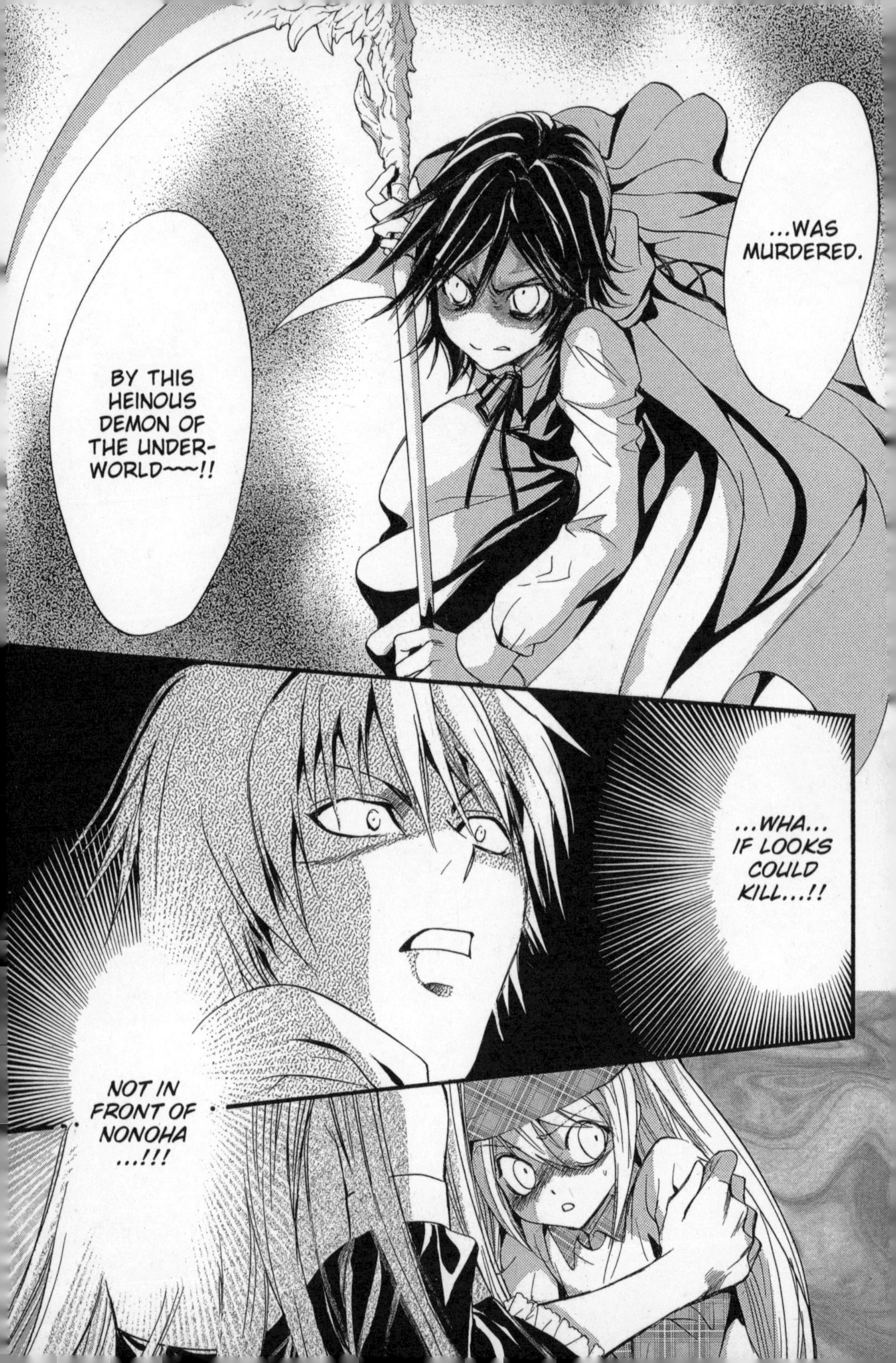
...WAS MURDERED.
BY THIS HEINOUS DEMON OF THE UNDER-WORLD~~~!!
...WHA... IF LOOKS COULD KILL...!!
NOT IN FRONT OF NONOHA ...!!!

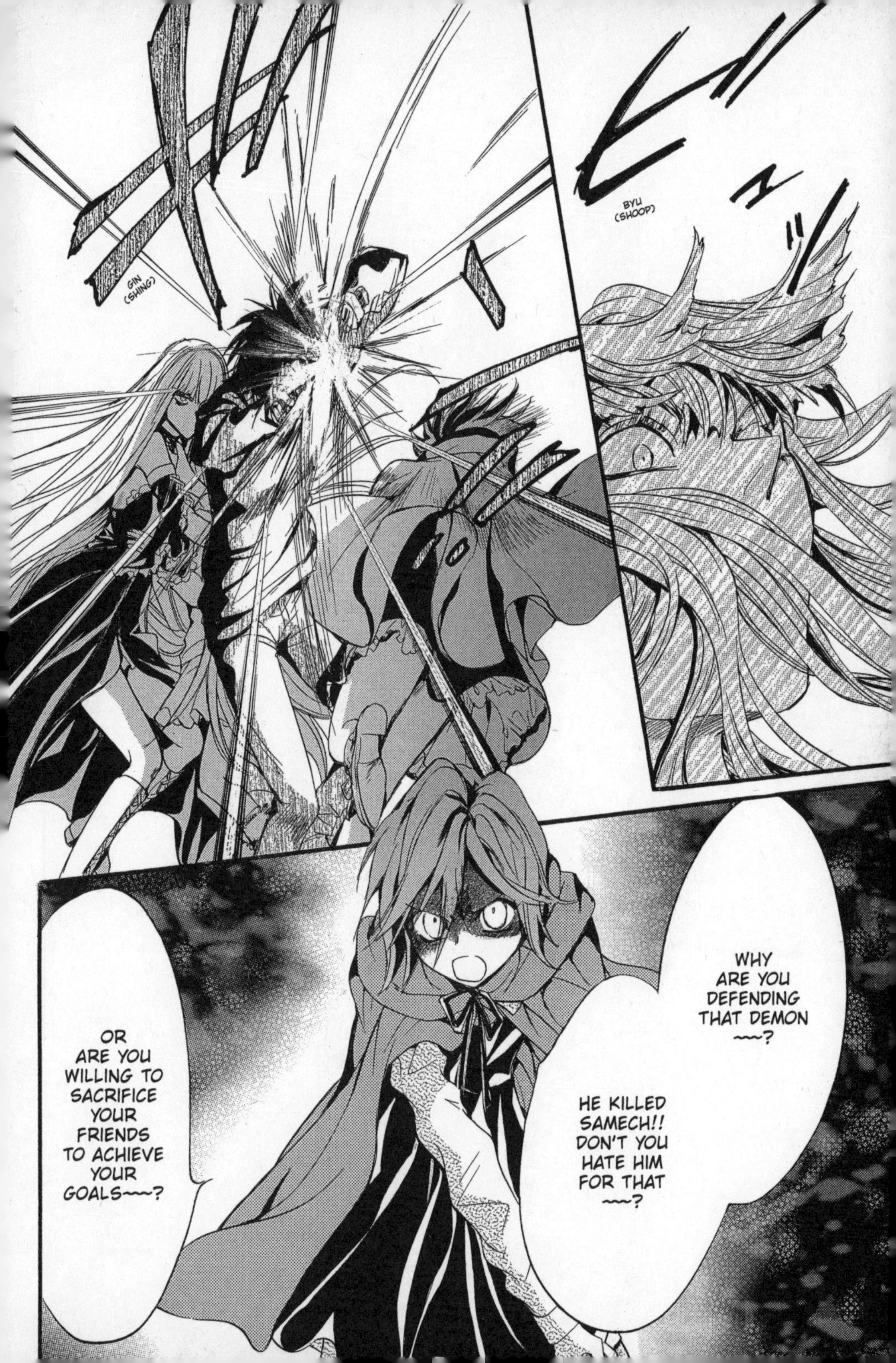
BYU (SHOOP)
GIN (SHING)
WHY ARE YOU DEFENDING THAT DEMON ~~~?
HE KILLED SAMECH!! DON'T YOU HATE HIM FOR THAT ~~~?
OR ARE YOU WILLING TO SACRIFICE YOUR FRIENDS TO ACHIEVE YOUR GOALS~~~?

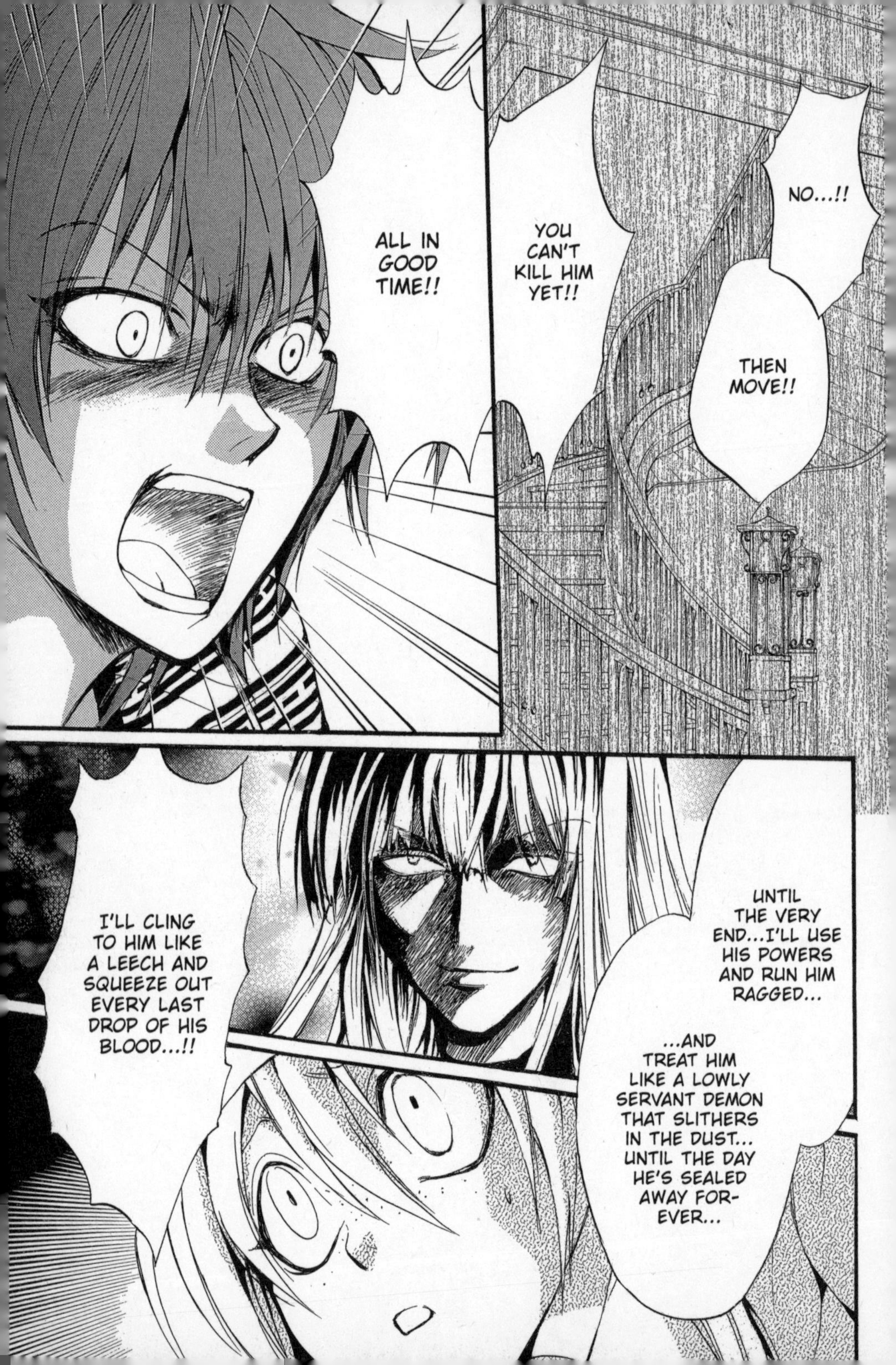

NO...!!
THEN MOVE!!
YOU CAN'T KILL HIM YET!!
ALL IN GOOD TIME!!
UNTIL THE VERY END...I'LL USE HIS POWERS AND RUN HIM RAGGED...
...AND TREAT HIM LIKE A LOWLY SERVANT DEMON THAT SLITHERS IN THE DUST... UNTIL THE DAY HE'S SEALED AWAY FOR-EVER...
I'LL CLING TO HIM LIKE A LEECH AND SQUEEZE OUT EVERY LAST DROP OF HIS BLOOD...!!

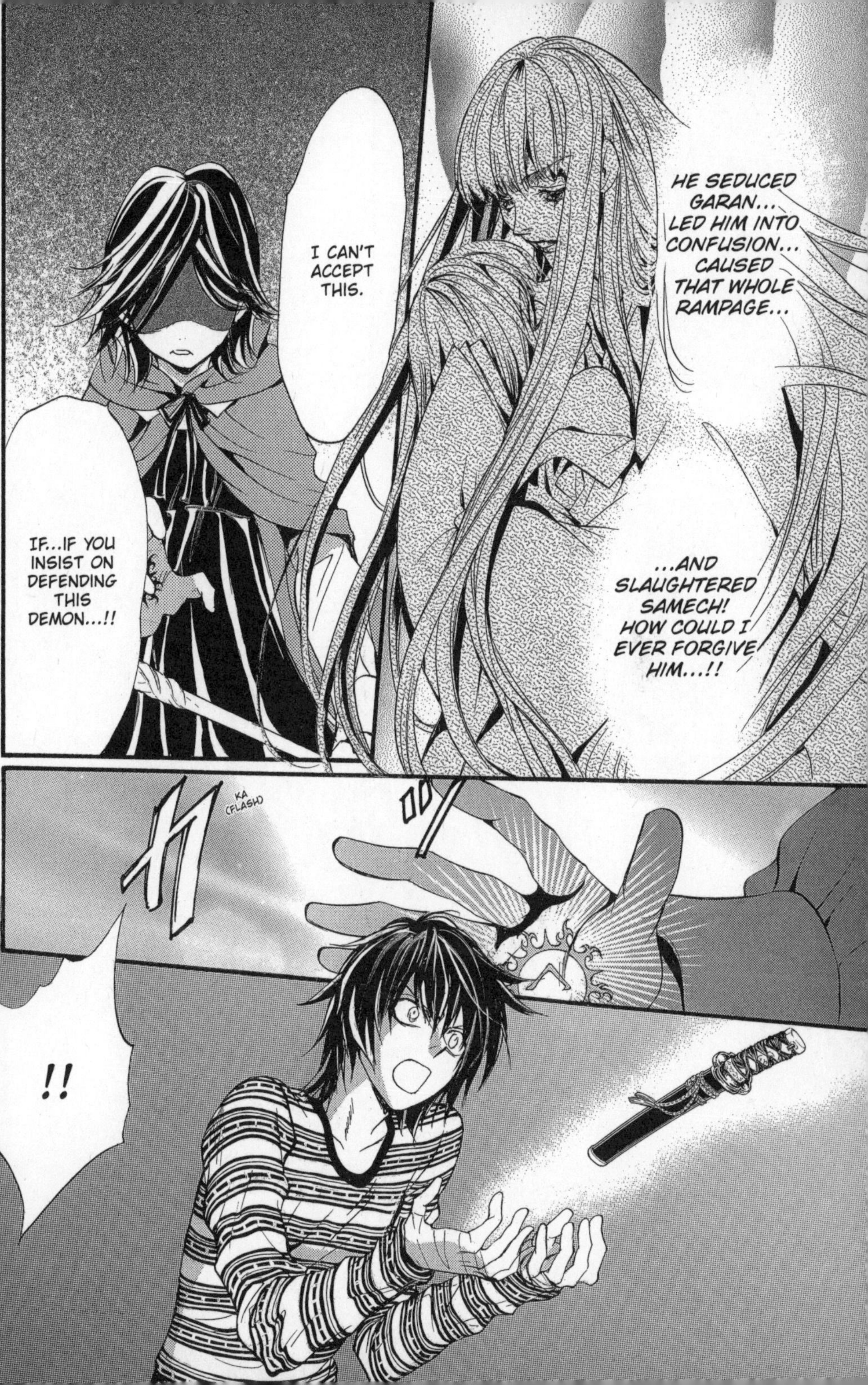
HE SEDUCED GARAN... LED HIM INTO CONFUSION... CAUSED THAT WHOLE RAMPAGE...
...AND SLAUGHTERED SAMECH! HOW COULD I EVER FORGIVE HIM...!!
I CAN'T ACCEPT THIS.
IF...IF YOU INSIST ON DEFENDING THIS DEMON...!!
KA (FLASH)
!!

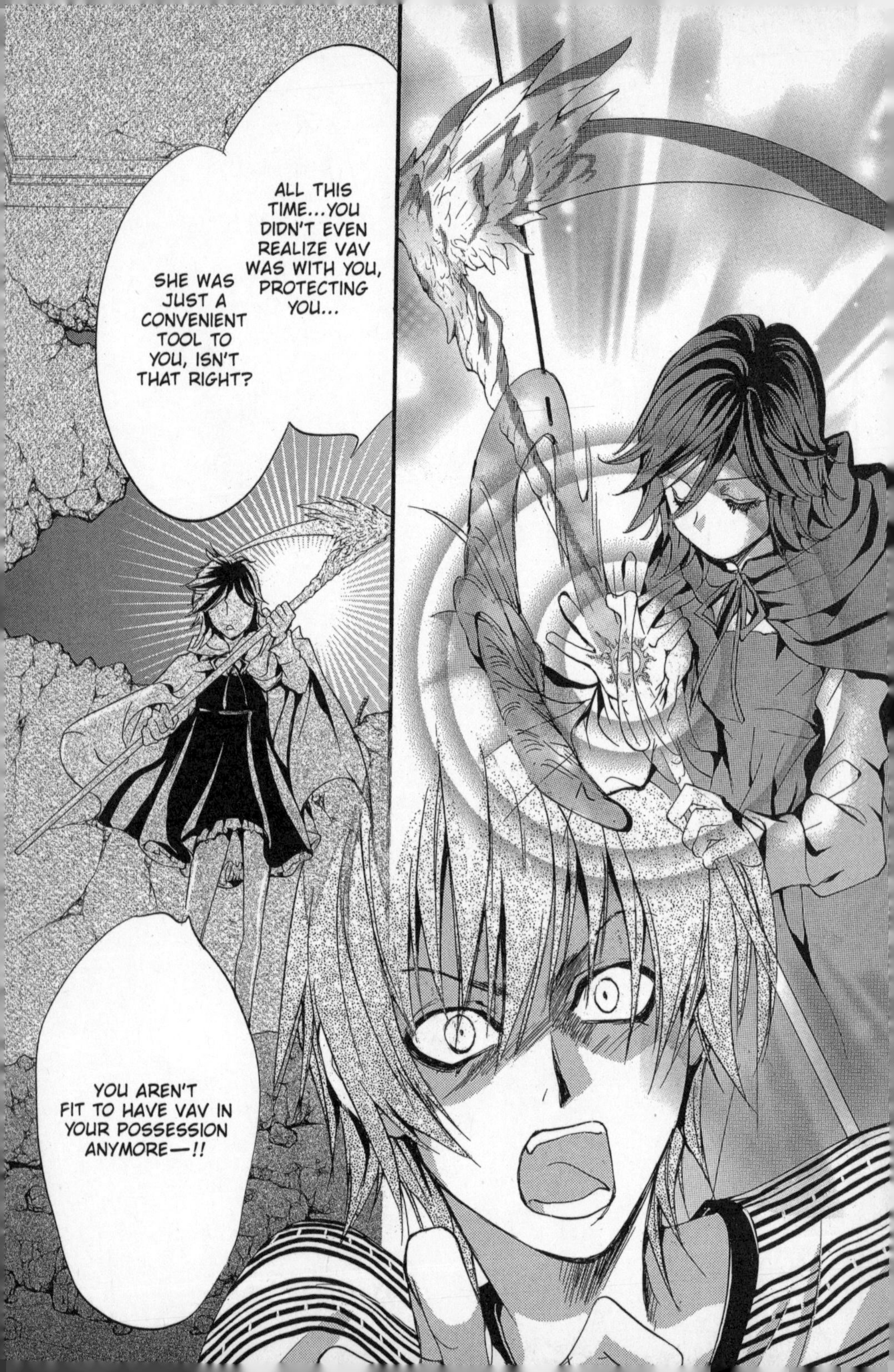
ALL THIS TIME...YOU DIDN'T EVEN REALIZE VAV WAS WITH YOU, PROTECTING YOU...
SHE WAS JUST A CONVENIENT TOOL TO YOU, ISN'T THAT RIGHT?
YOU AREN'T FIT TO HAVE VAV IN YOUR POSSESSION ANYMORE—!!

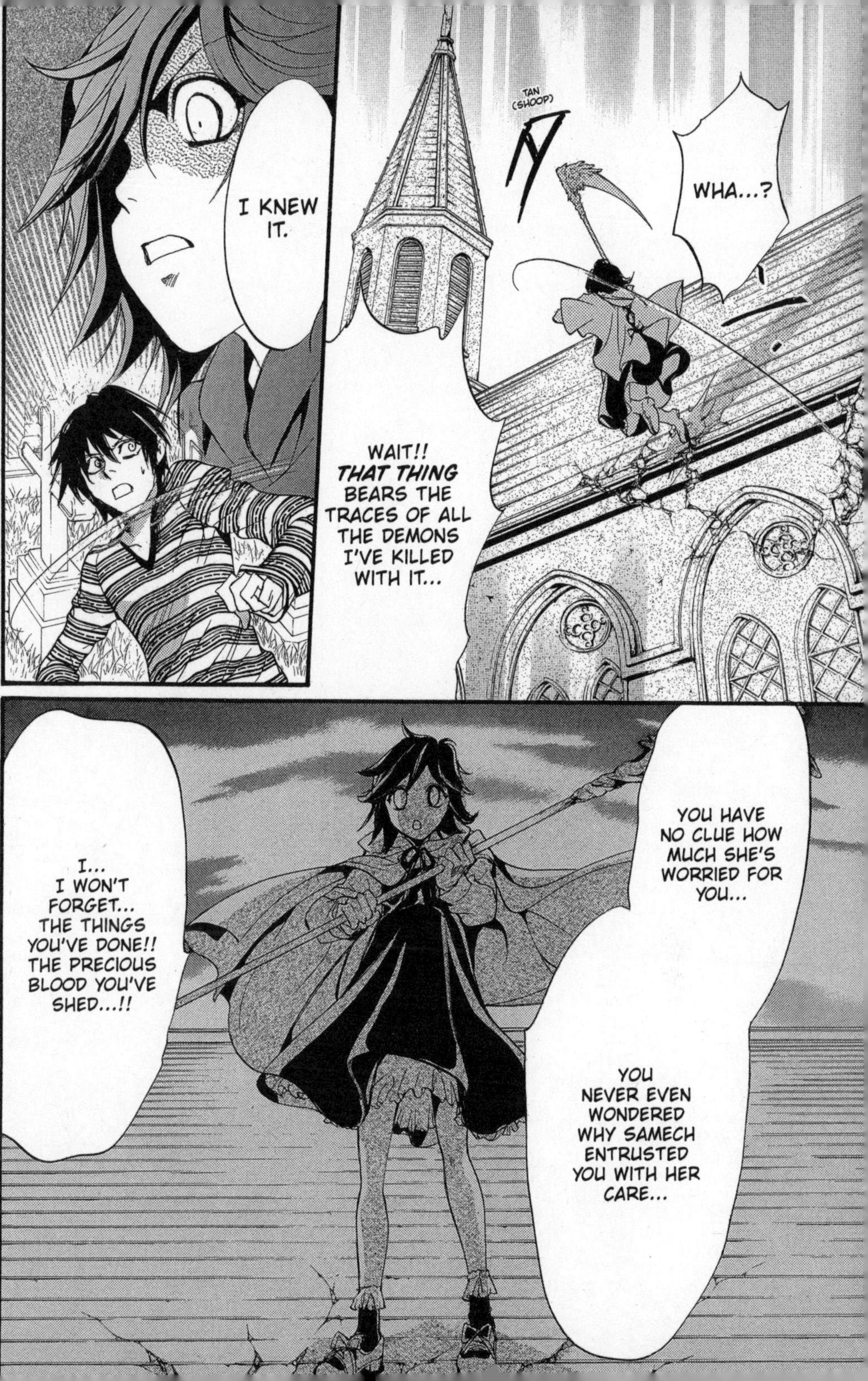
TAN (SHOOP)
WHA...?
I KNEW IT.
WAIT!! *THAT THING* BEARS THE TRACES OF ALL THE DEMONS I'VE KILLED WITH IT...
YOU HAVE NO CLUE HOW MUCH SHE'S WORRIED FOR YOU...
YOU NEVER EVEN WONDERED WHY SAMECH ENTRUSTED YOU WITH HER CARE...
I... I WON'T FORGET... THE THINGS YOU'VE DONE!! THE PRECIOUS BLOOD YOU'VE SHED...!!

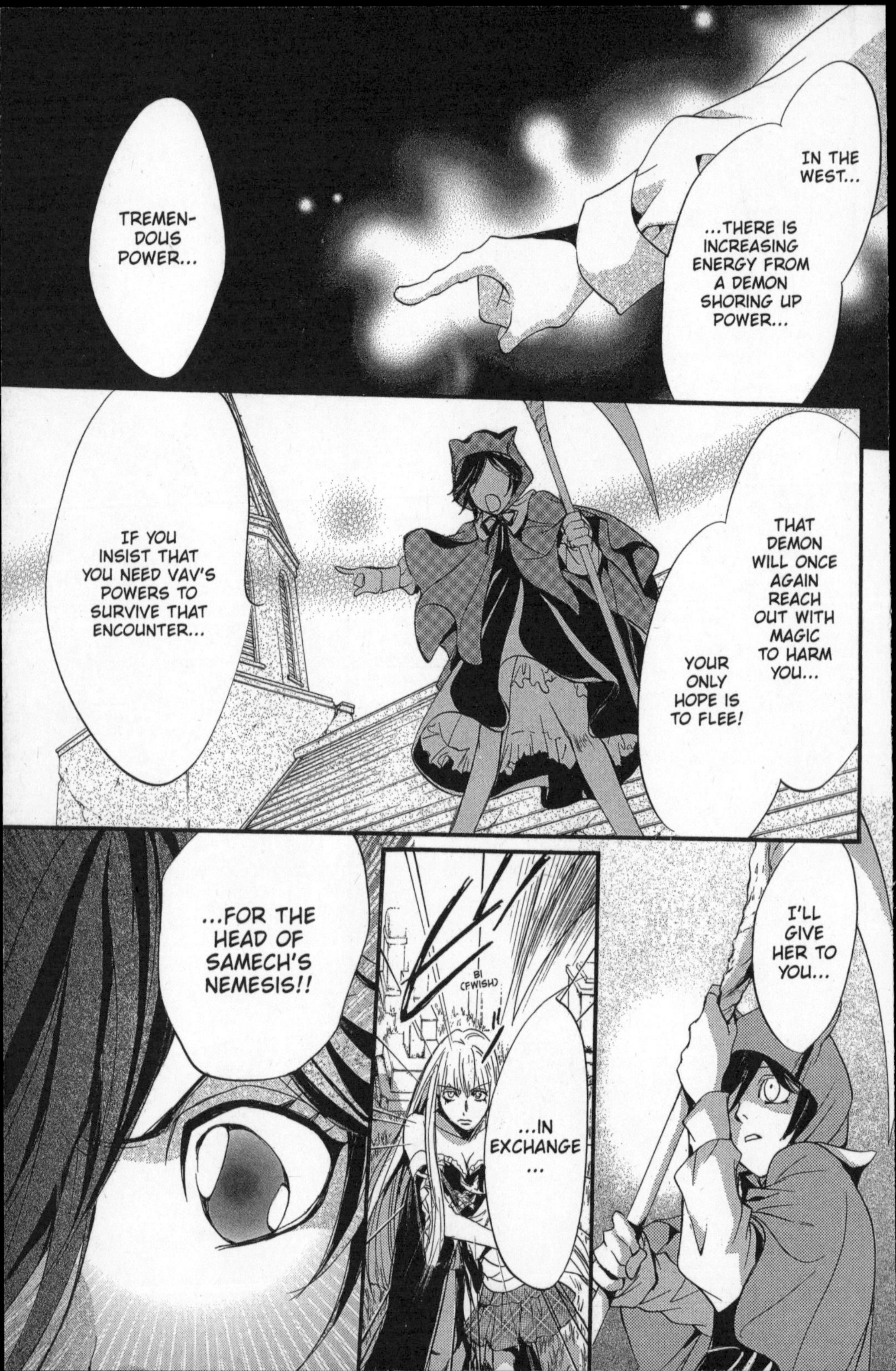
IN THE WEST...
...THERE IS INCREASING ENERGY FROM A DEMON SHORING UP POWER...
TREMEN-DOUS POWER...
THAT DEMON WILL ONCE AGAIN REACH OUT WITH MAGIC TO HARM YOU...
YOUR ONLY HOPE IS TO FLEE!
IF YOU INSIST THAT YOU NEED VAV'S POWERS TO SURVIVE THAT ENCOUNTER...
I'LL GIVE HER TO YOU...
...IN EXCHANGE...
BI (FWISH)
...FOR THE HEAD OF SAMECH'S NEMESIS!!

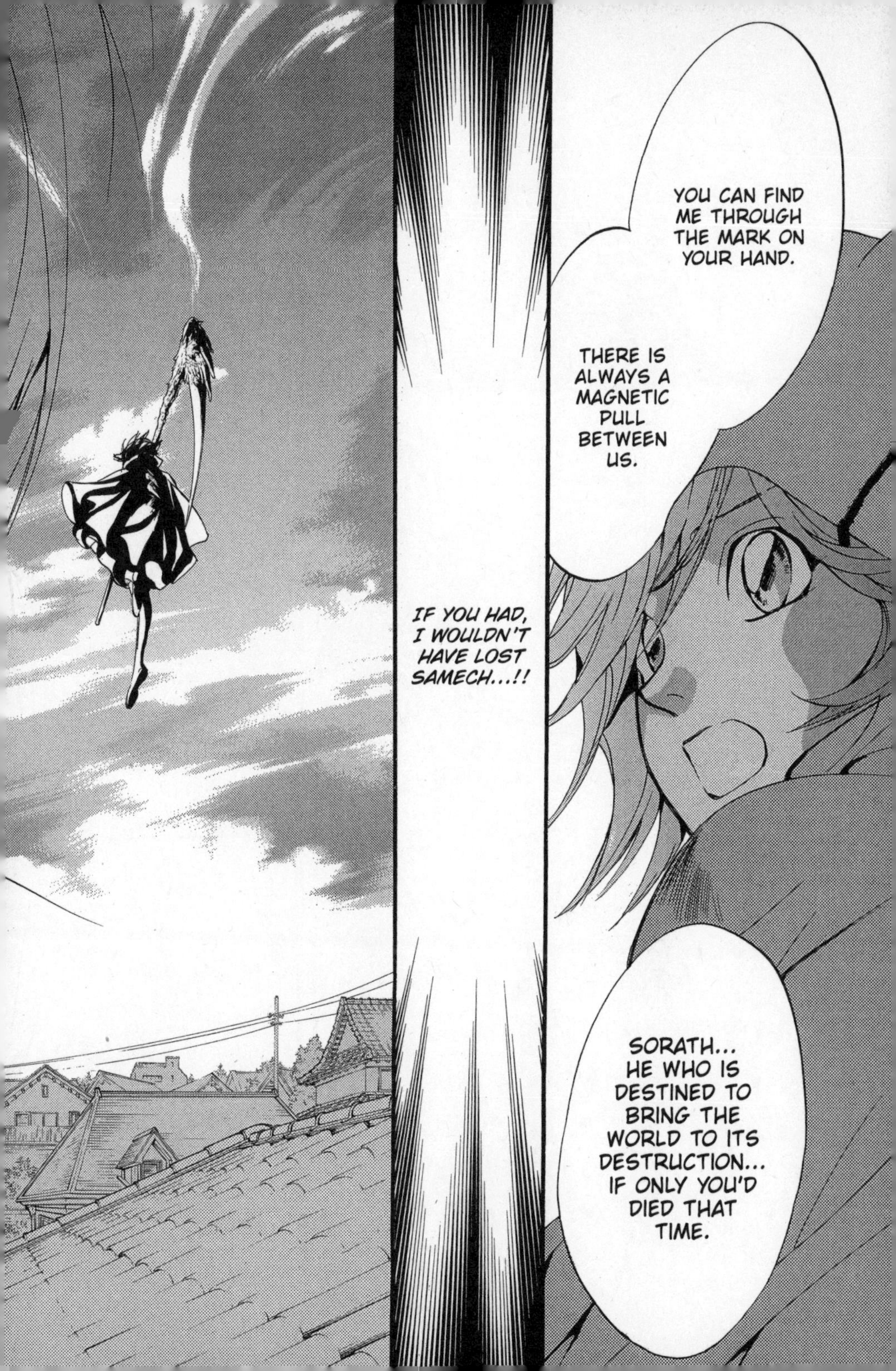
YOU CAN FIND ME THROUGH THE MARK ON YOUR HAND.
THERE IS ALWAYS A MAGNETIC PULL BETWEEN US.
SORATH... HE WHO IS DESTINED TO BRING THE WORLD TO ITS DESTRUCTION... IF ONLY YOU'D DIED THAT TIME.
IF YOU HAD, I WOULDN'T HAVE LOST SAMECH...!!

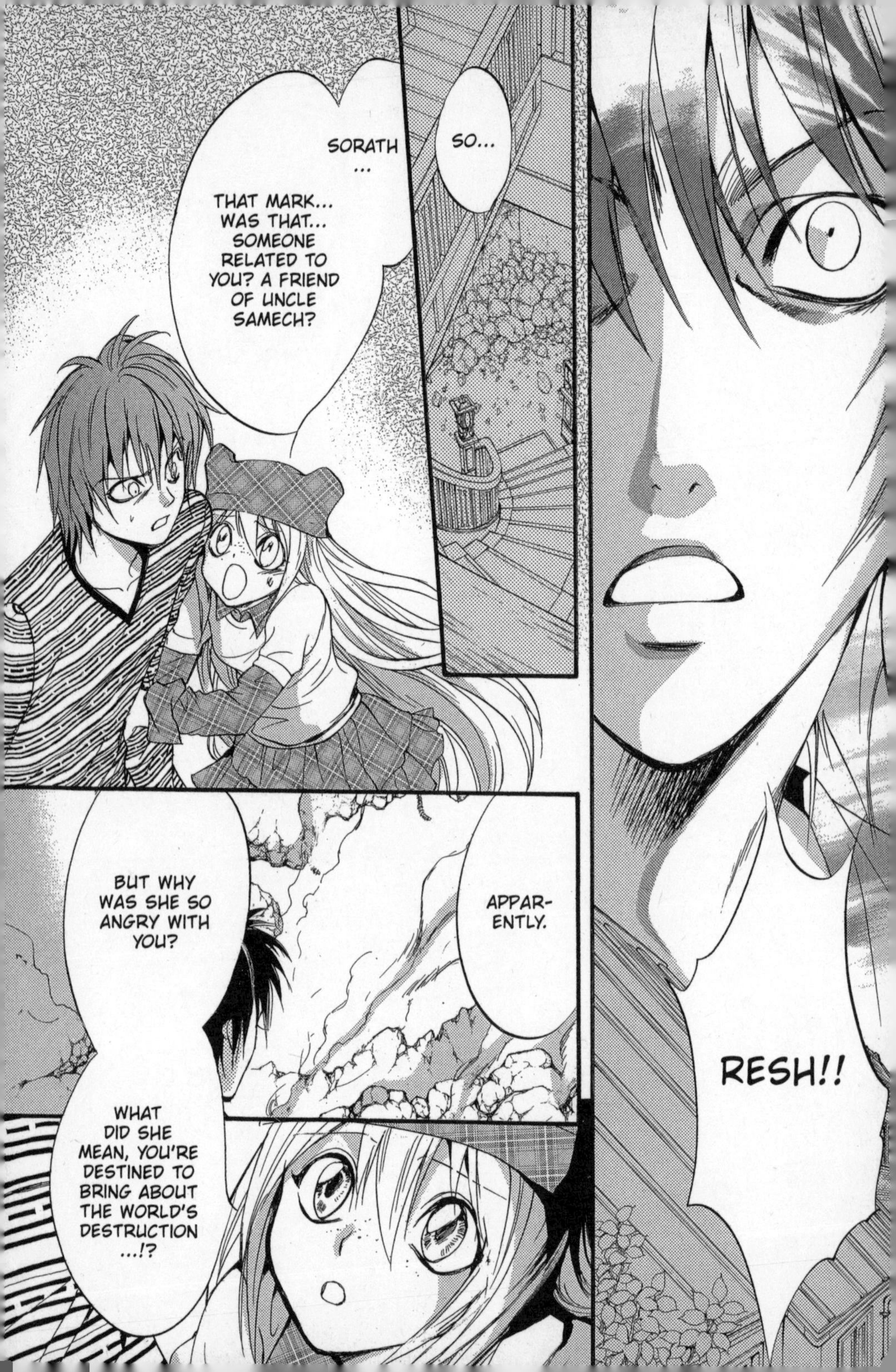
RESH!!
SO...
SORATH ...
THAT MARK... WAS THAT... SOMEONE RELATED TO YOU? A FRIEND OF UNCLE SAMECH?
APPAR-ENTLY.
BUT WHY WAS SHE SO ANGRY WITH YOU?
WHAT DID SHE MEAN, YOU'RE DESTINED TO BRING ABOUT THE WORLD'S DESTRUCTION ...!?

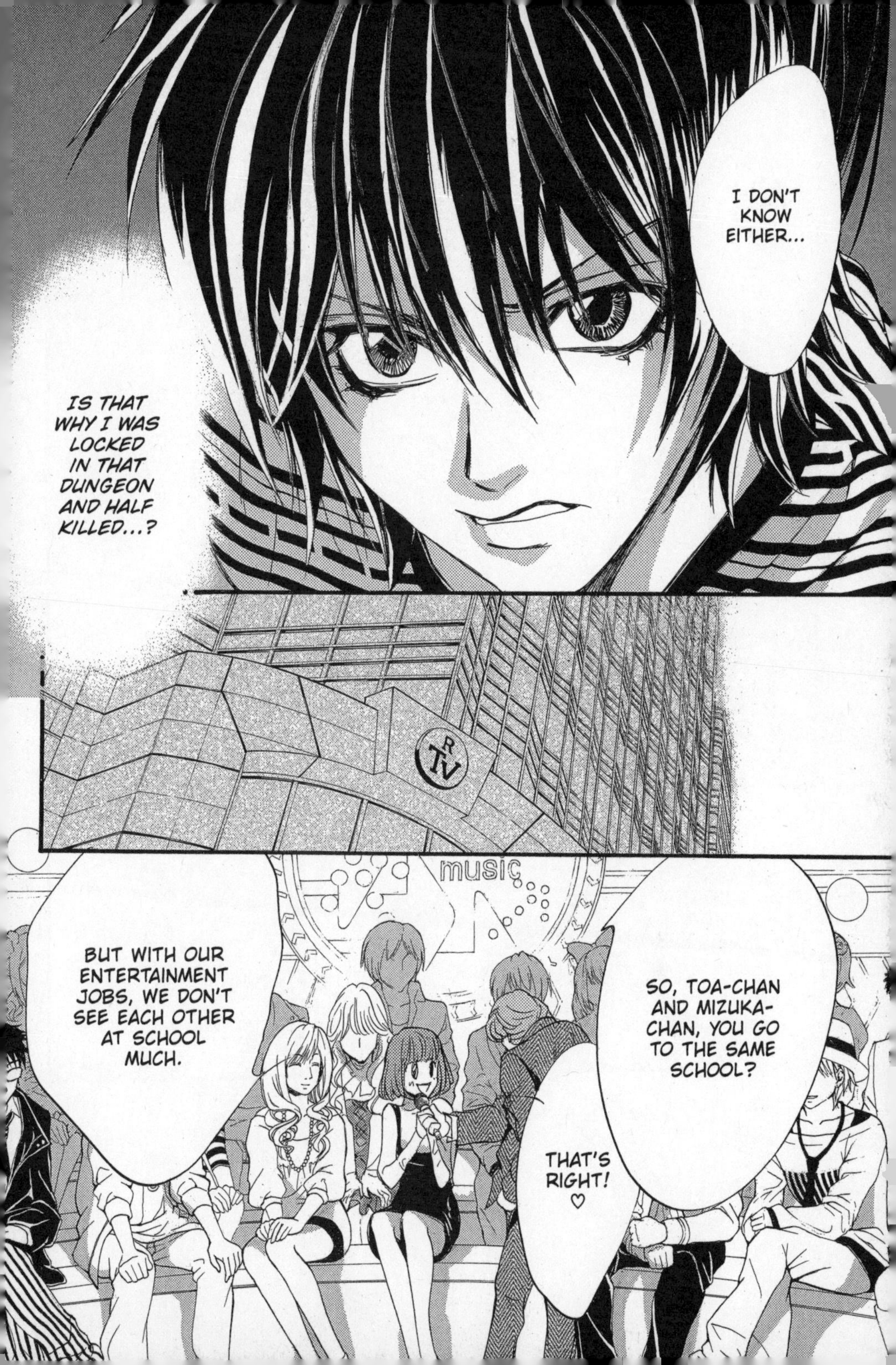
I DON'T KNOW EITHER...
IS THAT WHY I WAS LOCKED IN THAT DUNGEON AND HALF KILLED...?
music
SO, TOA-CHAN AND MIZUKA-CHAN, YOU GO TO THE SAME SCHOOL?
THAT'S RIGHT! ♡
BUT WITH OUR ENTERTAINMENT JOBS, WE DON'T SEE EACH OTHER AT SCHOOL MUCH.

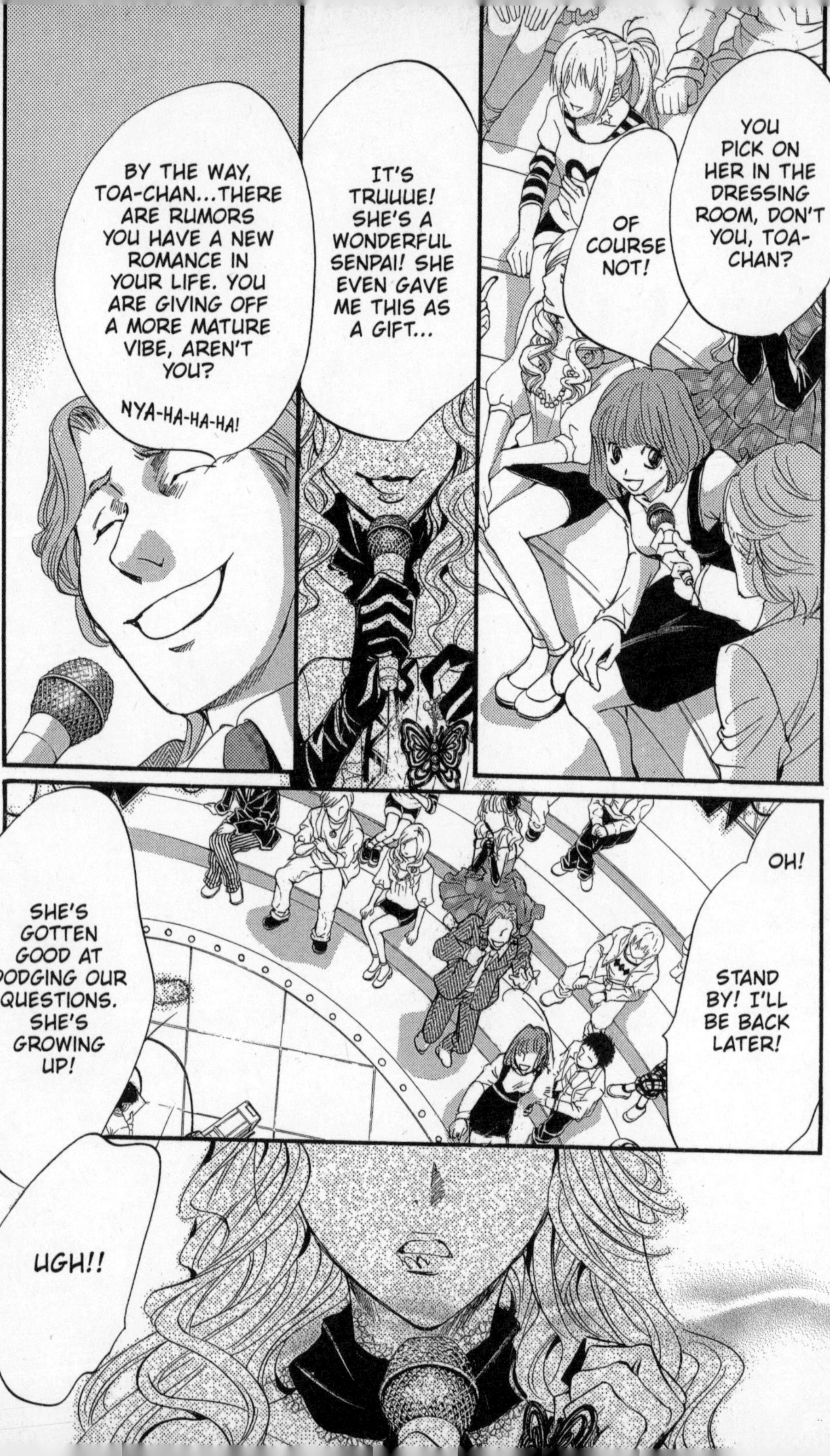
YOU PICK ON HER IN THE DRESSING ROOM, DON'T YOU, TOA-CHAN?
OF COURSE NOT!
IT'S TRUUUE! SHE'S A WONDERFUL SENPAI! SHE EVEN GAVE ME THIS AS A GIFT...
BY THE WAY, TOA-CHAN...THERE ARE RUMORS YOU HAVE A NEW ROMANCE IN YOUR LIFE. YOU ARE GIVING OFF A MORE MATURE VIBE, AREN'T YOU?
NYA-HA-HA-HA!
OH!
STAND BY! I'LL BE BACK LATER!
SHE'S GOTTEN GOOD AT DODGING OUR QUESTIONS. SHE'S GROWING UP!
UGH!!

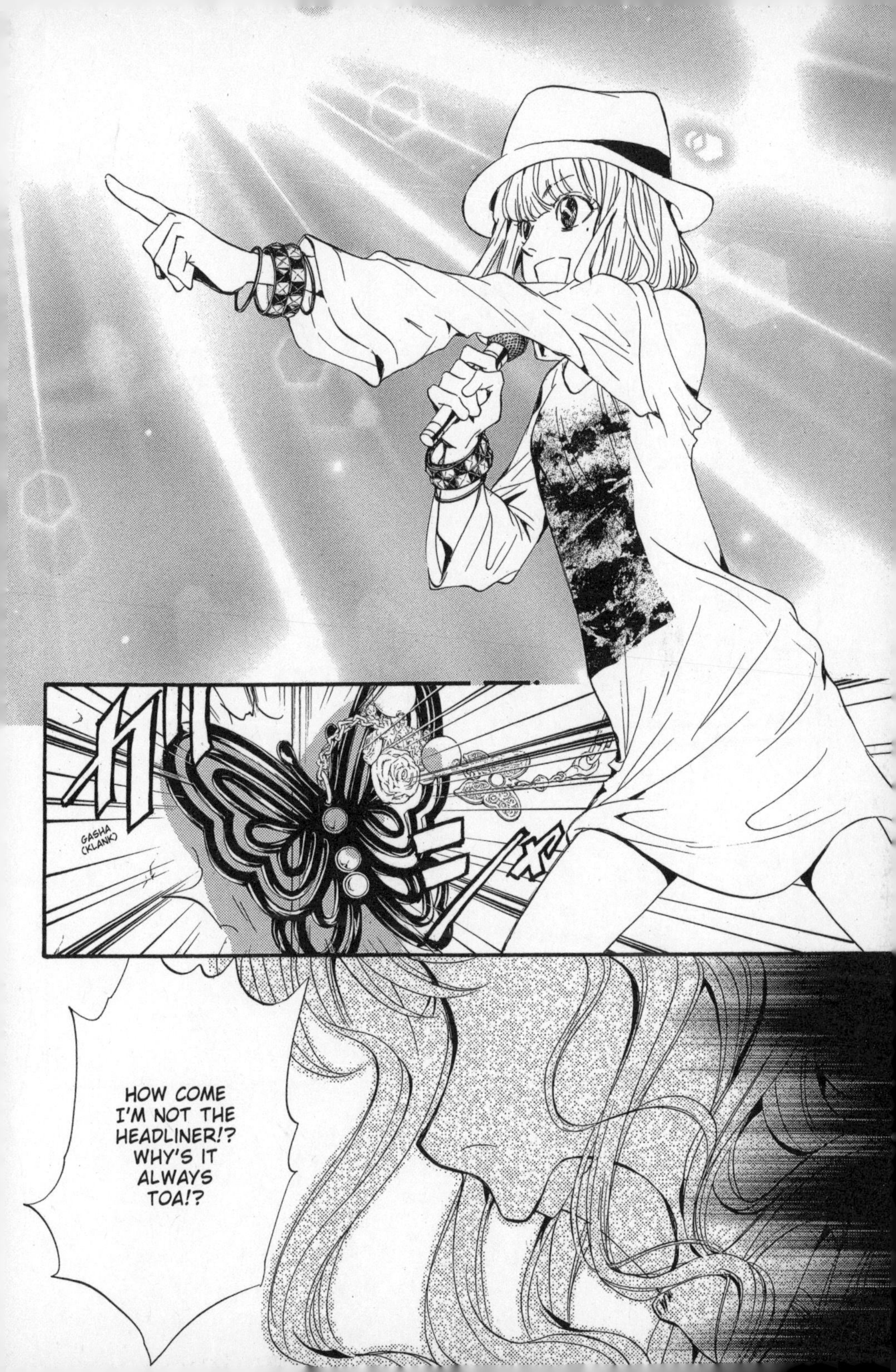
GASHA (KLANK)
HOW COME I'M NOT THE HEADLINER!? WHY'S IT ALWAYS TOA!?

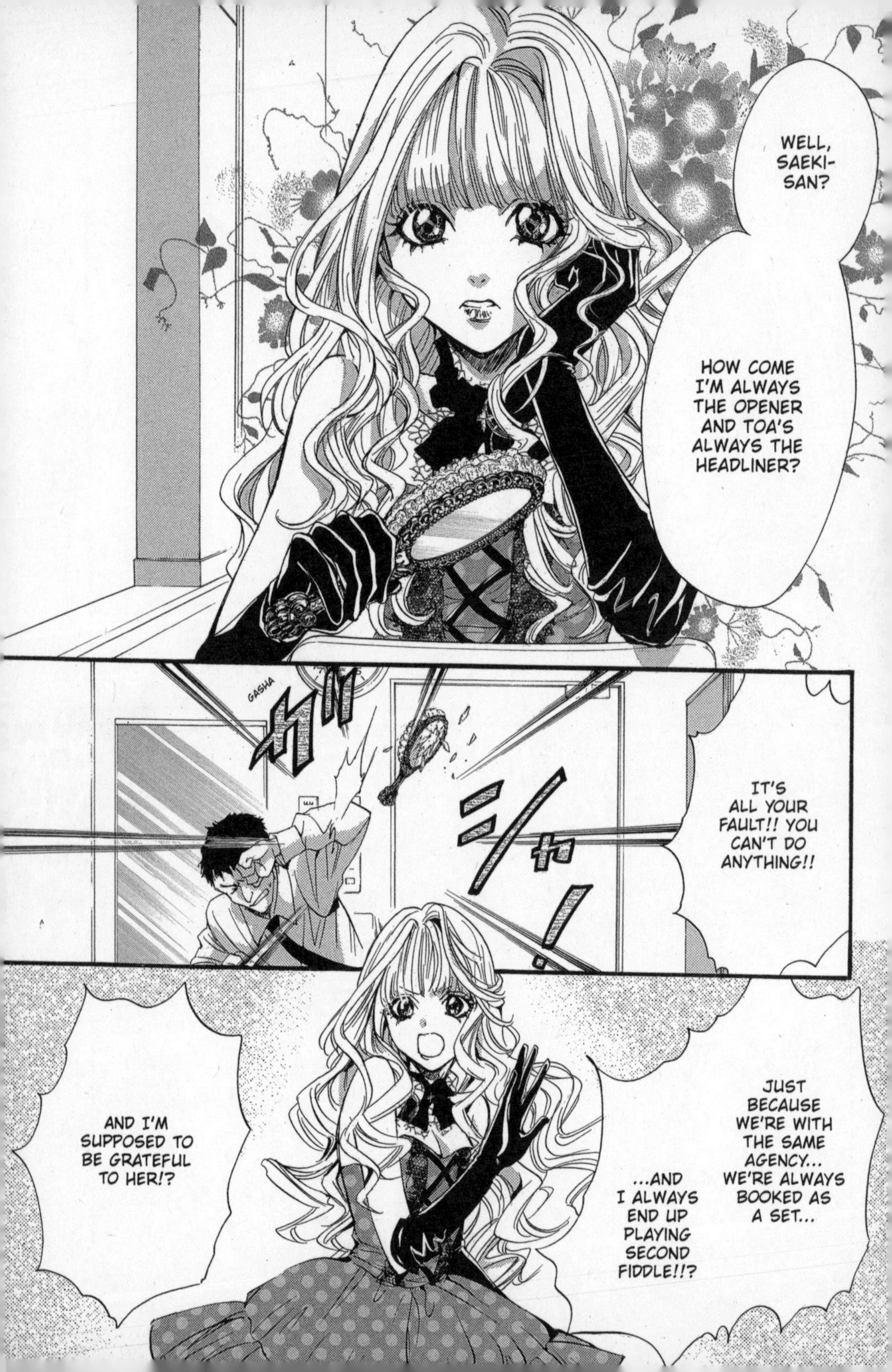
WELL, SAEKI-SAN?
HOW COME I'M ALWAYS THE OPENER AND TOA'S ALWAYS THE HEADLINER?
IT'S ALL YOUR FAULT!! YOU CAN'T DO ANYTHING!!
GASHA
JUST BECAUSE WE'RE WITH THE SAME AGENCY... WE'RE ALWAYS BOOKED AS A SET...
...AND I ALWAYS END UP PLAYING SECOND FIDDLE!!?
AND I'M SUPPOSED TO BE GRATEFUL TO HER!?

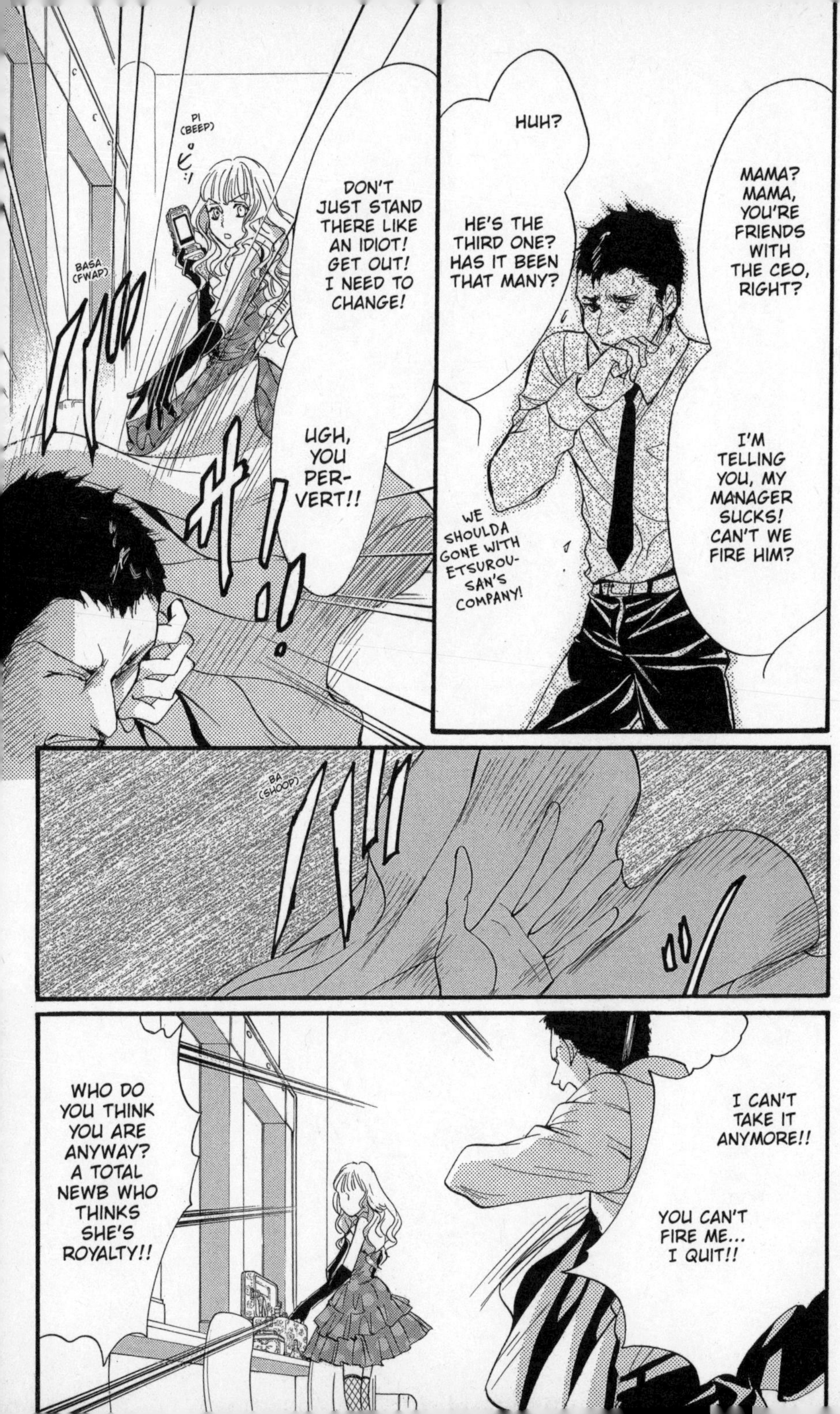
MAMA? MAMA, YOU'RE FRIENDS WITH THE CEO, RIGHT?
HUH?
HE'S THE THIRD ONE? HAS IT BEEN THAT MANY?
I'M TELLING YOU, MY MANAGER SUCKS! CAN'T WE FIRE HIM?
WE SHOULDA GONE WITH ETSUROU-SAN'S COMPANY!
DON'T JUST STAND THERE LIKE AN IDIOT! GET OUT! I NEED TO CHANGE!
PI (BEEP)
BASA (FWAP)
UGH, YOU PER-VERT!!
BA (SHOOP)
I CAN'T TAKE IT ANYMORE!!
YOU CAN'T FIRE ME... I QUIT!!
WHO DO YOU THINK YOU ARE ANYWAY? A TOTAL NEWB WHO THINKS SHE'S ROYALTY!!

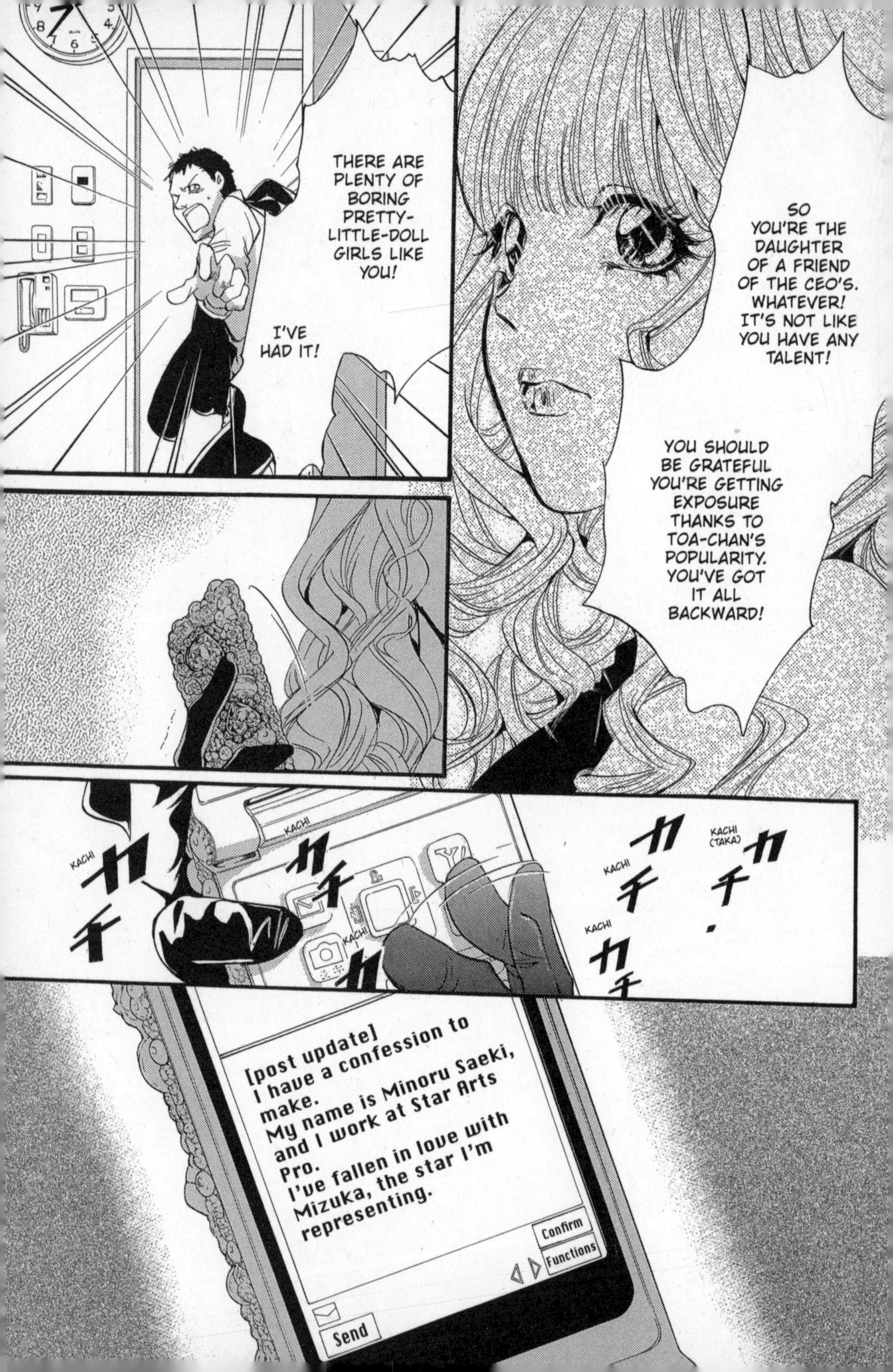
SO YOU'RE THE DAUGHTER OF A FRIEND OF THE CEO'S. WHATEVER! IT'S NOT LIKE YOU HAVE ANY TALENT!
YOU SHOULD BE GRATEFUL YOU'RE GETTING EXPOSURE THANKS TO TOA-CHAN'S POPULARITY. YOU'VE GOT IT ALL BACKWARD!
THERE ARE PLENTY OF BORING PRETTY-LITTLE-DOLL GIRLS LIKE YOU!
I'VE HAD IT!
KACHI (TAKA)
カチ
KACHI
カチ
KACHI
カチ
KACHI
カチ
KACHI
カチ
KACHI
カチ
[post update]
I have a confession to make.
My name is Minoru Saeki, and I work at Star Arts Pro.
I've fallen in love with Mizuka, the star I'm representing.
Confirm
Functions
Send

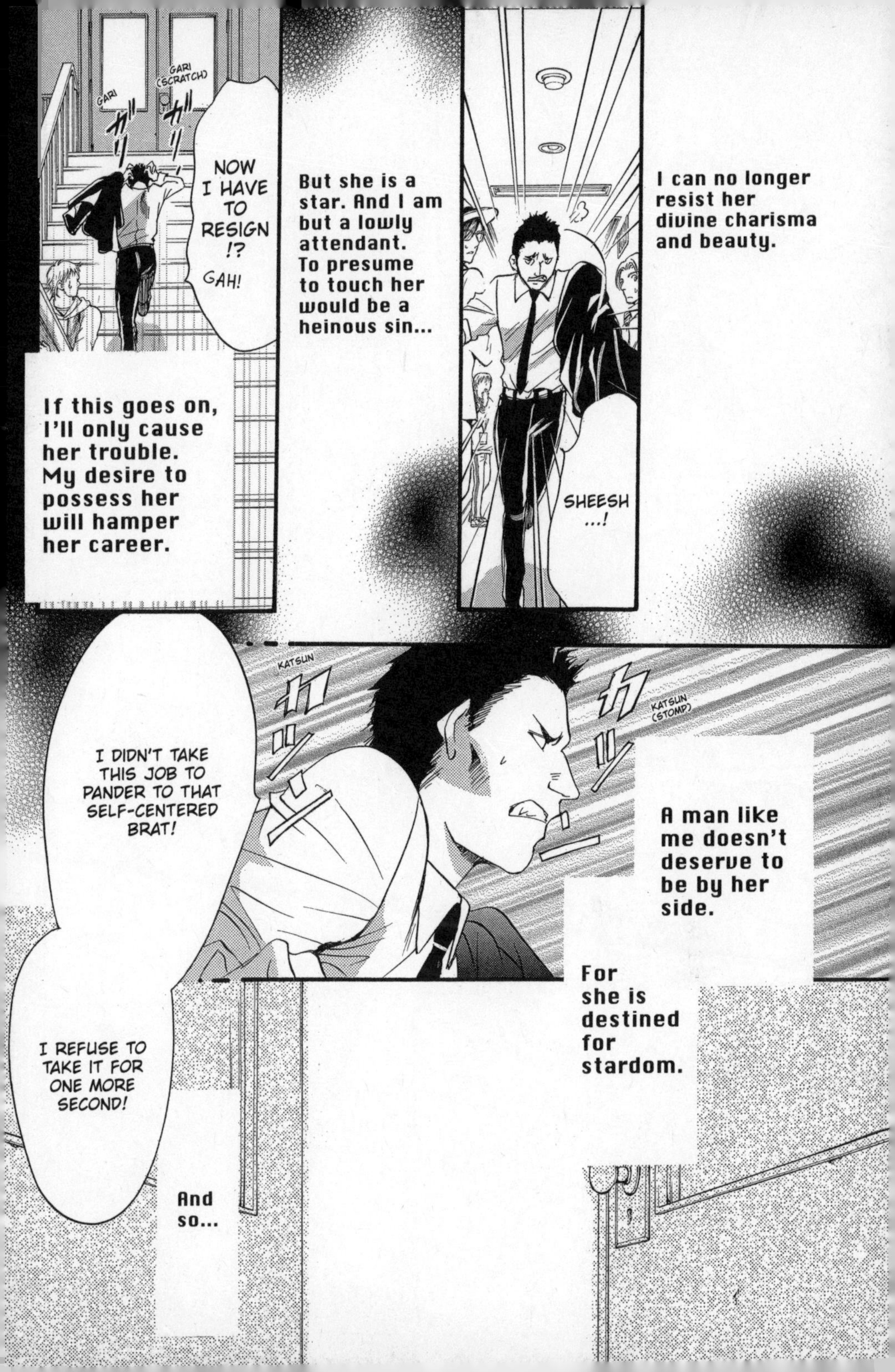
I can no longer resist her divine charisma and beauty.
SHEESH ...!
But she is a star. And I am but a lowly attendant. To presume to touch her would be a heinous sin...
GARI (SCRATCH)
GARI
NOW I HAVE TO RESIGN !?
GAH!
If this goes on, I'll only cause her trouble. My desire to possess her will hamper her career.
KATSUN (STOMP)
A man like me doesn't deserve to be by her side.
KATSUN
I DIDN'T TAKE THIS JOB TO PANDER TO THAT SELF-CENTERED BRAT!
For she is destined for stardom.
I REFUSE TO TAKE IT FOR ONE MORE SECOND!
And so...

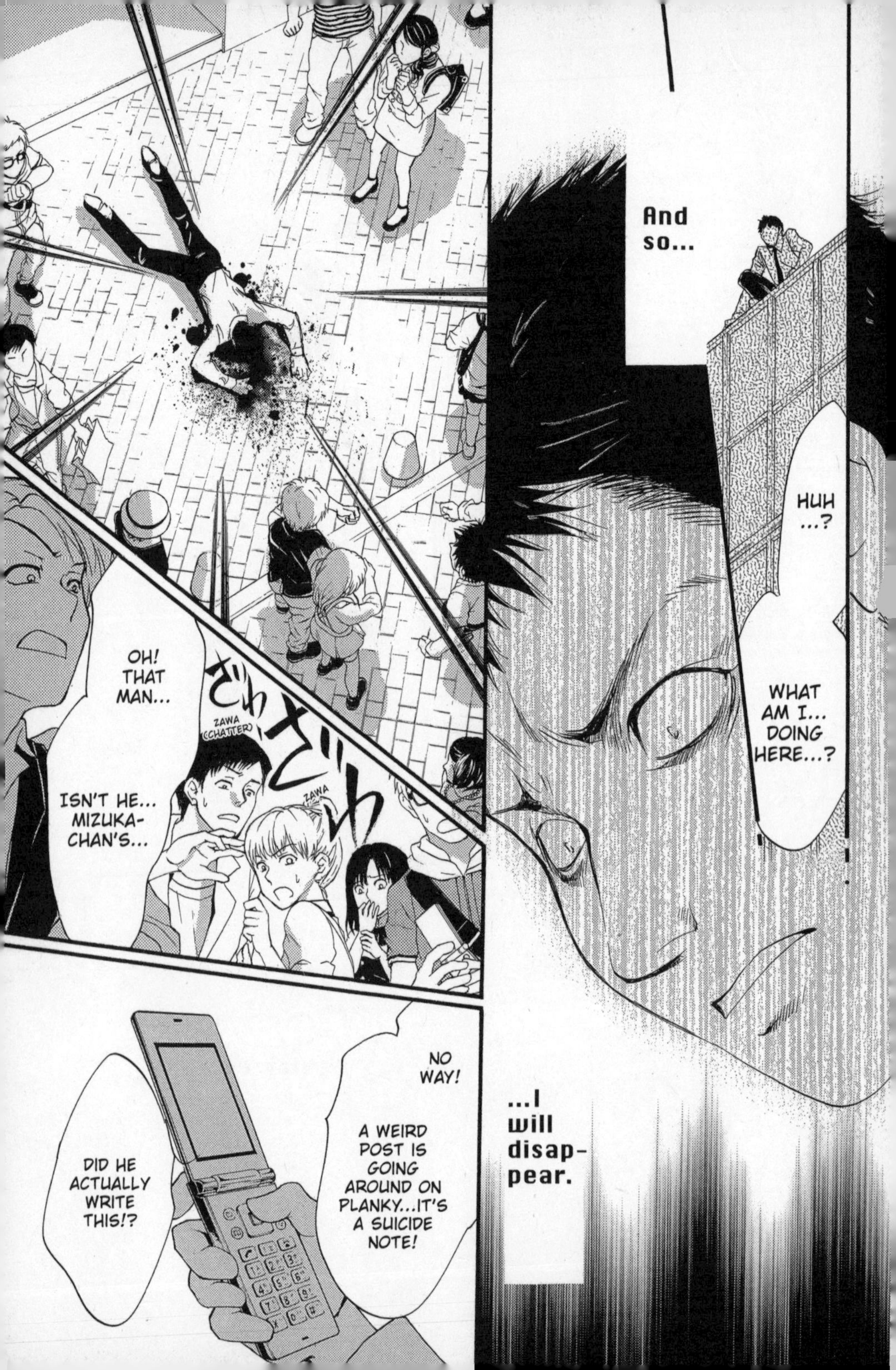

And so...
HUH ...?
WHAT AM I... DOING HERE...?
...I will disap-pear.
OH! THAT MAN...
ISN'T HE... MIZUKA-CHAN'S...
ざわ ざわ
ZAWA (CHATTER)
ZAWA
NO WAY!
A WEIRD POST IS GOING AROUND ON PLANKY...IT'S A SUICIDE NOTE!
DID HE ACTUALLY WRITE THIS!?

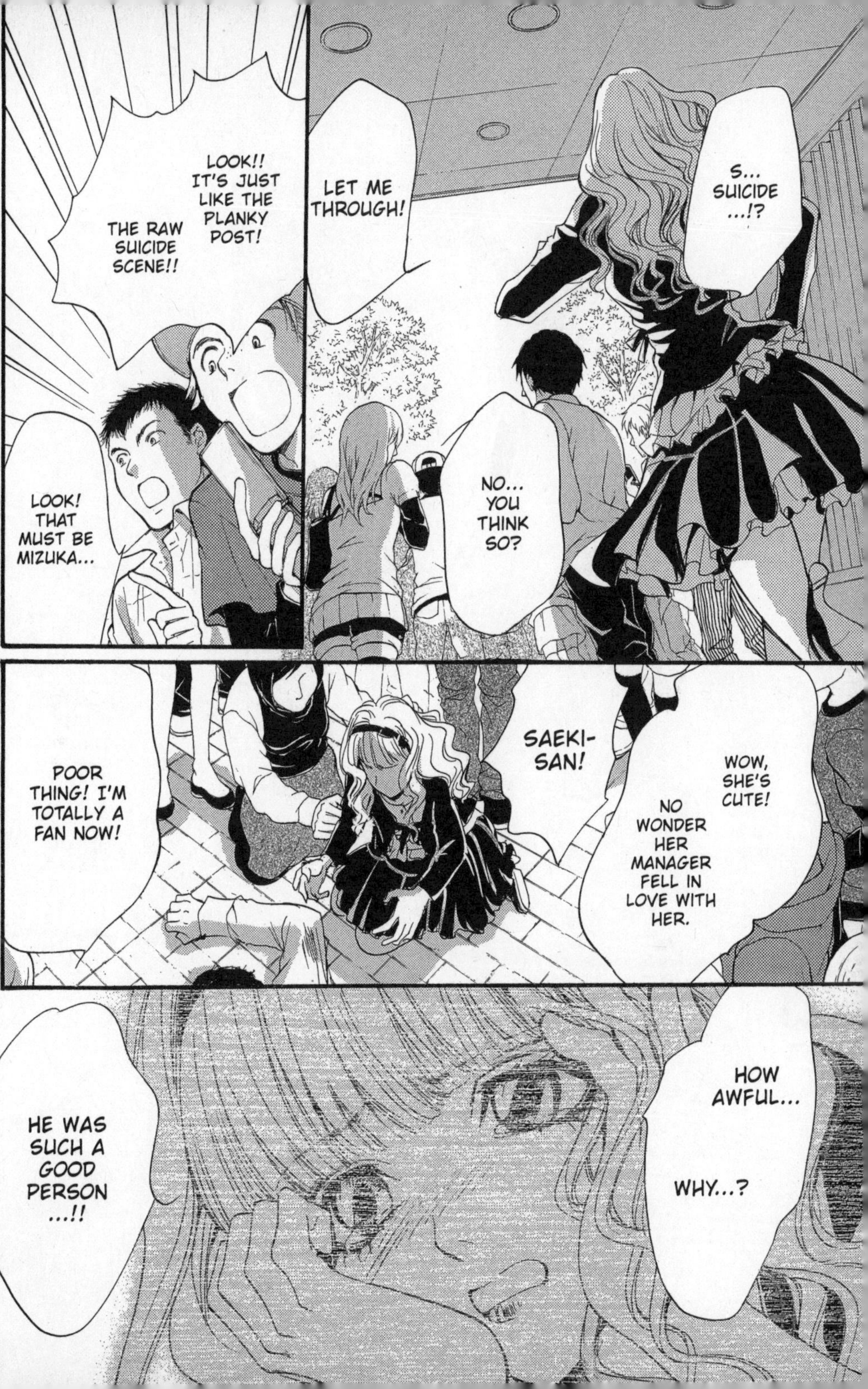
S... SUICIDE ...!?
LET ME THROUGH!
NO... YOU THINK SO?
LOOK!! IT'S JUST LIKE THE PLANKY POST!
THE RAW SUICIDE SCENE!!
LOOK! THAT MUST BE MIZUKA...
WOW, SHE'S CUTE!
NO WONDER HER MANAGER FELL IN LOVE WITH HER.
SAEKI-SAN!
POOR THING! I'M TOTALLY A FAN NOW!
HOW AWFUL...
WHY...?
HE WAS SUCH A GOOD PERSON ...!!

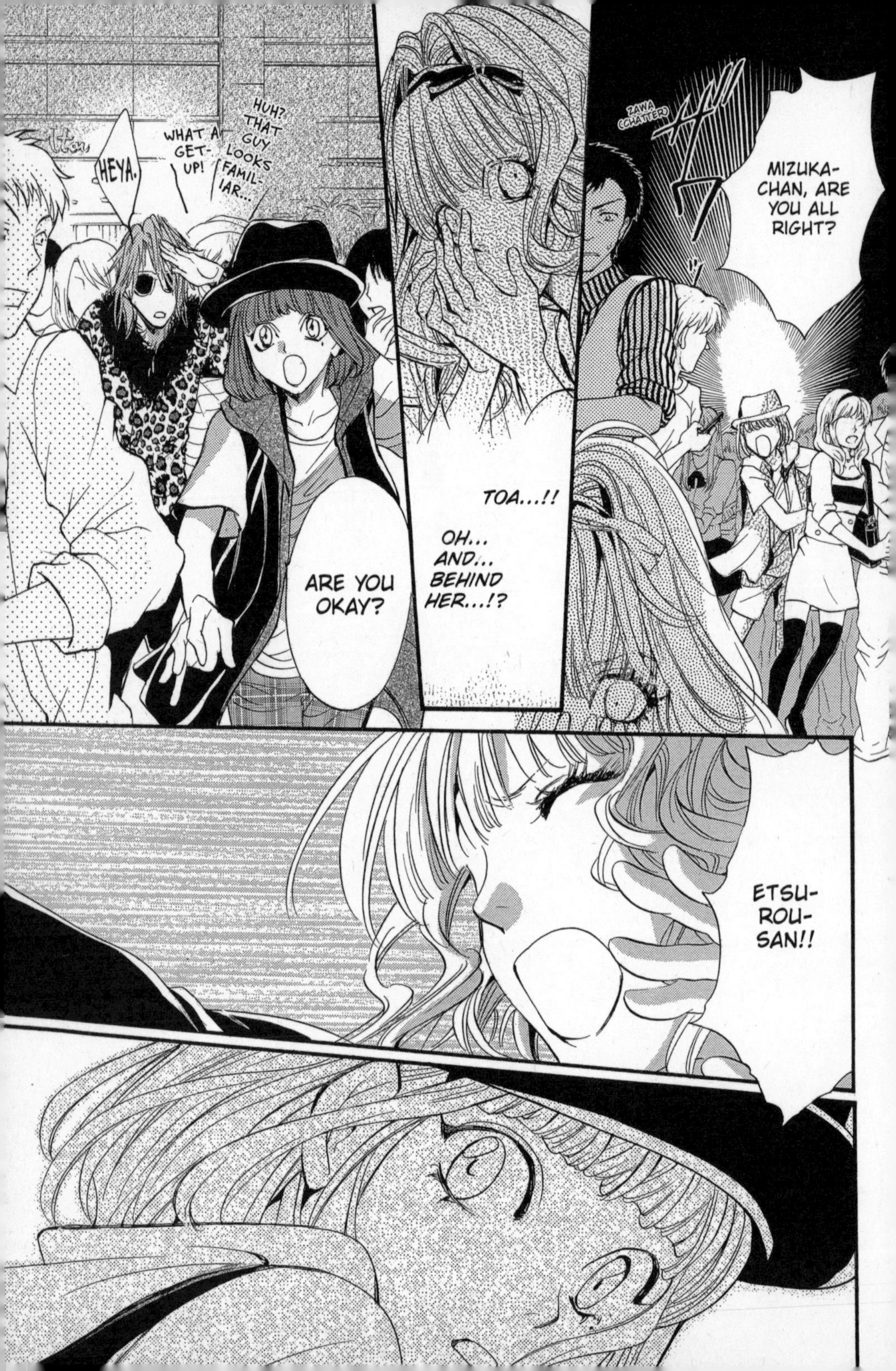
MIZUKA-CHAN, ARE YOU ALL RIGHT?
ZAWA (CHATTER)
TOA...!!
OH... AND... BEHIND HER...!?
HUH? THAT GUY LOOKS FAMIL-IAR...
WHAT A GET-UP!
HEYA.
ARE YOU OKAY?
ETSU-ROU-SAN!!

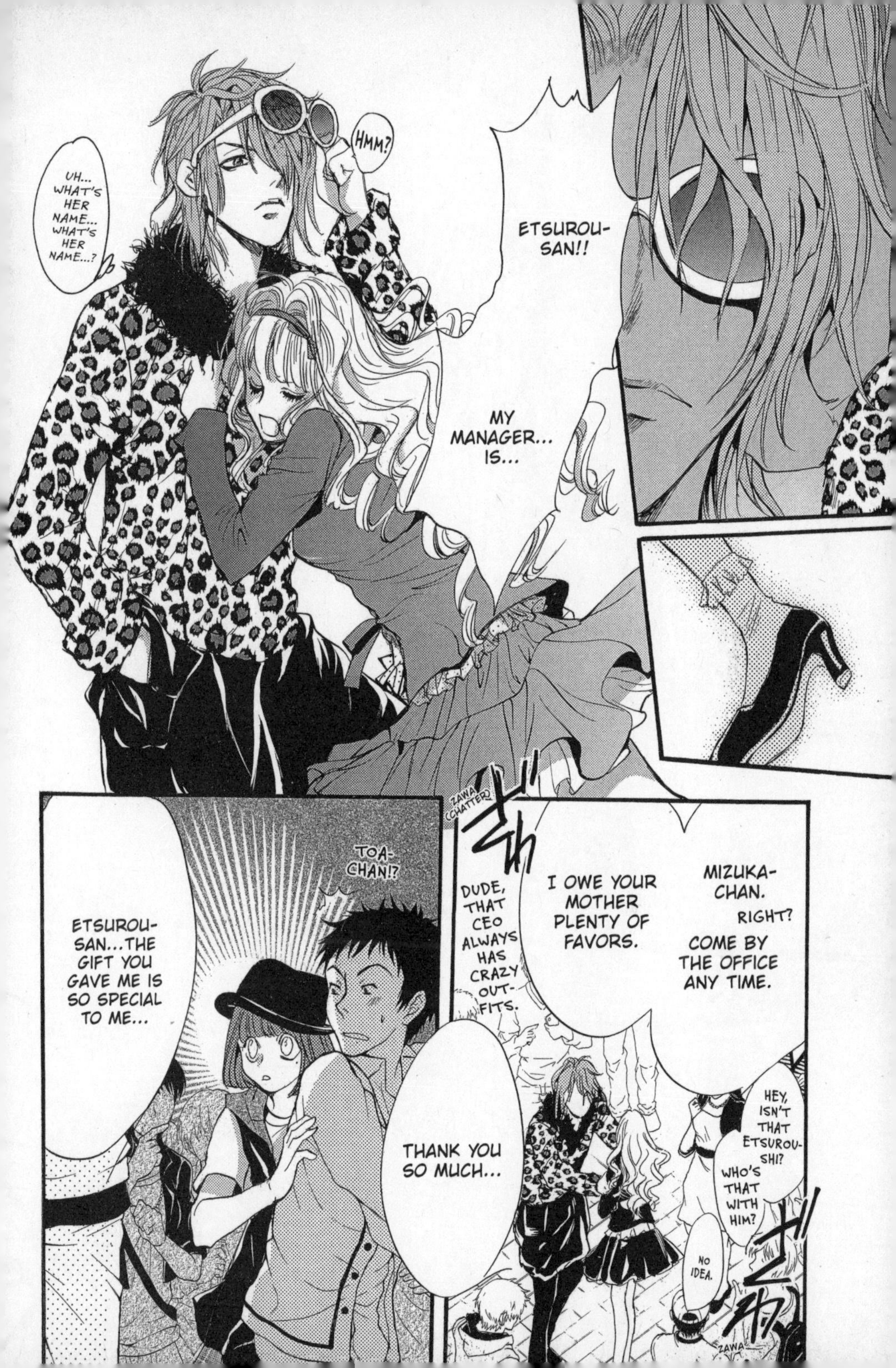
ETSUROU-SAN!!
MY MANAGER... IS...
HMM?
UH... WHAT'S HER NAME... WHAT'S HER NAME...?
ZAWA (CHATTER)
MIZUKA-CHAN.
RIGHT?
COME BY THE OFFICE ANY TIME.
I OWE YOUR MOTHER PLENTY OF FAVORS.
DUDE, THAT CEO ALWAYS HAS CRAZY OUT-FITS.
HEY, ISN'T THAT ETSUROU-SHI?
WHO'S THAT WITH HIM?
NO IDEA.
ZAWA
ETSUROU-SAN...THE GIFT YOU GAVE ME IS SO SPECIAL TO ME...
THANK YOU SO MUCH...
TOA-CHAN!?

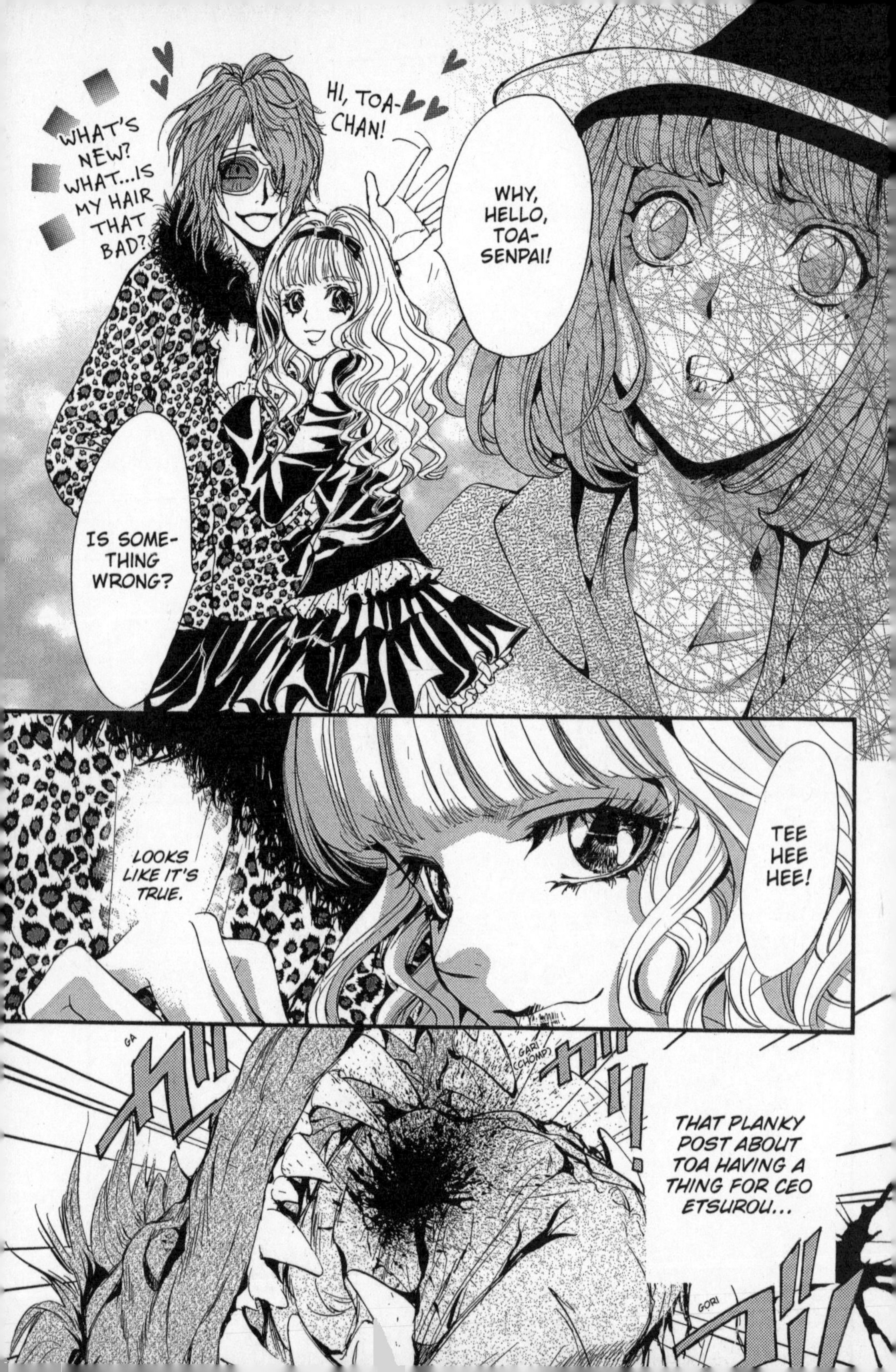
WHY, HELLO, TOA-SENPAI!
HI, TOA-CHAN!
WHAT'S NEW? WHAT...IS MY HAIR THAT BAD?
IS SOME-THING WRONG?
TEE HEE HEE!
LOOKS LIKE IT'S TRUE.
GARI (CHOMP)
GA
THAT PLANKY POST ABOUT TOA HAVING A THING FOR CEO ETSUROU...
GORI

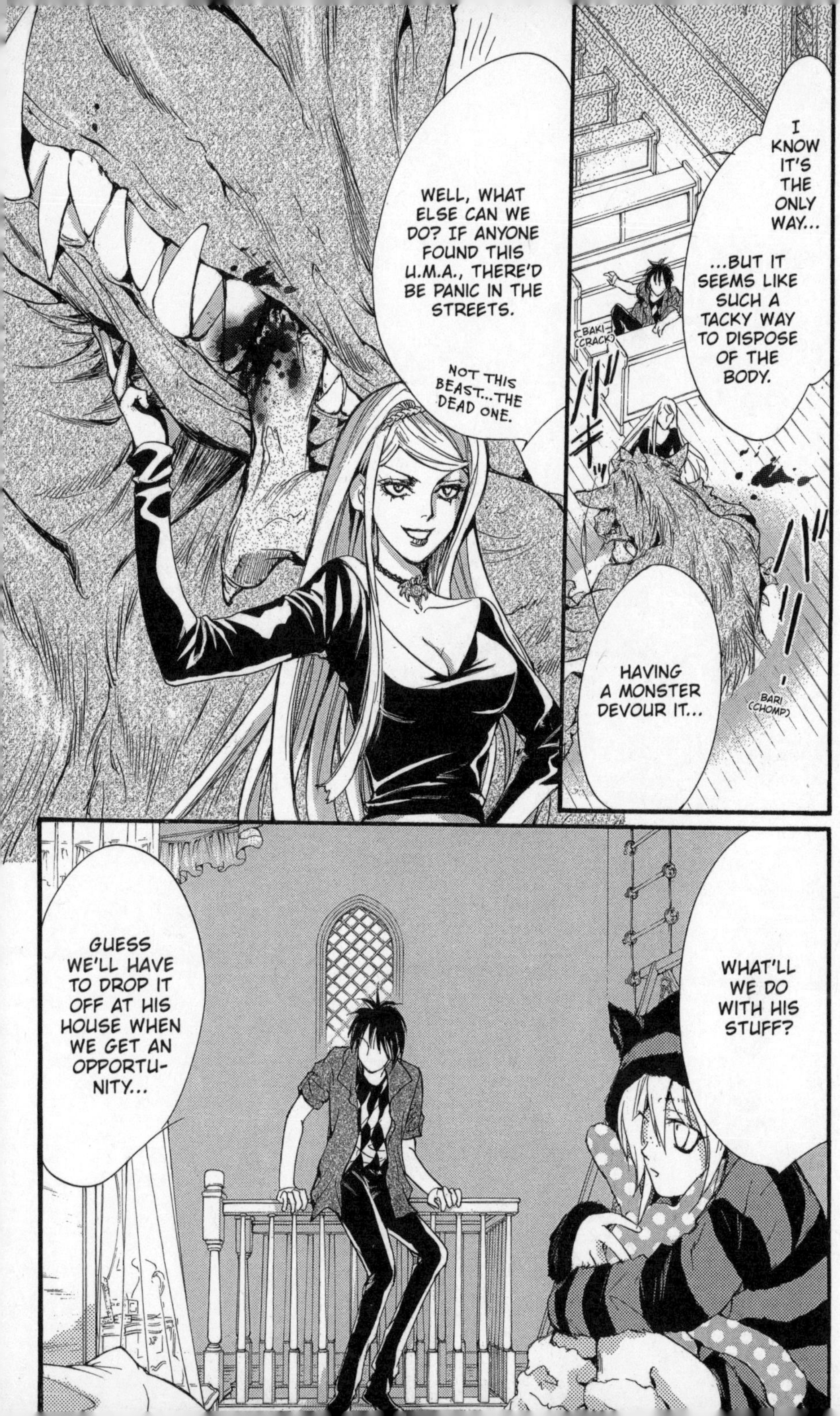
I KNOW IT'S THE ONLY WAY...
...BUT IT SEEMS LIKE SUCH A TACKY WAY TO DISPOSE OF THE BODY.
BAKI (CRACK)
HAVING A MONSTER DEVOUR IT...
BARI (CHOMP)
WELL, WHAT ELSE CAN WE DO? IF ANYONE FOUND THIS U.M.A., THERE'D BE PANIC IN THE STREETS.
NOT THIS BEAST...THE DEAD ONE.
WHAT'LL WE DO WITH HIS STUFF?
GUESS WE'LL HAVE TO DROP IT OFF AT HIS HOUSE WHEN WE GET AN OPPORTU-NITY...

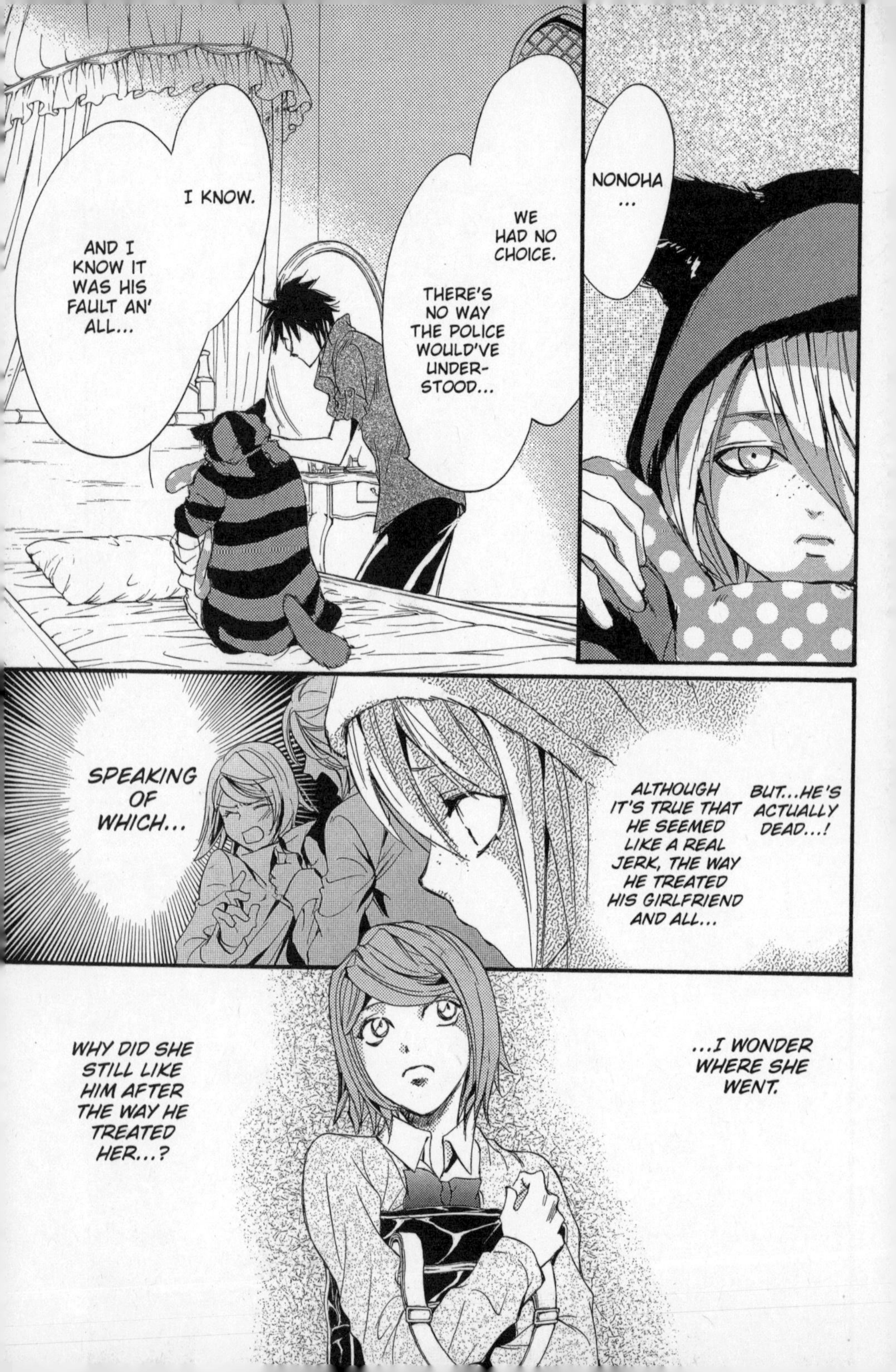
NONOHA...
WE HAD NO CHOICE.
THERE'S NO WAY THE POLICE WOULD'VE UNDERSTOOD...
I KNOW.
AND I KNOW IT WAS HIS FAULT AN' ALL...
BUT...HE'S ACTUALLY DEAD...!
ALTHOUGH IT'S TRUE THAT HE SEEMED LIKE A REAL JERK, THE WAY HE TREATED HIS GIRLFRIEND AND ALL...
SPEAKING OF WHICH...
...I WONDER WHERE SHE WENT.
WHY DID SHE STILL LIKE HIM AFTER THE WAY HE TREATED HER...?

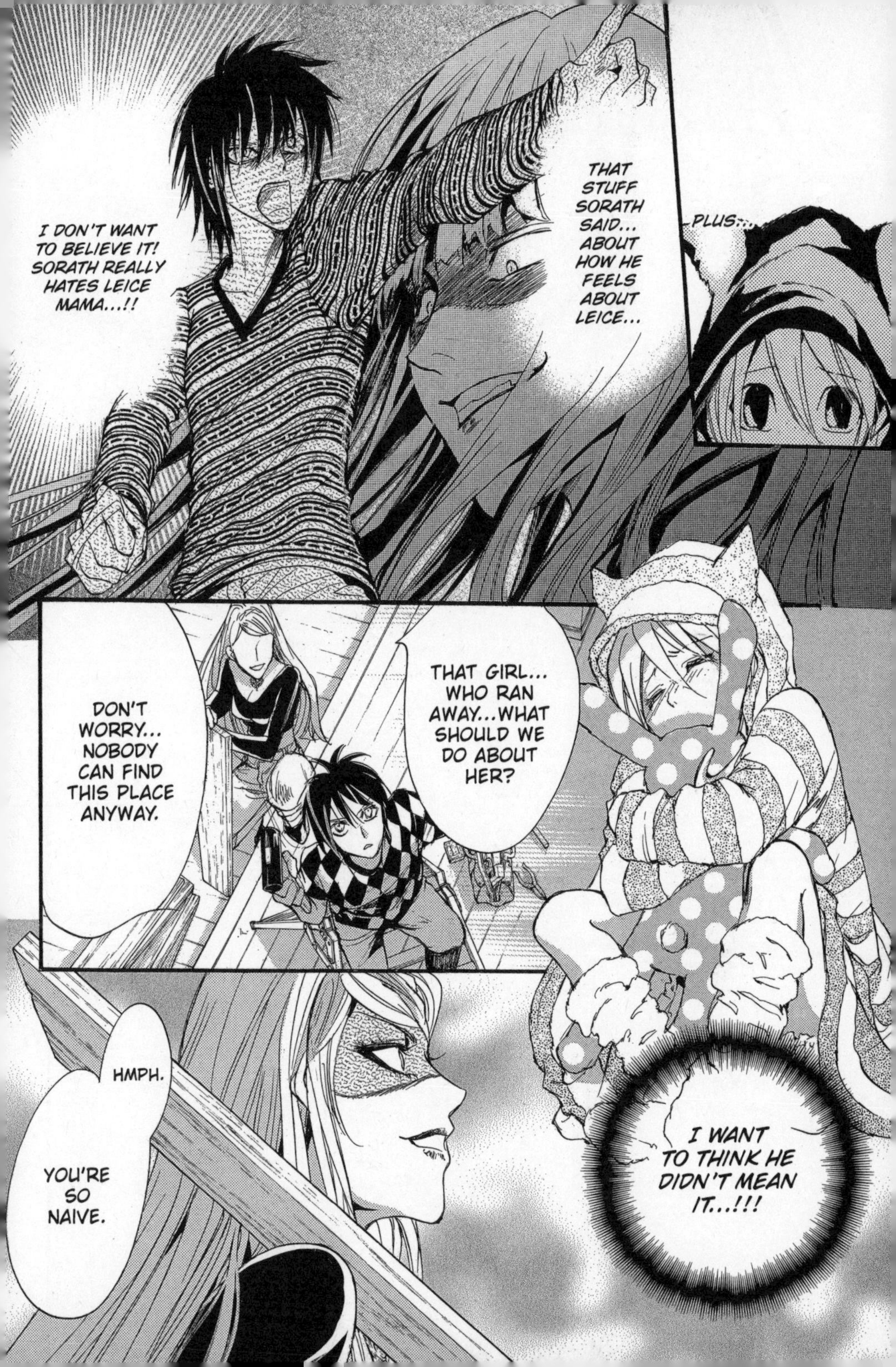
PLUS...
THAT STUFF SORATH SAID... ABOUT HOW HE FEELS ABOUT LEICE...
I DON'T WANT TO BELIEVE IT! SORATH REALLY HATES LEICE MAMA...!!
THAT GIRL... WHO RAN AWAY...WHAT SHOULD WE DO ABOUT HER?
DON'T WORRY... NOBODY CAN FIND THIS PLACE ANYWAY.
I WANT TO THINK HE DIDN'T MEAN IT...!!!
HMPH.
YOU'RE SO NAIVE.

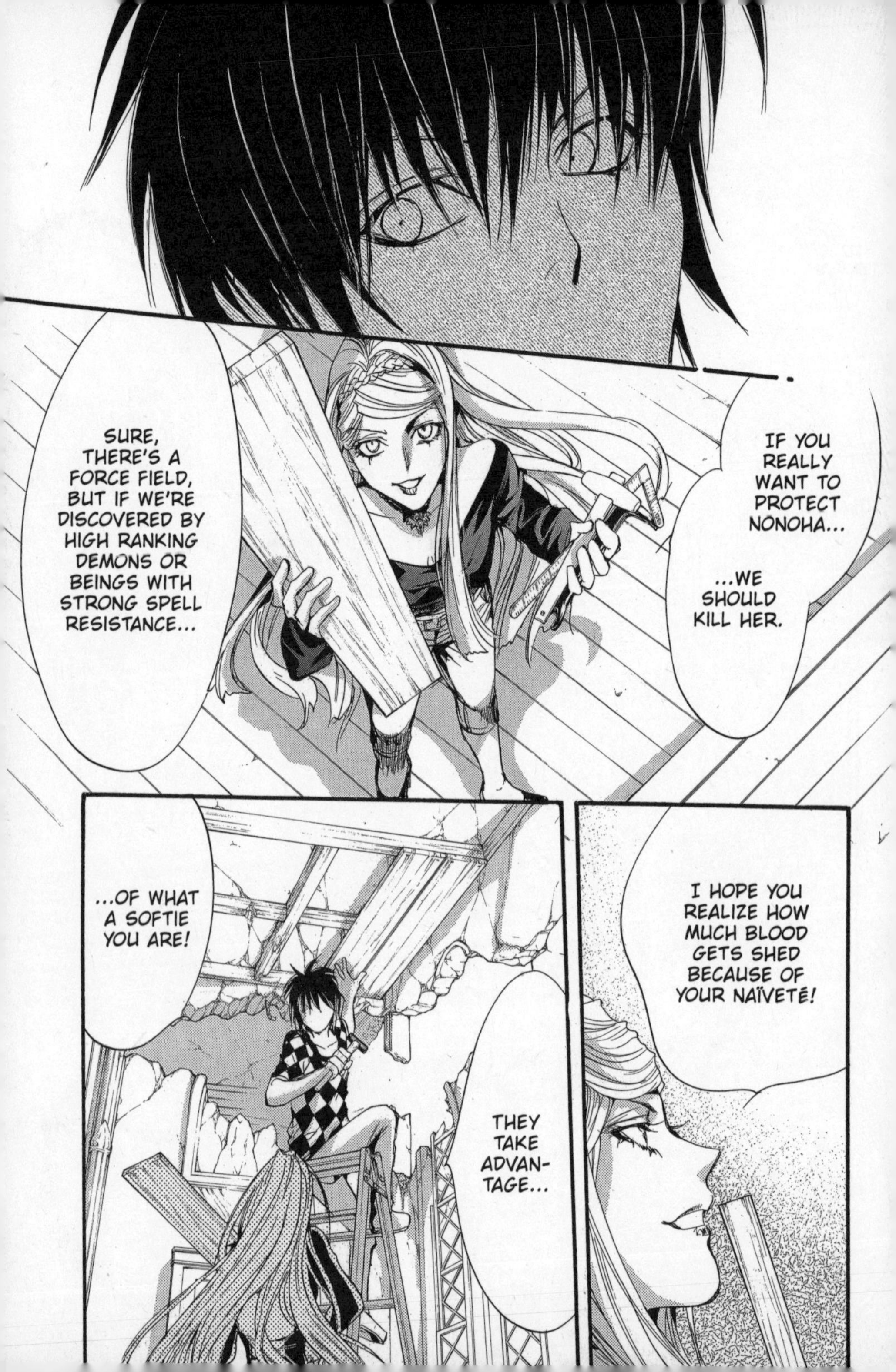
IF YOU REALLY WANT TO PROTECT NONOHA...
...WE SHOULD KILL HER.
SURE, THERE'S A FORCE FIELD, BUT IF WE'RE DISCOVERED BY HIGH RANKING DEMONS OR BEINGS WITH STRONG SPELL RESISTANCE...
I HOPE YOU REALIZE HOW MUCH BLOOD GETS SHED BECAUSE OF YOUR NAÏVETÉ!
THEY TAKE ADVAN-TAGE...
...OF WHAT A SOFTIE YOU ARE!

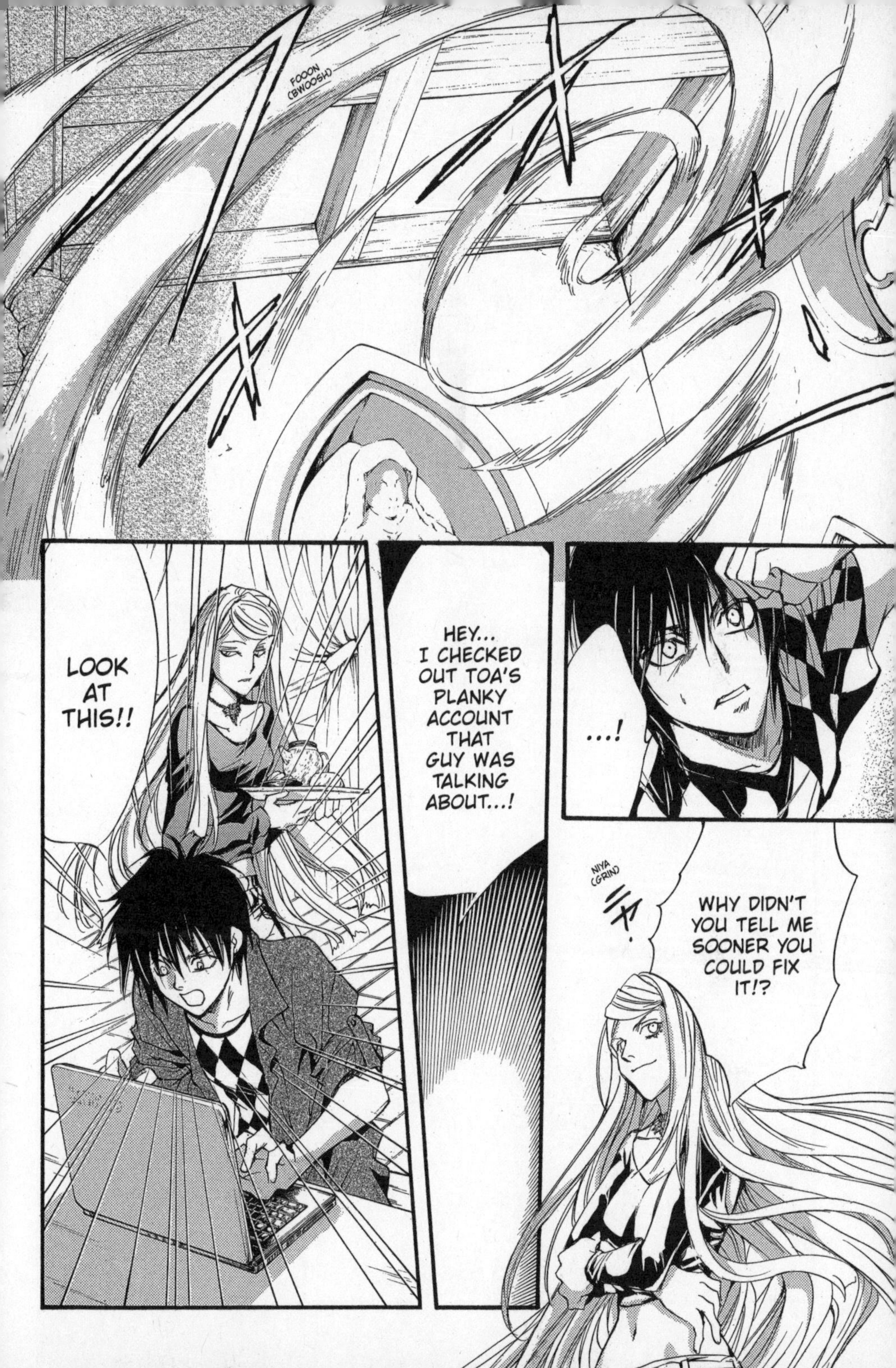
FOOON
(BWOOSH)
...!
NIYA
(GRIN)
WHY DIDN'T YOU TELL ME SOONER YOU COULD FIX IT!?
HEY... I CHECKED OUT TOA'S PLANKY ACCOUNT THAT GUY WAS TALKING ABOUT...!
LOOK AT THIS!!

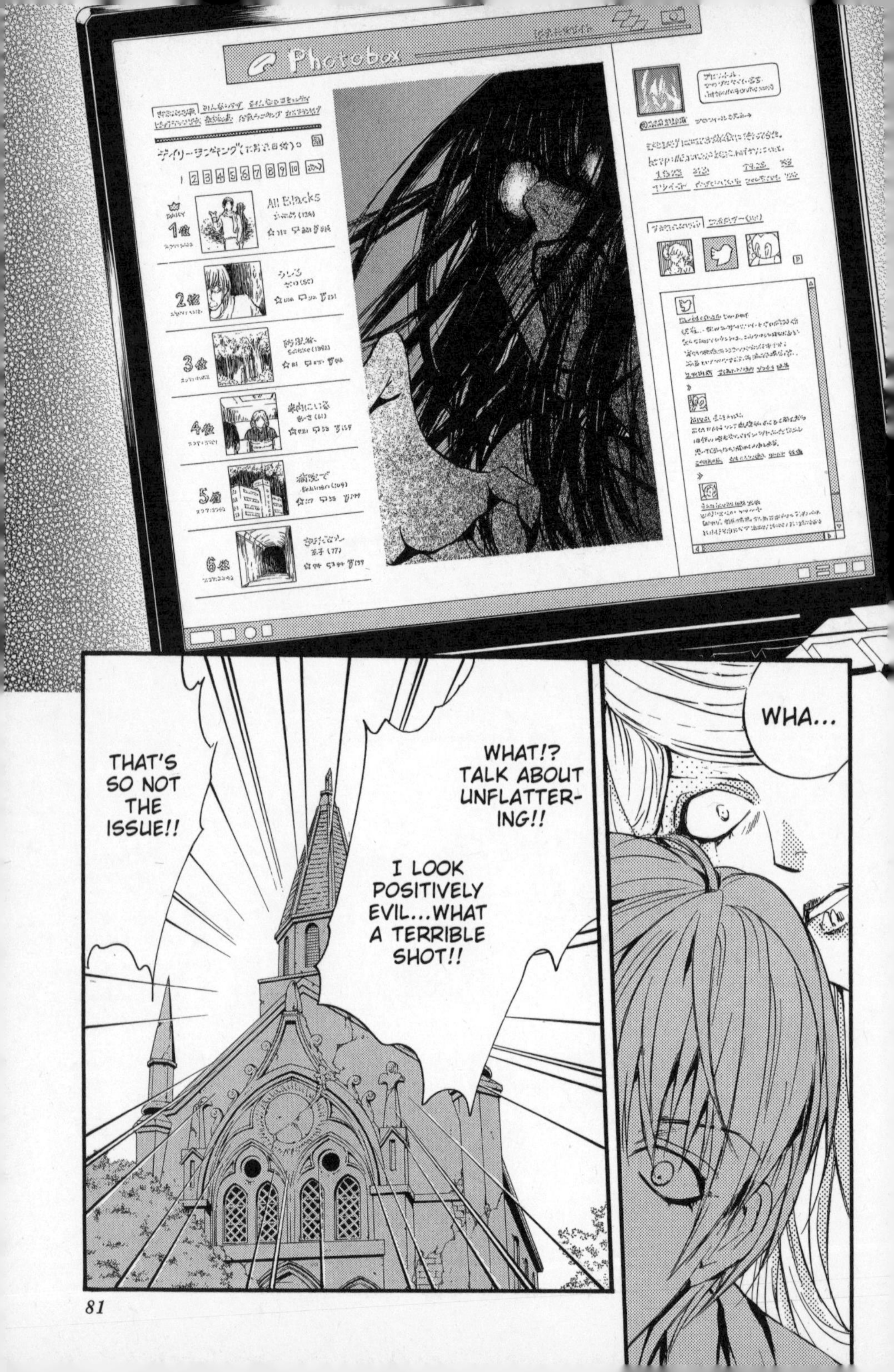
Photobox
All Blacks
WHA...
WHAT!? TALK ABOUT UNFLATTERING!!
I LOOK POSITIVELY EVIL...WHAT A TERRIBLE SHOT!!
THAT'S SO NOT THE ISSUE!!

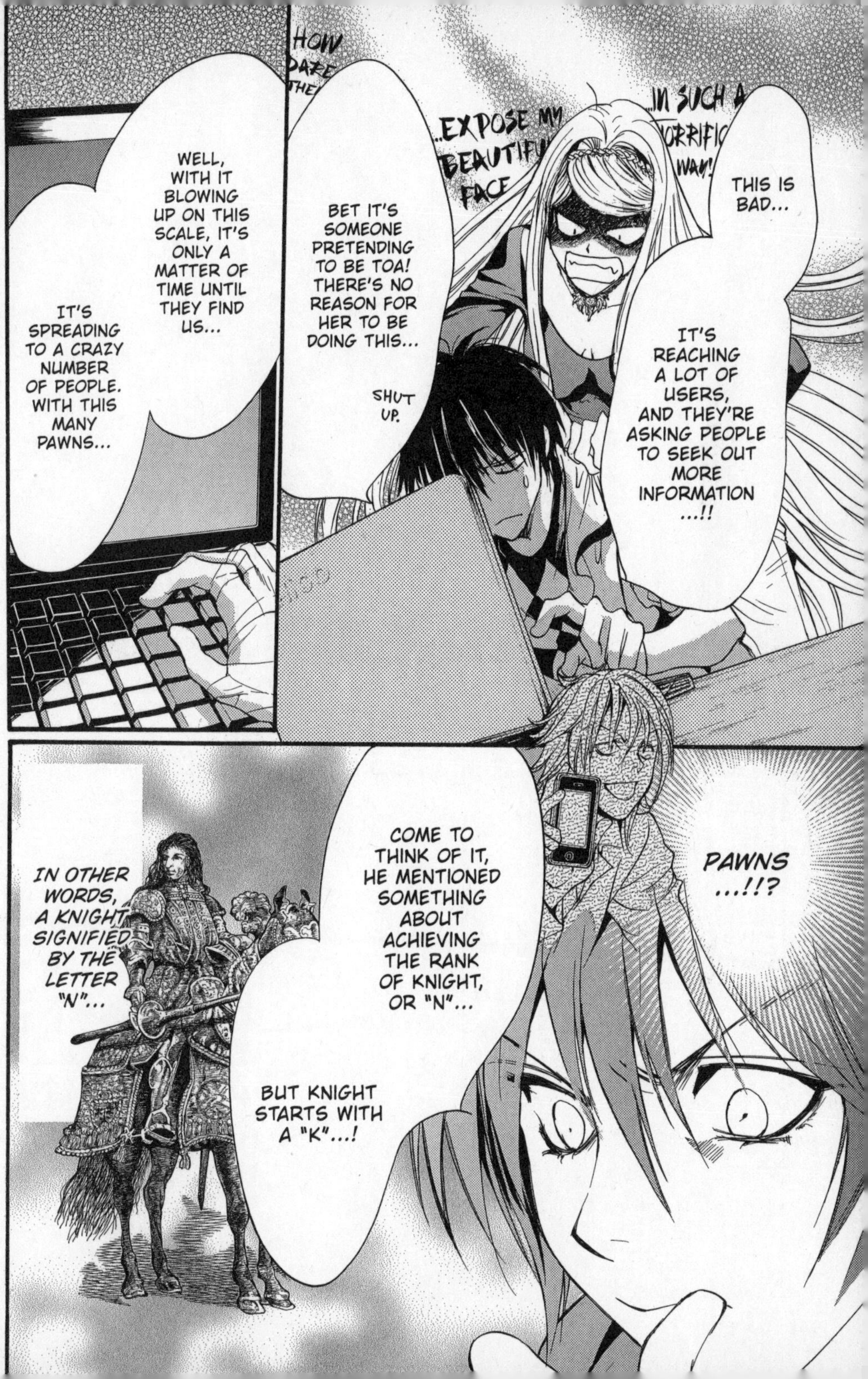
HOW DARE THE
...EXPOSE MY BEAUTIFU FACE
...IN SUCH A ORRIFIC WAY!
THIS IS BAD...
IT'S REACHING A LOT OF USERS, AND THEY'RE ASKING PEOPLE TO SEEK OUT MORE INFORMATION ...!!
BET IT'S SOMEONE PRETENDING TO BE TOA! THERE'S NO REASON FOR HER TO BE DOING THIS...
SHUT UP.
WELL, WITH IT BLOWING UP ON THIS SCALE, IT'S ONLY A MATTER OF TIME UNTIL THEY FIND US...
IT'S SPREADING TO A CRAZY NUMBER OF PEOPLE. WITH THIS MANY PAWNS...
PAWNS ...!!?
COME TO THINK OF IT, HE MENTIONED SOMETHING ABOUT ACHIEVING THE RANK OF KNIGHT, OR "N"...
BUT KNIGHT STARTS WITH A "K"...!
IN OTHER WORDS, A KNIGHT SIGNIFIED BY THE LETTER "N"...

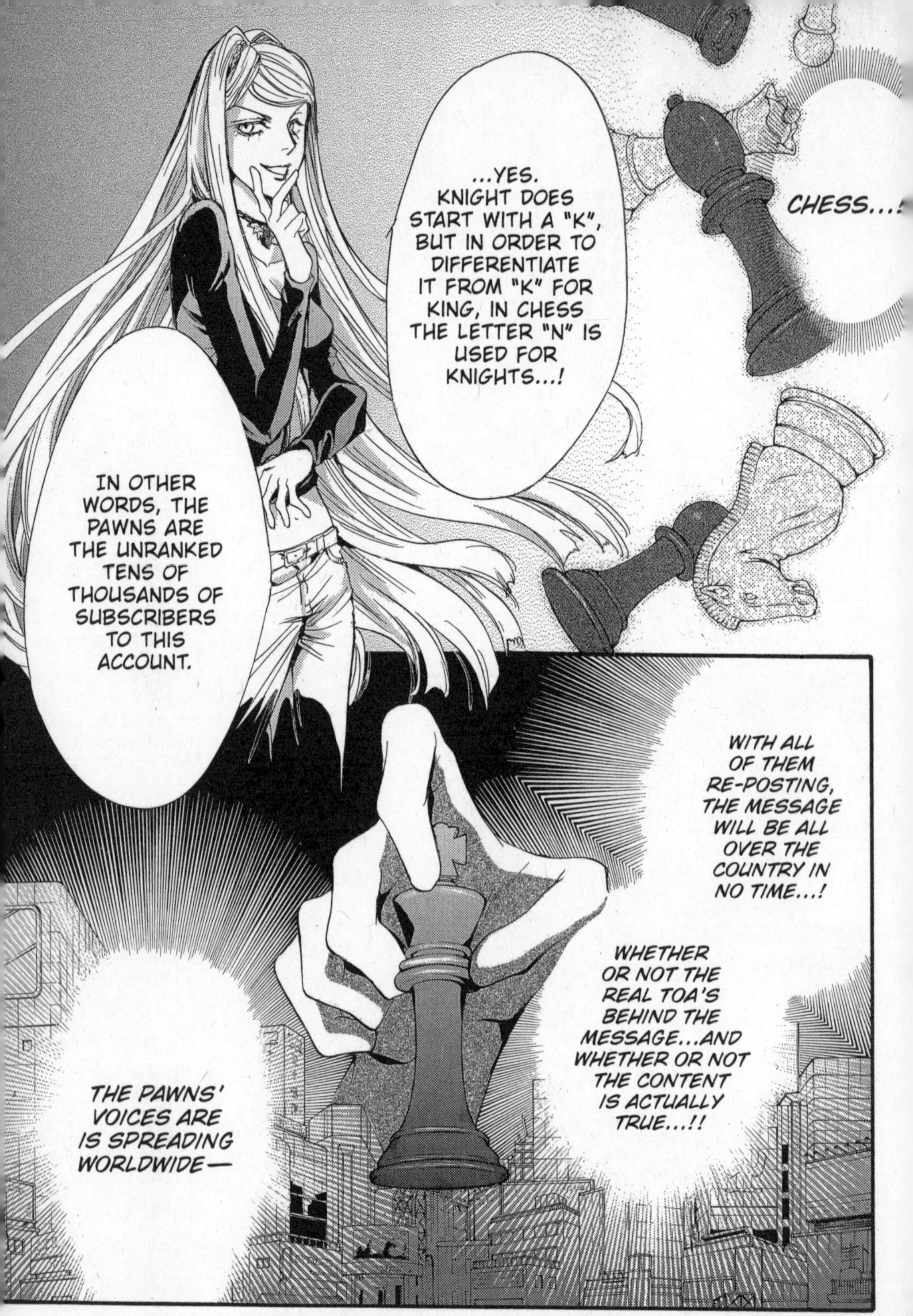
CHESS...!
...YES. KNIGHT DOES START WITH A "K", BUT IN ORDER TO DIFFERENTIATE IT FROM "K" FOR KING, IN CHESS THE LETTER "N" IS USED FOR KNIGHTS...!
IN OTHER WORDS, THE PAWNS ARE THE UNRANKED TENS OF THOUSANDS OF SUBSCRIBERS TO THIS ACCOUNT.
WITH ALL OF THEM RE-POSTING, THE MESSAGE WILL BE ALL OVER THE COUNTRY IN NO TIME...!
WHETHER OR NOT THE REAL TOA'S BEHIND THE MESSAGE...AND WHETHER OR NOT THE CONTENT IS ACTUALLY TRUE...!!
THE PAWNS' VOICES ARE IS SPREADING WORLDWIDE—

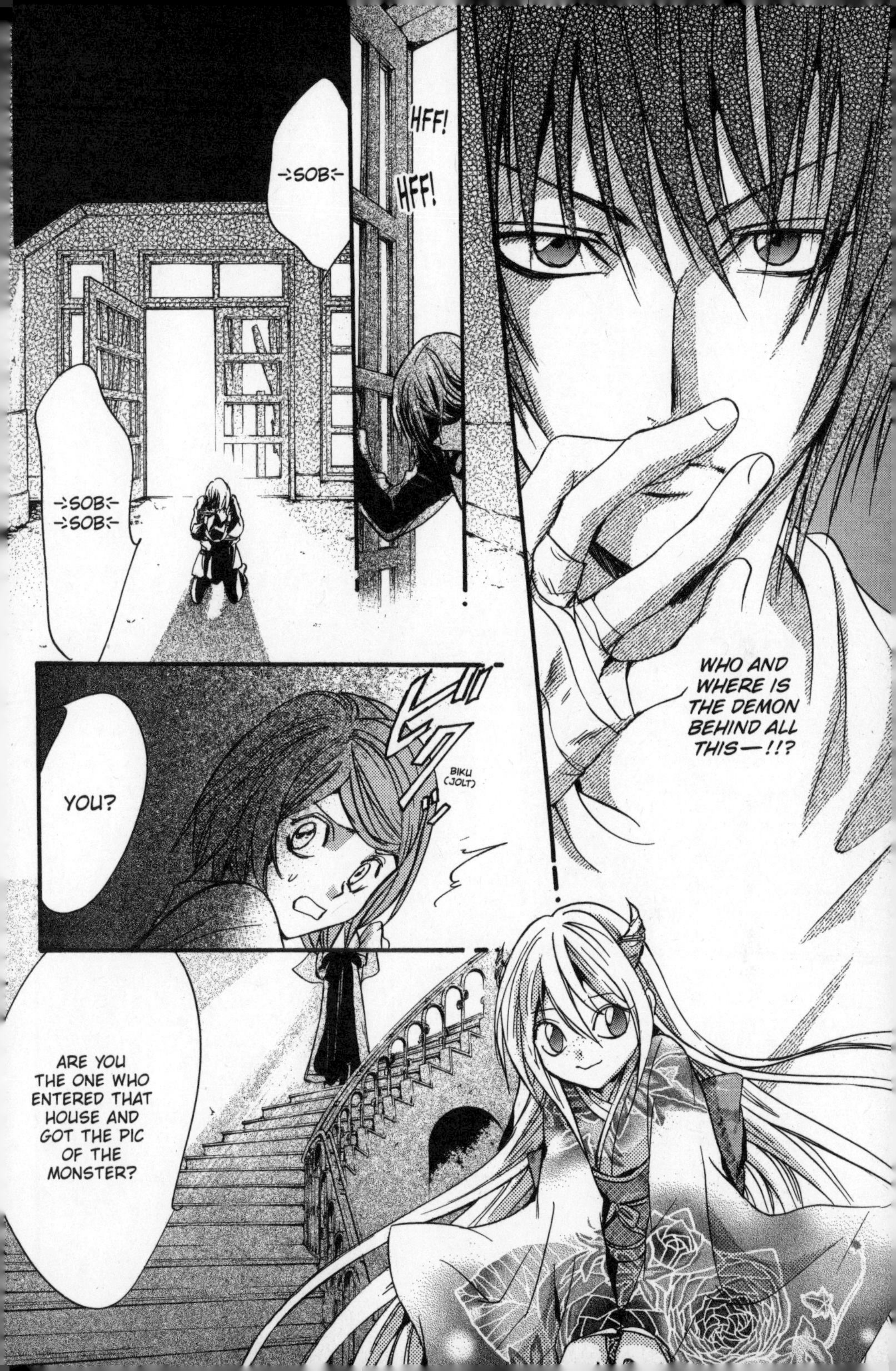
WHO AND WHERE IS THE DEMON BEHIND ALL THIS—!!?
HFF!
HFF!
-SOB-
-SOB-
-SOB-
BIKU (JOLT)
YOU?
ARE YOU THE ONE WHO ENTERED THAT HOUSE AND GOT THE PIC OF THE MONSTER?

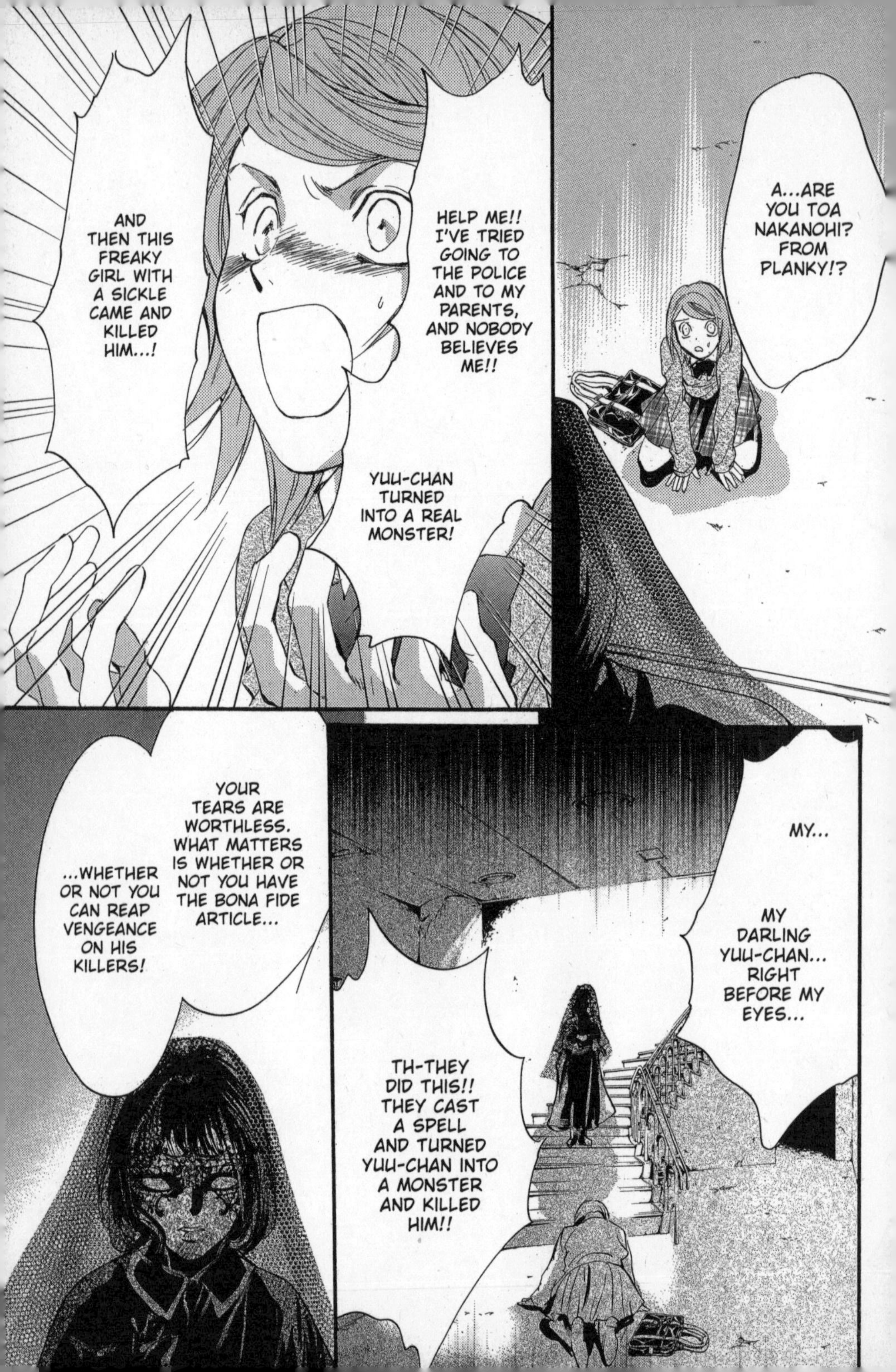
A...ARE YOU TOA NAKANOHI? FROM PLANKY!?
HELP ME!! I'VE TRIED GOING TO THE POLICE AND TO MY PARENTS, AND NOBODY BELIEVES ME!!
YUU-CHAN TURNED INTO A REAL MONSTER!
AND THEN THIS FREAKY GIRL WITH A SICKLE CAME AND KILLED HIM...!
MY...
MY DARLING YUU-CHAN... RIGHT BEFORE MY EYES...
TH-THEY DID THIS!! THEY CAST A SPELL AND TURNED YUU-CHAN INTO A MONSTER AND KILLED HIM!!
YOUR TEARS ARE WORTHLESS. WHAT MATTERS IS WHETHER OR NOT YOU HAVE THE BONA FIDE ARTICLE...
...WHETHER OR NOT YOU CAN REAP VENGEANCE ON HIS KILLERS!

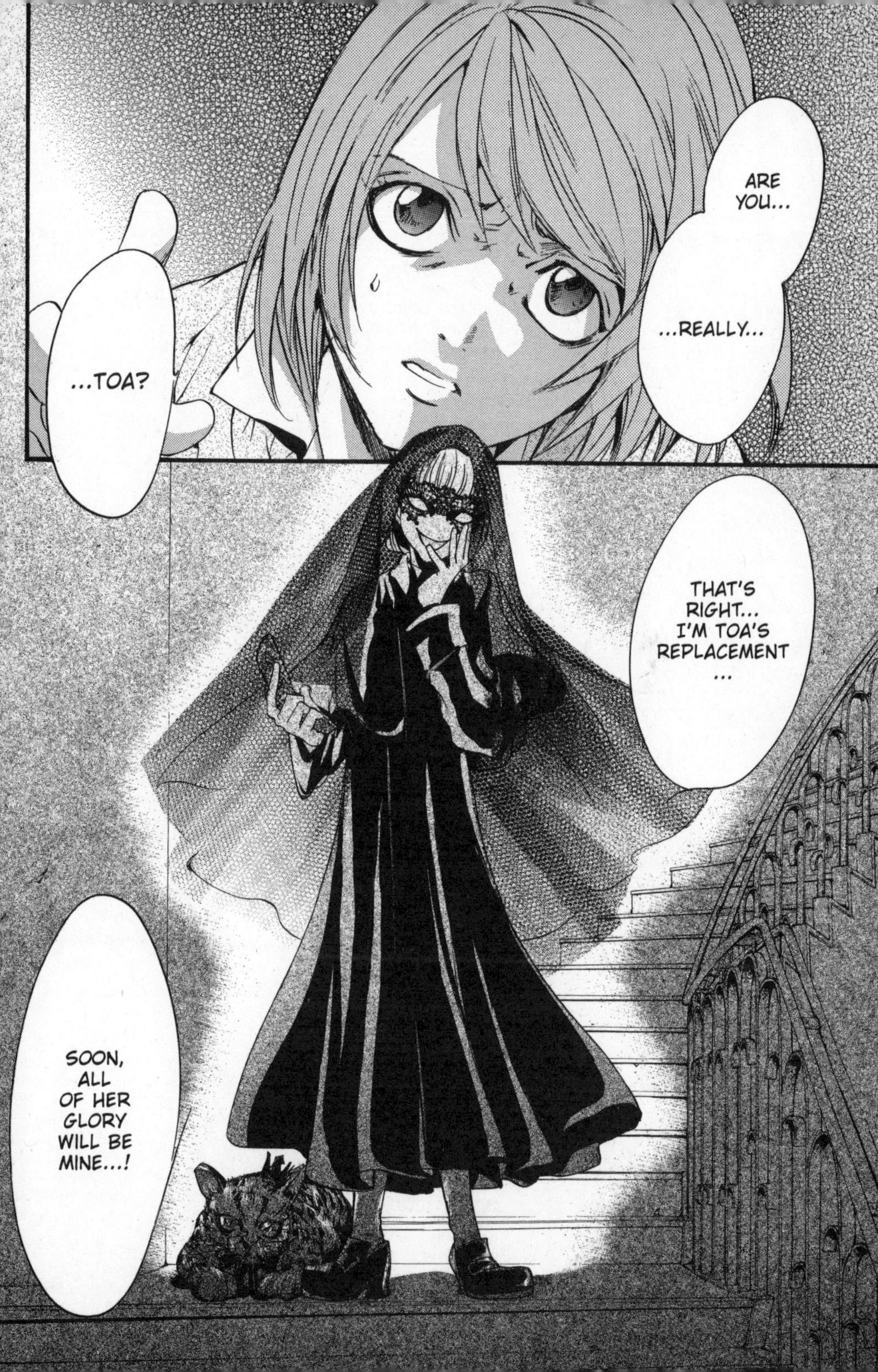
ARE YOU...
...REALLY...
...TOA?
THAT'S RIGHT... I'M TOA'S REPLACEMENT ...
SOON, ALL OF HER GLORY WILL BE MINE...!

Modern Day Arc

Chapter 10

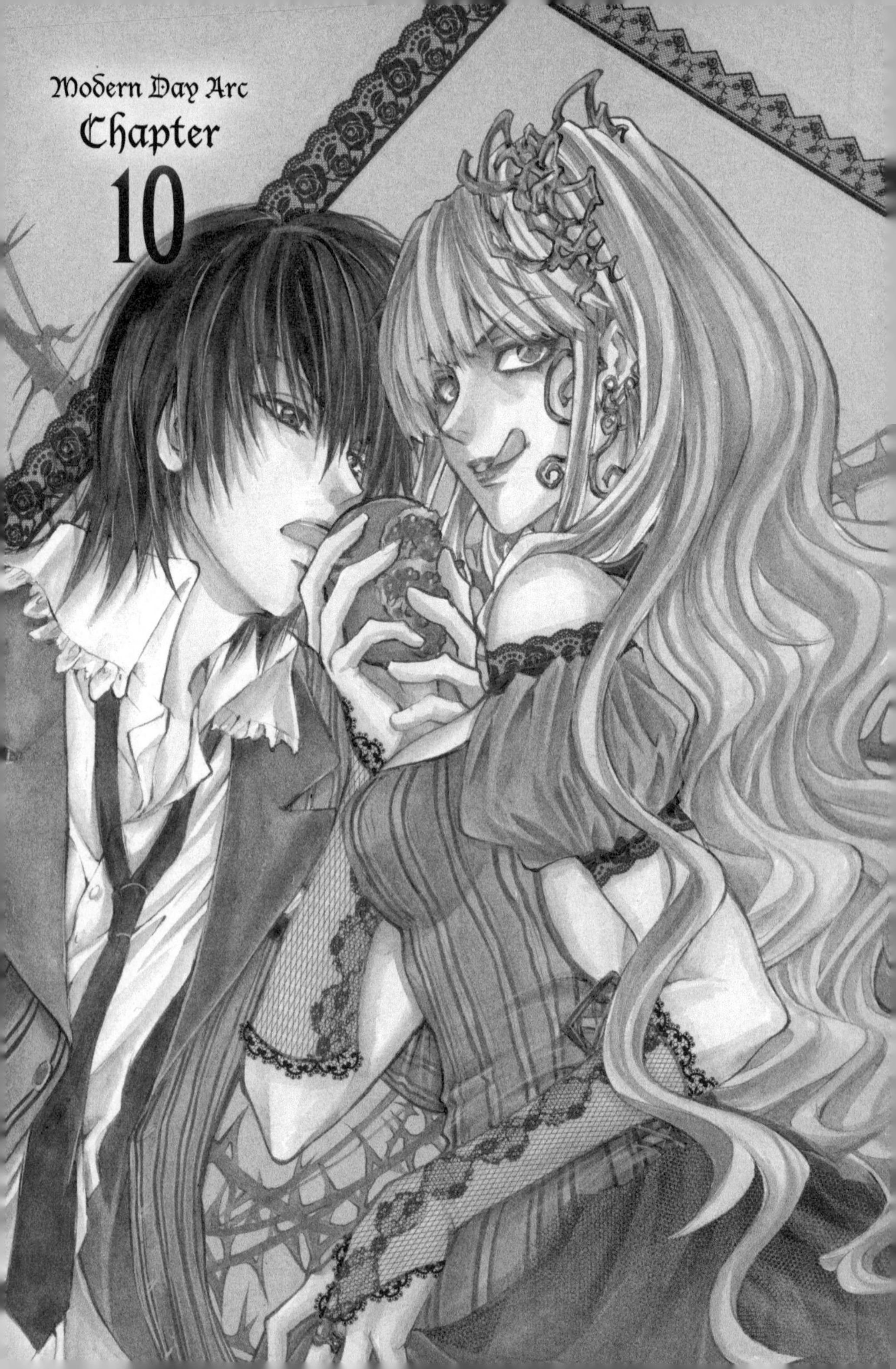

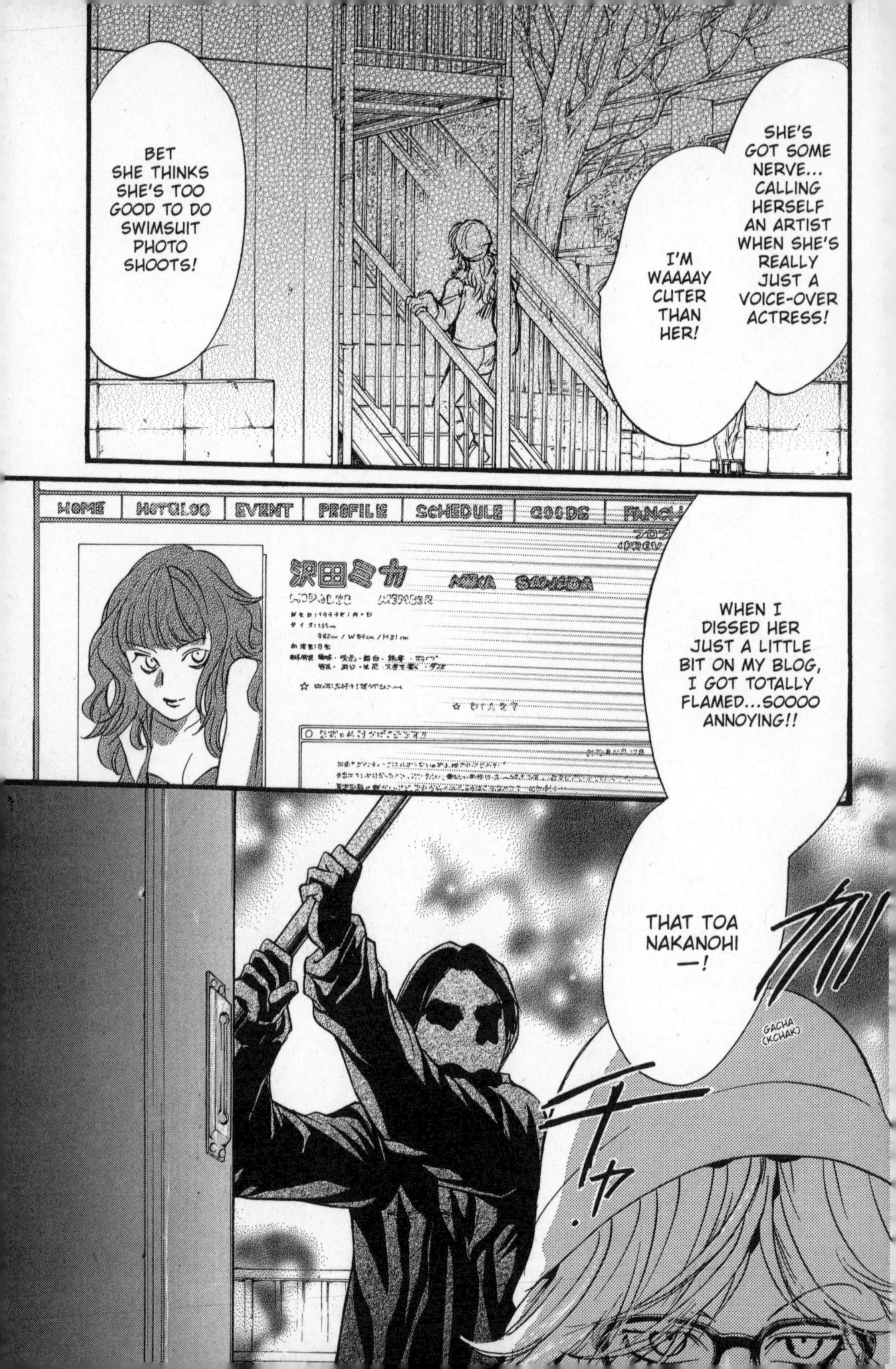
SHE'S GOT SOME NERVE... CALLING HERSELF AN ARTIST WHEN SHE'S REALLY JUST A VOICE-OVER ACTRESS!
I'M WAAAAY CUTER THAN HER!
BET SHE THINKS SHE'S TOO GOOD TO DO SWIMSUIT PHOTO SHOOTS!
WHEN I DISSED HER JUST A LITTLE BIT ON MY BLOG, I GOT TOTALLY FLAMED...SOOOO ANNOYING!!
HOME
EVENT
PROFILE
SCHEDULE
沢田ミカ
MIKA SAWADA
MEMBER
THAT TOA NAKANOHI—!
GACHA (KCHAK)

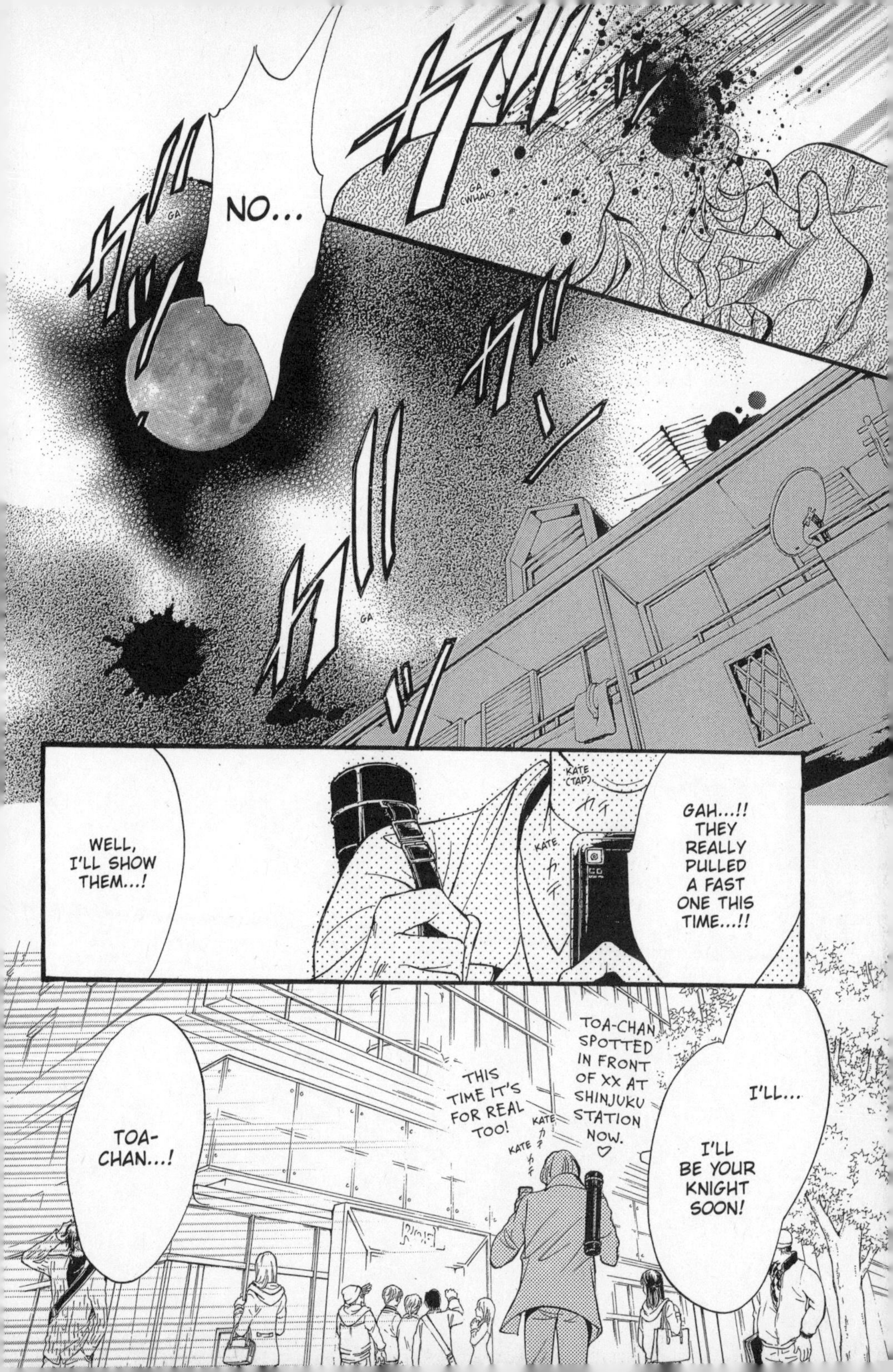
GA (WHAK)
NO...
GA
GAN
GA
KATE (TAP)
GAH...!! THEY REALLY PULLED A FAST ONE THIS TIME...!!
KATE
WELL, I'LL SHOW THEM...!
I'LL...
I'LL BE YOUR KNIGHT SOON!
TOA-CHAN SPOTTED IN FRONT OF XX AT SHINJUKU STATION NOW. ♡
THIS TIME IT'S FOR REAL TOO!
KATE
KATE
TOA-CHAN...!

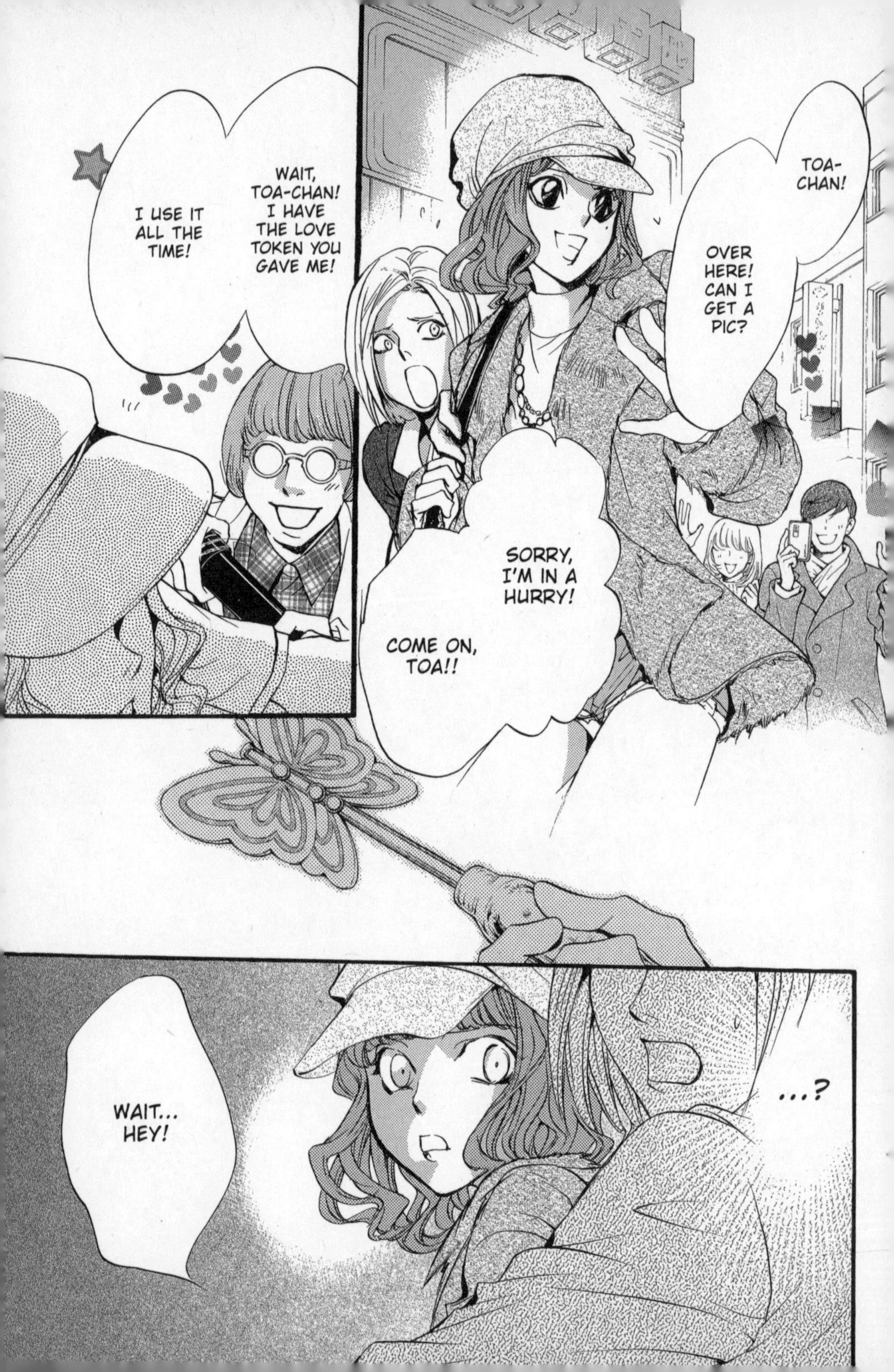
TOA-CHAN!
OVER HERE! CAN I GET A PIC?
SORRY, I'M IN A HURRY!
COME ON, TOA!!
WAIT, TOA-CHAN! I HAVE THE LOVE TOKEN YOU GAVE ME!
I USE IT ALL THE TIME!
...?
WAIT... HEY!

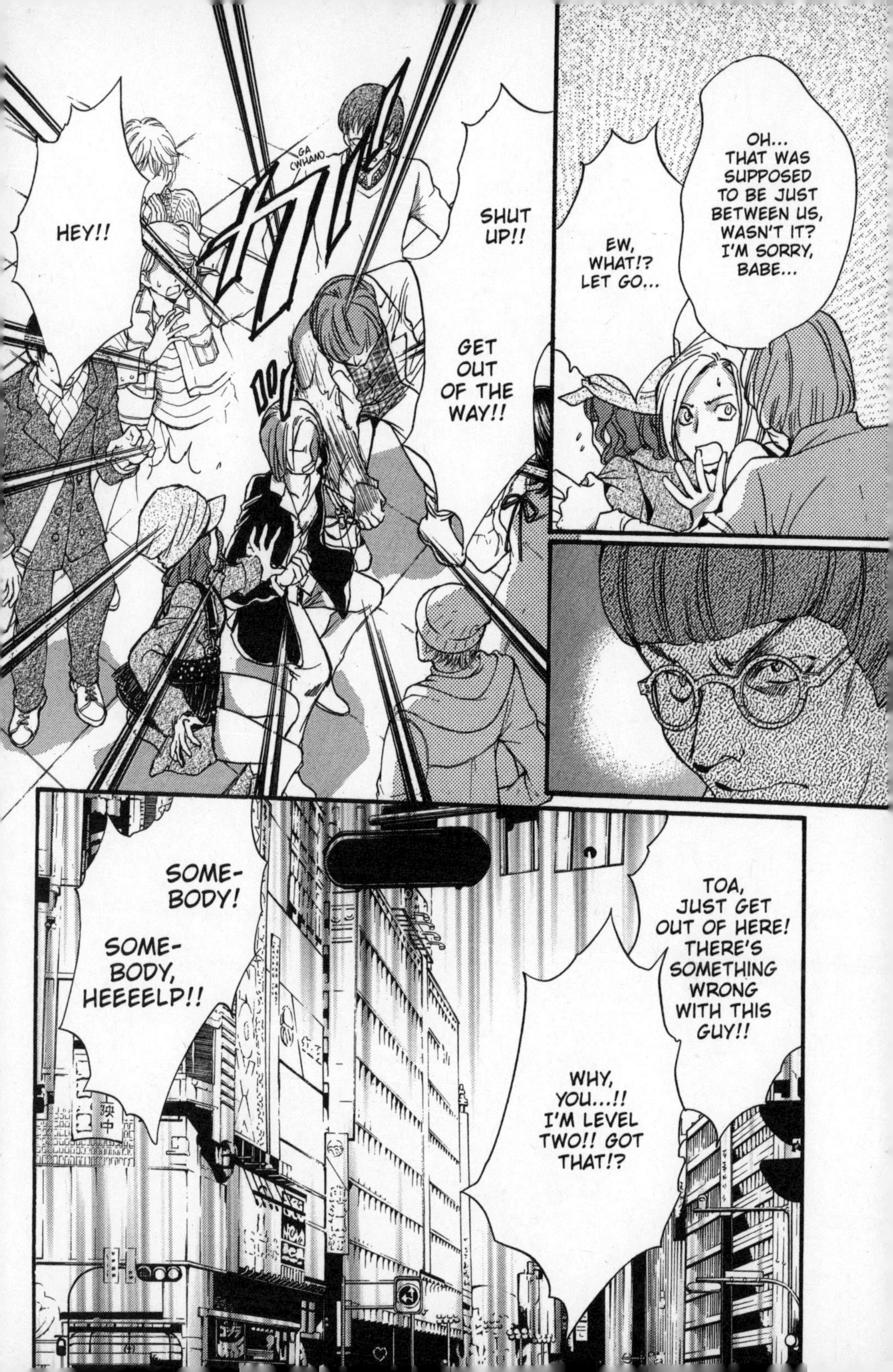
OH... THAT WAS SUPPOSED TO BE JUST BETWEEN US, WASN'T IT? I'M SORRY, BABE...
EW, WHAT!? LET GO...
SHUT UP!!
GET OUT OF THE WAY!!
GA (WHAM)
HEY!!
TOA, JUST GET OUT OF HERE! THERE'S SOMETHING WRONG WITH THIS GUY!!
WHY, YOU...!! I'M LEVEL TWO!! GOT THAT!?
SOME-BODY!
SOME-BODY, HEEEELP!!

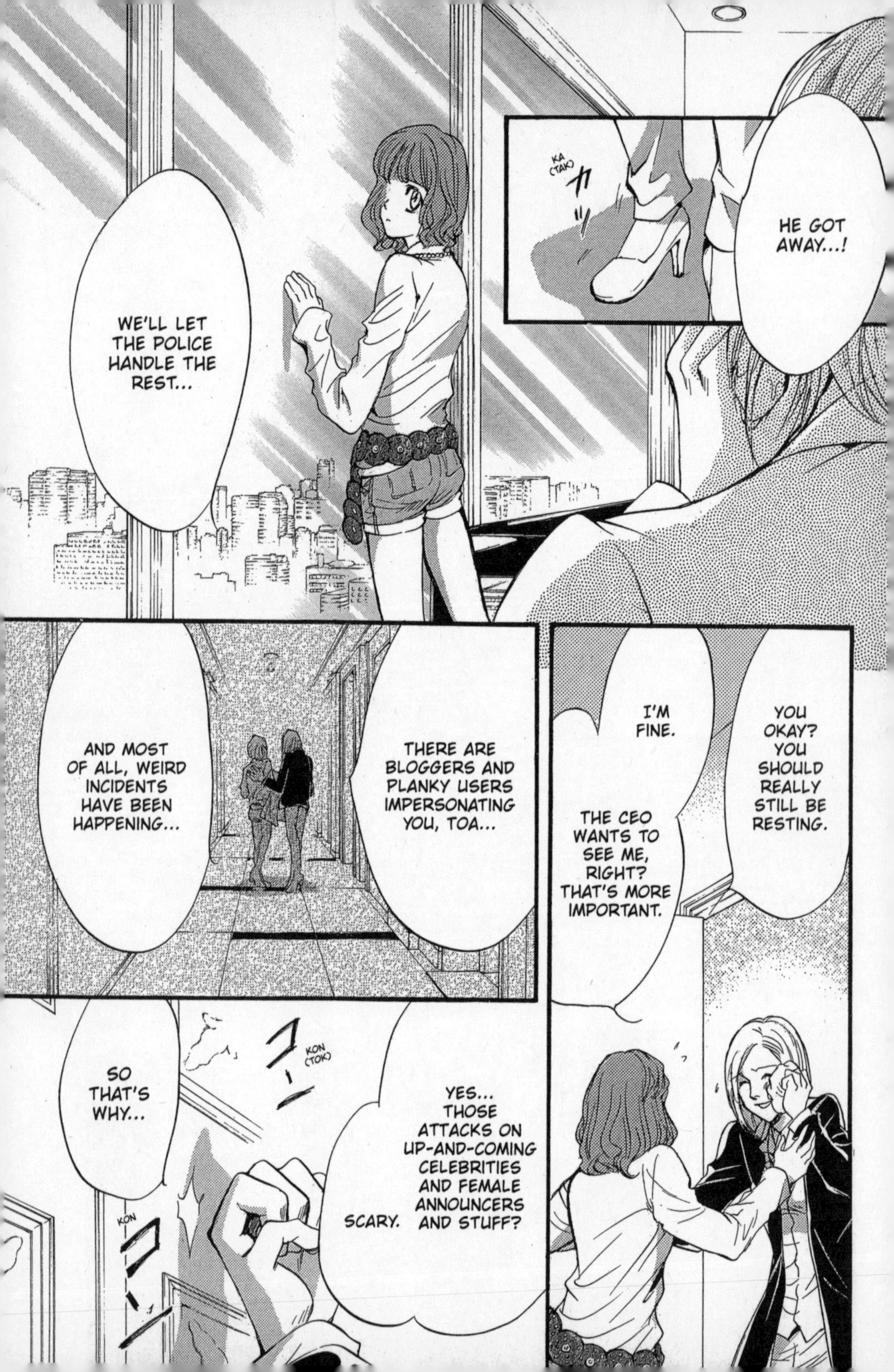
HE GOT AWAY...!
KA (TAK)
WE'LL LET THE POLICE HANDLE THE REST...
YOU OKAY? YOU SHOULD REALLY STILL BE RESTING.
I'M FINE.
THE CEO WANTS TO SEE ME, RIGHT? THAT'S MORE IMPORTANT.
THERE ARE BLOGGERS AND PLANKY USERS IMPERSONATING YOU, TOA...
AND MOST OF ALL, WEIRD INCIDENTS HAVE BEEN HAPPENING...
KON (TOK)
YES... THOSE ATTACKS ON UP-AND-COMING CELEBRITIES AND FEMALE ANNOUNCERS AND STUFF?
SCARY.
SO THAT'S WHY...
KON

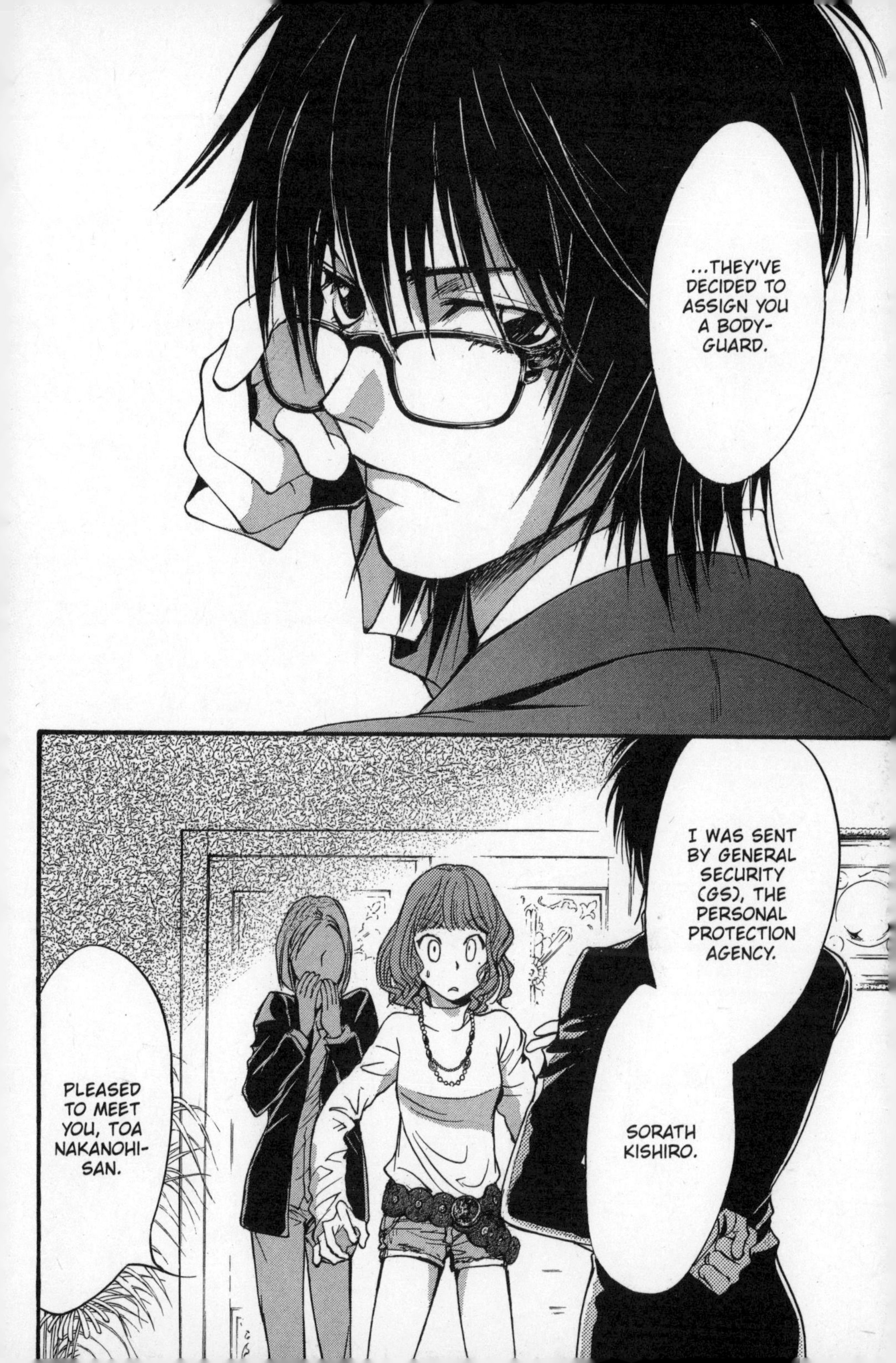
...THEY'VE DECIDED TO ASSIGN YOU A BODY-GUARD.
I WAS SENT BY GENERAL SECURITY (GS), THE PERSONAL PROTECTION AGENCY.
SORATH KISHIRO.
PLEASED TO MEET YOU, TOA NAKANOHI-SAN.

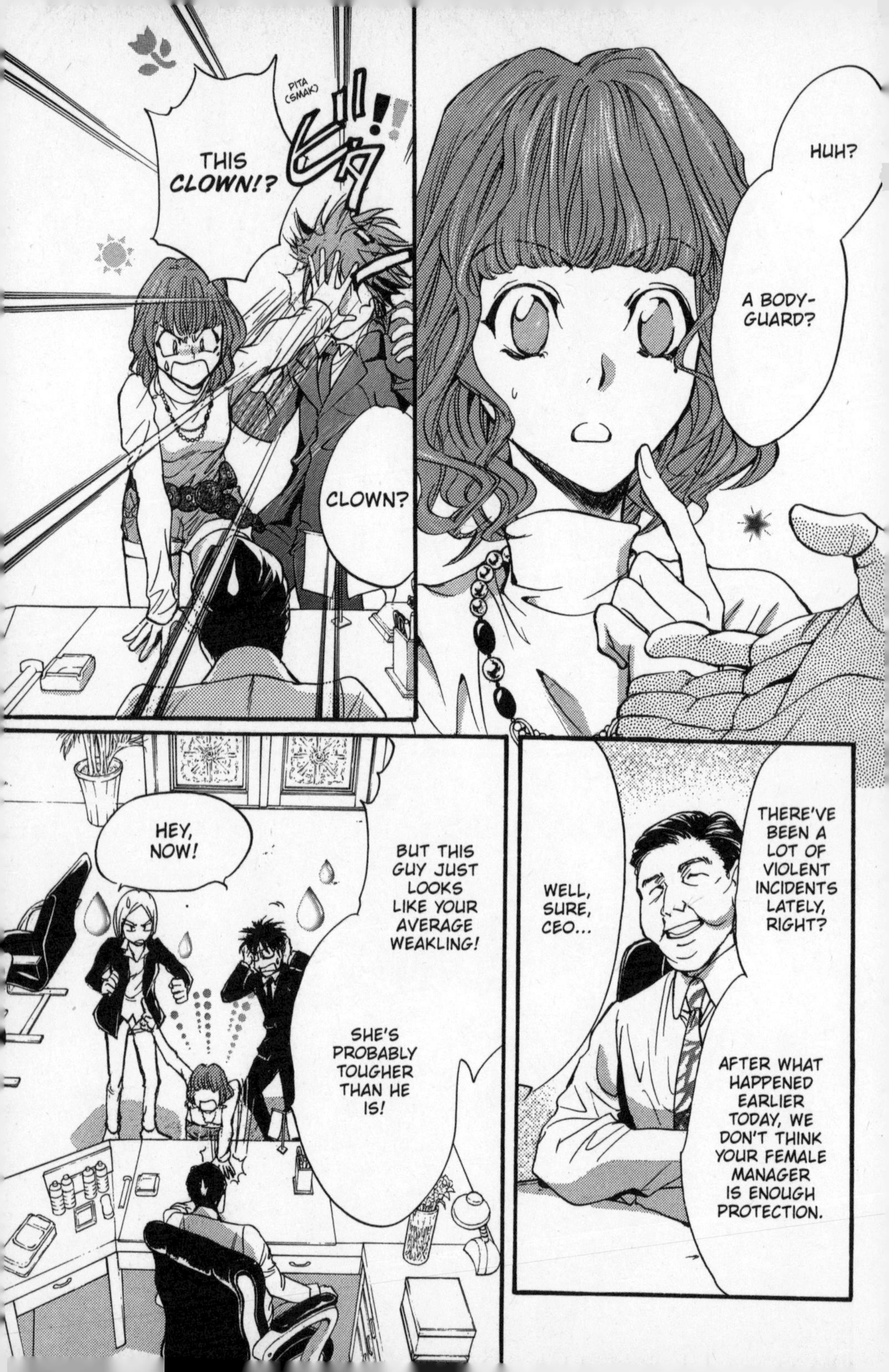
HUH?
A BODY-GUARD?
PITA (SMAK)
THIS CLOWN!?
CLOWN?
THERE'VE BEEN A LOT OF VIOLENT INCIDENTS LATELY, RIGHT?
AFTER WHAT HAPPENED EARLIER TODAY, WE DON'T THINK YOUR FEMALE MANAGER IS ENOUGH PROTECTION.
WELL, SURE, CEO...
BUT THIS GUY JUST LOOKS LIKE YOUR AVERAGE WEAKLING!
SHE'S PROBABLY TOUGHER THAN HE IS!
HEY, NOW!

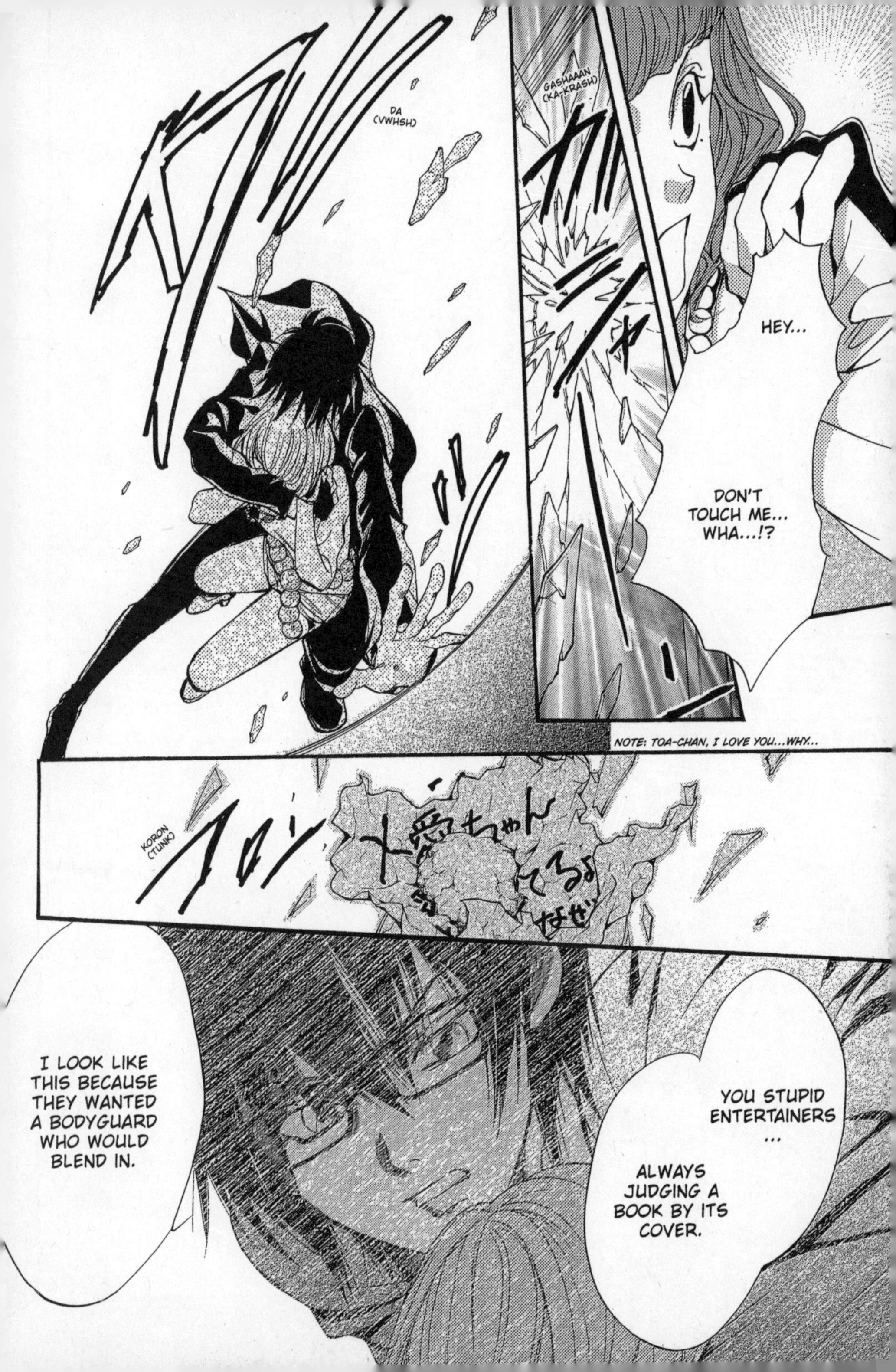
GASHAAAN (KA-KRASH)
HEY...
DON'T TOUCH ME... WHA...!?
DA (VWHSH)
NOTE: TOA-CHAN, I LOVE YOU...WHY...
KORON (TUNK)
YOU STUPID ENTERTAINERS ...
ALWAYS JUDGING A BOOK BY ITS COVER.
I LOOK LIKE THIS BECAUSE THEY WANTED A BODYGUARD WHO WOULD BLEND IN.

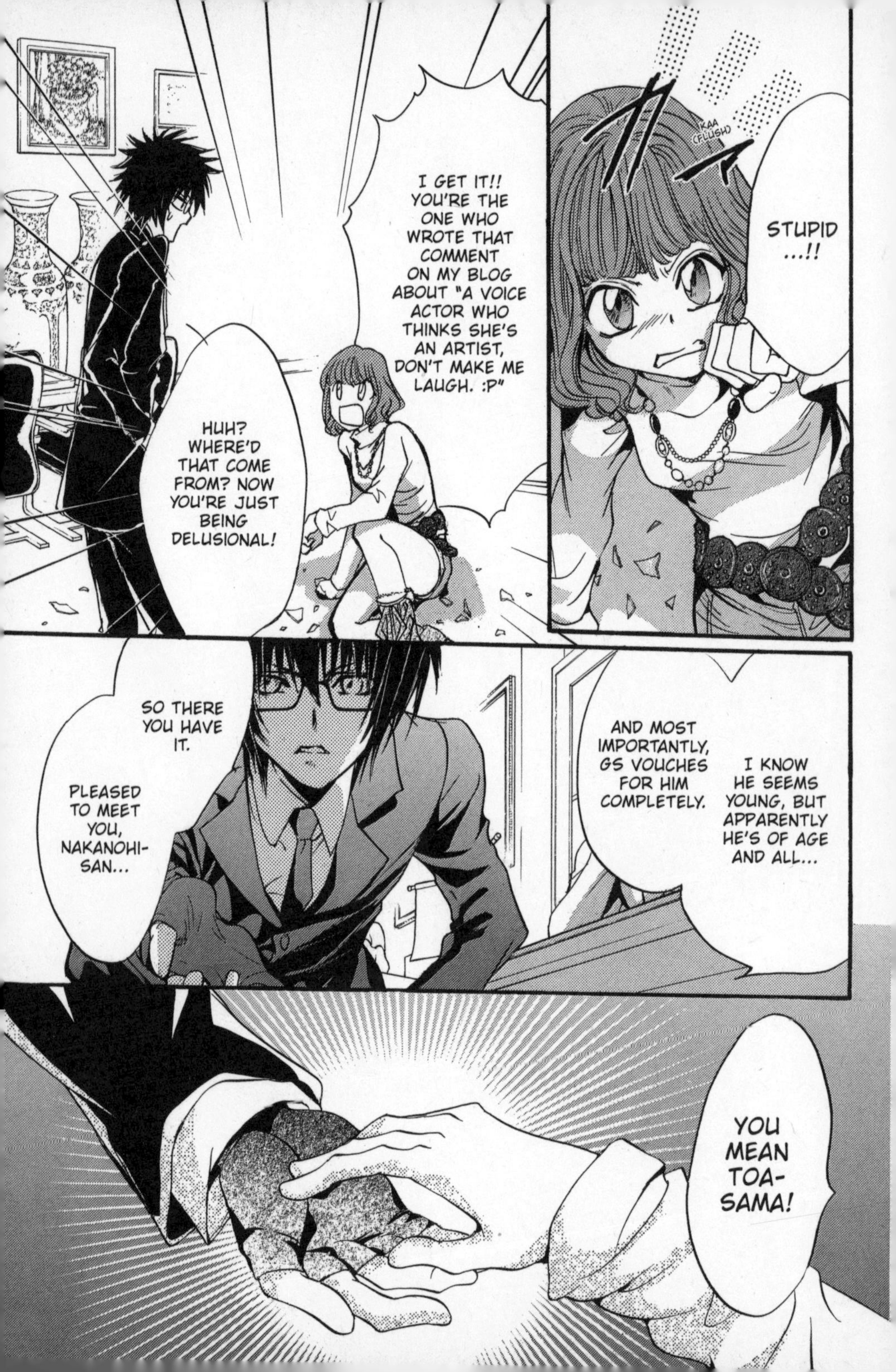
KAA (FLUSH)
STUPID ...!!
I GET IT!! YOU'RE THE ONE WHO WROTE THAT COMMENT ON MY BLOG ABOUT "A VOICE ACTOR WHO THINKS SHE'S AN ARTIST, DON'T MAKE ME LAUGH. :P"
HUH? WHERE'D THAT COME FROM? NOW YOU'RE JUST BEING DELUSIONAL!
I KNOW HE SEEMS YOUNG, BUT APPARENTLY HE'S OF AGE AND ALL...
AND MOST IMPORTANTLY, GS VOUCHES FOR HIM COMPLETELY.
SO THERE YOU HAVE IT.
PLEASED TO MEET YOU, NAKANOHI-SAN...
YOU MEAN TOA-SAMA!

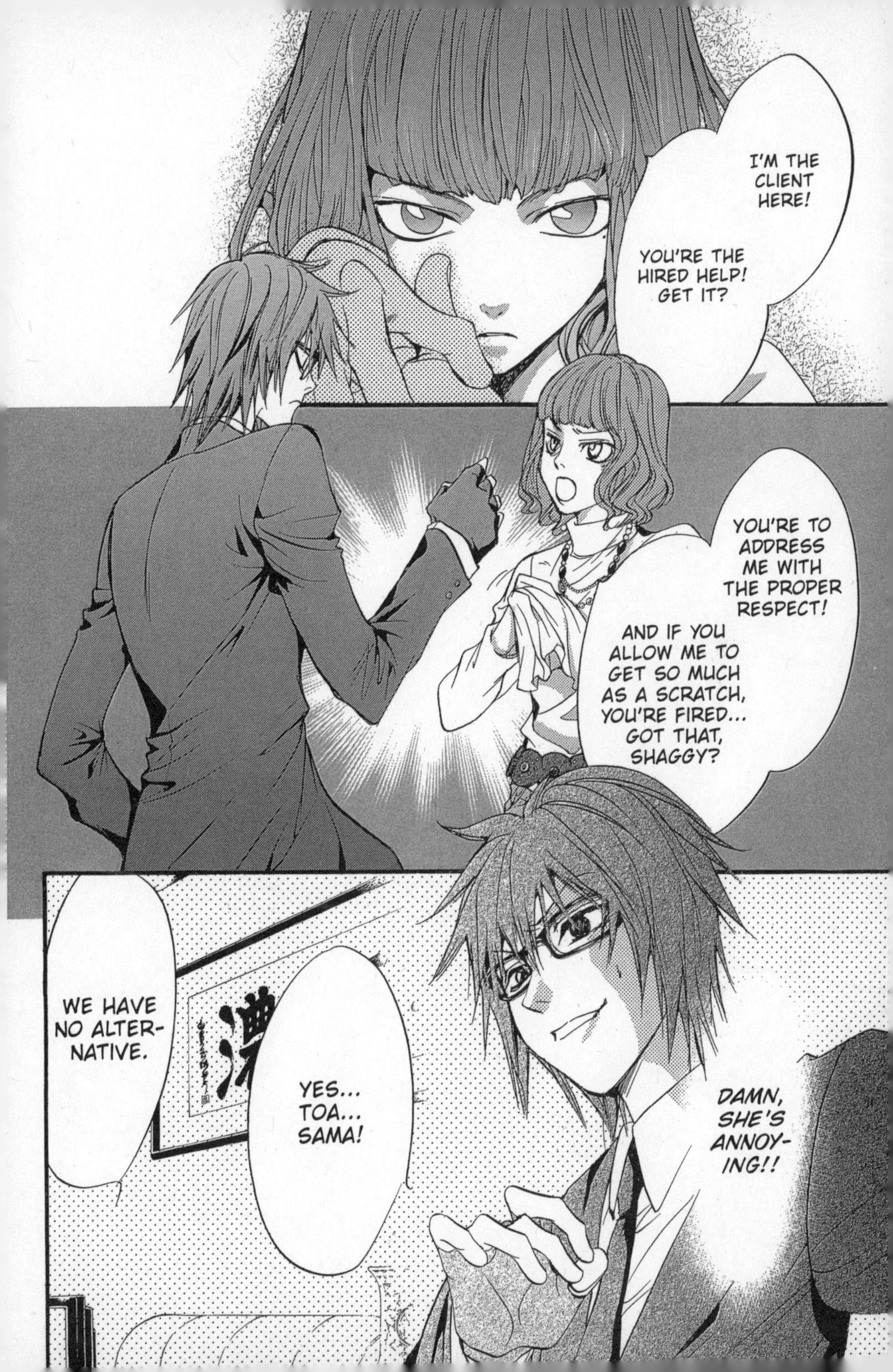
I'M THE CLIENT HERE!
YOU'RE THE HIRED HELP! GET IT?
YOU'RE TO ADDRESS ME WITH THE PROPER RESPECT!
AND IF YOU ALLOW ME TO GET SO MUCH AS A SCRATCH, YOU'RE FIRED... GOT THAT, SHAGGY?
DAMN, SHE'S ANNOYING!!
YES... TOA... SAMA!
WE HAVE NO ALTERNATIVE.

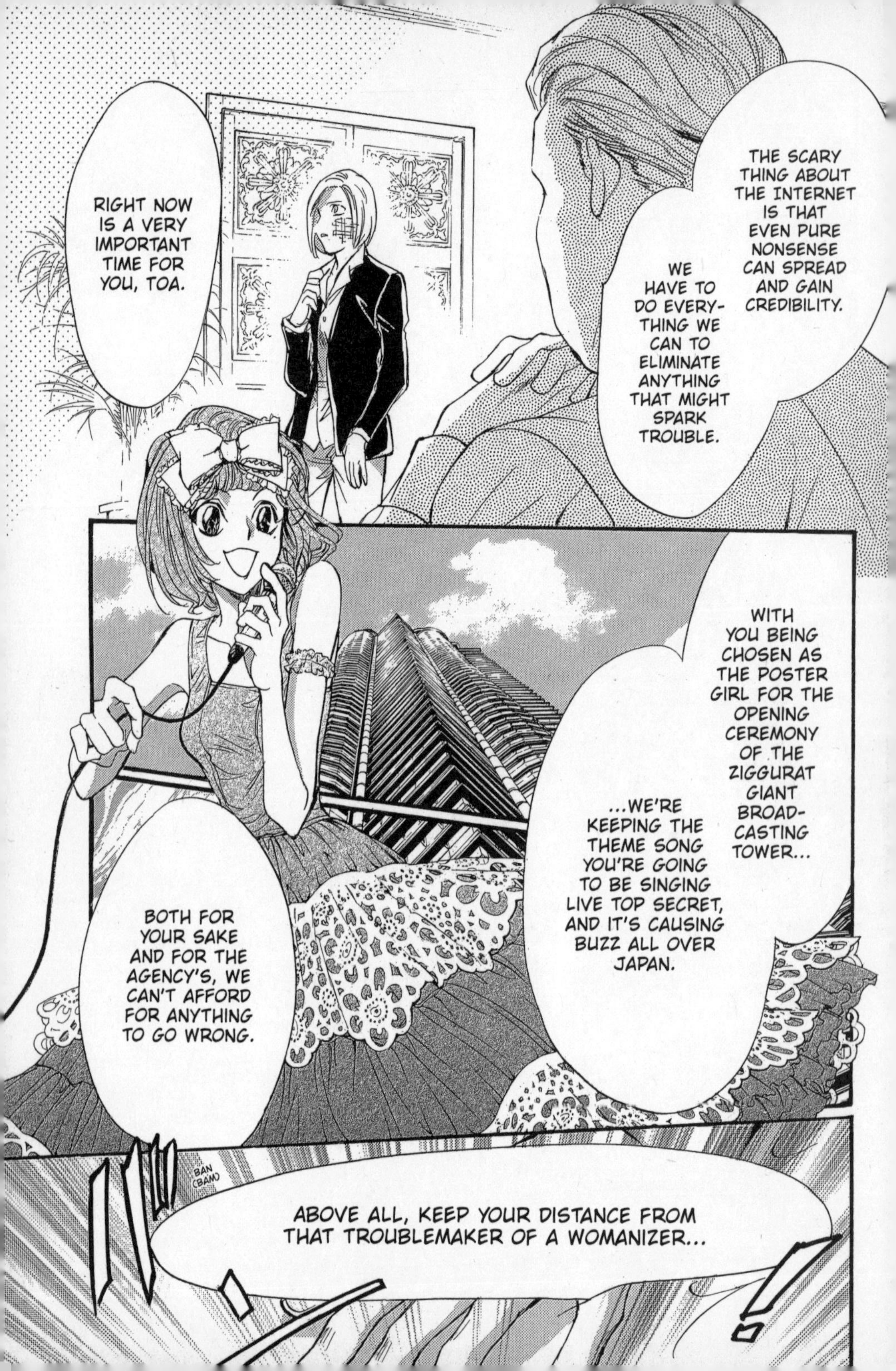
THE SCARY THING ABOUT THE INTERNET IS THAT EVEN PURE NONSENSE CAN SPREAD AND GAIN CREDIBILITY.
WE HAVE TO DO EVERY-THING WE CAN TO ELIMINATE ANYTHING THAT MIGHT SPARK TROUBLE.
RIGHT NOW IS A VERY IMPORTANT TIME FOR YOU, TOA.
WITH YOU BEING CHOSEN AS THE POSTER GIRL FOR THE OPENING CEREMONY OF THE ZIGGURAT GIANT BROAD-CASTING TOWER...
...WE'RE KEEPING THE THEME SONG YOU'RE GOING TO BE SINGING LIVE TOP SECRET, AND IT'S CAUSING BUZZ ALL OVER JAPAN.
BOTH FOR YOUR SAKE AND FOR THE AGENCY'S, WE CAN'T AFFORD FOR ANYTHING TO GO WRONG.
BAN (BAM)
ABOVE ALL, KEEP YOUR DISTANCE FROM THAT TROUBLEMAKER OF A WOMANIZER...

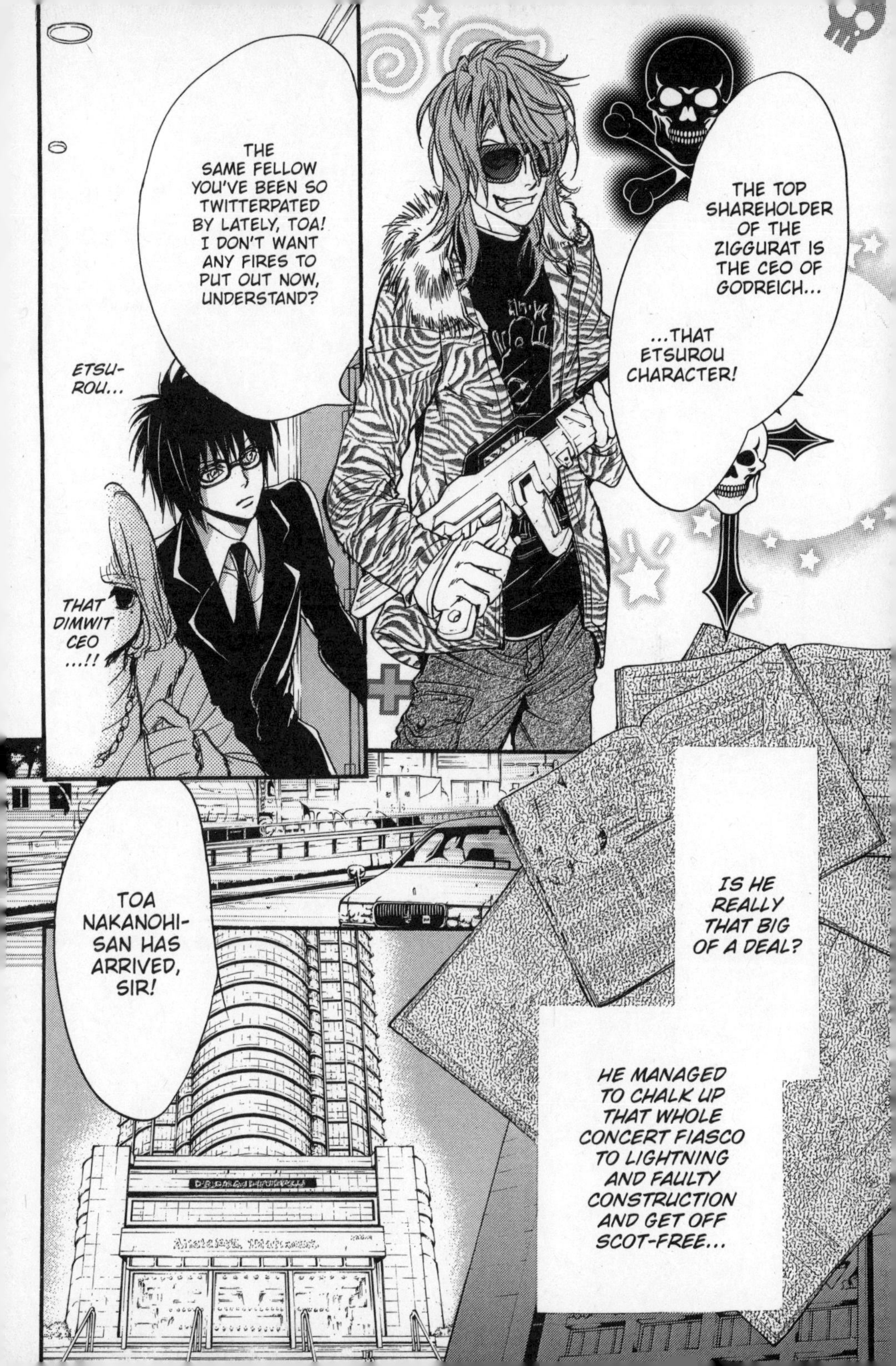
THE TOP SHAREHOLDER OF THE ZIGGURAT IS THE CEO OF GODREICH...
...THAT ETSUROU CHARACTER!
THE SAME FELLOW YOU'VE BEEN SO TWITTERPATED BY LATELY, TOA! I DON'T WANT ANY FIRES TO PUT OUT NOW, UNDERSTAND?
ETSU-ROU...
THAT DIMWIT CEO ...!!
IS HE REALLY THAT BIG OF A DEAL?
HE MANAGED TO CHALK UP THAT WHOLE CONCERT FIASCO TO LIGHTNING AND FAULTY CONSTRUCTION AND GET OFF SCOT-FREE...
TOA NAKANOHI-SAN HAS ARRIVED, SIR!

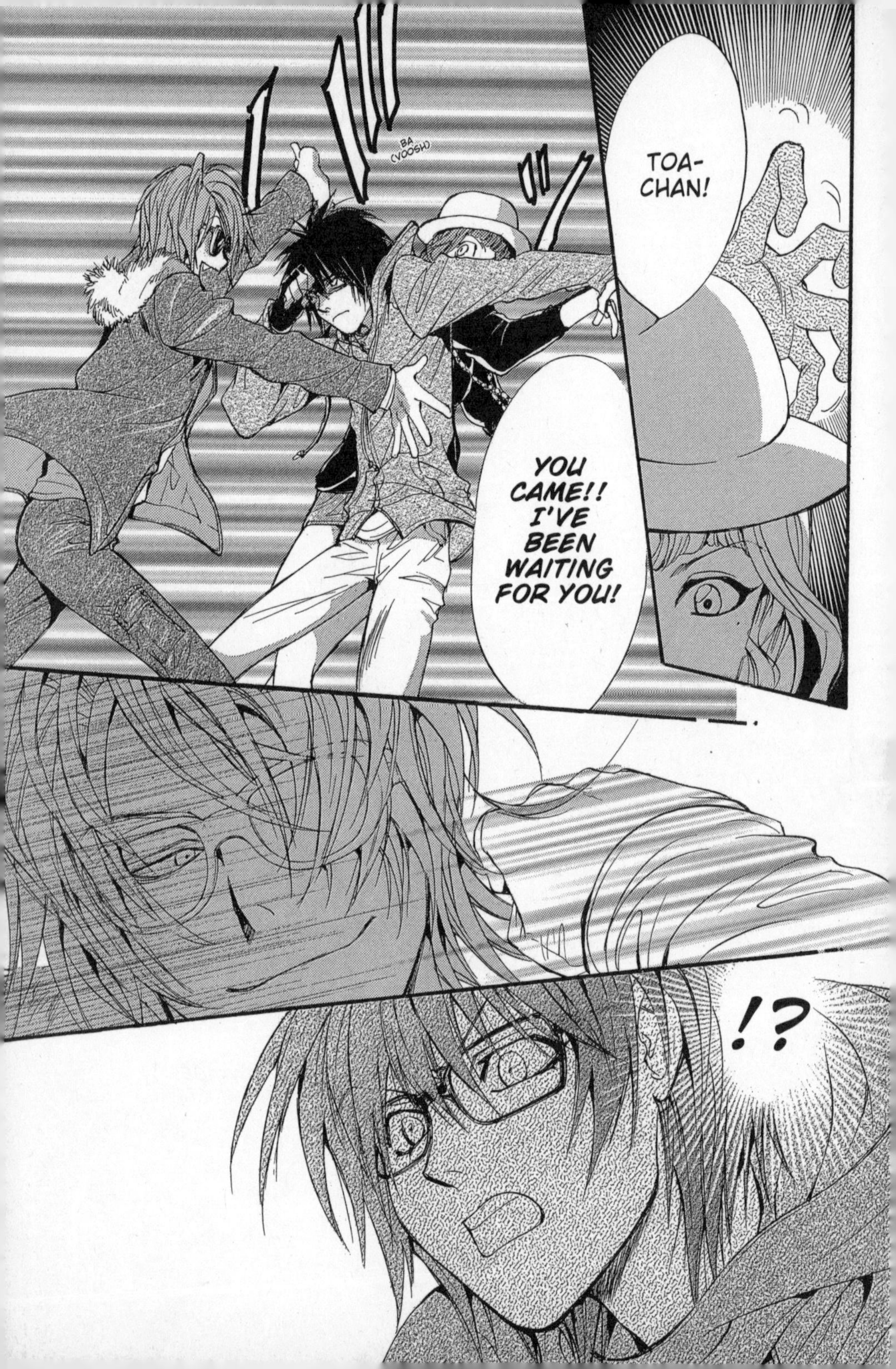
TOA-CHAN!
YOU CAME!! I'VE BEEN WAITING FOR YOU!
BA (VOOSH)
!?

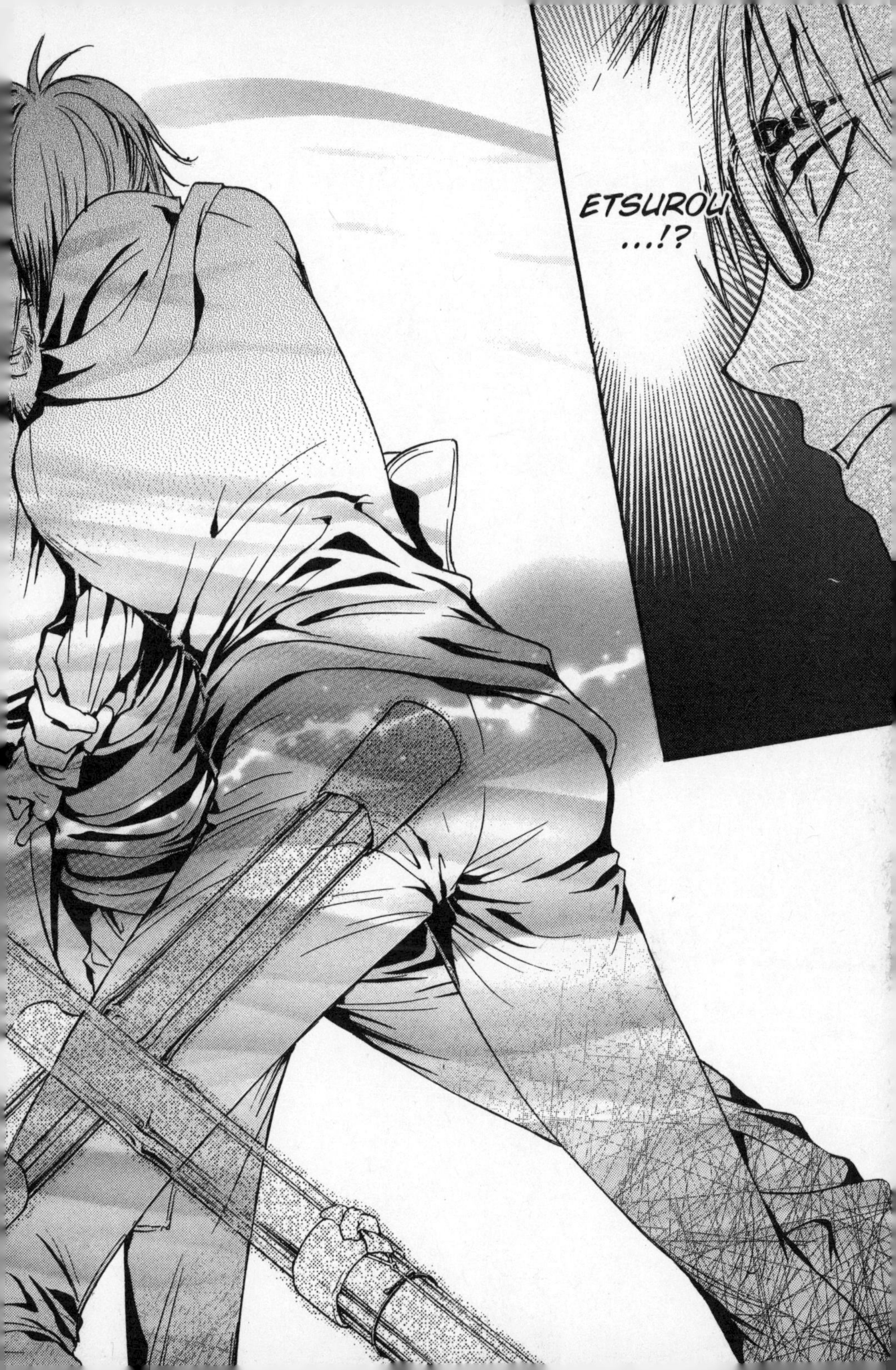
ETSUROU ...!?

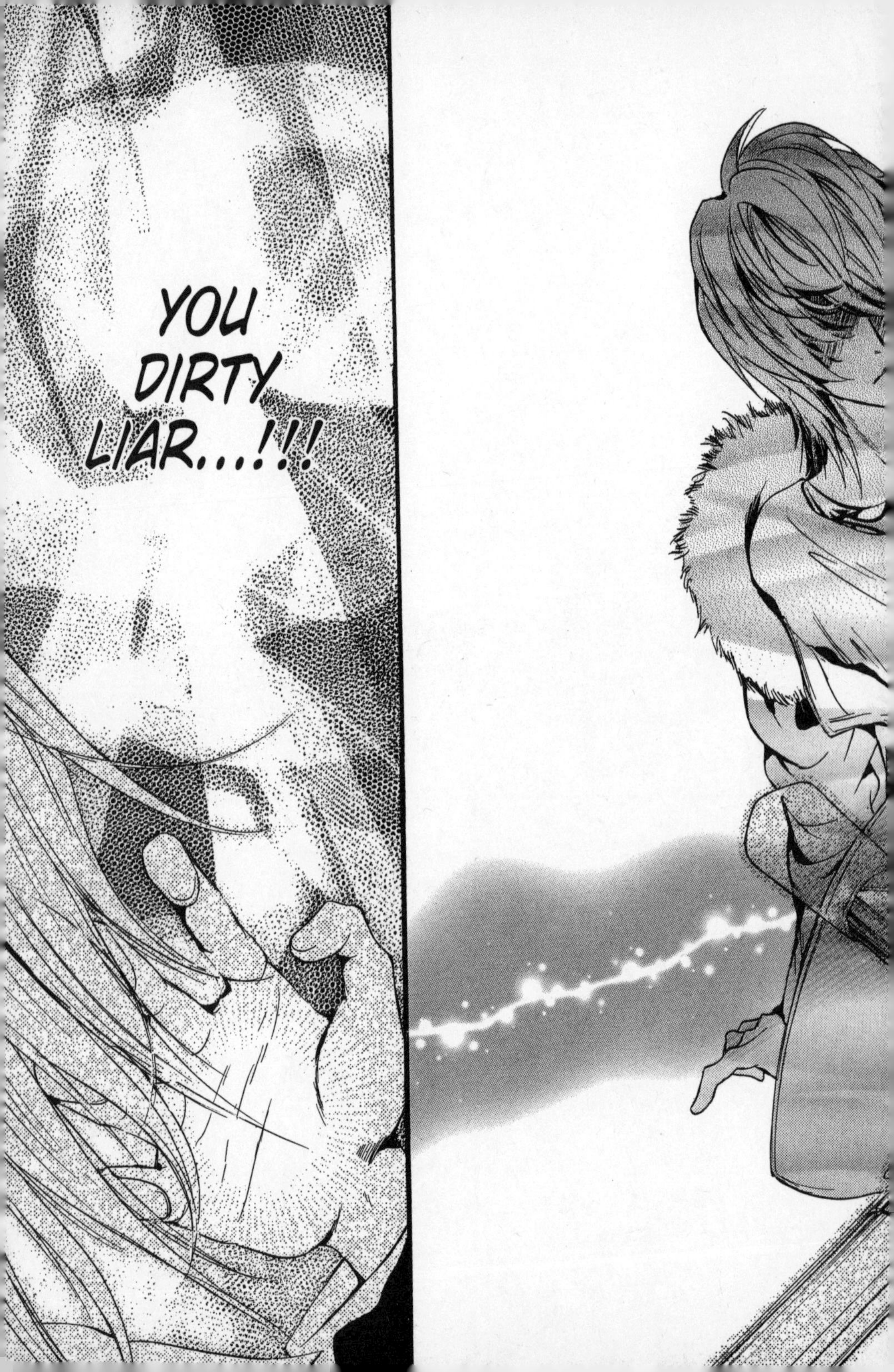
YOU DIRTY LIAR...!!!

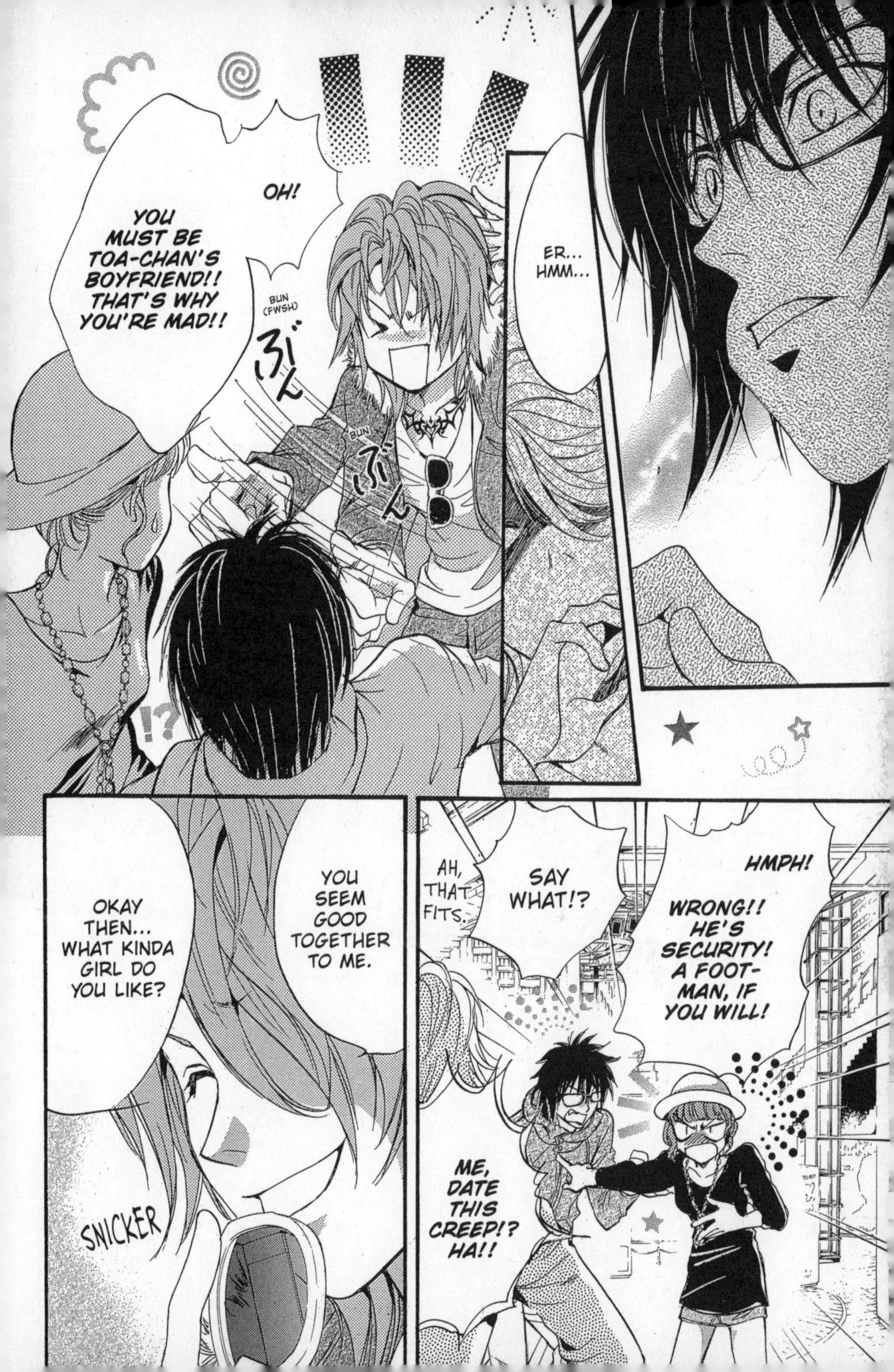
ER... HMM...
OH!
YOU MUST BE TOA-CHAN'S BOYFRIEND!! THAT'S WHY YOU'RE MAD!!
BUN (FWSH)
ぶん
BUN
ぶん
!?
HMPH!
WRONG!! HE'S SECURITY! A FOOT-MAN, IF YOU WILL!
SAY WHAT!?
AH, THAT FITS.
ME, DATE THIS CREEP!? HA!!
YOU SEEM GOOD TOGETHER TO ME.
OKAY THEN... WHAT KINDA GIRL DO YOU LIKE?
SNICKER

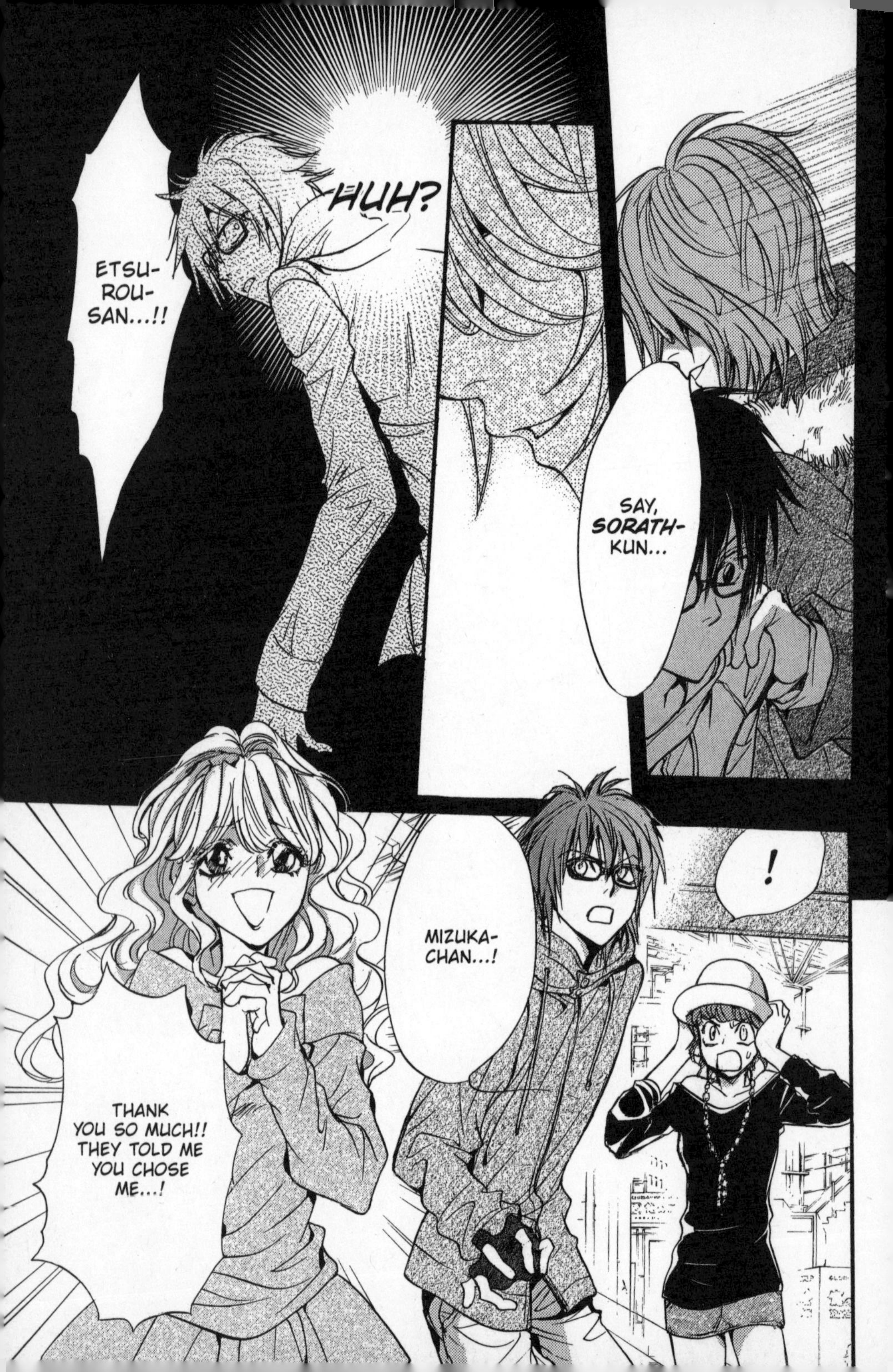
SAY, SORATH-KUN...
HUH?
ETSU-ROU-SAN...!!
!
MIZUKA-CHAN...!
THANK YOU SO MUCH!! THEY TOLD ME YOU CHOSE ME...!

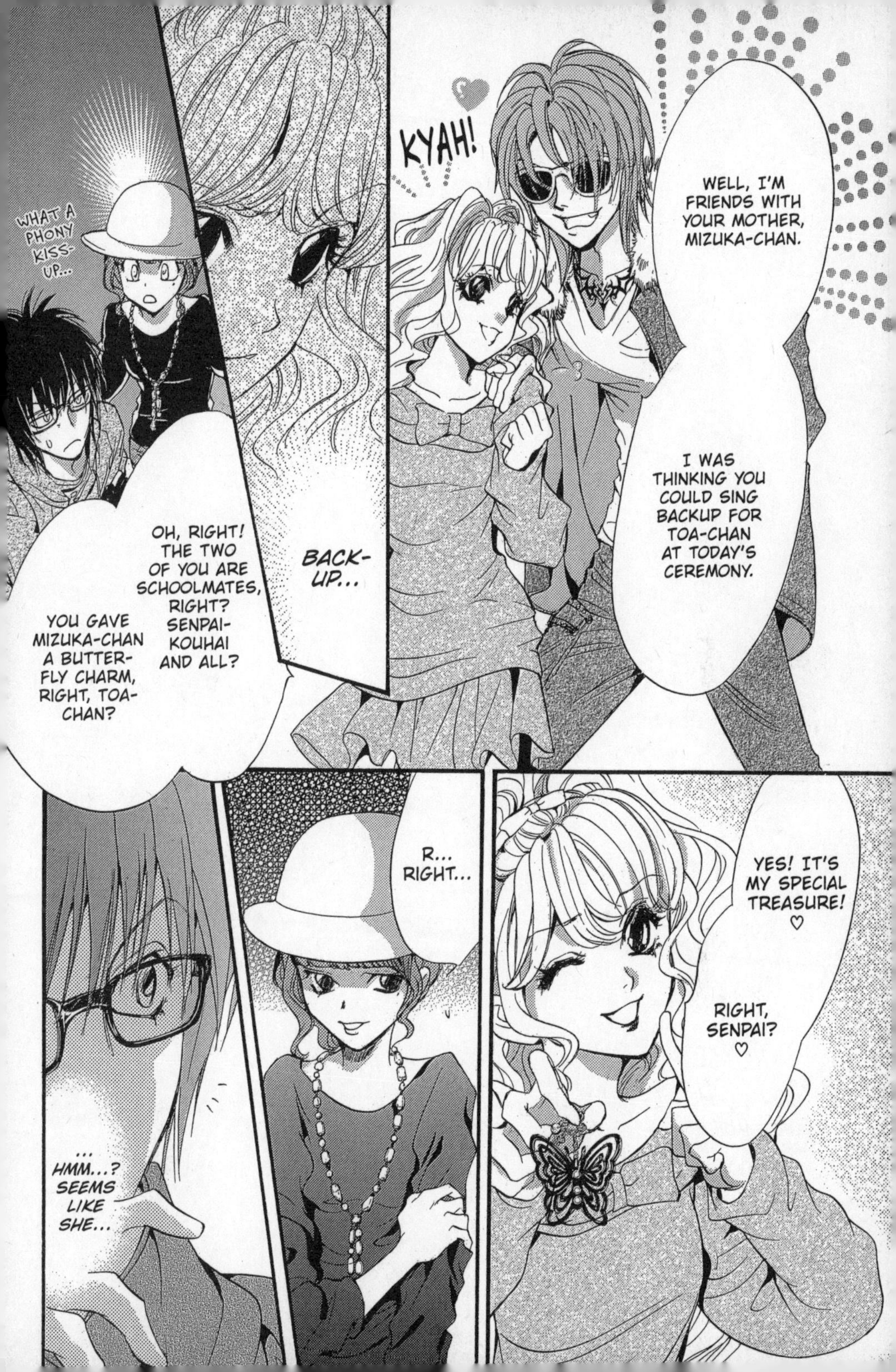
WELL, I'M FRIENDS WITH YOUR MOTHER, MIZUKA-CHAN.
KYAH!
I WAS THINKING YOU COULD SING BACKUP FOR TOA-CHAN AT TODAY'S CEREMONY.
BACK-UP...
WHAT A PHONY KISS-UP...
OH, RIGHT! THE TWO OF YOU ARE SCHOOLMATES, RIGHT? SENPAI-KOUHAI AND ALL?
YOU GAVE MIZUKA-CHAN A BUTTER-FLY CHARM, RIGHT, TOA-CHAN?
YES! IT'S MY SPECIAL TREASURE! ♡
RIGHT, SENPAI? ♡
R... RIGHT...
... HMM...? SEEMS LIKE SHE...

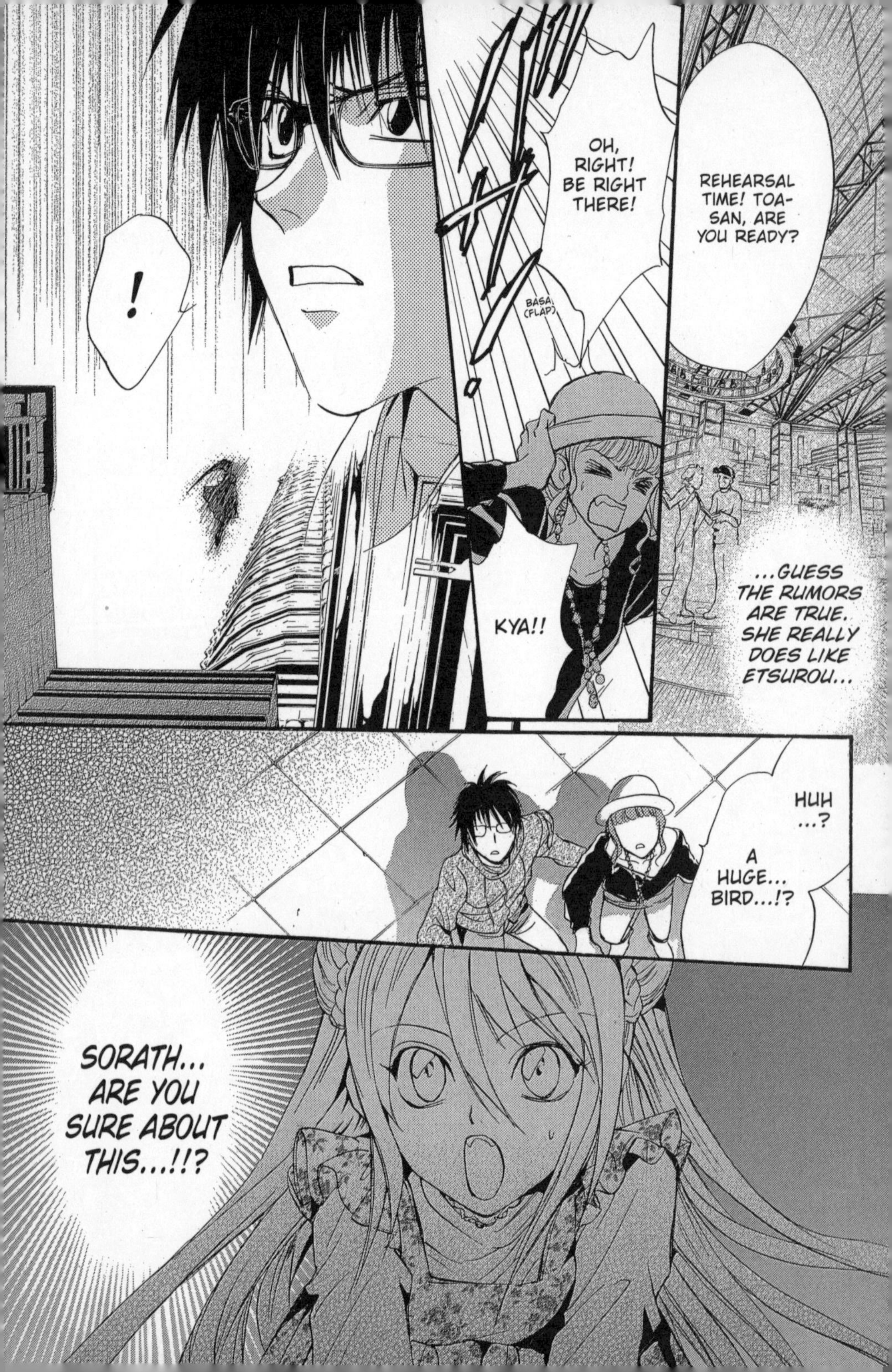
REHEARSAL TIME! TOA-SAN, ARE YOU READY?
...GUESS THE RUMORS ARE TRUE. SHE REALLY DOES LIKE ETSUROU...
OH, RIGHT! BE RIGHT THERE!
BASA (FLAP)
KYA!!
!
HUH ...?
A HUGE... BIRD...!?
SORATH... ARE YOU SURE ABOUT THIS...!!?

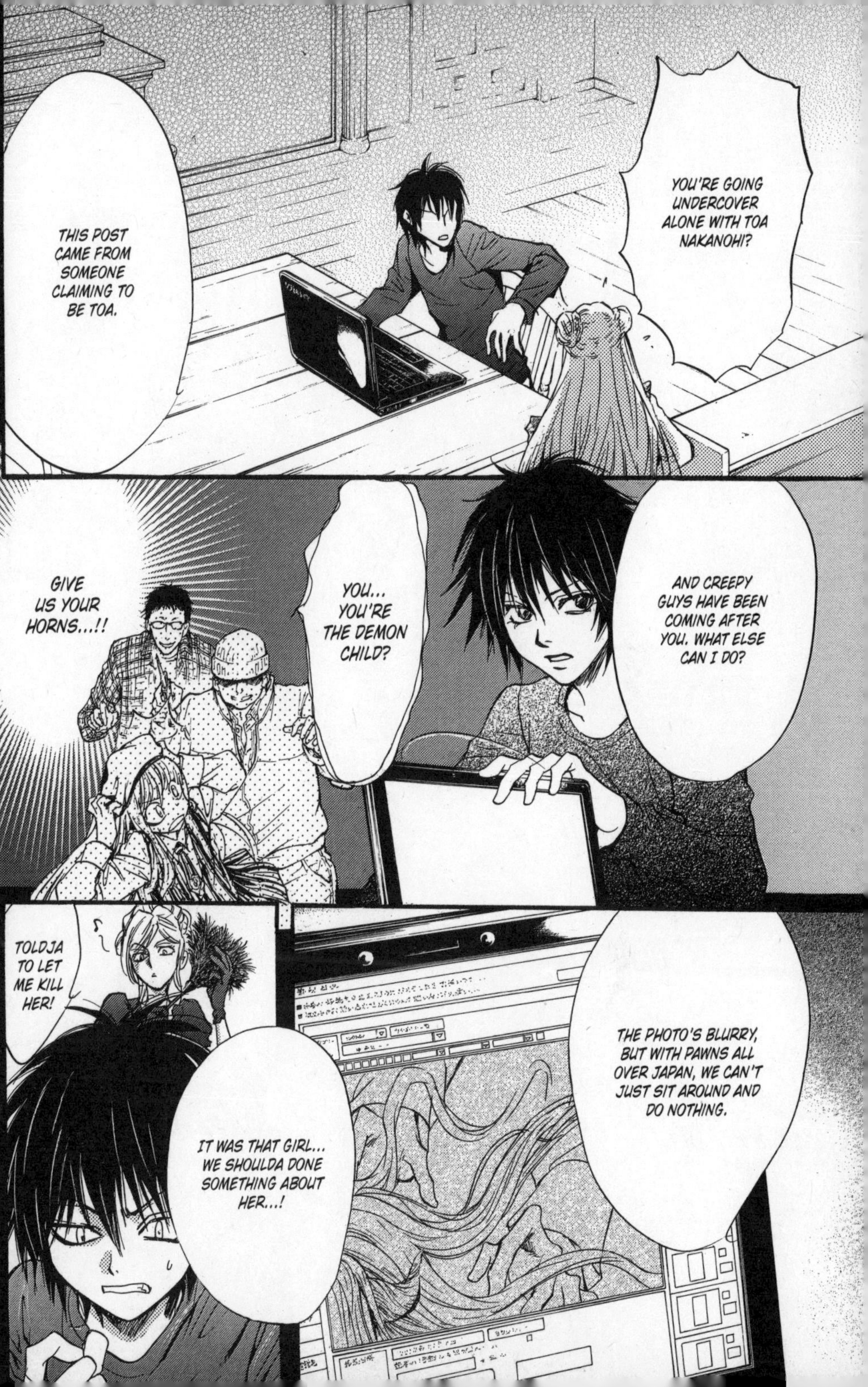
YOU'RE GOING UNDERCOVER ALONE WITH TOA NAKANOHI?
THIS POST CAME FROM SOMEONE CLAIMING TO BE TOA.
AND CREEPY GUYS HAVE BEEN COMING AFTER YOU. WHAT ELSE CAN I DO?
YOU... YOU'RE THE DEMON CHILD?
GIVE US YOUR HORNS...!!
THE PHOTO'S BLURRY, BUT WITH PAWNS ALL OVER JAPAN, WE CAN'T JUST SIT AROUND AND DO NOTHING.
IT WAS THAT GIRL... WE SHOULDA DONE SOMETHING ABOUT HER...!
TOLDJA TO LET ME KILL HER!

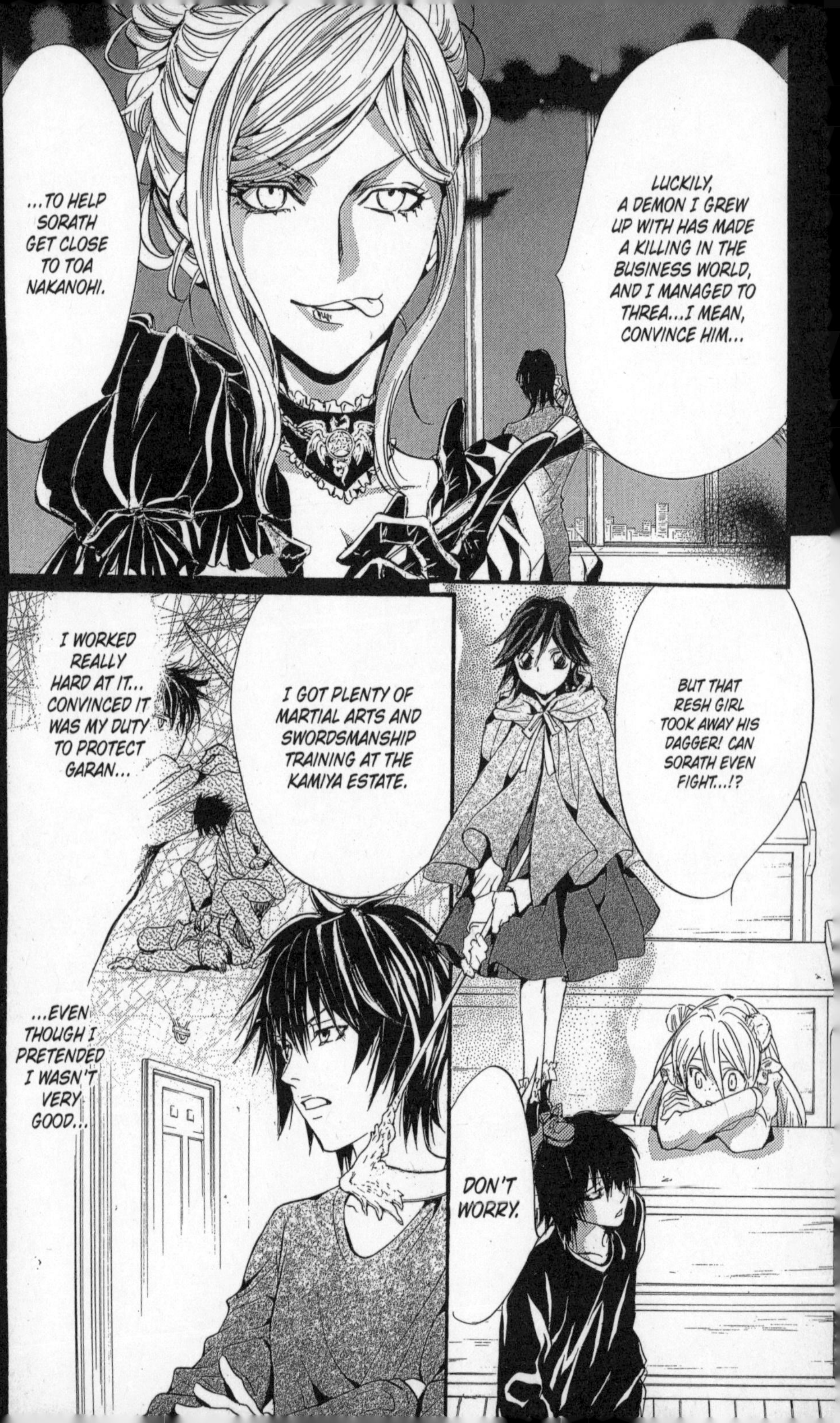
LUCKILY, A DEMON I GREW UP WITH HAS MADE A KILLING IN THE BUSINESS WORLD, AND I MANAGED TO THREA...I MEAN, CONVINCE HIM...
...TO HELP SORATH GET CLOSE TO TOA NAKANOHI.
BUT THAT RESH GIRL TOOK AWAY HIS DAGGER! CAN SORATH EVEN FIGHT...!?
DON'T WORRY.
I GOT PLENTY OF MARTIAL ARTS AND SWORDSMANSHIP TRAINING AT THE KAMIYA ESTATE.
I WORKED REALLY HARD AT IT... CONVINCED IT WAS MY DUTY TO PROTECT GARAN...
...EVEN THOUGH I PRETENDED I WASN'T VERY GOOD...

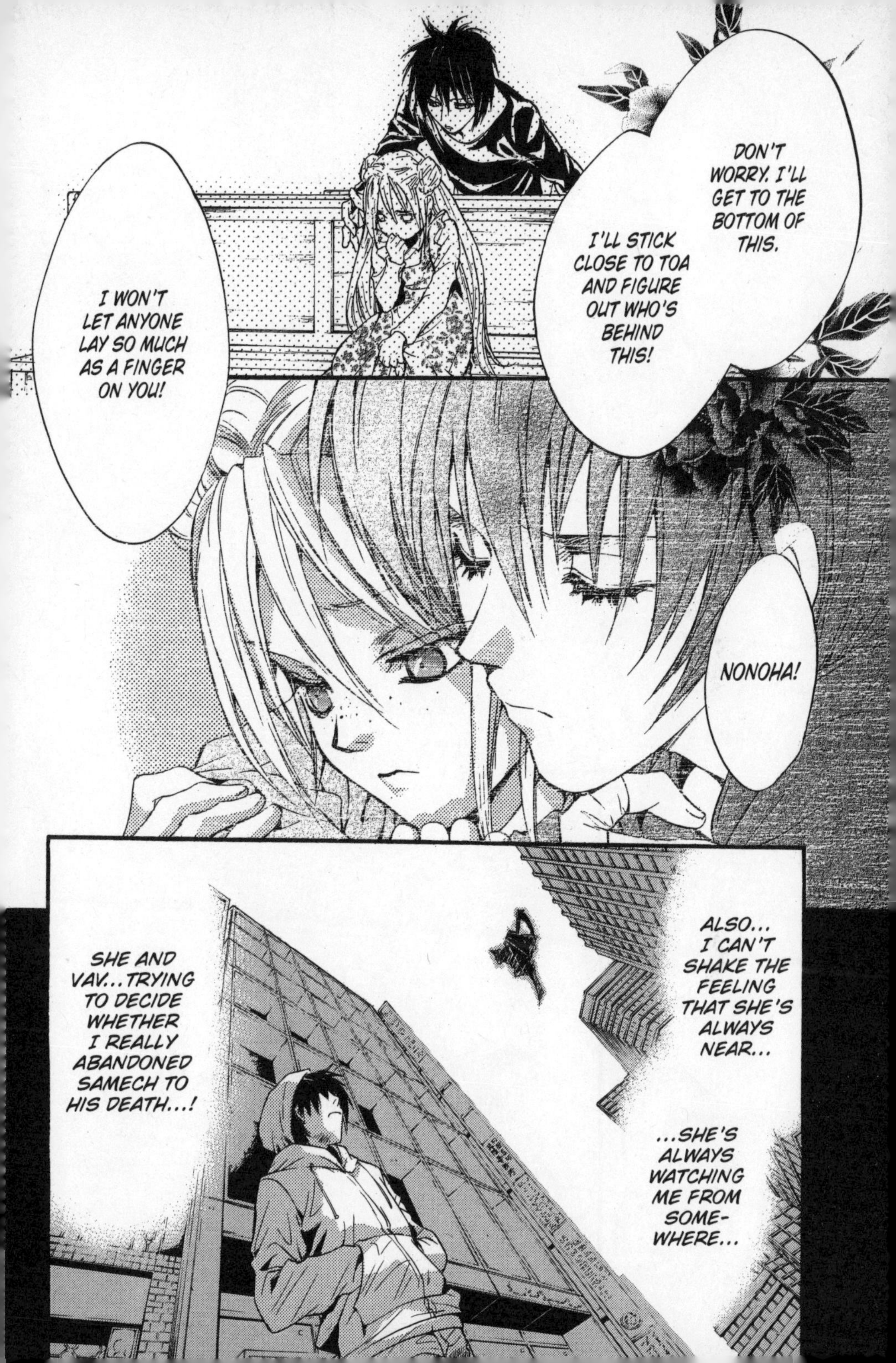
DON'T WORRY. I'LL GET TO THE BOTTOM OF THIS.
I'LL STICK CLOSE TO TOA AND FIGURE OUT WHO'S BEHIND THIS!
I WON'T LET ANYONE LAY SO MUCH AS A FINGER ON YOU!
NONOHA!
ALSO... I CAN'T SHAKE THE FEELING THAT SHE'S ALWAYS NEAR...
SHE AND VAV...TRYING TO DECIDE WHETHER I REALLY ABANDONED SAMECH TO HIS DEATH...!
...SHE'S ALWAYS WATCHING ME FROM SOME-WHERE...

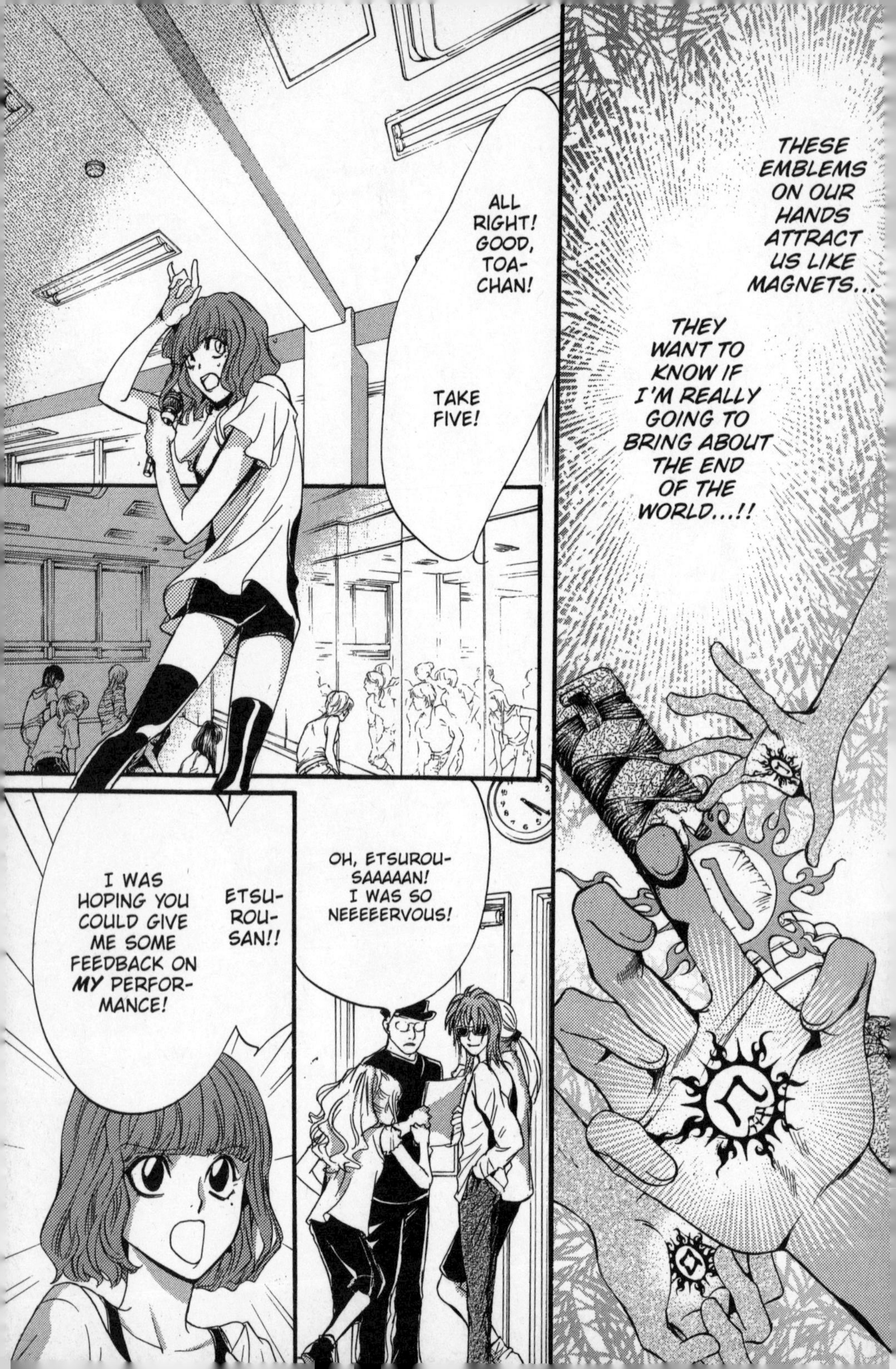
THESE EMBLEMS ON OUR HANDS ATTRACT US LIKE MAGNETS...
THEY WANT TO KNOW IF I'M REALLY GOING TO BRING ABOUT THE END OF THE WORLD...!!
ALL RIGHT! GOOD, TOA-CHAN!
TAKE FIVE!
OH, ETSUROU-SAAAAAN! I WAS SO NEEEEERVOUS!
ETSU-ROU-SAN!!
I WAS HOPING YOU COULD GIVE ME SOME FEEDBACK ON *MY* PERFOR-MANCE!

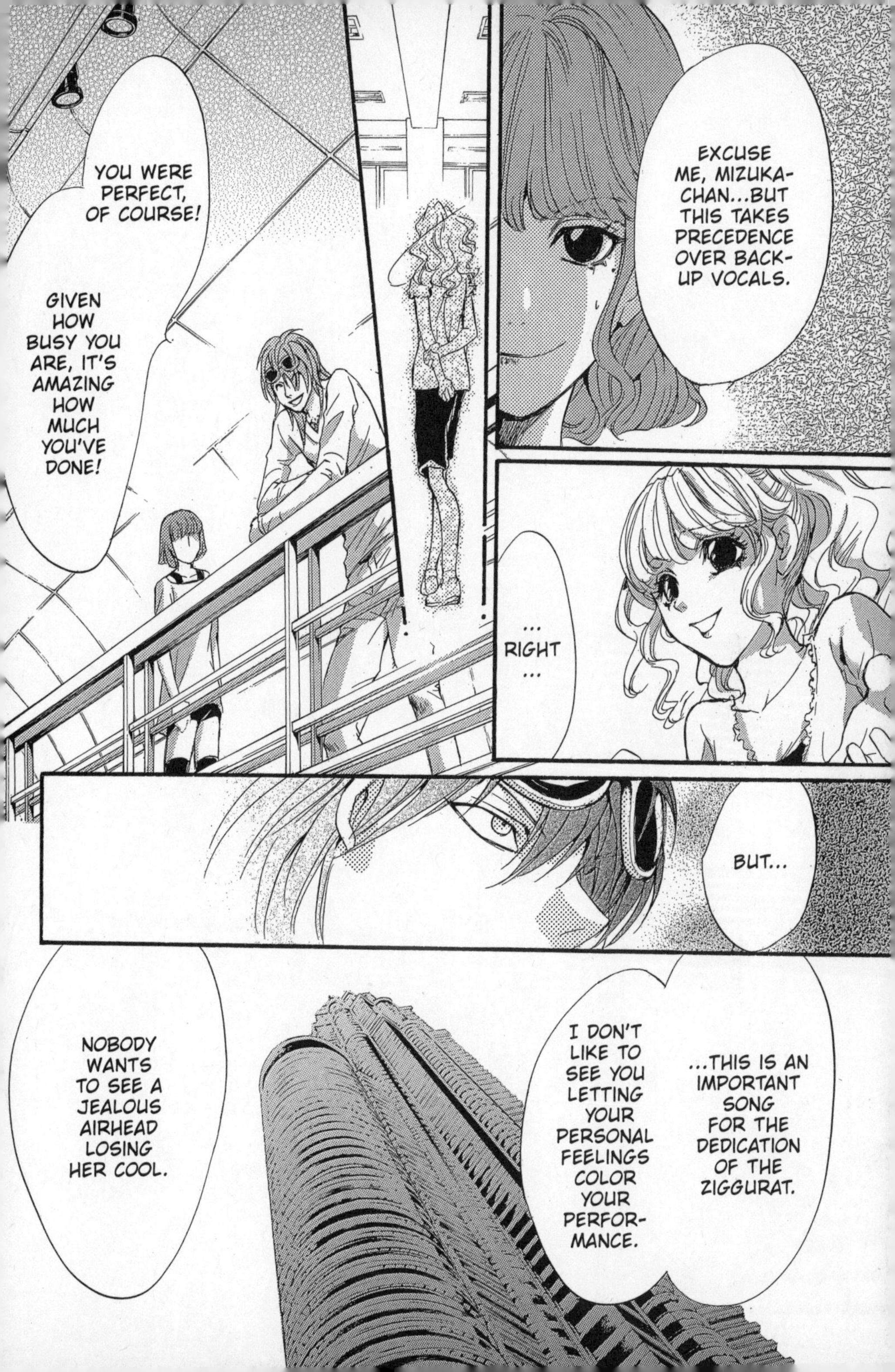
EXCUSE ME, MIZUKA-CHAN...BUT THIS TAKES PRECEDENCE OVER BACK-UP VOCALS.
...RIGHT...
YOU WERE PERFECT, OF COURSE!
GIVEN HOW BUSY YOU ARE, IT'S AMAZING HOW MUCH YOU'VE DONE!
BUT...
...THIS IS AN IMPORTANT SONG FOR THE DEDICATION OF THE ZIGGURAT.
I DON'T LIKE TO SEE YOU LETTING YOUR PERSONAL FEELINGS COLOR YOUR PERFOR-MANCE.
NOBODY WANTS TO SEE A JEALOUS AIRHEAD LOSING HER COOL.

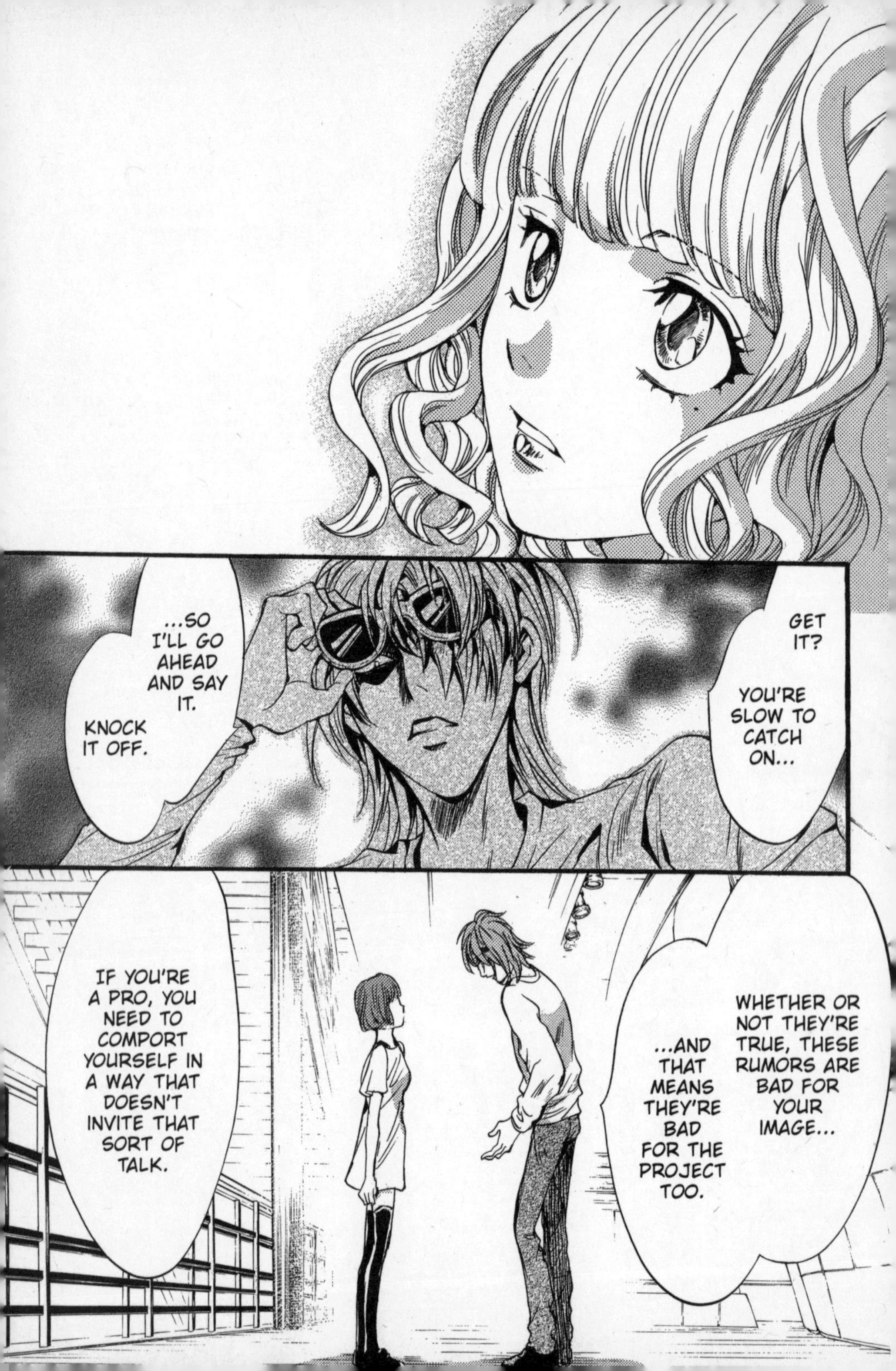
GET IT?
YOU'RE SLOW TO CATCH ON...
...SO I'LL GO AHEAD AND SAY IT.
KNOCK IT OFF.
WHETHER OR NOT THEY'RE TRUE, THESE RUMORS ARE BAD FOR YOUR IMAGE...
...AND THAT MEANS THEY'RE BAD FOR THE PROJECT TOO.
IF YOU'RE A PRO, YOU NEED TO COMPORT YOURSELF IN A WAY THAT DOESN'T INVITE THAT SORT OF TALK.

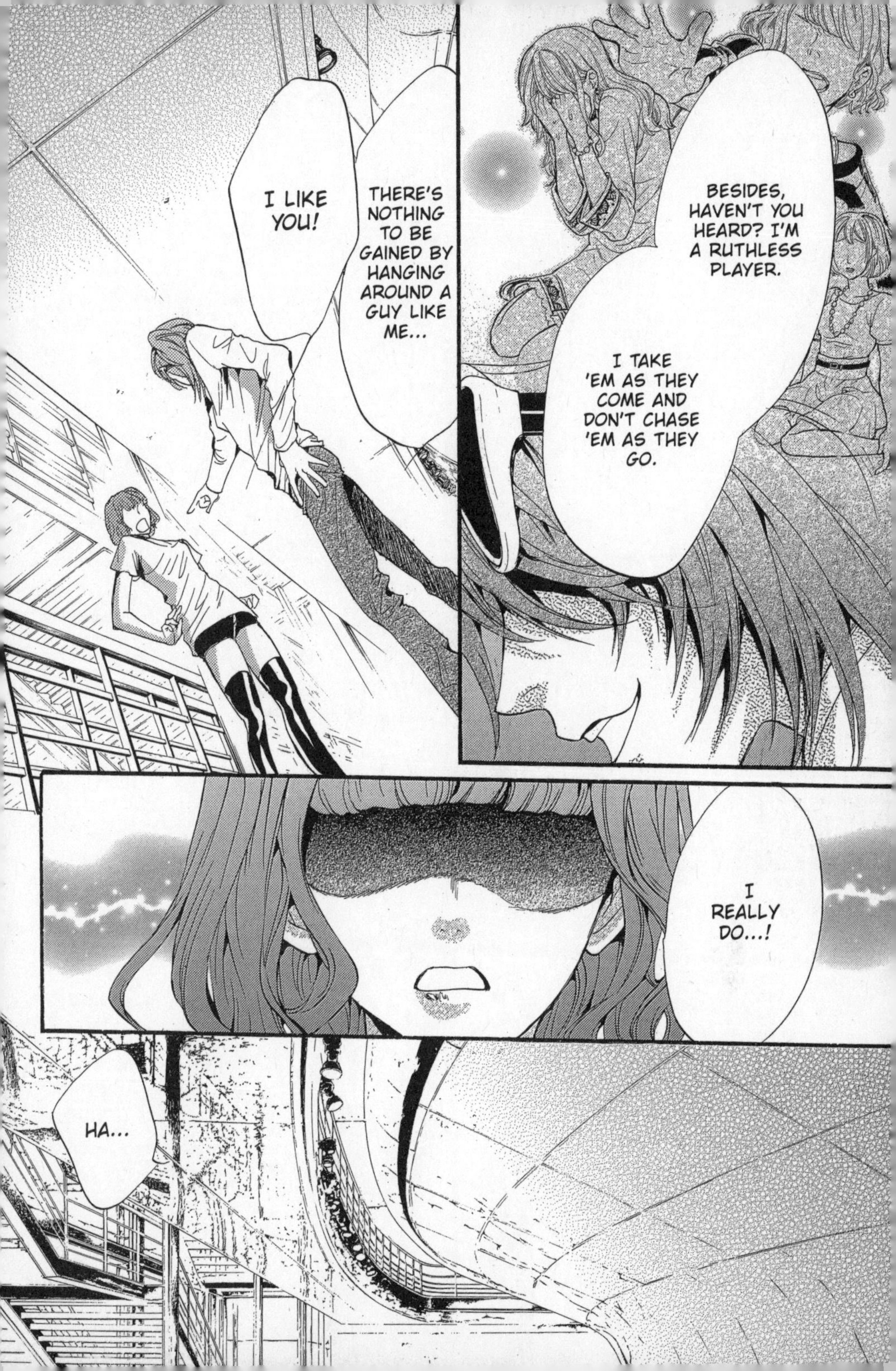
BESIDES, HAVEN'T YOU HEARD? I'M A RUTHLESS PLAYER.
I TAKE 'EM AS THEY COME AND DON'T CHASE 'EM AS THEY GO.
THERE'S NOTHING TO BE GAINED BY HANGING AROUND A GUY LIKE ME...
I LIKE YOU!
I REALLY DO...!
HA...

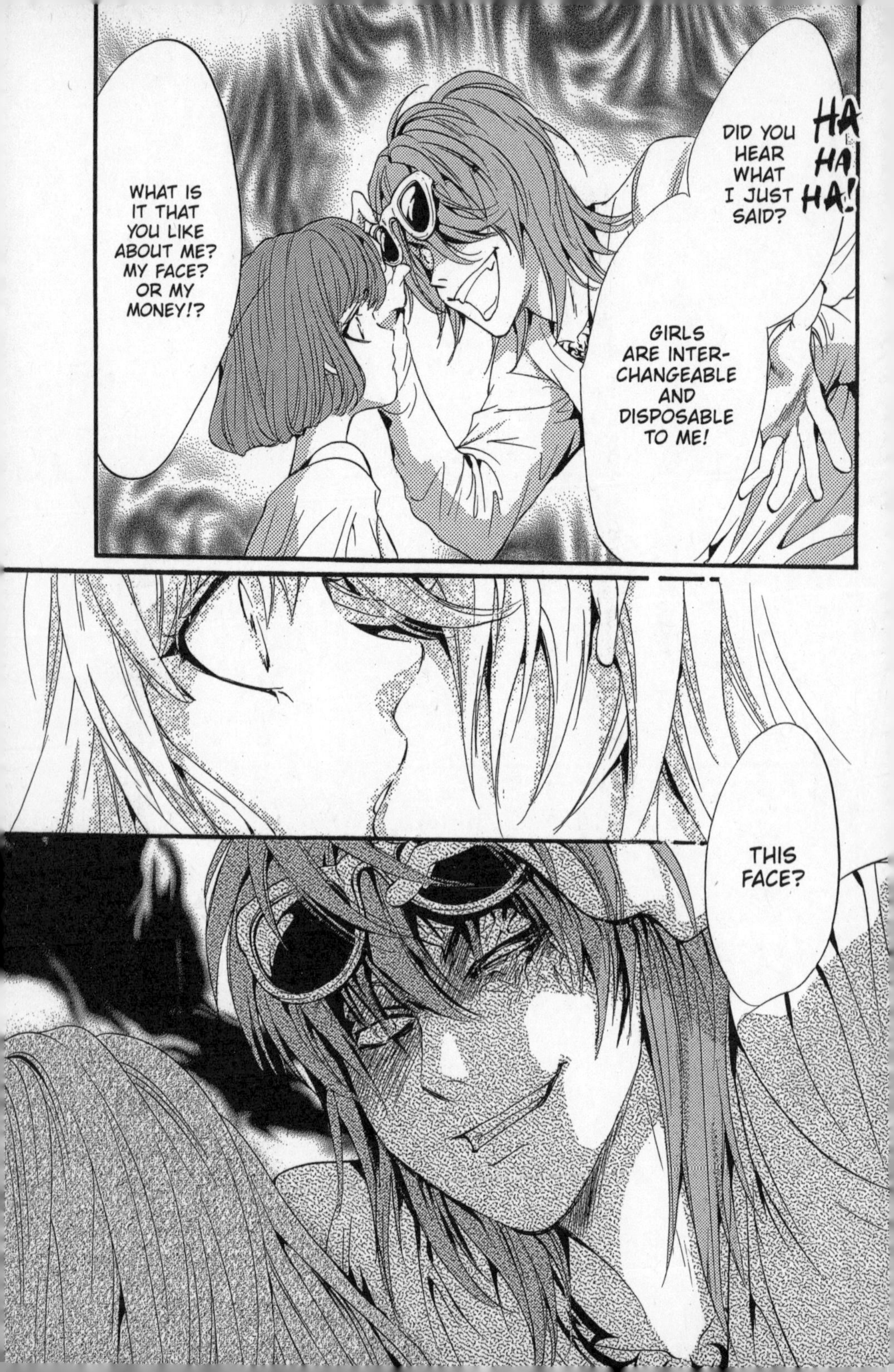
HA HA HA!
DID YOU HEAR WHAT I JUST SAID?
WHAT IS IT THAT YOU LIKE ABOUT ME? MY FACE? OR MY MONEY!?
GIRLS ARE INTER-CHANGEABLE AND DISPOSABLE TO ME!
THIS FACE?

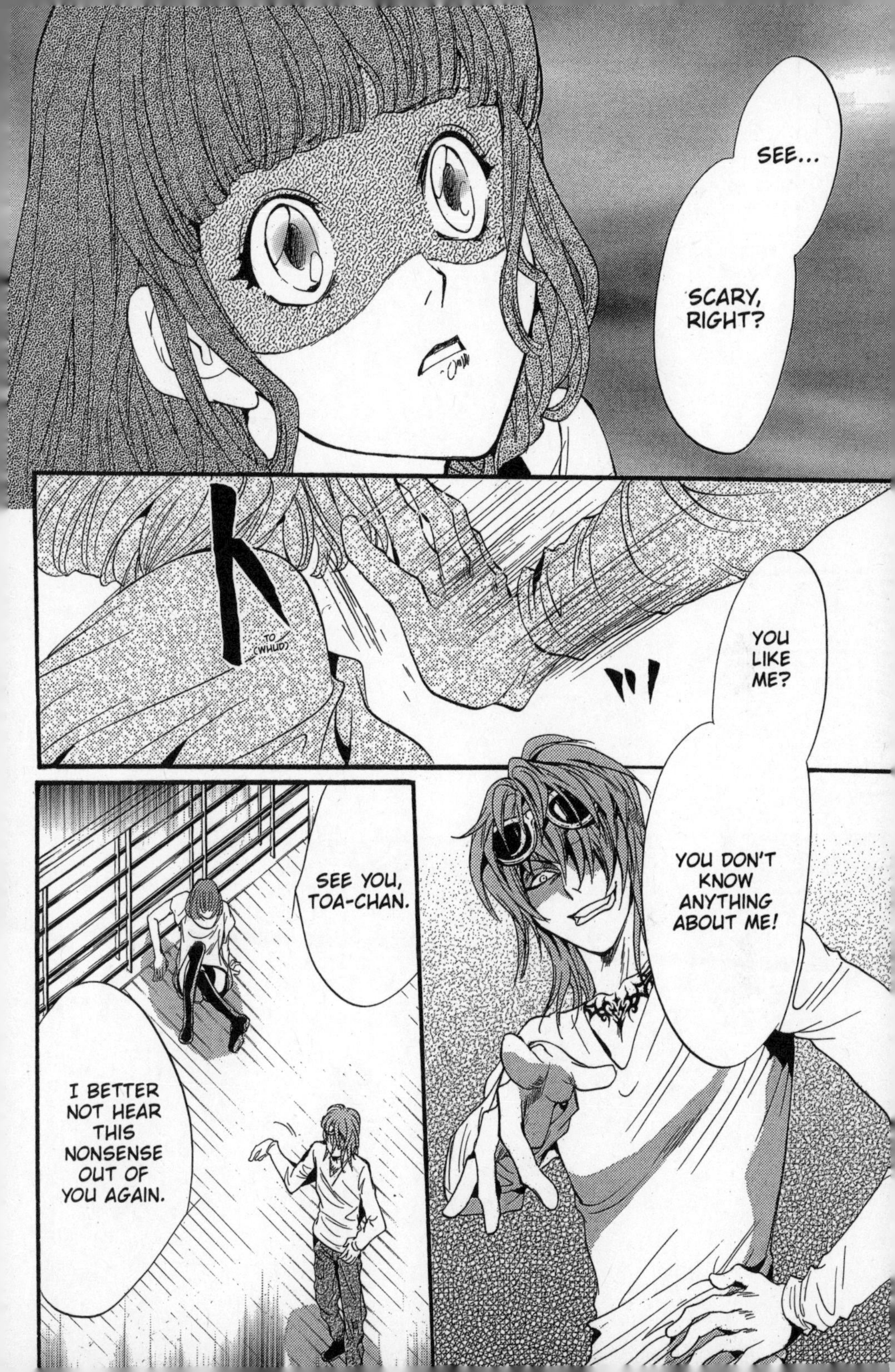
SEE...
SCARY, RIGHT?
YOU LIKE ME?
TO (WHUD)
YOU DON'T KNOW ANYTHING ABOUT ME!
SEE YOU, TOA-CHAN.
I BETTER NOT HEAR THIS NONSENSE OUT OF YOU AGAIN.

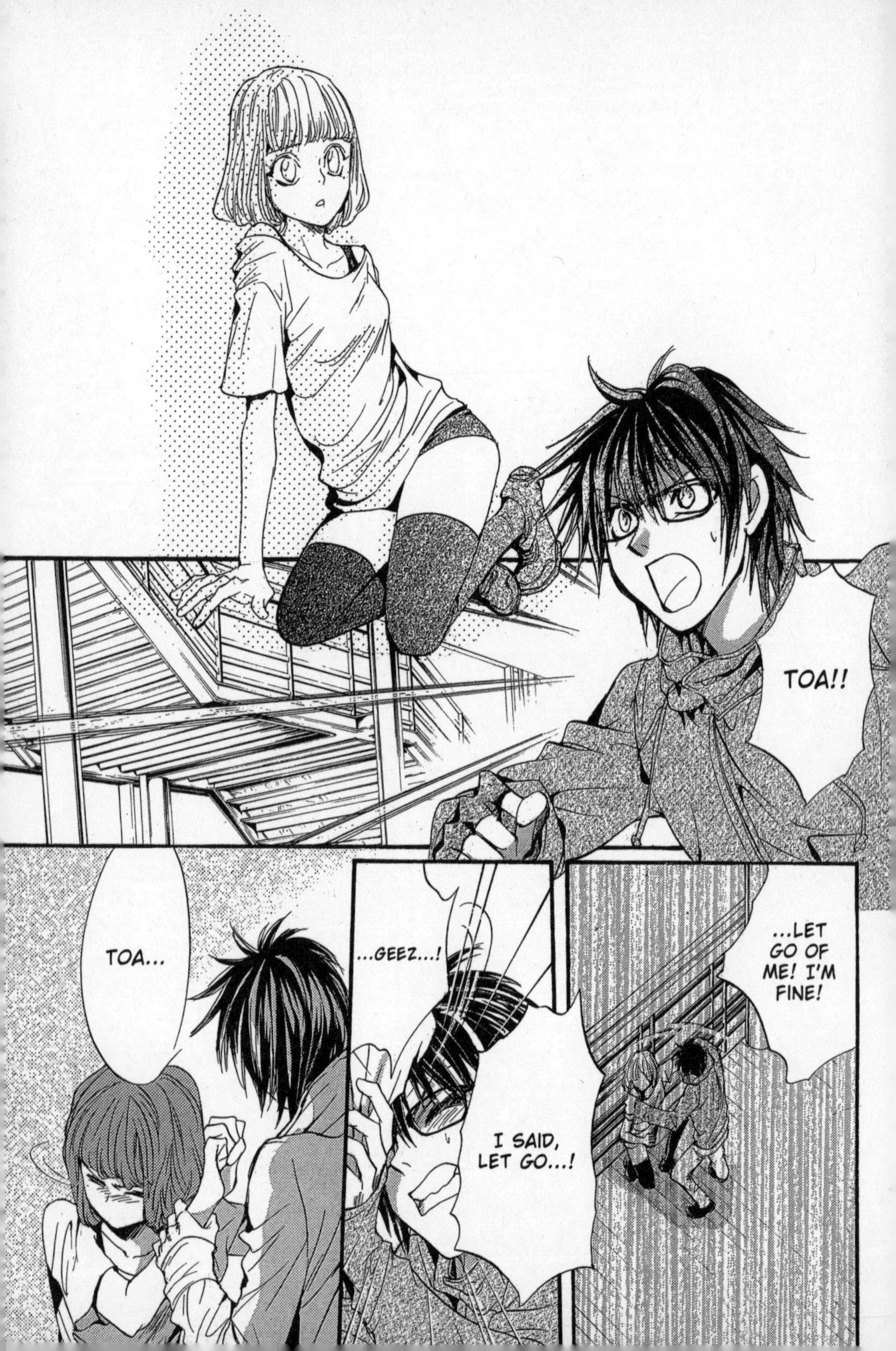
TOA!!
...LET GO OF ME! I'M FINE!
...GEEZ...!
I SAID, LET GO...!
TOA...

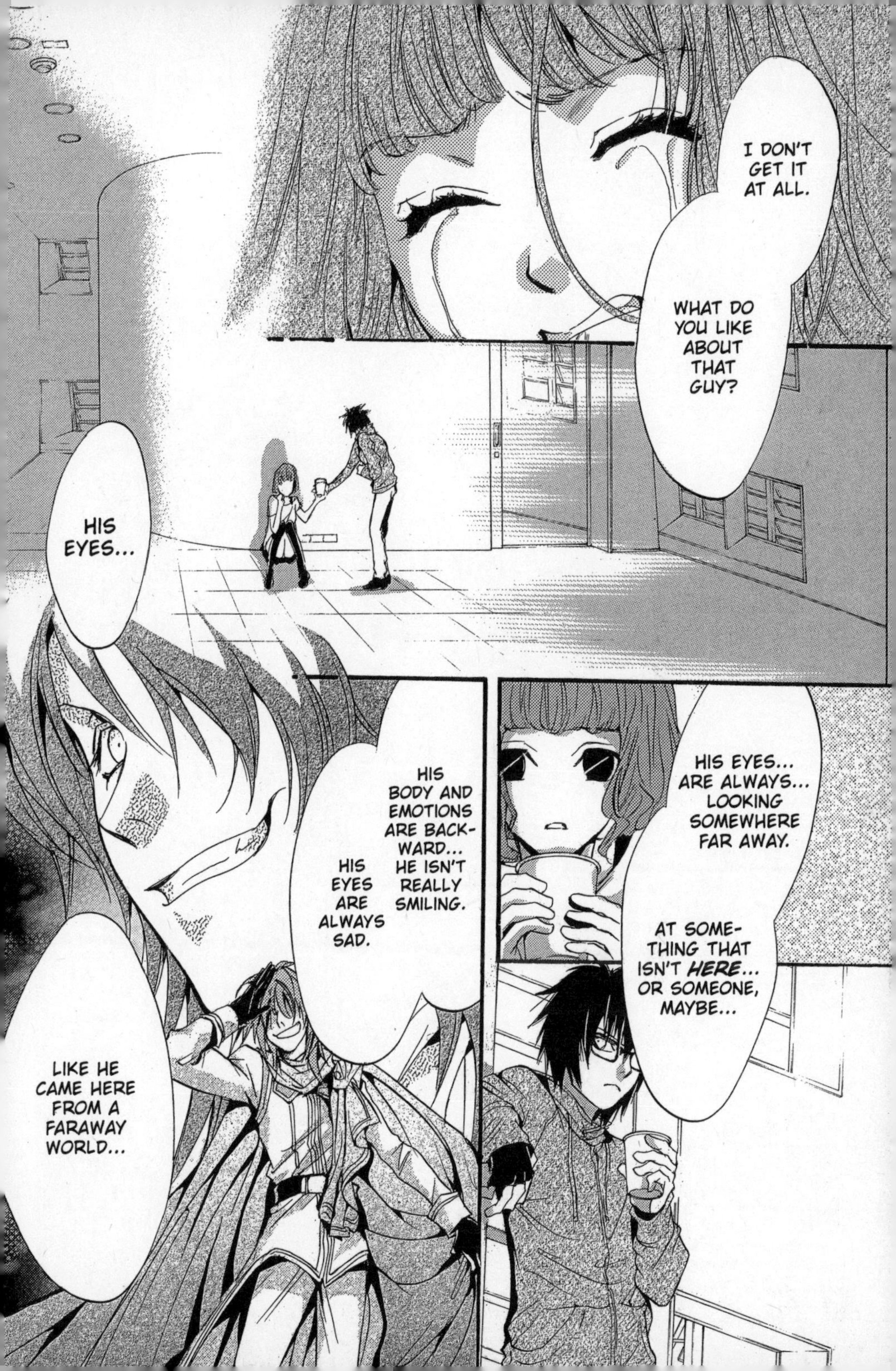
I DON'T GET IT AT ALL.
WHAT DO YOU LIKE ABOUT THAT GUY?
HIS EYES...
HIS EYES... ARE ALWAYS... LOOKING SOMEWHERE FAR AWAY.
AT SOMETHING THAT ISN'T *HERE*... OR SOMEONE, MAYBE...
HIS BODY AND EMOTIONS ARE BACKWARD... HE ISN'T REALLY SMILING.
HIS EYES ARE ALWAYS SAD.
LIKE HE CAME HERE FROM A FARAWAY WORLD...

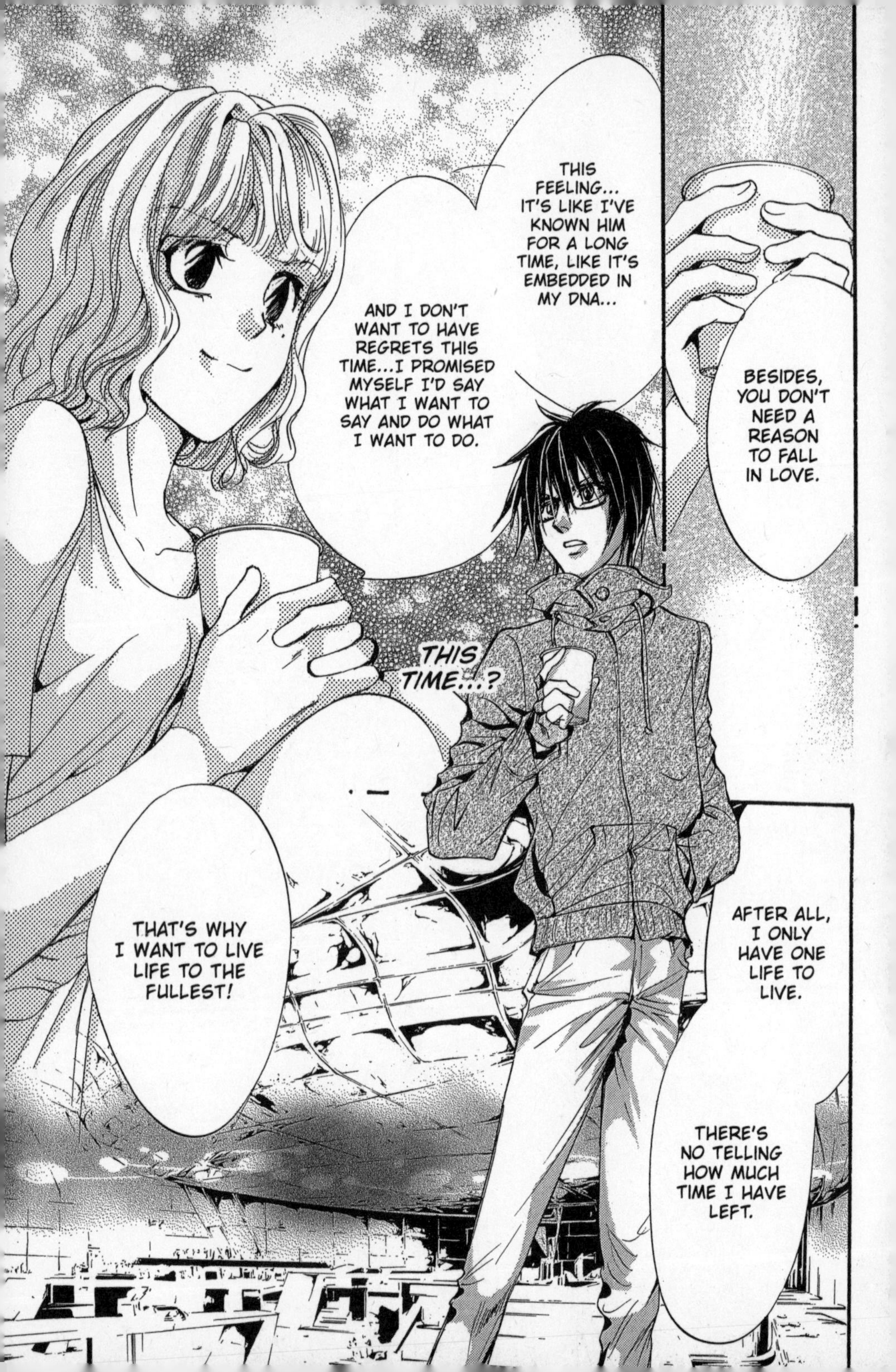
THIS FEELING... IT'S LIKE I'VE KNOWN HIM FOR A LONG TIME, LIKE IT'S EMBEDDED IN MY DNA...
BESIDES, YOU DON'T NEED A REASON TO FALL IN LOVE.
AND I DON'T WANT TO HAVE REGRETS THIS TIME...I PROMISED MYSELF I'D SAY WHAT I WANT TO SAY AND DO WHAT I WANT TO DO.
THIS TIME...?
THAT'S WHY I WANT TO LIVE LIFE TO THE FULLEST!
AFTER ALL, I ONLY HAVE ONE LIFE TO LIVE.
THERE'S NO TELLING HOW MUCH TIME I HAVE LEFT.

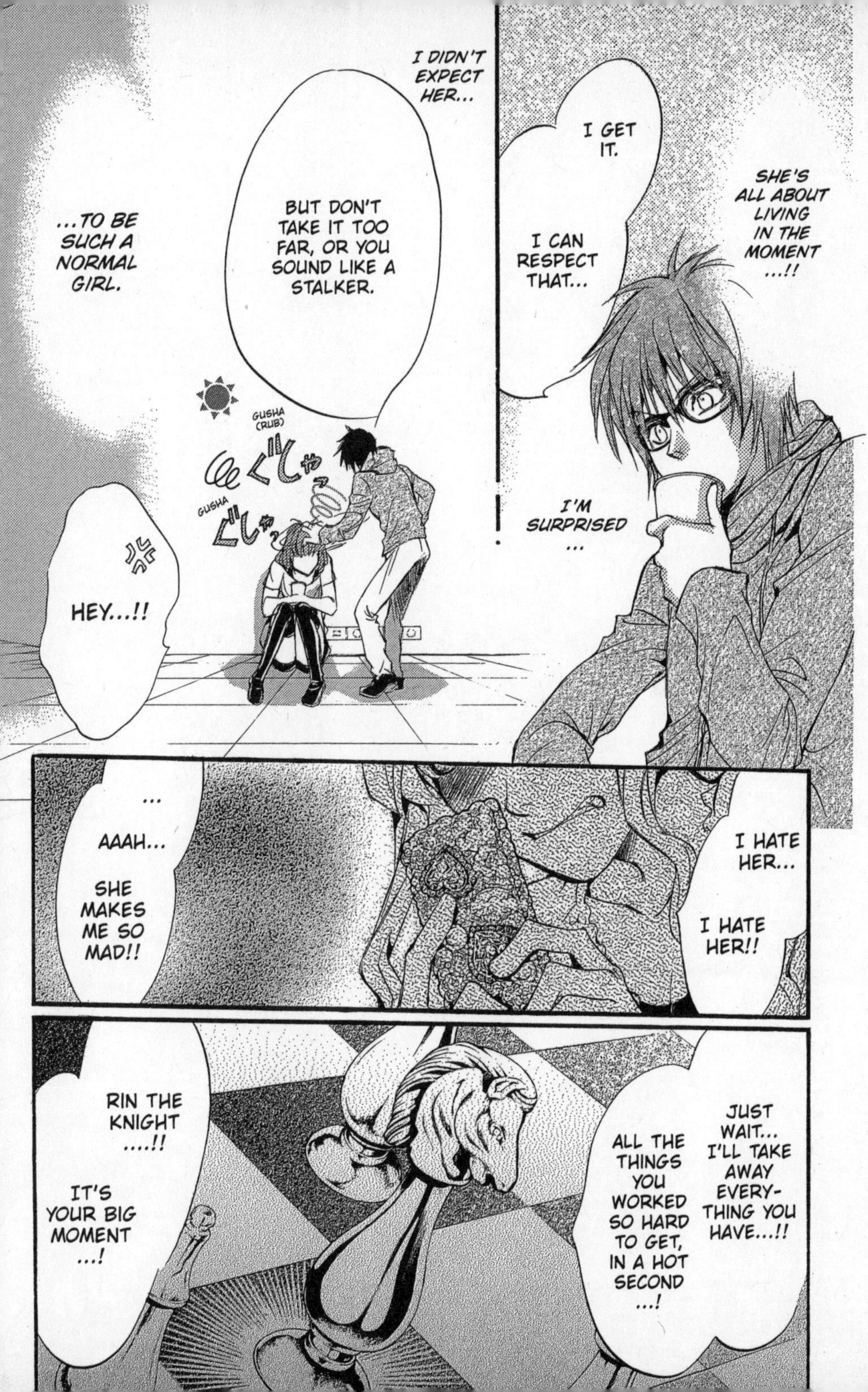

SHE'S ALL ABOUT LIVING IN THE MOMENT ...!!
I GET IT.
I CAN RESPECT THAT...
I'M SURPRISED ...
I DIDN'T EXPECT HER...
...TO BE SUCH A NORMAL GIRL.
BUT DON'T TAKE IT TOO FAR, OR YOU SOUND LIKE A STALKER.
GUSHA (RUB)
GUSHA
HEY...!!
I HATE HER...
I HATE HER!!
...
AAAH...
SHE MAKES ME SO MAD!!
JUST WAIT... I'LL TAKE AWAY EVERY-THING YOU HAVE...!!
ALL THE THINGS YOU WORKED SO HARD TO GET, IN A HOT SECOND ...!
RIN THE KNIGHT ....!!
IT'S YOUR BIG MOMENT ...!

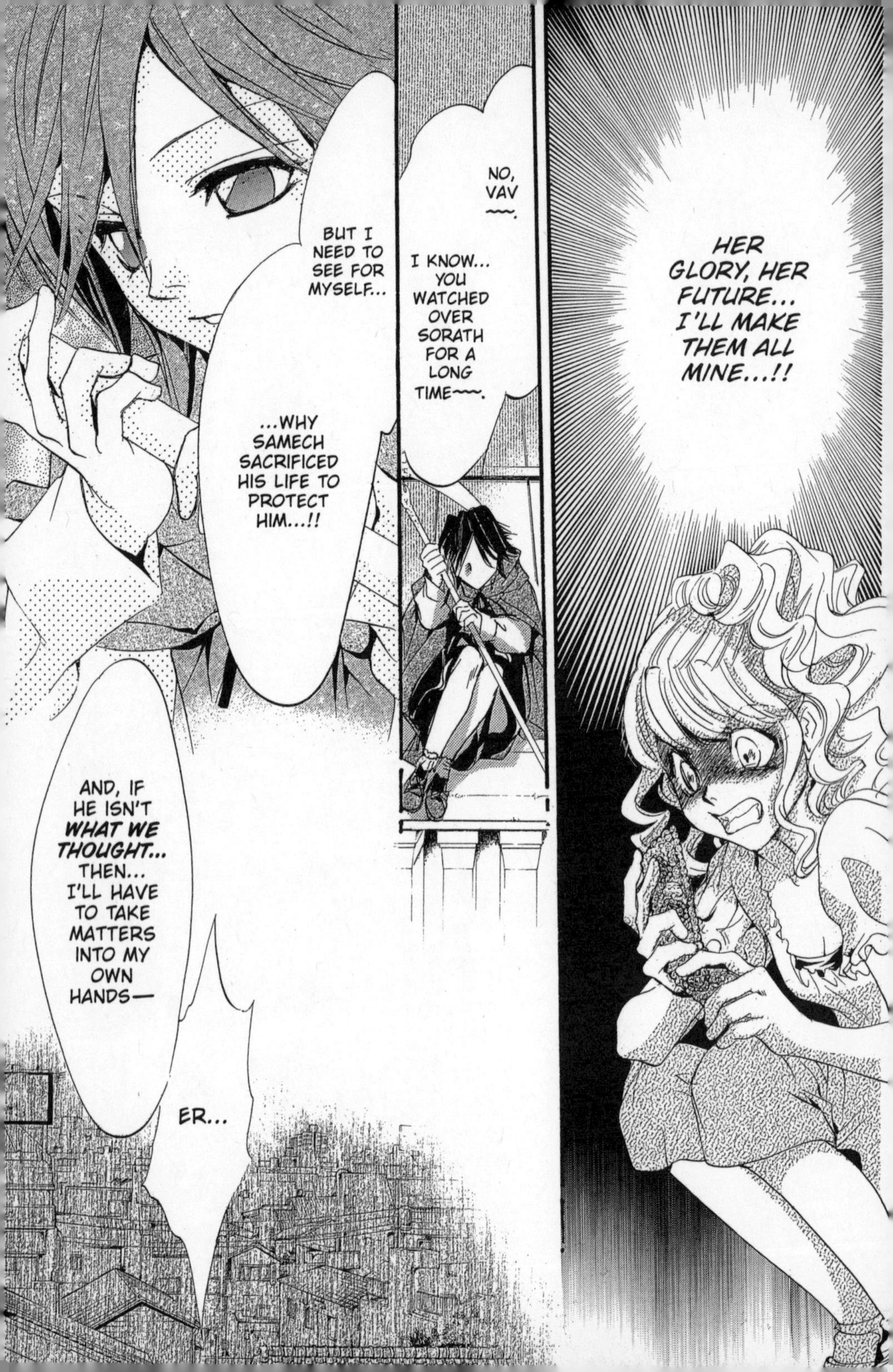
HER GLORY, HER FUTURE... I'LL MAKE THEM ALL MINE...!!
NO, VAV~~.
I KNOW... YOU WATCHED OVER SORATH FOR A LONG TIME~~.
BUT I NEED TO SEE FOR MYSELF...
...WHY SAMECH SACRIFICED HIS LIFE TO PROTECT HIM...!!
AND, IF HE ISN'T *WHAT WE THOUGHT...* THEN... I'LL HAVE TO TAKE MATTERS INTO MY OWN HANDS—
ER...

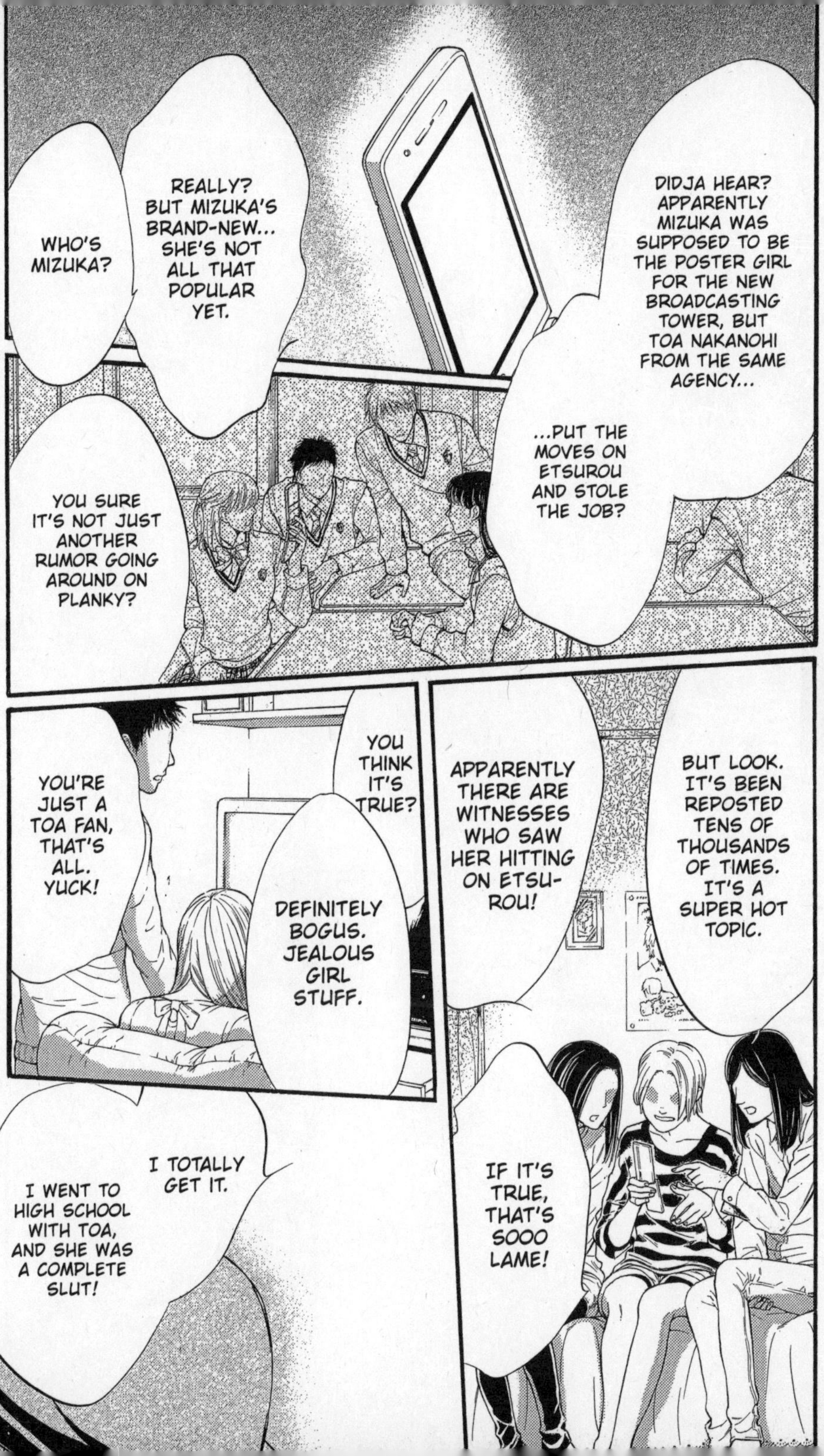
DIDJA HEAR? APPARENTLY MIZUKA WAS SUPPOSED TO BE THE POSTER GIRL FOR THE NEW BROADCASTING TOWER, BUT TOA NAKANOHI FROM THE SAME AGENCY...
...PUT THE MOVES ON ETSUROU AND STOLE THE JOB?
REALLY? BUT MIZUKA'S BRAND-NEW... SHE'S NOT ALL THAT POPULAR YET.
WHO'S MIZUKA?
YOU SURE IT'S NOT JUST ANOTHER RUMOR GOING AROUND ON PLANKY?
BUT LOOK. IT'S BEEN REPOSTED TENS OF THOUSANDS OF TIMES. IT'S A SUPER HOT TOPIC.
APPARENTLY THERE ARE WITNESSES WHO SAW HER HITTING ON ETSU-ROU!
IF IT'S TRUE, THAT'S SOOO LAME!
YOU THINK IT'S TRUE?
YOU'RE JUST A TOA FAN, THAT'S ALL. YUCK!
DEFINITELY BOGUS. JEALOUS GIRL STUFF.
I TOTALLY GET IT.
I WENT TO HIGH SCHOOL WITH TOA, AND SHE WAS A COMPLETE SLUT!

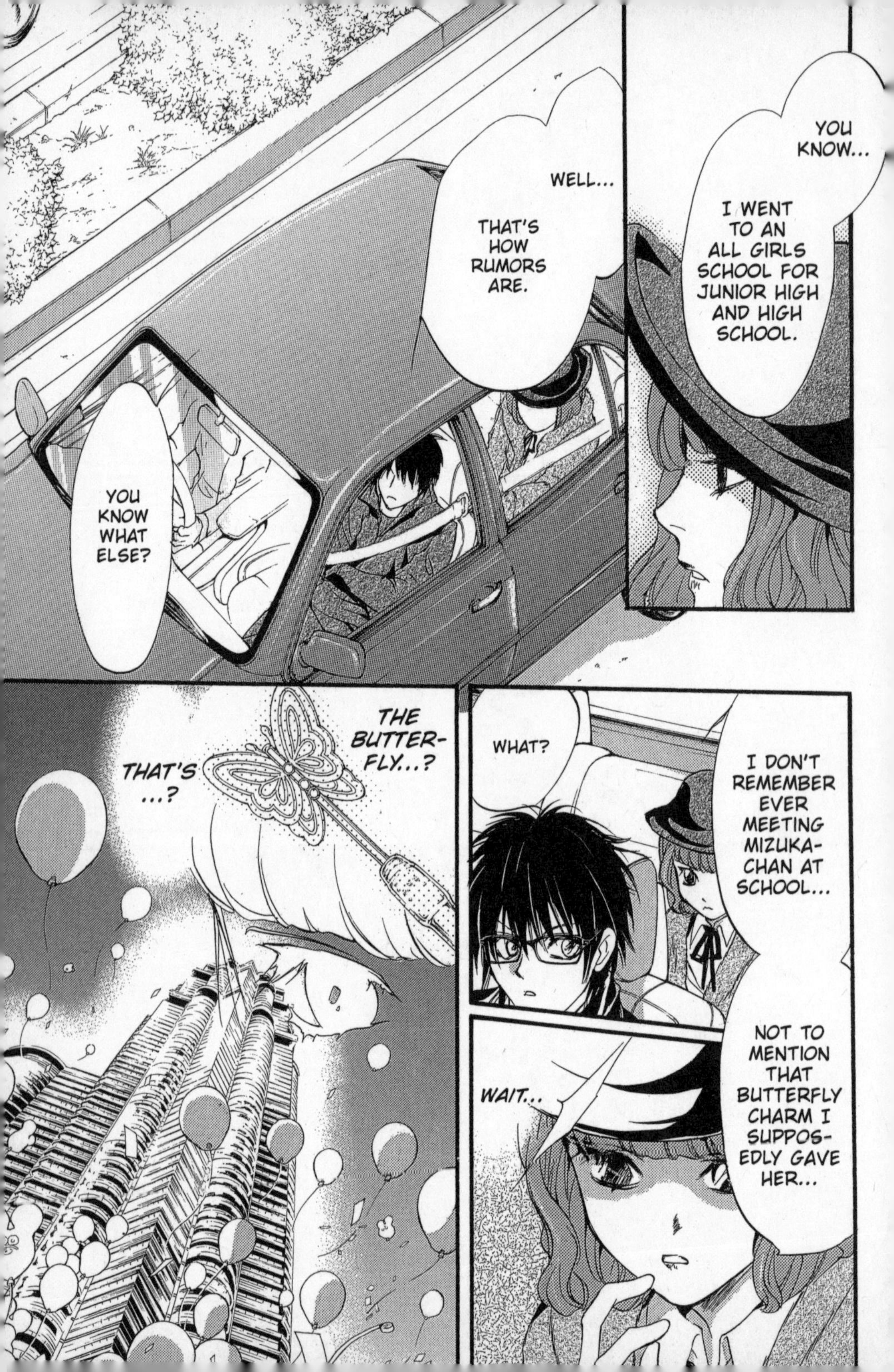
YOU KNOW...
I WENT TO AN ALL GIRLS SCHOOL FOR JUNIOR HIGH AND HIGH SCHOOL.
WELL...
THAT'S HOW RUMORS ARE.
YOU KNOW WHAT ELSE?
I DON'T REMEMBER EVER MEETING MIZUKA-CHAN AT SCHOOL...
WHAT?
NOT TO MENTION THAT BUTTERFLY CHARM I SUPPOS-EDLY GAVE HER...
WAIT...
THE BUTTER-FLY...?
THAT'S ...?

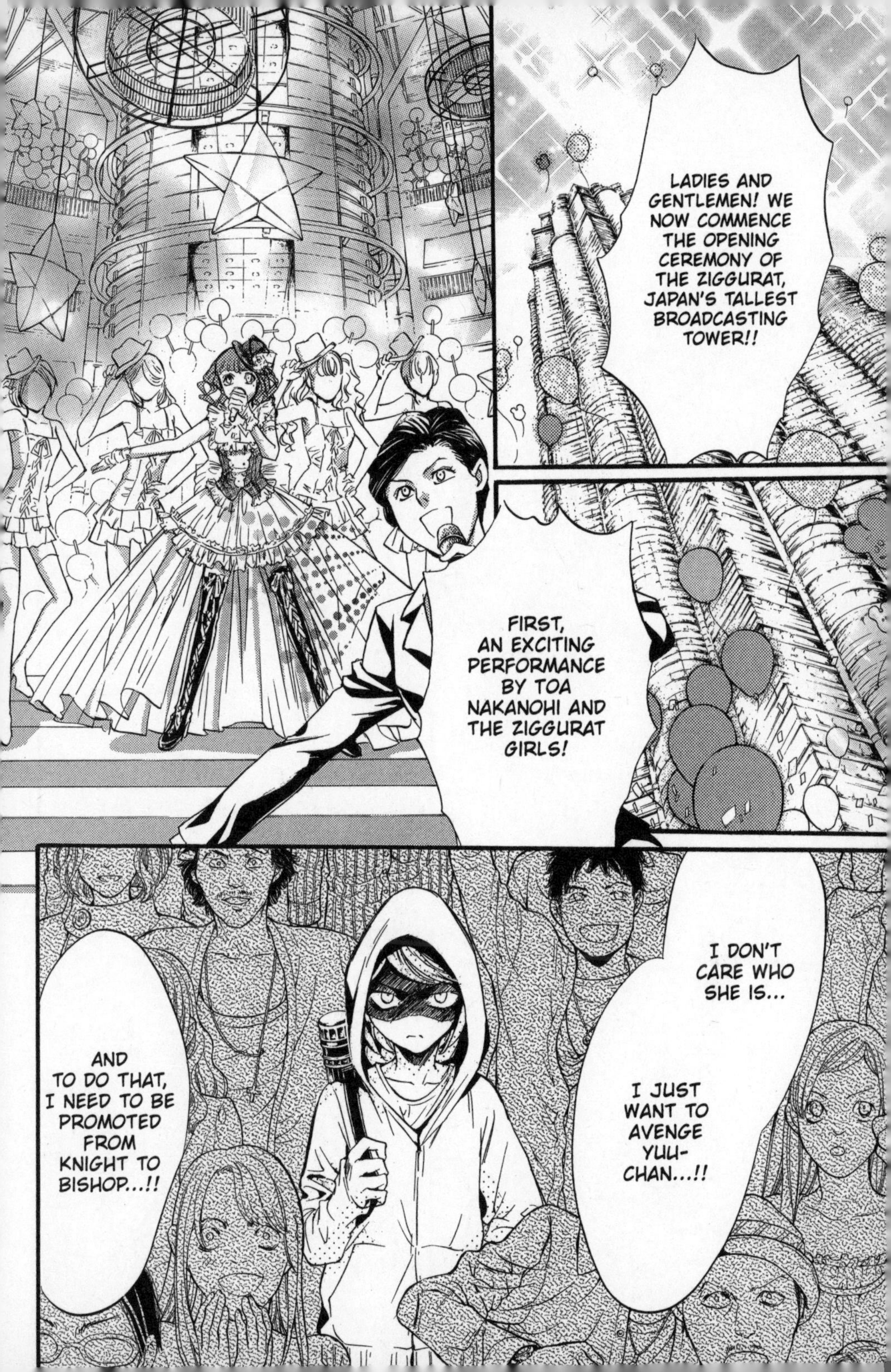

LADIES AND GENTLEMEN! WE NOW COMMENCE THE OPENING CEREMONY OF THE ZIGGURAT, JAPAN'S TALLEST BROADCASTING TOWER!!
FIRST, AN EXCITING PERFORMANCE BY TOA NAKANOHI AND THE ZIGGURAT GIRLS!
I DON'T CARE WHO SHE IS...
I JUST WANT TO AVENGE YUU-CHAN...!!
AND TO DO THAT, I NEED TO BE PROMOTED FROM KNIGHT TO BISHOP...!!

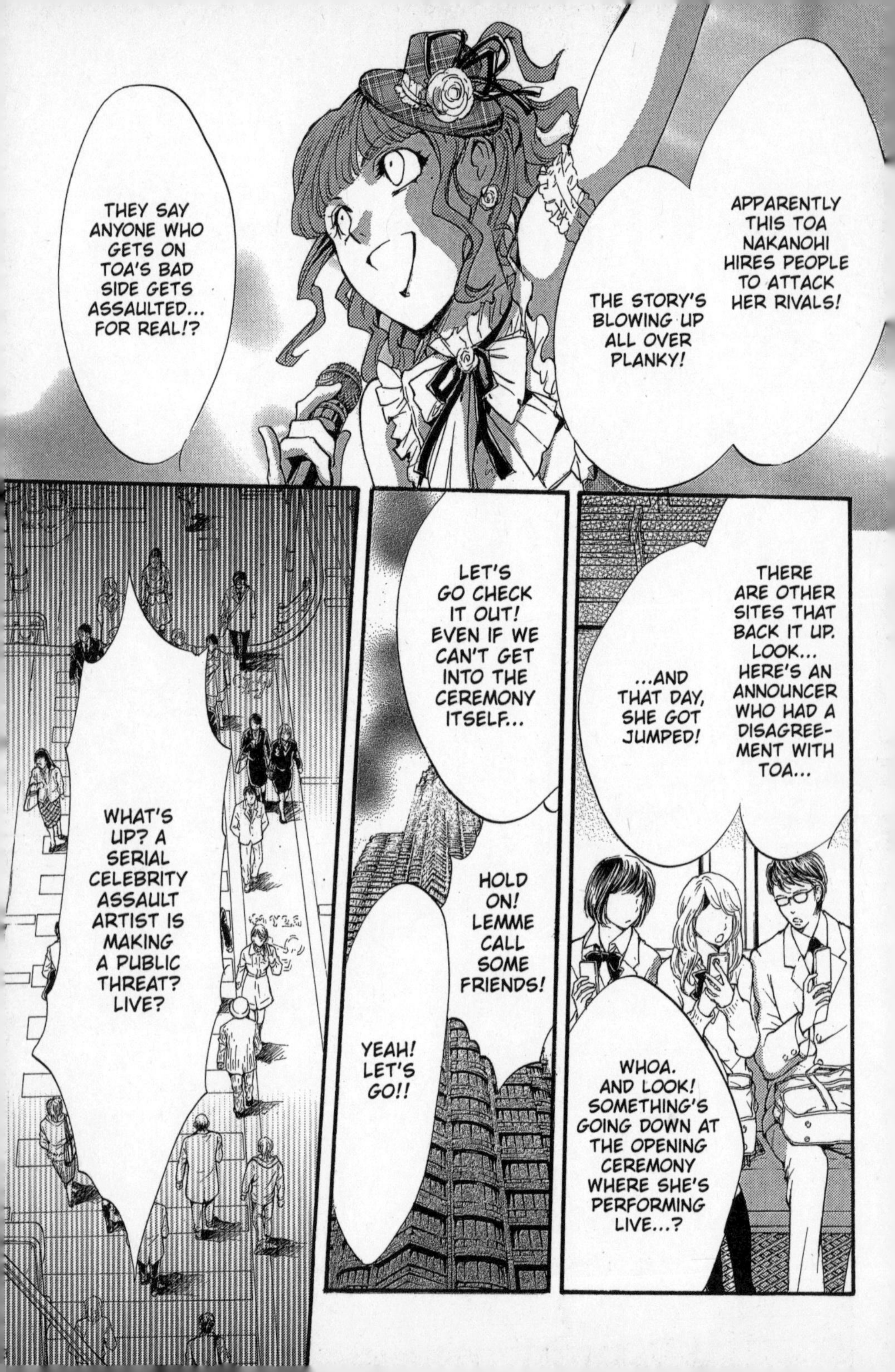
APPARENTLY THIS TOA NAKANOHI HIRES PEOPLE TO ATTACK HER RIVALS!
THE STORY'S BLOWING UP ALL OVER PLANKY!
THEY SAY ANYONE WHO GETS ON TOA'S BAD SIDE GETS ASSAULTED... FOR REAL!?
THERE ARE OTHER SITES THAT BACK IT UP. LOOK... HERE'S AN ANNOUNCER WHO HAD A DISAGREE-MENT WITH TOA...
...AND THAT DAY, SHE GOT JUMPED!
WHOA. AND LOOK! SOMETHING'S GOING DOWN AT THE OPENING CEREMONY WHERE SHE'S PERFORMING LIVE...?
LET'S GO CHECK IT OUT! EVEN IF WE CAN'T GET INTO THE CEREMONY ITSELF...
HOLD ON! LEMME CALL SOME FRIENDS!
YEAH! LET'S GO!!
WHAT'S UP? A SERIAL CELEBRITY ASSAULT ARTIST IS MAKING A PUBLIC THREAT? LIVE?

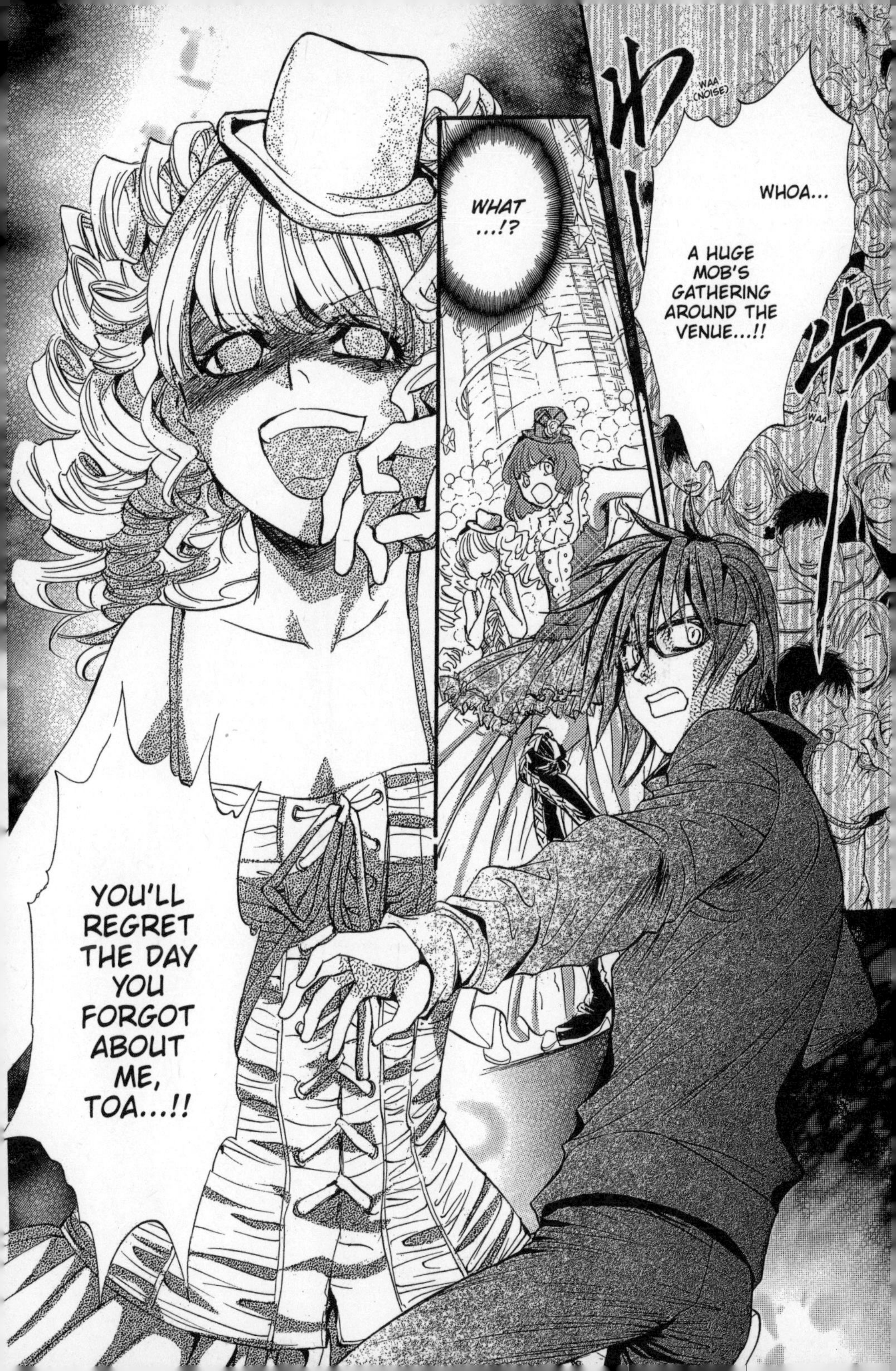
WAA (NOISE)
WHOA...
A HUGE MOB'S GATHERING AROUND THE VENUE...!!
WAA
WHAT ...!?
YOU'LL REGRET THE DAY YOU FORGOT ABOUT ME, TOA...!!

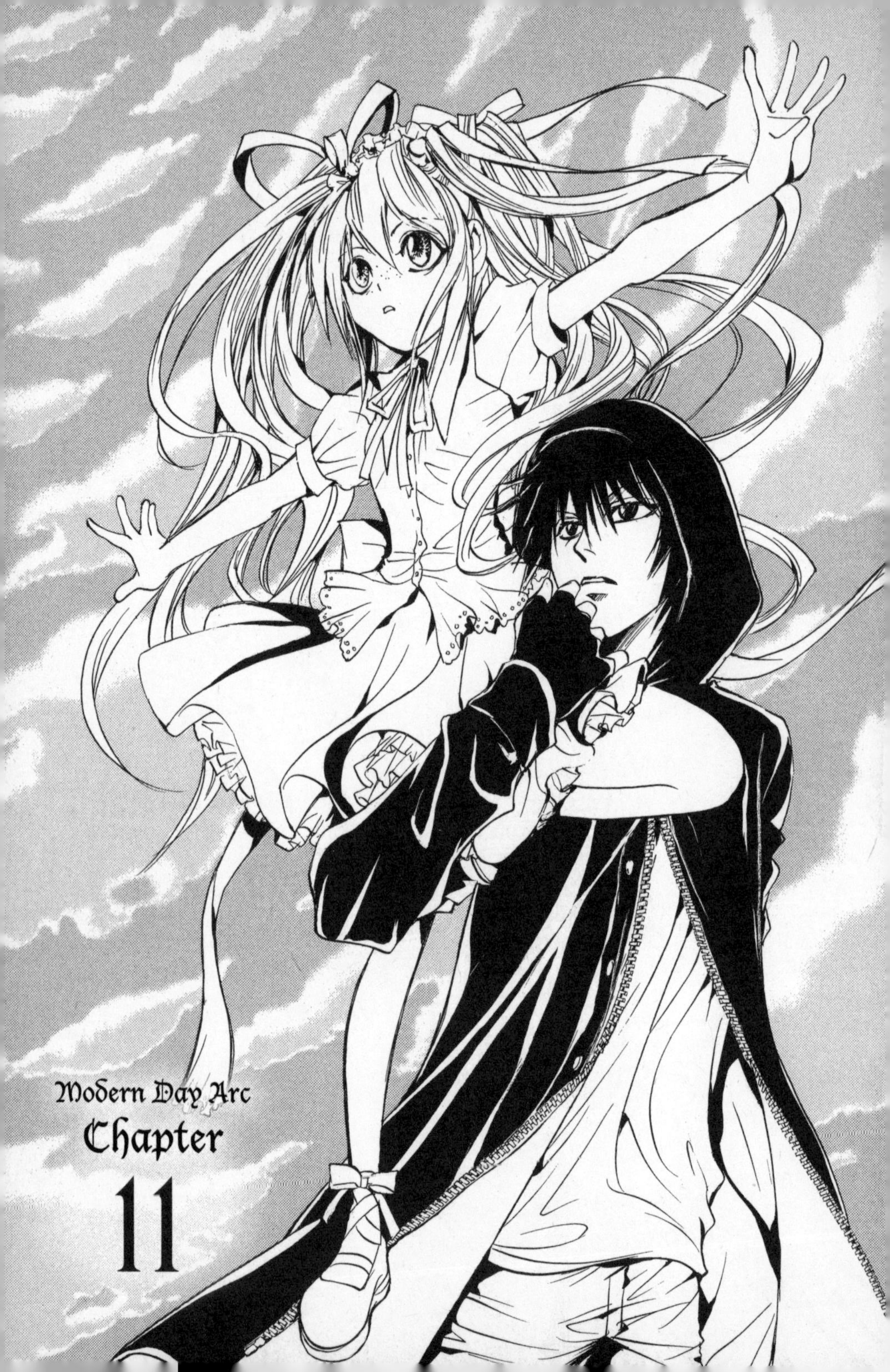
Modern Day Arc
Chapter
11

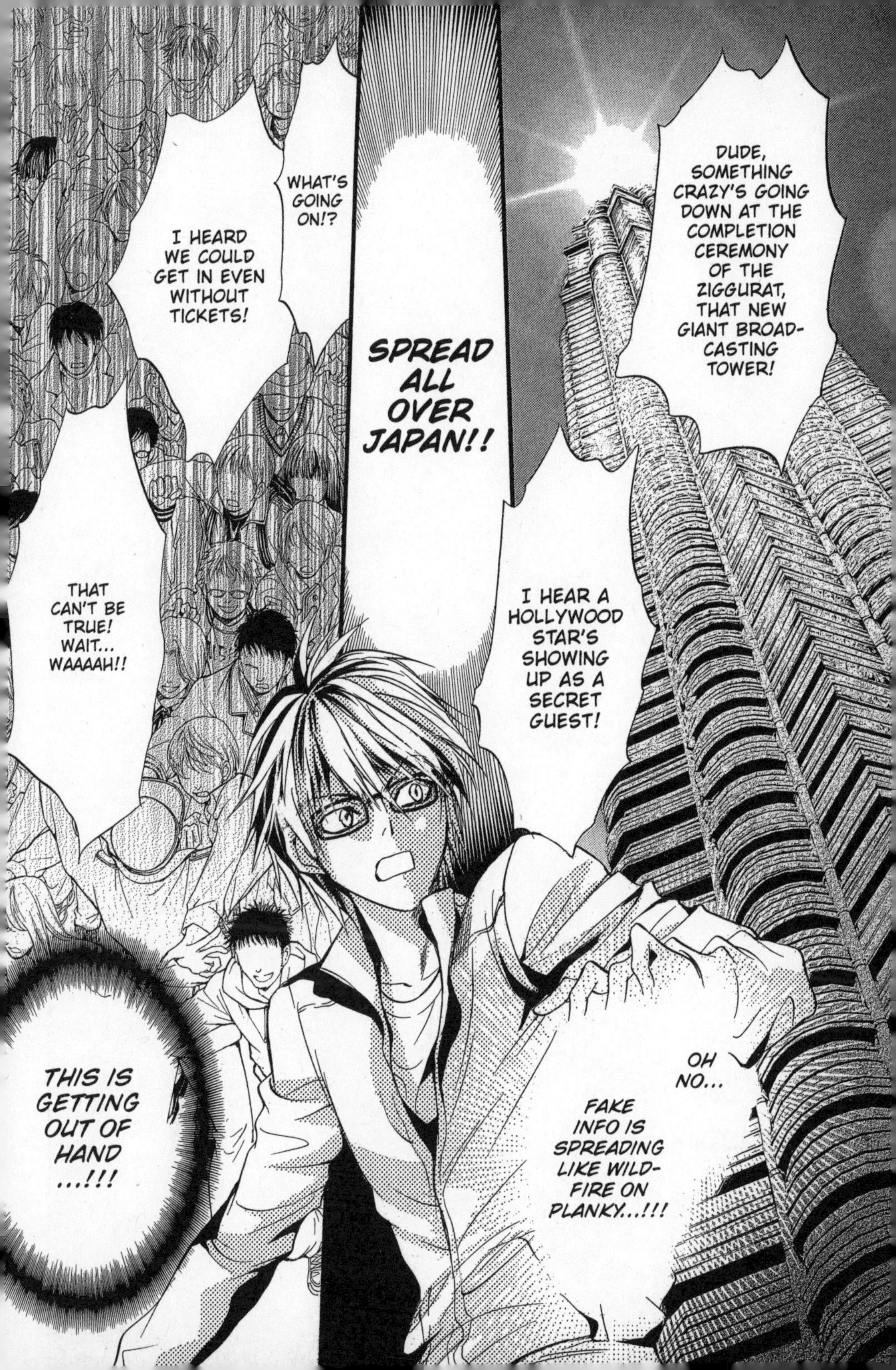
DUDE, SOMETHING CRAZY'S GOING DOWN AT THE COMPLETION CEREMONY OF THE ZIGGURAT, THAT NEW GIANT BROAD-CASTING TOWER!
I HEAR A HOLLYWOOD STAR'S SHOWING UP AS A SECRET GUEST!
SPREAD ALL OVER JAPAN!!
WHAT'S GOING ON!?
I HEARD WE COULD GET IN EVEN WITHOUT TICKETS!
THAT CAN'T BE TRUE! WAIT... WAAAAH!!
OH NO...
FAKE INFO IS SPREADING LIKE WILD-FIRE ON PLANKY...!!!
THIS IS GETTING OUT OF HAND ...!!!

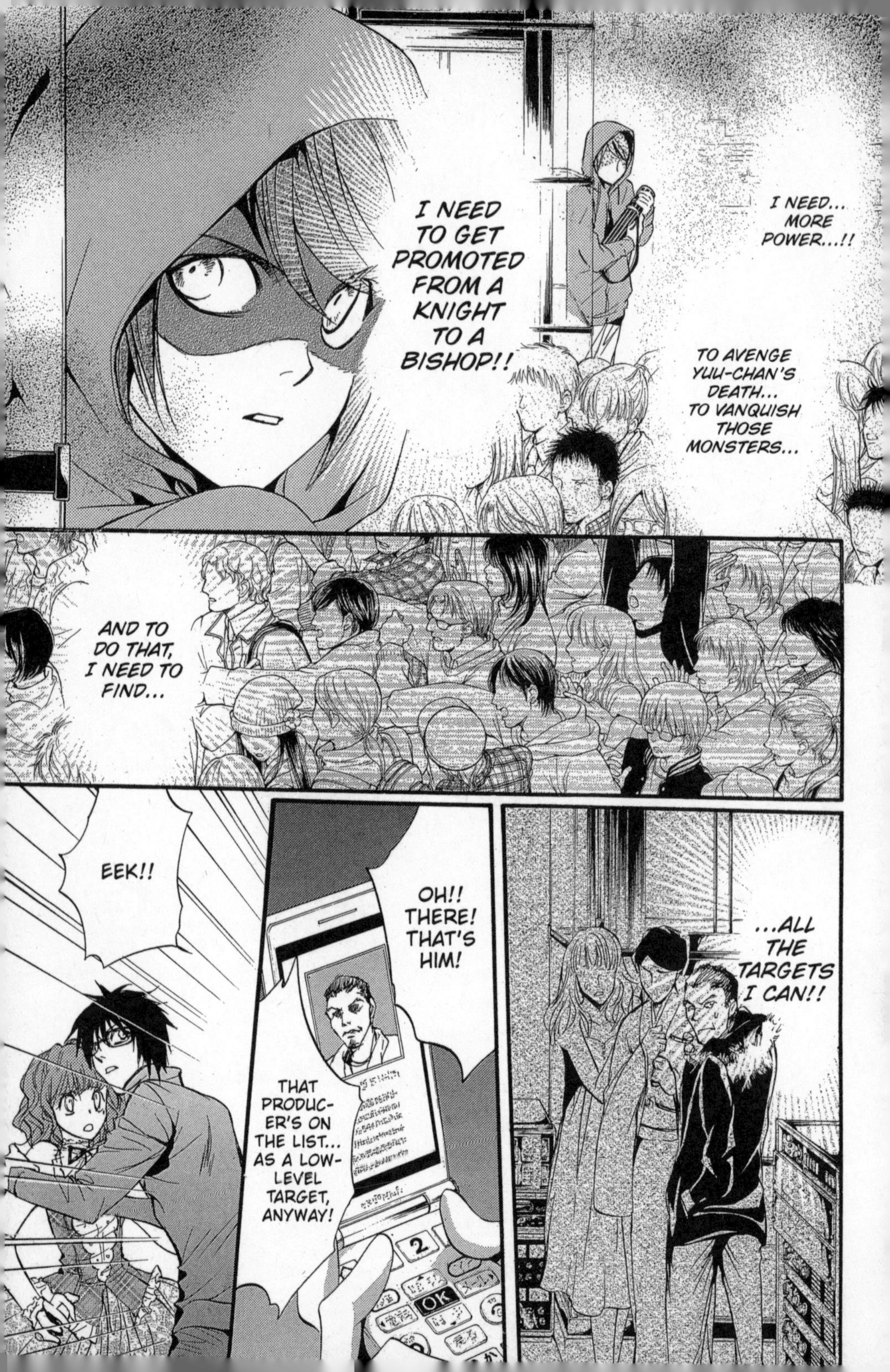
I NEED... MORE POWER...!!
TO AVENGE YUU-CHAN'S DEATH... TO VANQUISH THOSE MONSTERS...
I NEED TO GET PROMOTED FROM A KNIGHT TO A BISHOP!!
AND TO DO THAT, I NEED TO FIND...
...ALL THE TARGETS I CAN!!
OH!! THERE! THAT'S HIM!
THAT PRODUCER'S ON THE LIST... AS A LOW-LEVEL TARGET, ANYWAY!
EEK!!

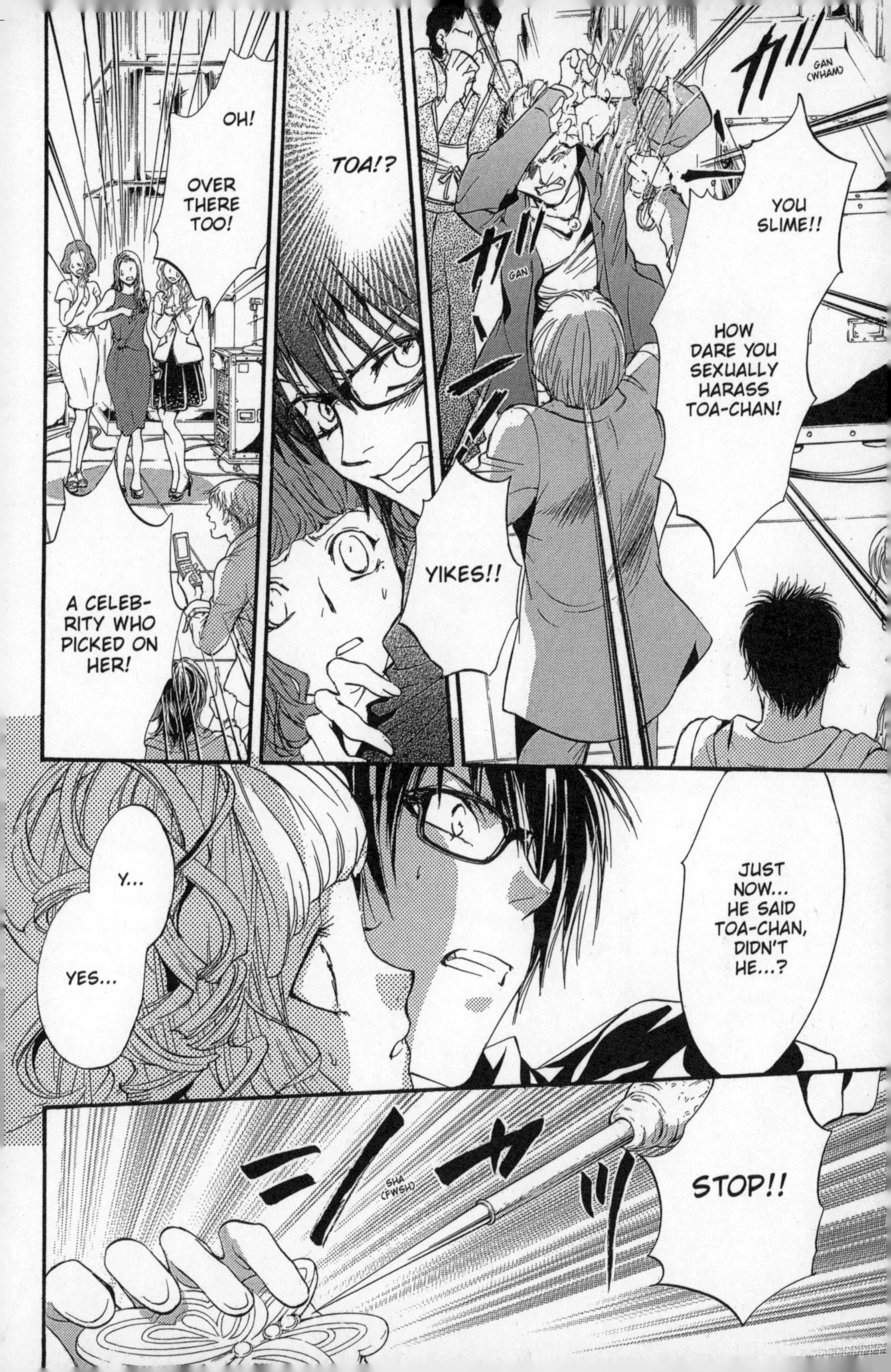
GAN (WHAM)
YOU SLIME!!
GAN
HOW DARE YOU SEXUALLY HARASS TOA-CHAN!
YIKES!!
TOA!?
OH!
OVER THERE TOO!
A CELEBRITY WHO PICKED ON HER!
JUST NOW... HE SAID TOA-CHAN, DIDN'T HE...?
Y...
YES...
STOP!!
SHA (FWSH)

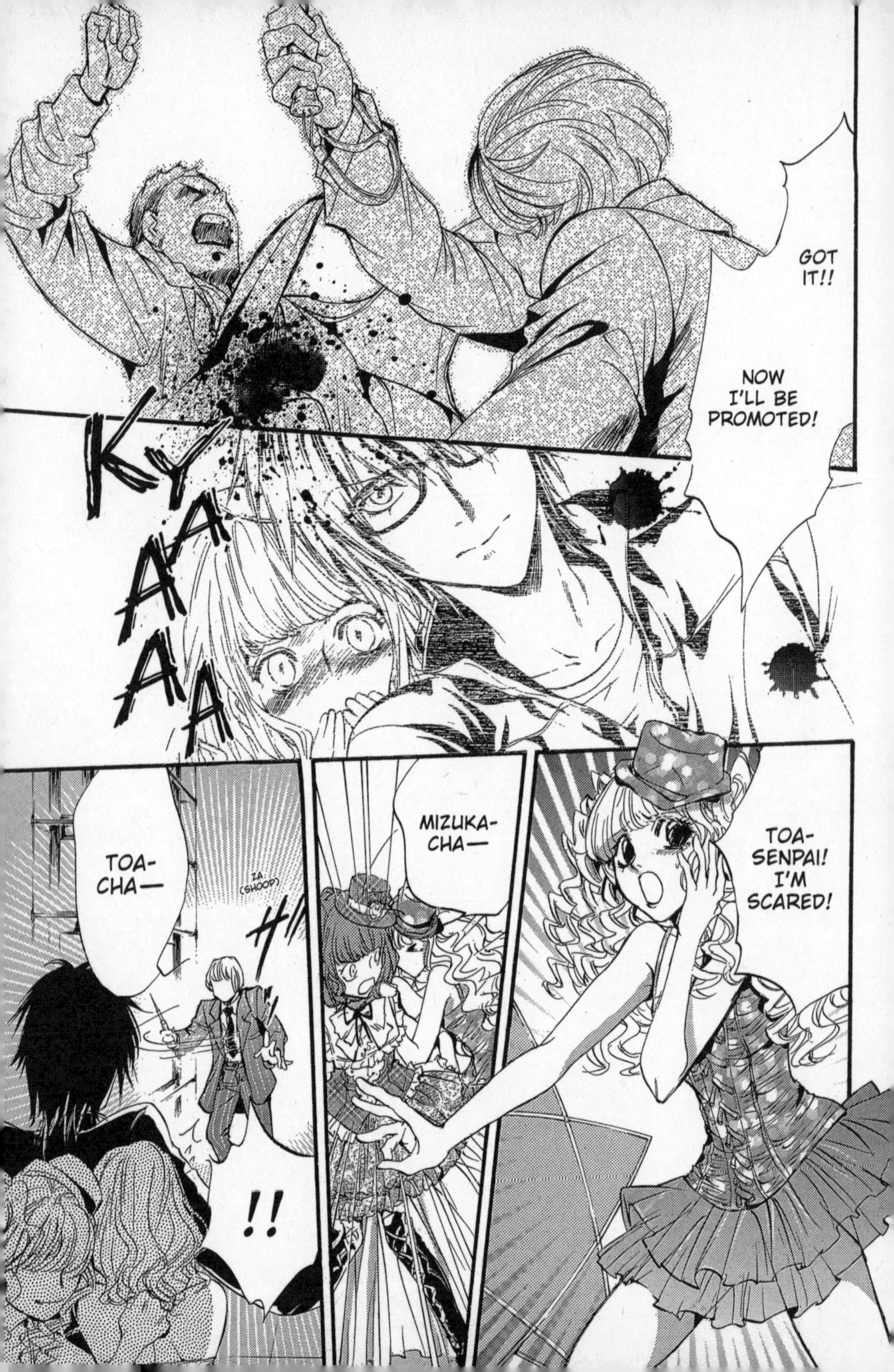
GOT IT!!
NOW I'LL BE PROMOTED!
KYAAAA
TOA-SENPAI! I'M SCARED!
MIZUKA-CHA—
TOA-CHA—
ZA (SHOOP)
!!

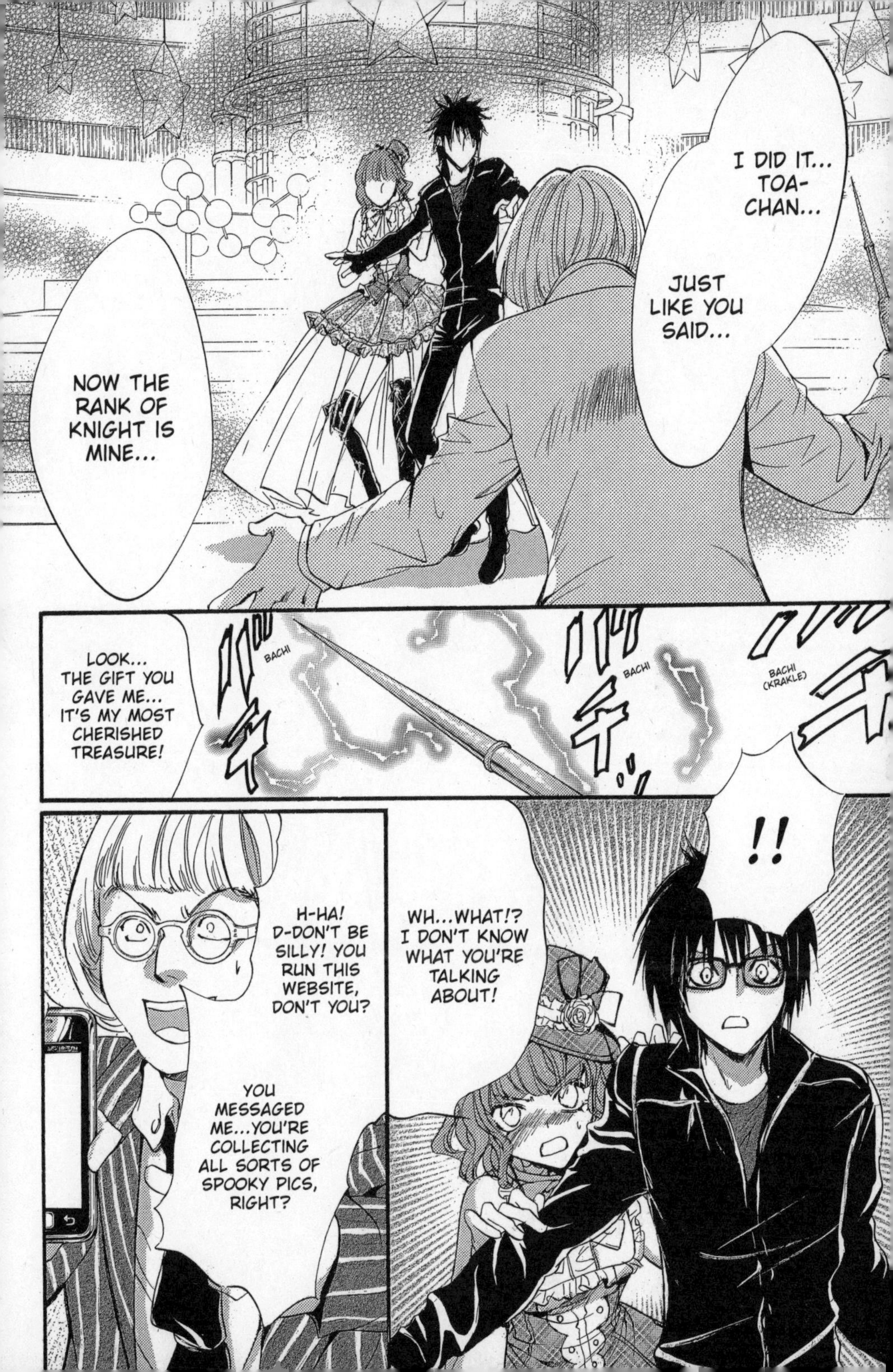
I DID IT... TOA-CHAN...
JUST LIKE YOU SAID...
NOW THE RANK OF KNIGHT IS MINE...
BACHI (KRAKLE)
BACHI
BACHI
LOOK... THE GIFT YOU GAVE ME... IT'S MY MOST CHERISHED TREASURE!
!!
WH...WHAT!? I DON'T KNOW WHAT YOU'RE TALKING ABOUT!
H-HA! D-DON'T BE SILLY! YOU RUN THIS WEBSITE, DON'T YOU?
YOU MESSAGED ME...YOU'RE COLLECTING ALL SORTS OF SPOOKY PICS, RIGHT?

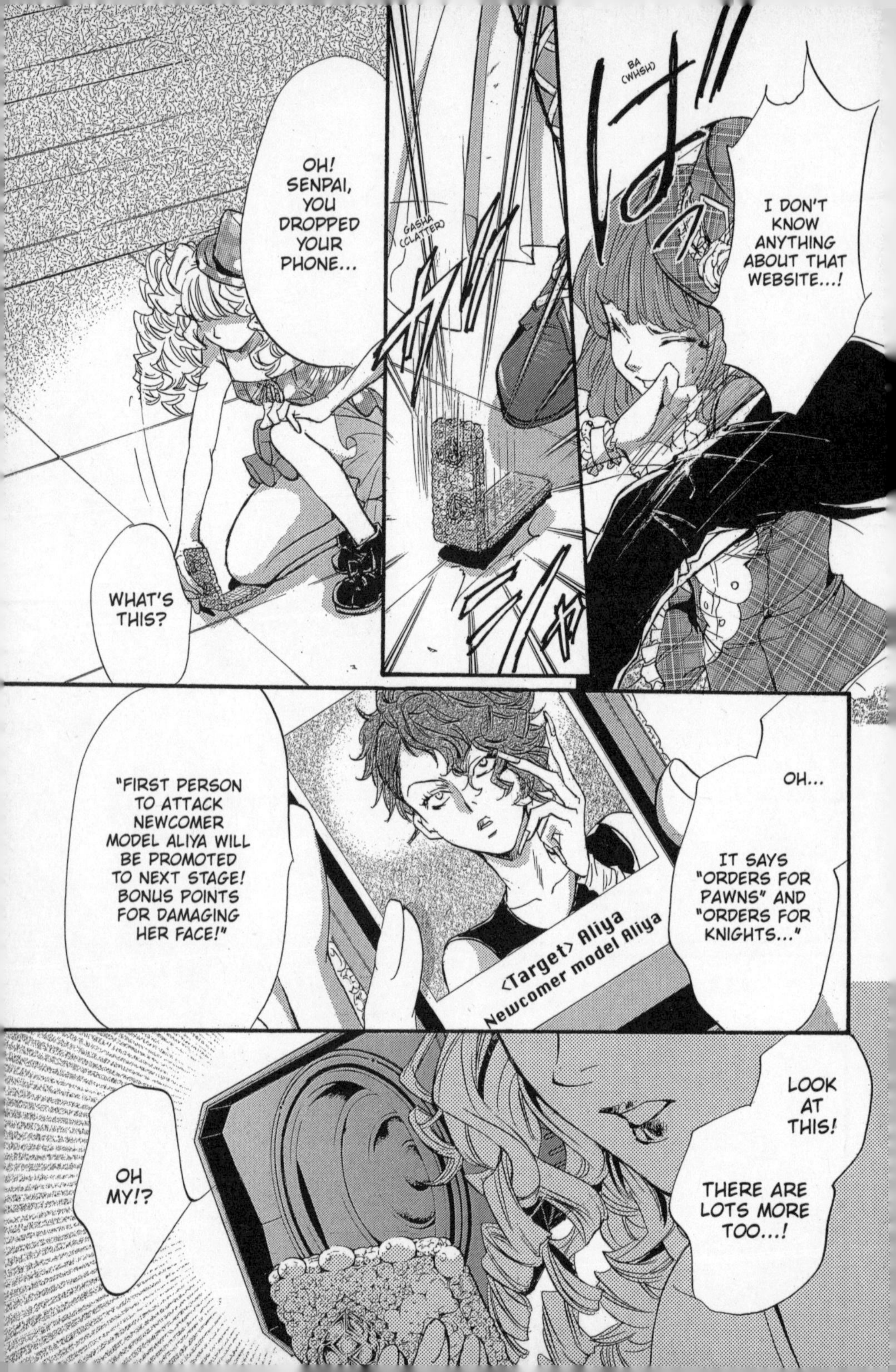
BA (WHSH)
I DON'T KNOW ANYTHING ABOUT THAT WEBSITE...!
GASHA (CLATTER)
OH! SENPAI, YOU DROPPED YOUR PHONE...
WHAT'S THIS?
OH...
IT SAYS "ORDERS FOR PAWNS" AND "ORDERS FOR KNIGHTS..."
<Target> Aliya
Newcomer model Aliya
"FIRST PERSON TO ATTACK NEWCOMER MODEL ALIYA WILL BE PROMOTED TO NEXT STAGE! BONUS POINTS FOR DAMAGING HER FACE!"
LOOK AT THIS!
THERE ARE LOTS MORE TOO...!
OH MY!?

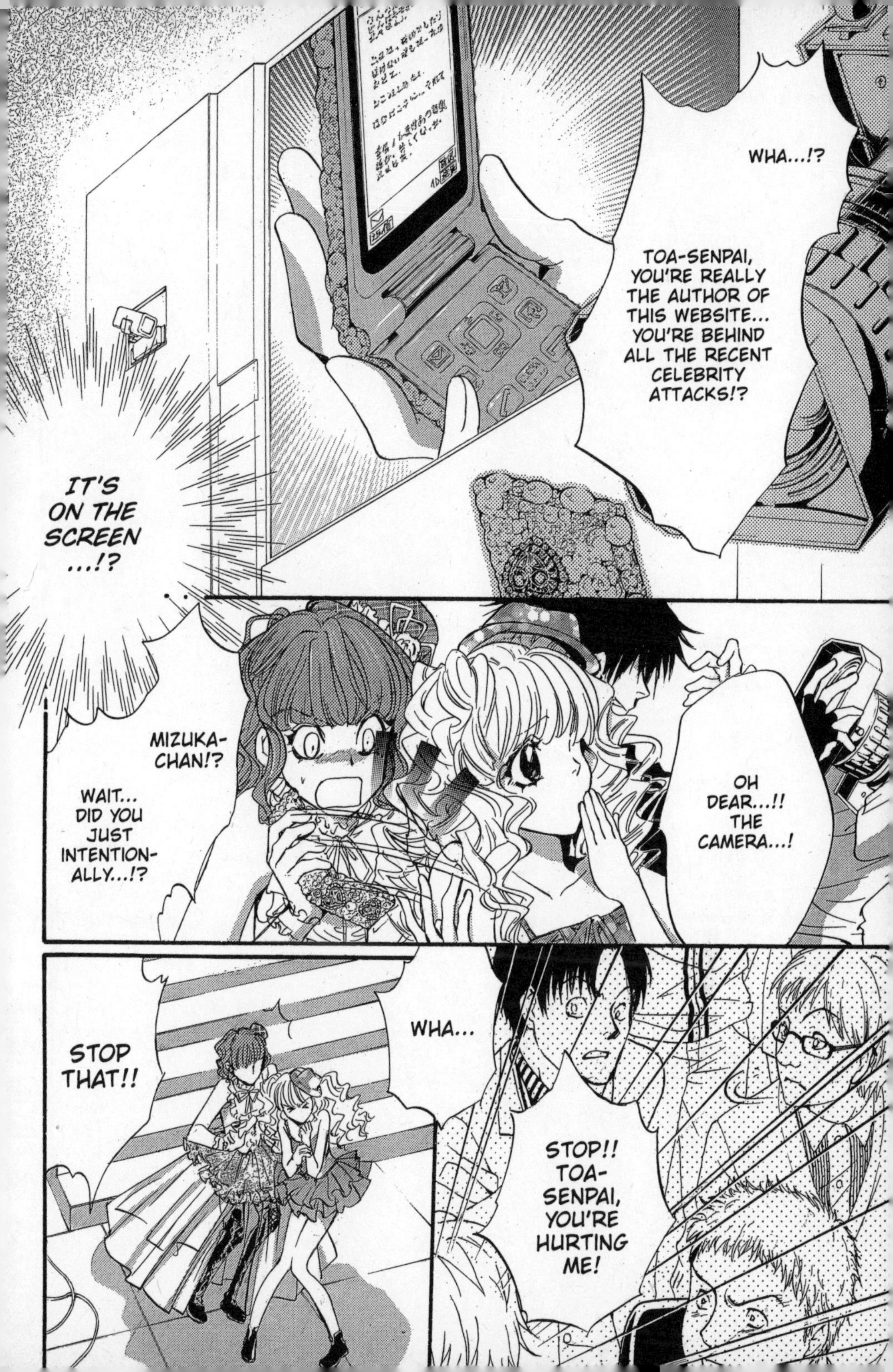
WHA...!?
TOA-SENPAI, YOU'RE REALLY THE AUTHOR OF THIS WEBSITE... YOU'RE BEHIND ALL THE RECENT CELEBRITY ATTACKS!?
IT'S ON THE SCREEN ...!?
OH DEAR...!! THE CAMERA...!
MIZUKA-CHAN!?
WAIT... DID YOU JUST INTENTION-ALLY...!?
WHA...
STOP!! TOA-SENPAI, YOU'RE HURTING ME!
STOP THAT!!

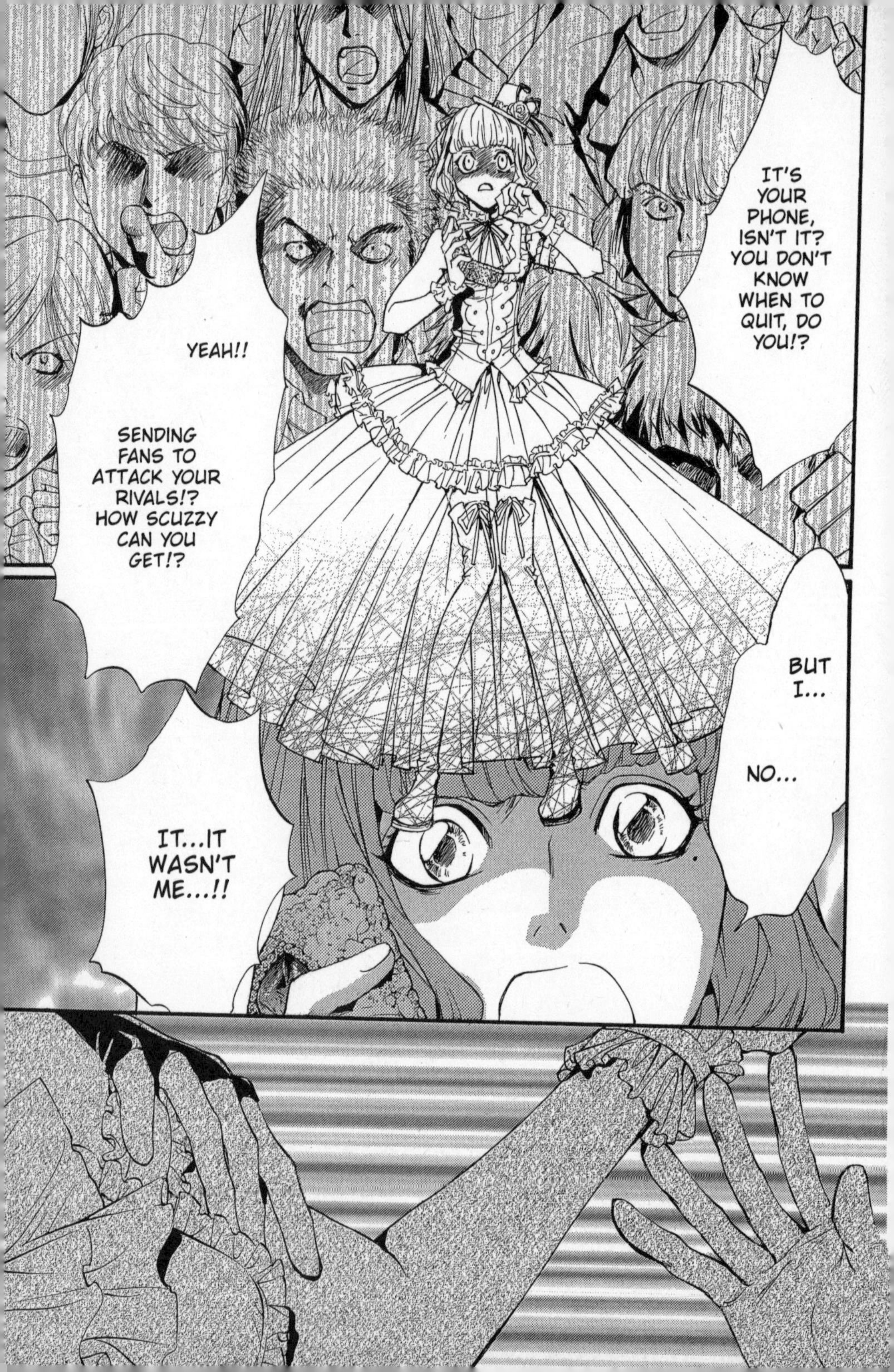
IT'S YOUR PHONE, ISN'T IT? YOU DON'T KNOW WHEN TO QUIT, DO YOU!?
YEAH!!
SENDING FANS TO ATTACK YOUR RIVALS!? HOW SCUZZY CAN YOU GET!?
BUT I...
NO...
IT...IT WASN'T ME...!!

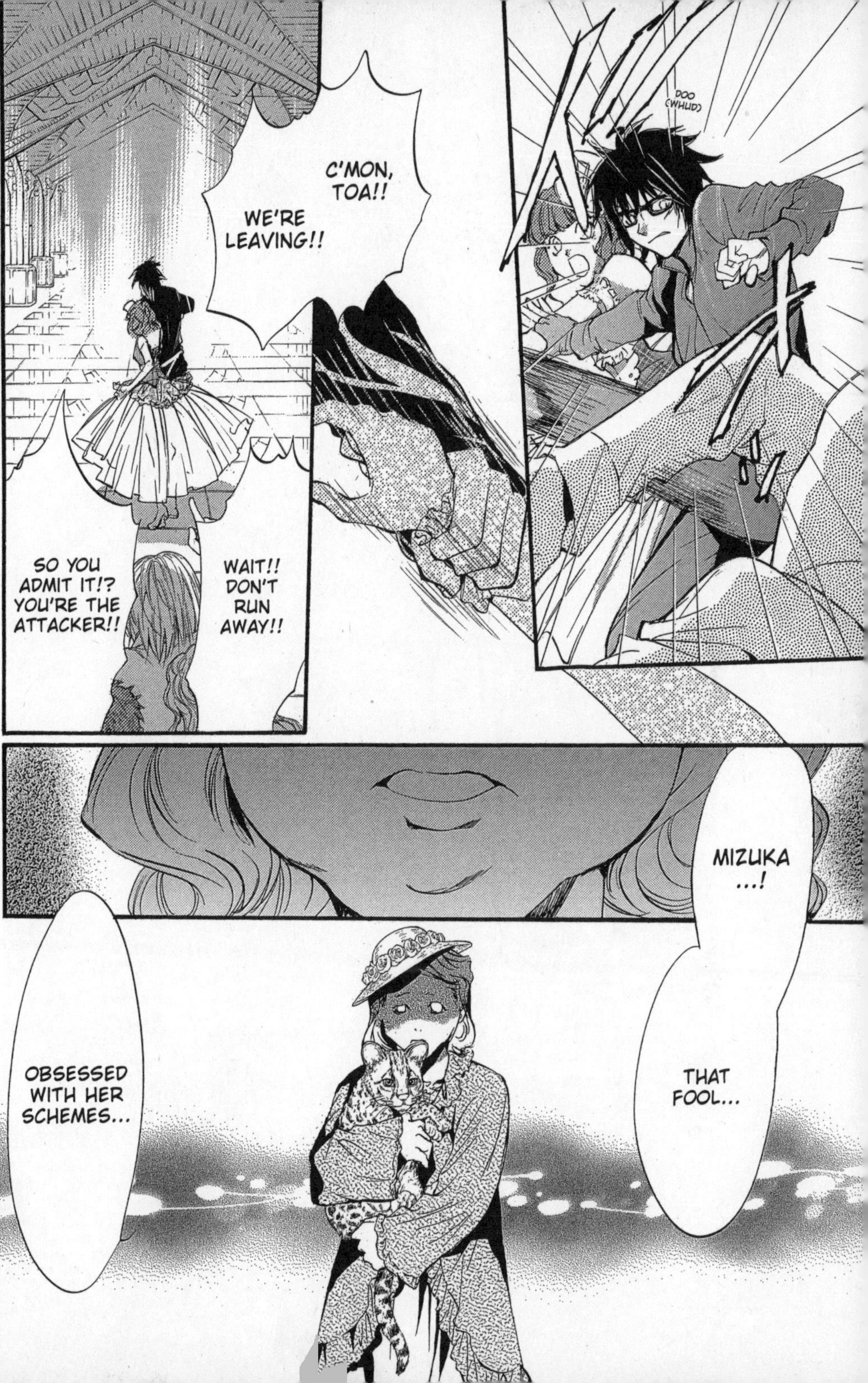
DOO (WHUD)
C'MON, TOA!! WE'RE LEAVING!!
WAIT!! DON'T RUN AWAY!!
SO YOU ADMIT IT!? YOU'RE THE ATTACKER!!
MIZUKA ...!
THAT FOOL...
OBSESSED WITH HER SCHEMES...

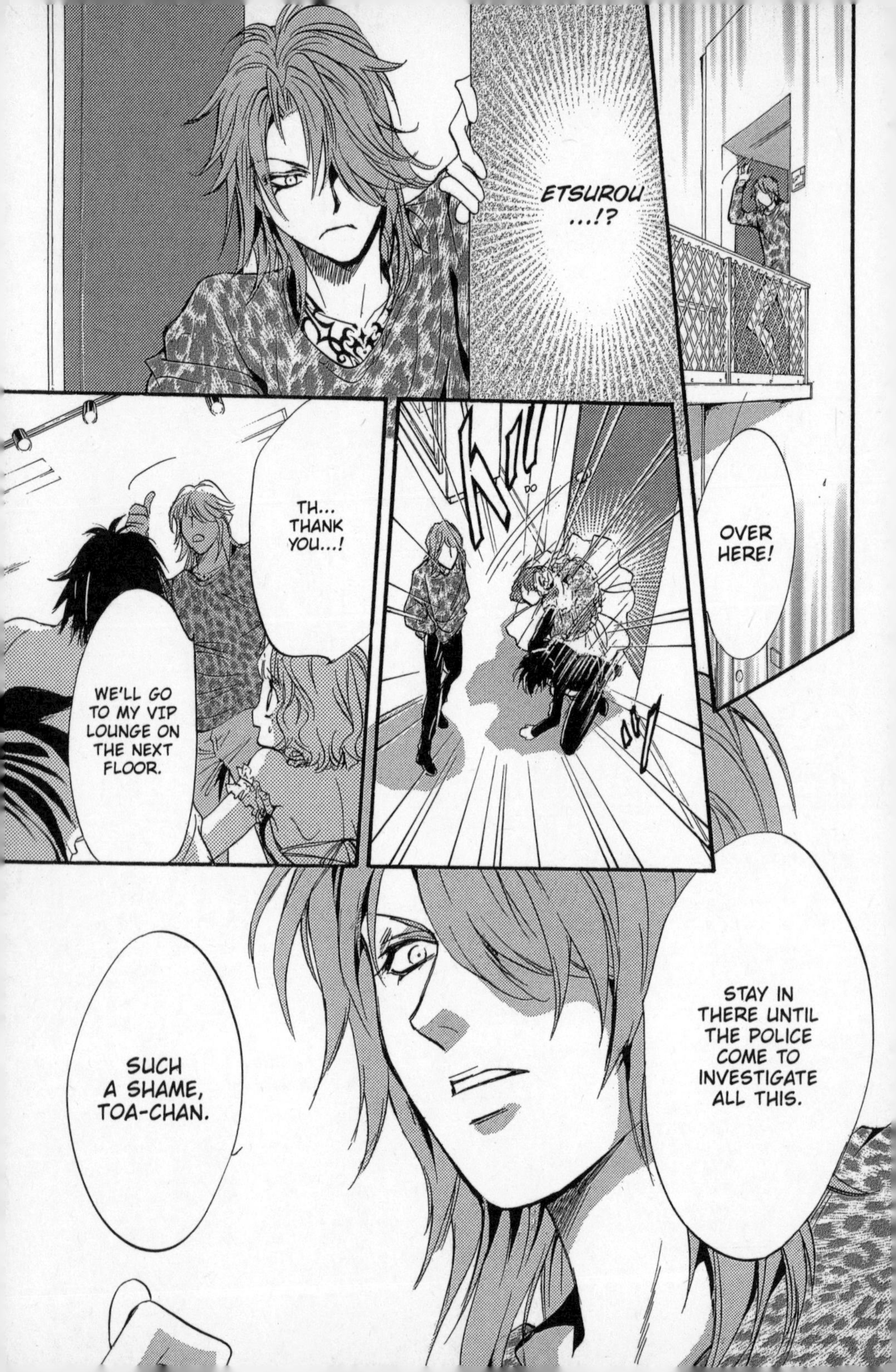
ETSUROU ...!?
OVER HERE!
DO
TH... THANK YOU...!
WE'LL GO TO MY VIP LOUNGE ON THE NEXT FLOOR.
STAY IN THERE UNTIL THE POLICE COME TO INVESTIGATE ALL THIS.
SUCH A SHAME, TOA-CHAN.

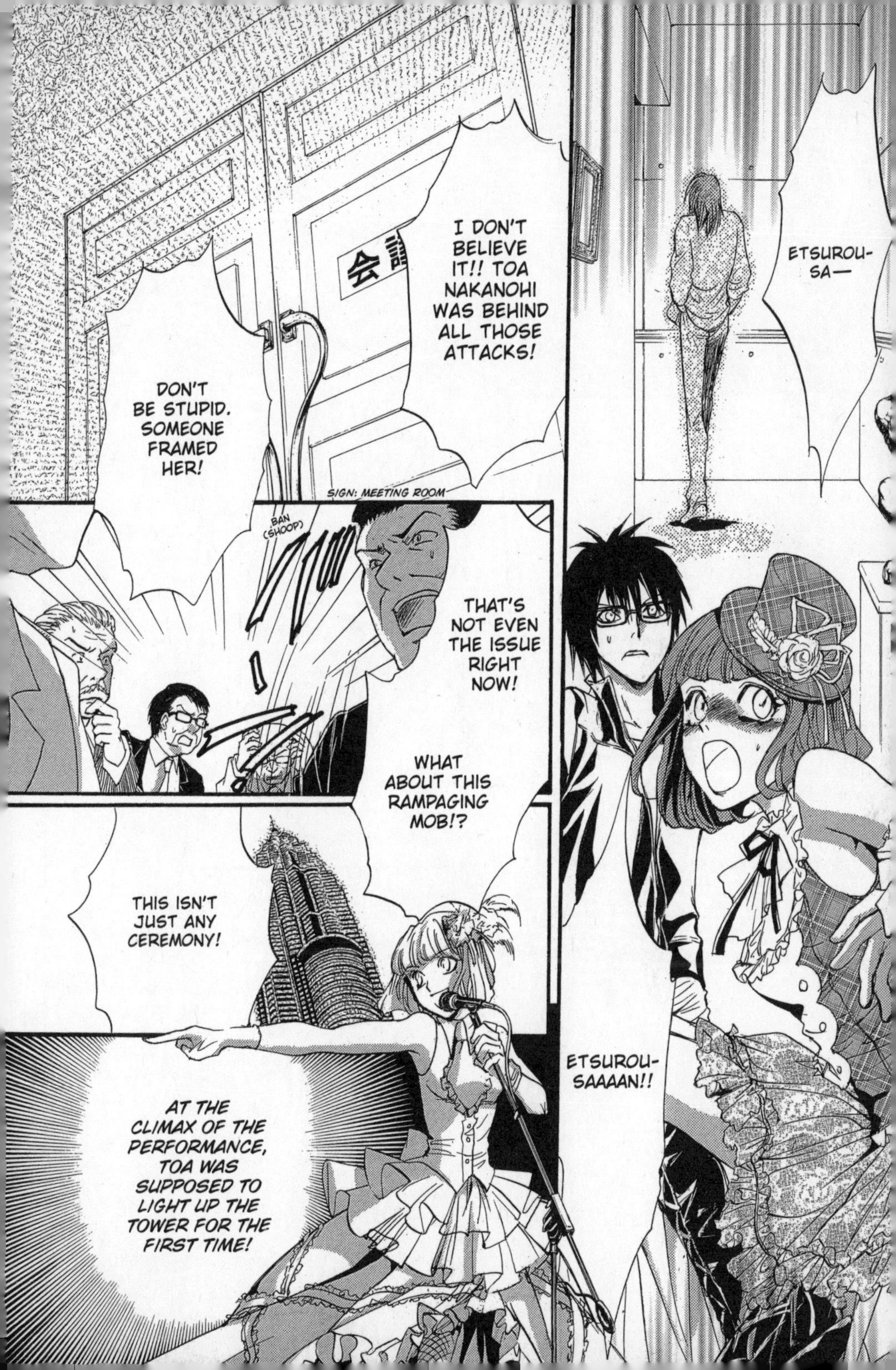
ETSUROU-SA—
ETSUROU-SAAAAN!!
I DON'T BELIEVE IT!! TOA NAKANOHI WAS BEHIND ALL THOSE ATTACKS!
DON'T BE STUPID. SOMEONE FRAMED HER!
SIGN: MEETING ROOM
BAN (SHOOP)
THAT'S NOT EVEN THE ISSUE RIGHT NOW!
WHAT ABOUT THIS RAMPAGING MOB!?
THIS ISN'T JUST ANY CEREMONY!
AT THE CLIMAX OF THE PERFORMANCE, TOA WAS SUPPOSED TO LIGHT UP THE TOWER FOR THE FIRST TIME!

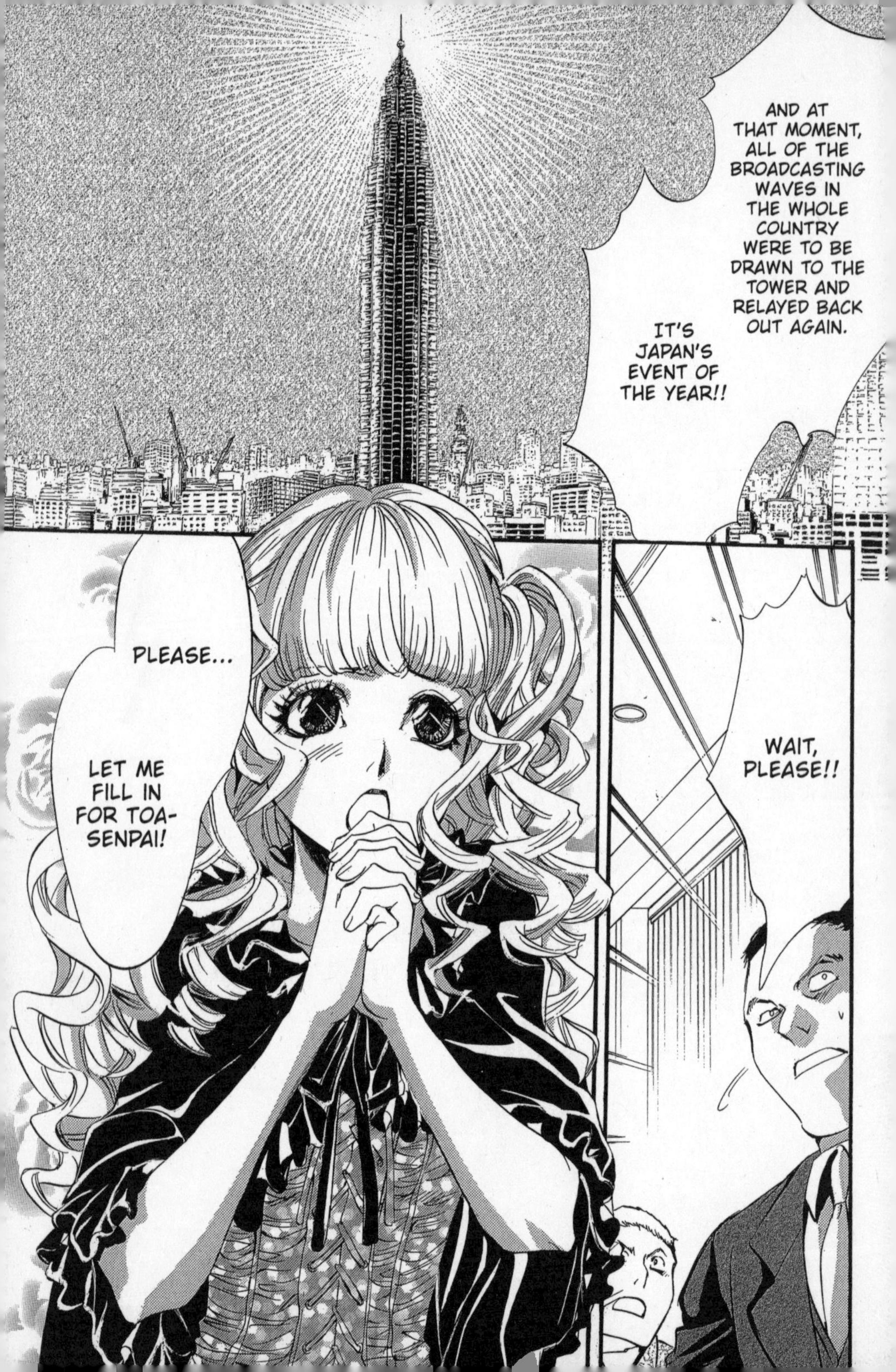
AND AT THAT MOMENT, ALL OF THE BROADCASTING WAVES IN THE WHOLE COUNTRY WERE TO BE DRAWN TO THE TOWER AND RELAYED BACK OUT AGAIN.
IT'S JAPAN'S EVENT OF THE YEAR!!
WAIT, PLEASE!!
PLEASE...
LET ME FILL IN FOR TOA-SENPAI!

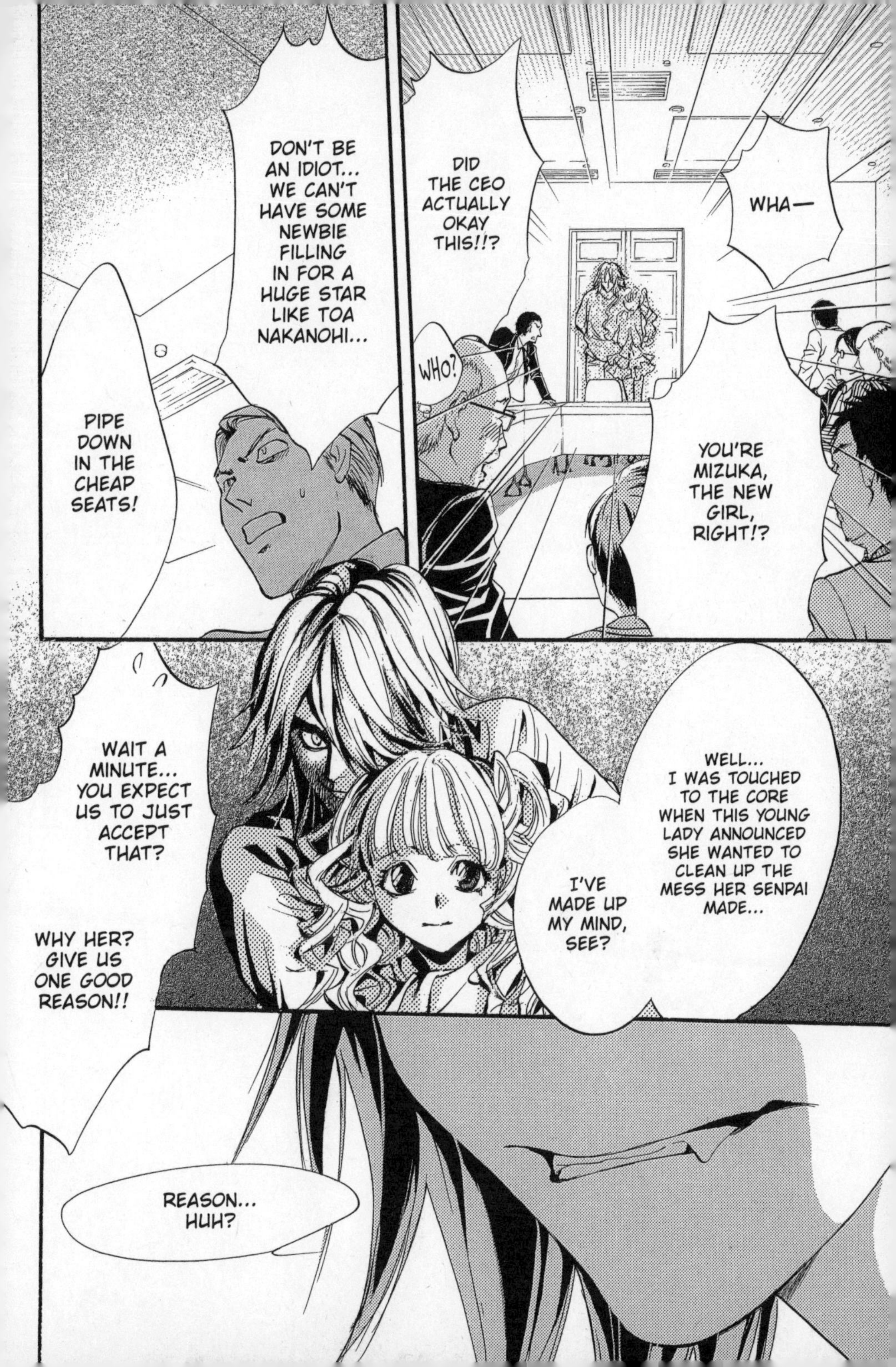
WHA—
DID THE CEO ACTUALLY OKAY THIS!!?
WHO?
YOU'RE MIZUKA, THE NEW GIRL, RIGHT!?
DON'T BE AN IDIOT... WE CAN'T HAVE SOME NEWBIE FILLING IN FOR A HUGE STAR LIKE TOA NAKANOHI...
PIPE DOWN IN THE CHEAP SEATS!
WELL... I WAS TOUCHED TO THE CORE WHEN THIS YOUNG LADY ANNOUNCED SHE WANTED TO CLEAN UP THE MESS HER SENPAI MADE...
I'VE MADE UP MY MIND, SEE?
WAIT A MINUTE... YOU EXPECT US TO JUST ACCEPT THAT?
WHY HER? GIVE US ONE GOOD REASON!!
REASON... HUH?

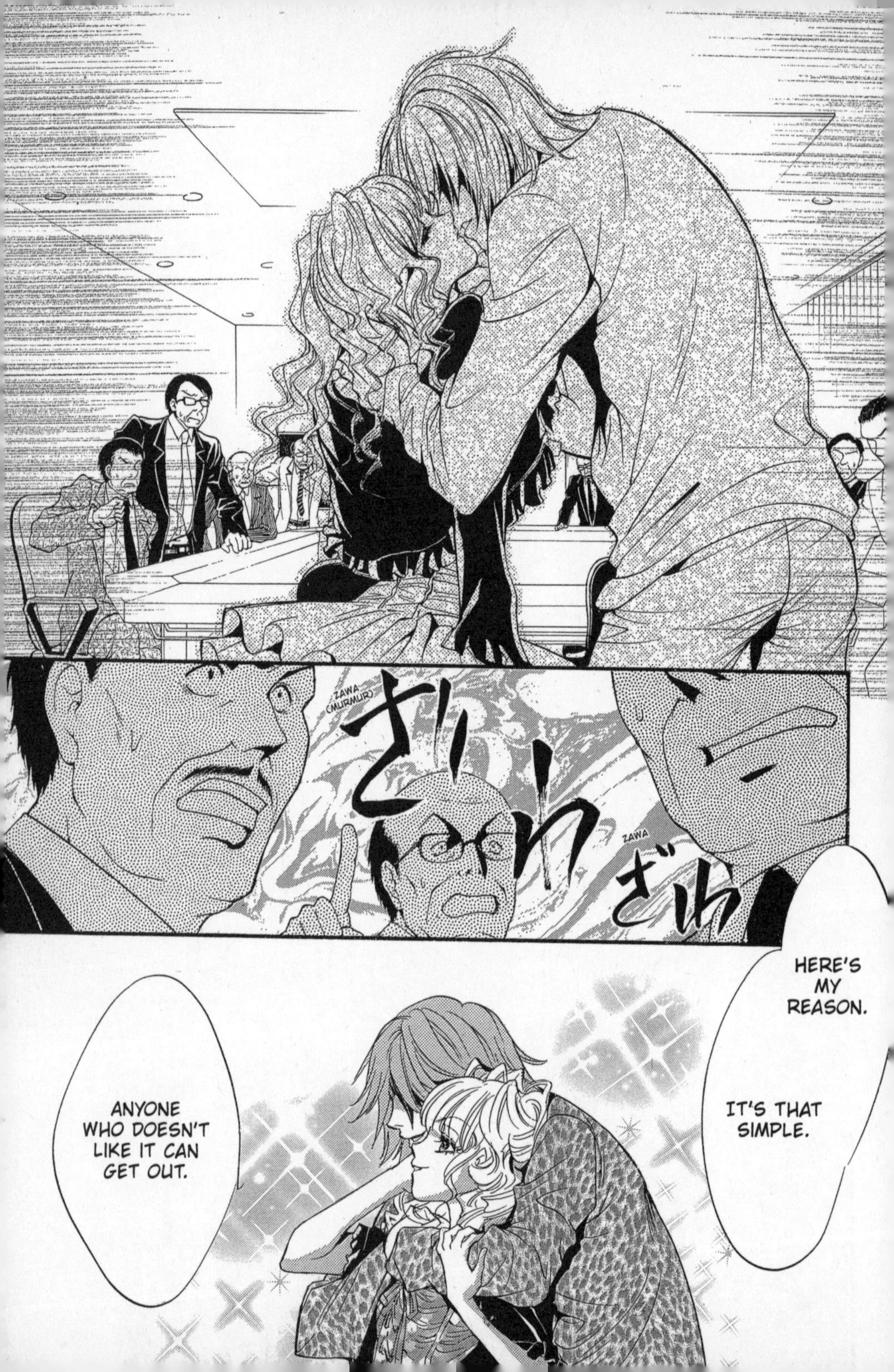
ZAWA (MURMUR)
ざわ
ZAWA
ざわ
HERE'S MY REASON.
IT'S THAT SIMPLE.
ANYONE WHO DOESN'T LIKE IT CAN GET OUT.

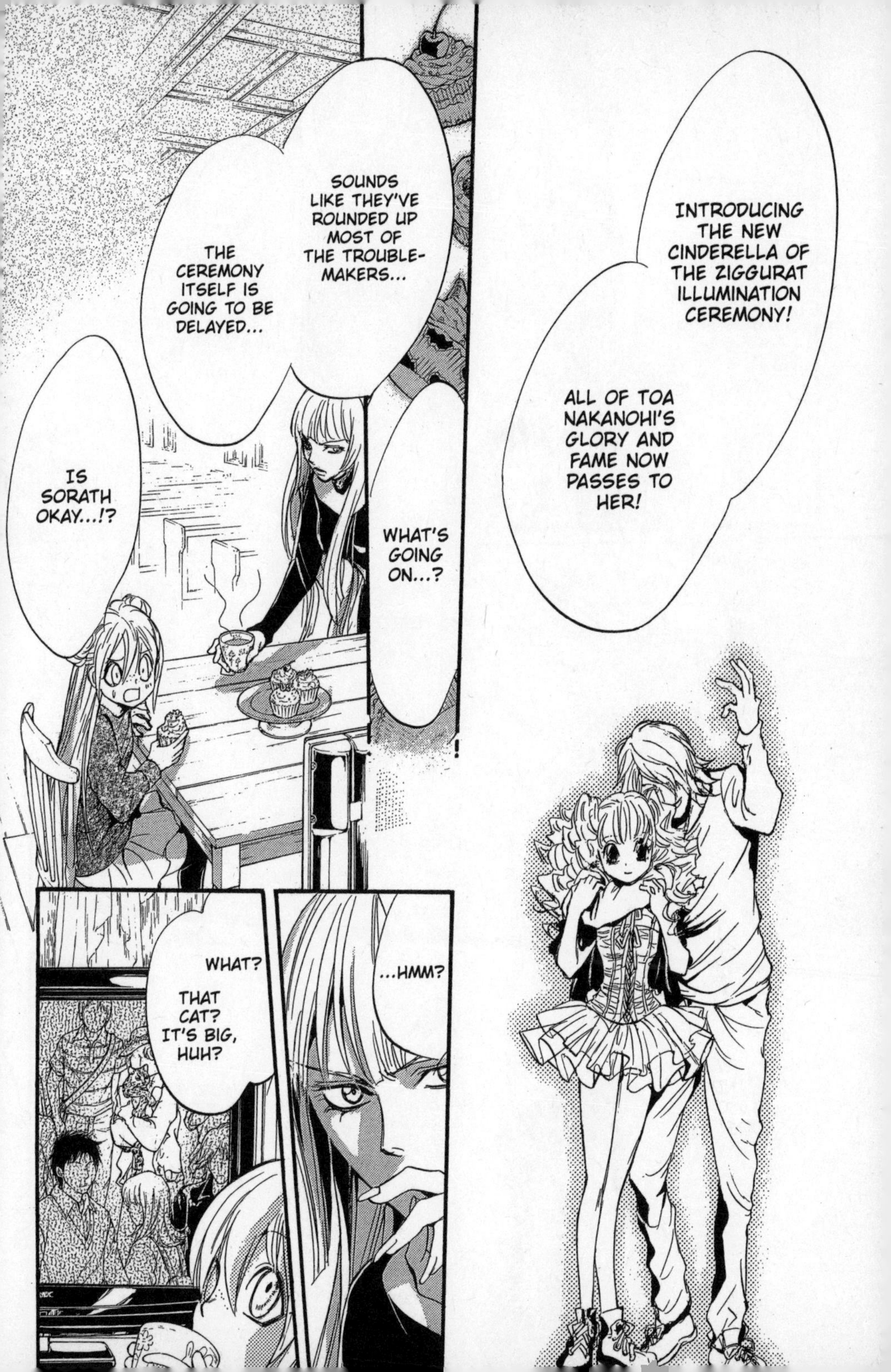
INTRODUCING THE NEW CINDERELLA OF THE ZIGGURAT ILLUMINATION CEREMONY!
ALL OF TOA NAKANOHI'S GLORY AND FAME NOW PASSES TO HER!
SOUNDS LIKE THEY'VE ROUNDED UP MOST OF THE TROUBLE-MAKERS...
THE CEREMONY ITSELF IS GOING TO BE DELAYED...
WHAT'S GOING ON...?
IS SORATH OKAY...!?
...HMM?
WHAT?
THAT CAT? IT'S BIG, HUH?

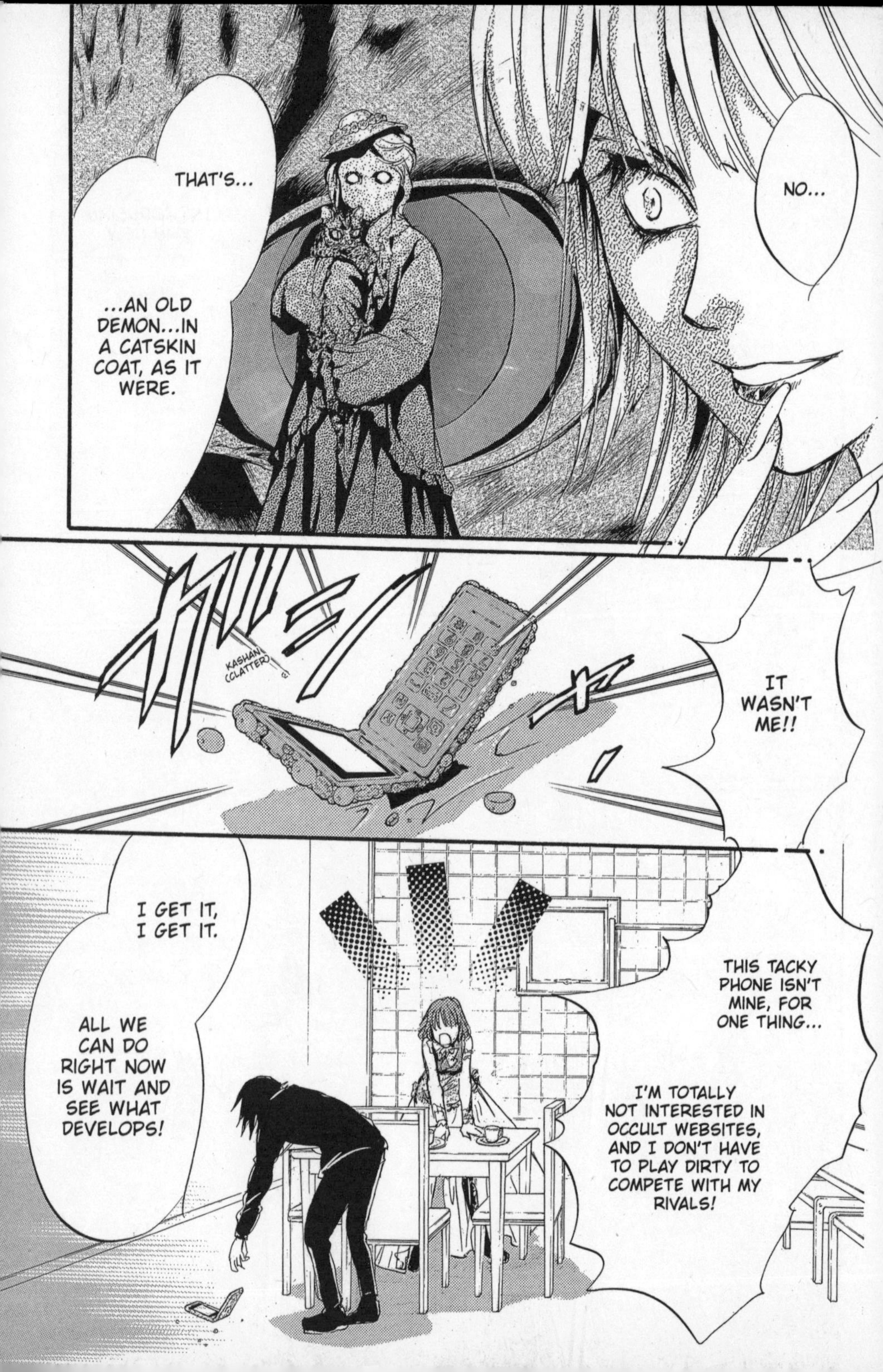
NO...
THAT'S...
...AN OLD DEMON...IN A CATSKIN COAT, AS IT WERE.
IT WASN'T ME!!
KASHAN (CLATTER)
THIS TACKY PHONE ISN'T MINE, FOR ONE THING...
I'M TOTALLY NOT INTERESTED IN OCCULT WEBSITES, AND I DON'T HAVE TO PLAY DIRTY TO COMPETE WITH MY RIVALS!
I GET IT, I GET IT.
ALL WE CAN DO RIGHT NOW IS WAIT AND SEE WHAT DEVELOPS!

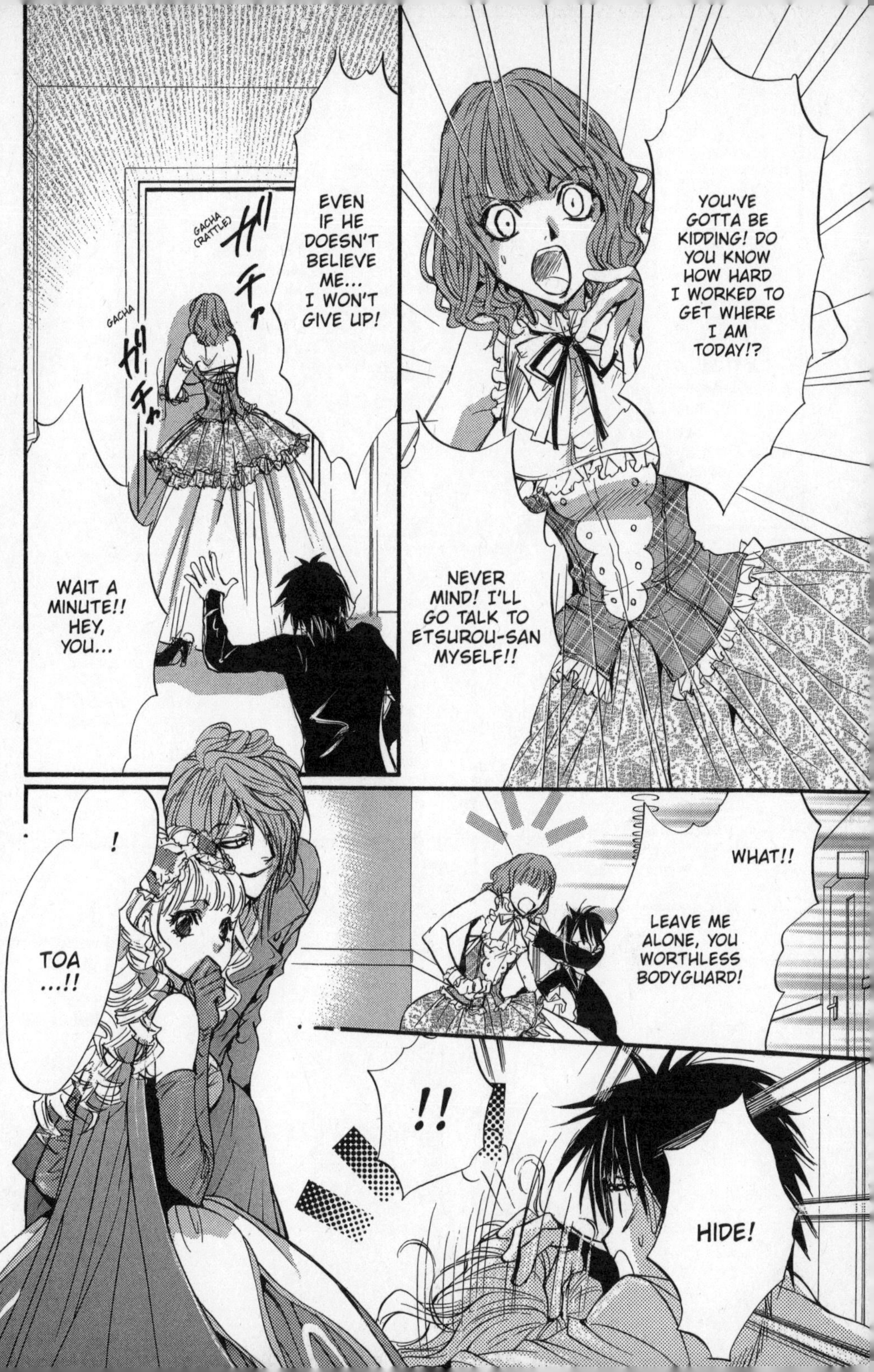
YOU'VE GOTTA BE KIDDING! DO YOU KNOW HOW HARD I WORKED TO GET WHERE I AM TODAY!?
NEVER MIND! I'LL GO TALK TO ETSUROU-SAN MYSELF!!
EVEN IF HE DOESN'T BELIEVE ME... I WON'T GIVE UP!
GACHA (RATTLE)
ガチャ
GACHA
ガチャ
WAIT A MINUTE!! HEY, YOU...
WHAT!!
LEAVE ME ALONE, YOU WORTHLESS BODYGUARD!
HIDE!
!!
!
TOA ...!!

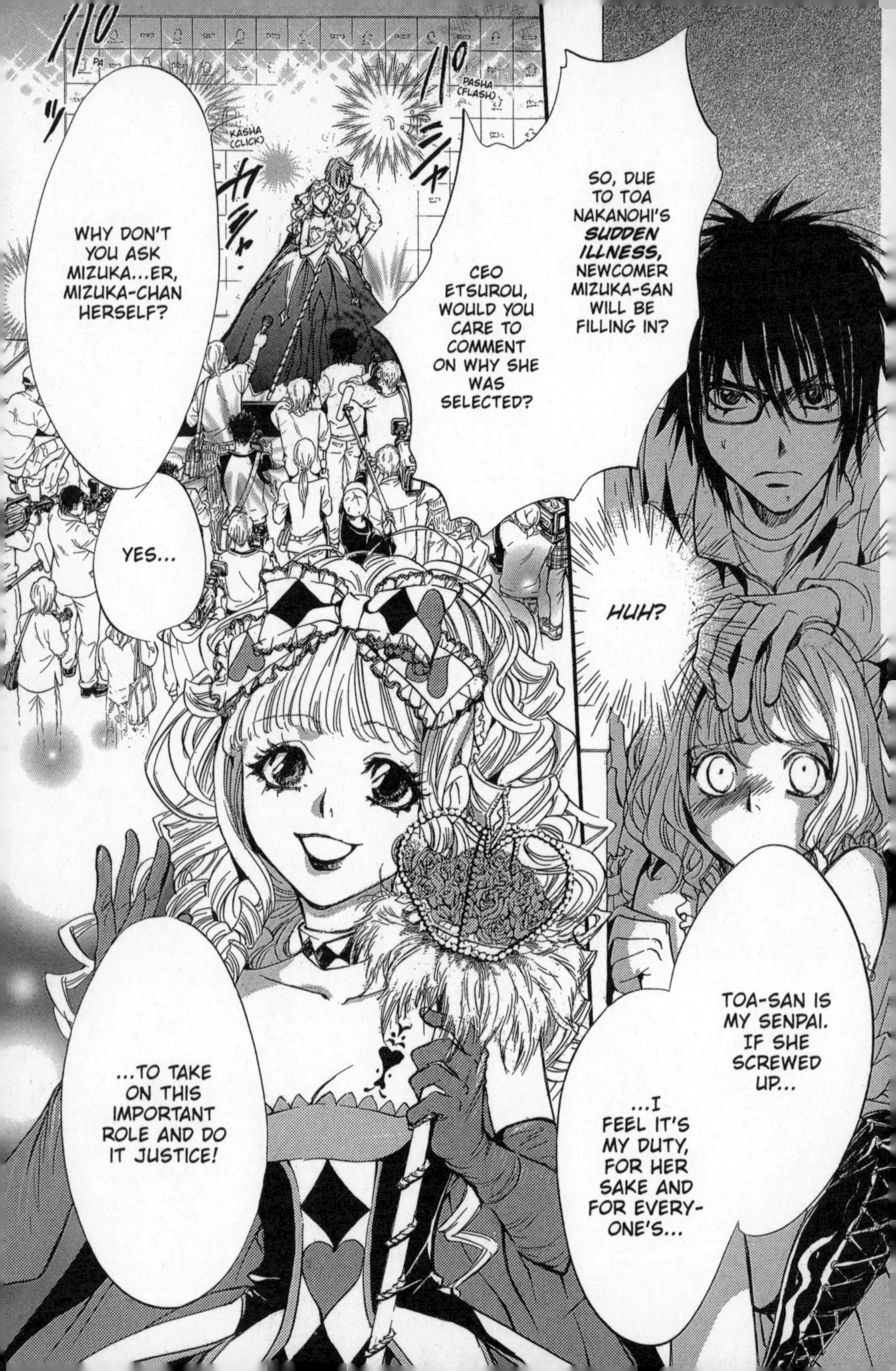
SO, DUE TO TOA NAKANOHI'S ***SUDDEN ILLNESS,*** NEWCOMER MIZUKA-SAN WILL BE FILLING IN?
CEO ETSUROU, WOULD YOU CARE TO COMMENT ON WHY SHE WAS SELECTED?
PASHA (FLASH)
KASHA (CLICK)
PA
WHY DON'T YOU ASK MIZUKA...ER, MIZUKA-CHAN HERSELF?
YES...
HUH?
TOA-SAN IS MY SENPAI. IF SHE SCREWED UP...
...I FEEL IT'S MY DUTY, FOR HER SAKE AND FOR EVERY-ONE'S...
...TO TAKE ON THIS IMPORTANT ROLE AND DO IT JUSTICE!

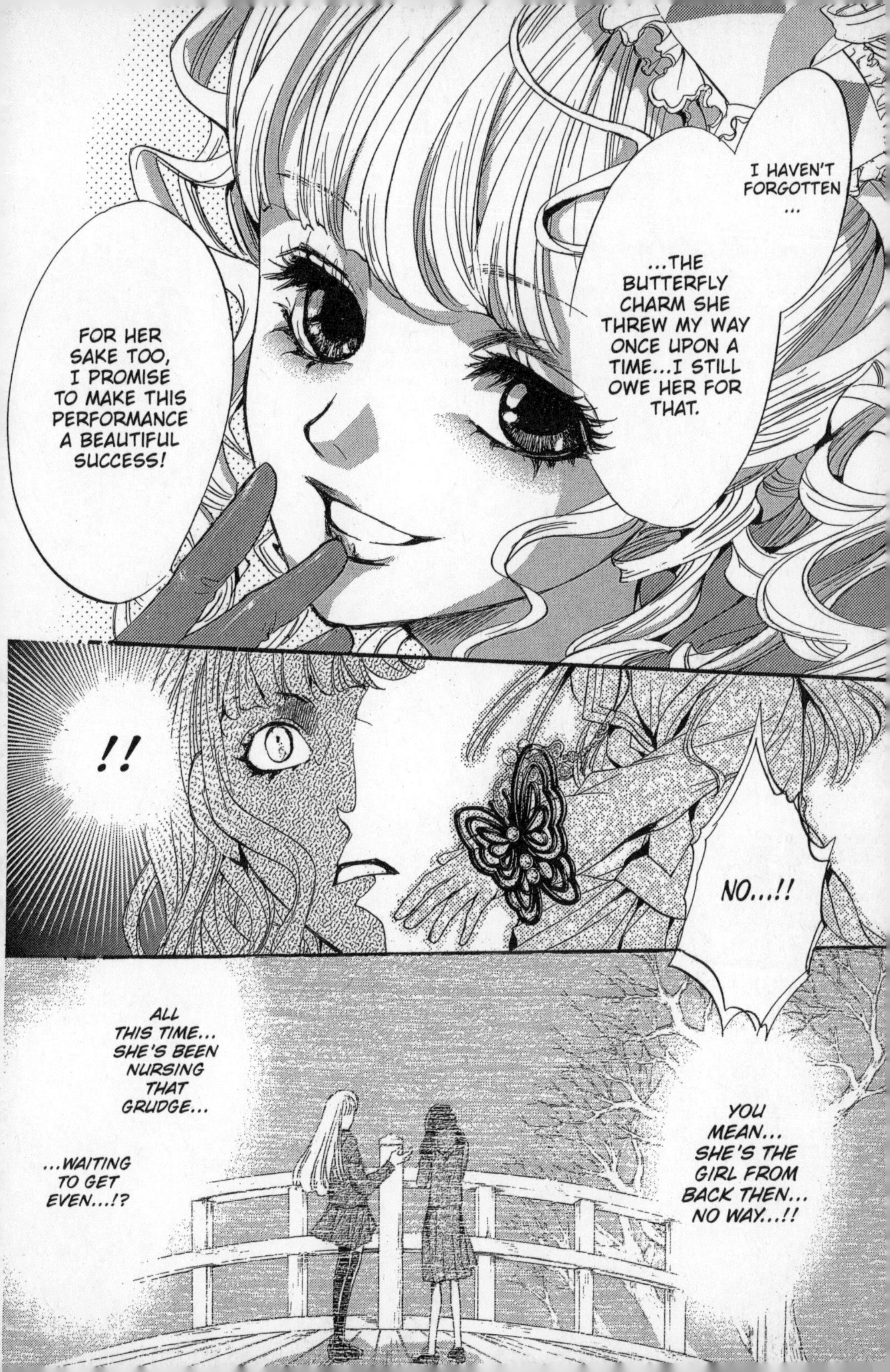

I HAVEN'T FORGOTTEN...
...THE BUTTERFLY CHARM SHE THREW MY WAY ONCE UPON A TIME...I STILL OWE HER FOR THAT.
FOR HER SAKE TOO, I PROMISE TO MAKE THIS PERFORMANCE A BEAUTIFUL SUCCESS!
NO...!!
!!
YOU MEAN... SHE'S THE GIRL FROM BACK THEN... NO WAY...!!
ALL THIS TIME... SHE'S BEEN NURSING THAT GRUDGE...
...WAITING TO GET EVEN...!?

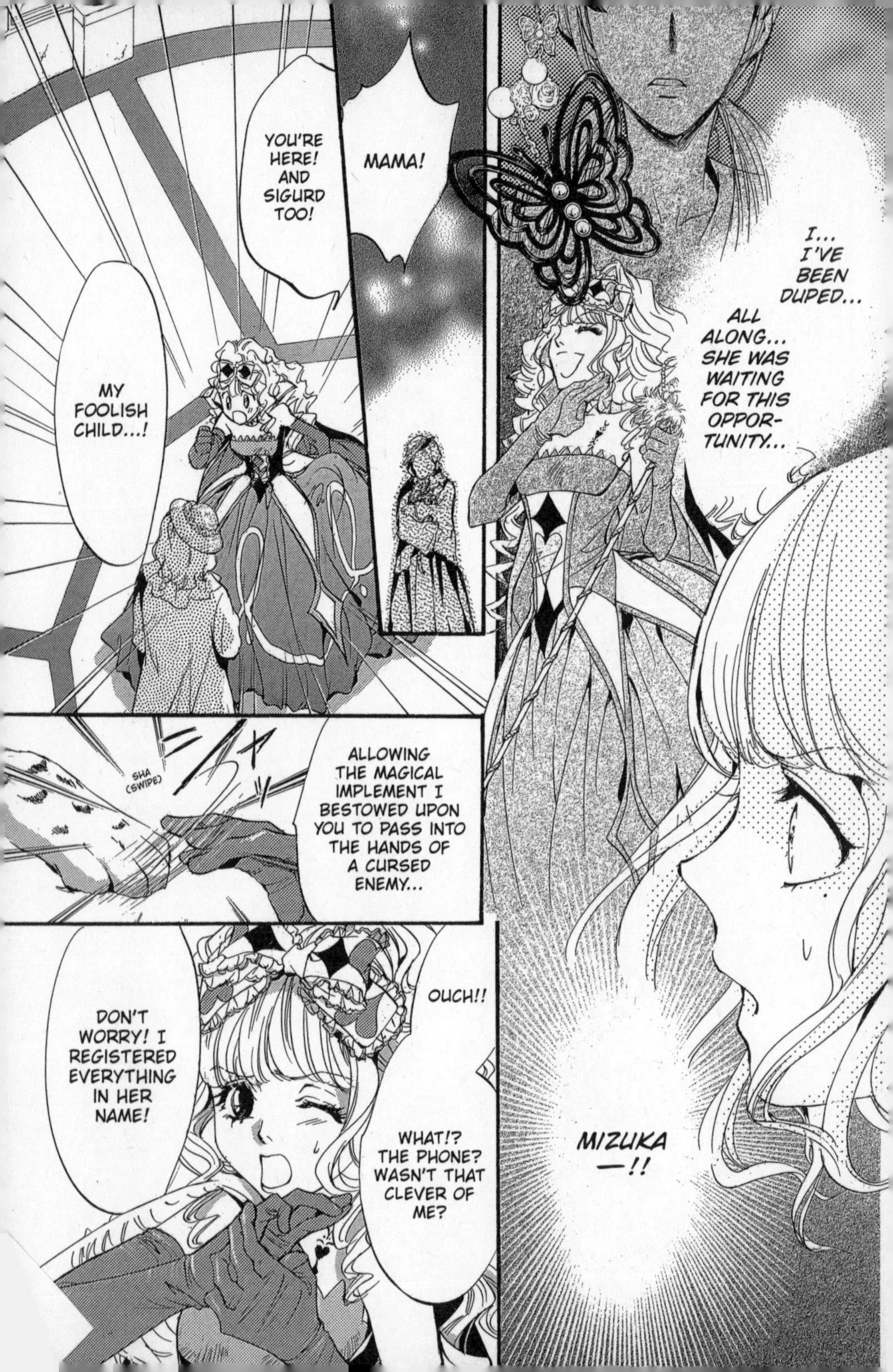

I... I'VE BEEN DUPED...
ALL ALONG... SHE WAS WAITING FOR THIS OPPORTUNITY...
MIZUKA—!!
MAMA!
YOU'RE HERE! AND SIGURD TOO!
MY FOOLISH CHILD...!
ALLOWING THE MAGICAL IMPLEMENT I BESTOWED UPON YOU TO PASS INTO THE HANDS OF A CURSED ENEMY...
SHA (SWIPE)
OUCH!!
WHAT!? THE PHONE? WASN'T THAT CLEVER OF ME?
DON'T WORRY! I REGISTERED EVERYTHING IN HER NAME!

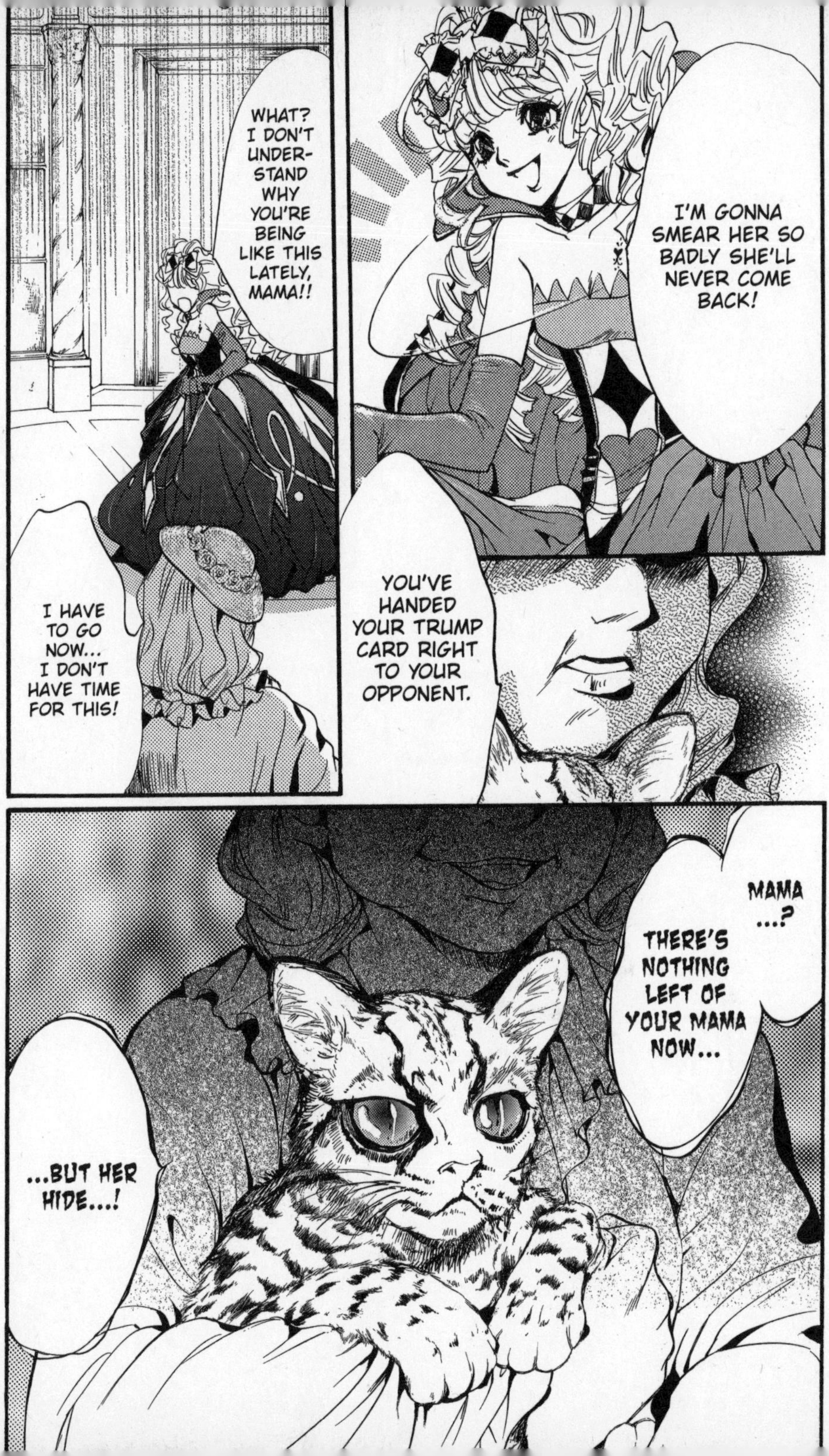
I'M GONNA SMEAR HER SO BADLY SHE'LL NEVER COME BACK!
YOU'VE HANDED YOUR TRUMP CARD RIGHT TO YOUR OPPONENT.
WHAT? I DON'T UNDER-STAND WHY YOU'RE BEING LIKE THIS LATELY, MAMA!!
I HAVE TO GO NOW... I DON'T HAVE TIME FOR THIS!
MAMA ...?
THERE'S NOTHING LEFT OF YOUR MAMA NOW...
...BUT HER HIDE...!

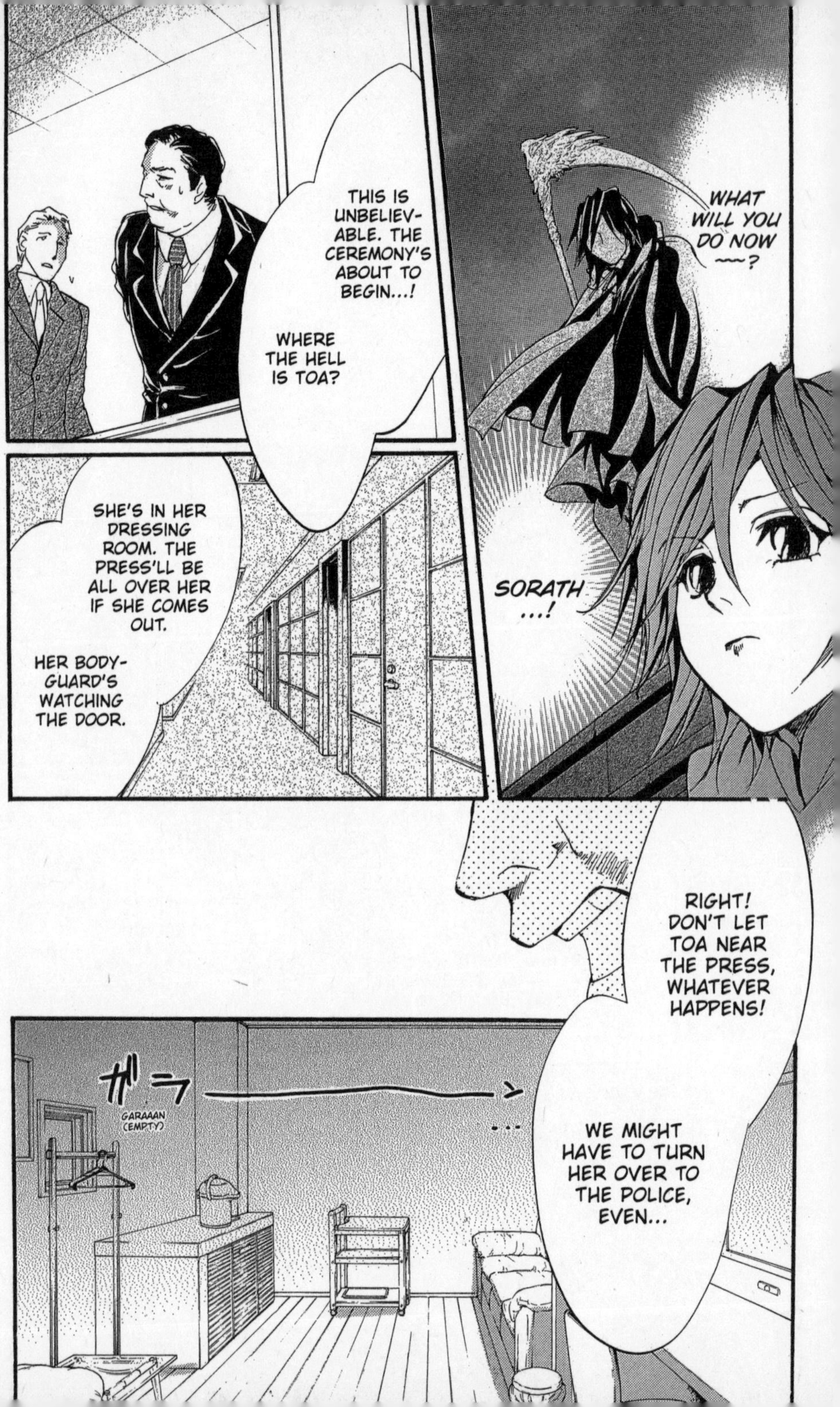
WHAT WILL YOU DO NOW ~~~?
SORATH ...!
THIS IS UNBELIEV-ABLE. THE CEREMONY'S ABOUT TO BEGIN...!
WHERE THE HELL IS TOA?
SHE'S IN HER DRESSING ROOM. THE PRESS'LL BE ALL OVER HER IF SHE COMES OUT.
HER BODY-GUARD'S WATCHING THE DOOR.
RIGHT! DON'T LET TOA NEAR THE PRESS, WHATEVER HAPPENS!
WE MIGHT HAVE TO TURN HER OVER TO THE POLICE, EVEN...
...
ガラ
GARAAAN (EMPTY)

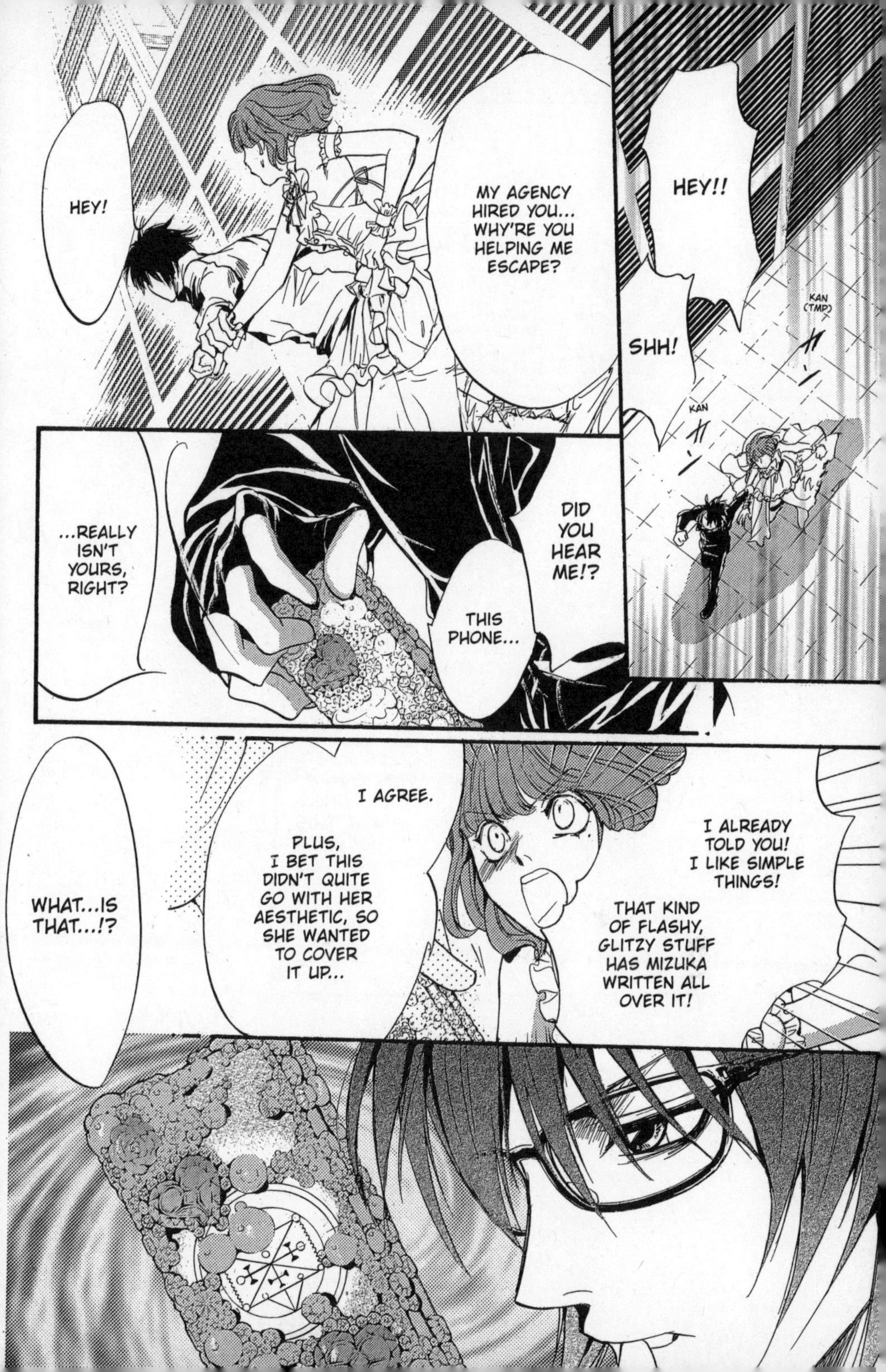
HEY!!
SHH!
KAN (TMP)
KAN
MY AGENCY HIRED YOU... WHY'RE YOU HELPING ME ESCAPE?
HEY!
DID YOU HEAR ME!?
THIS PHONE...
...REALLY ISN'T YOURS, RIGHT?
I ALREADY TOLD YOU! I LIKE SIMPLE THINGS!
THAT KIND OF FLASHY, GLITZY STUFF HAS MIZUKA WRITTEN ALL OVER IT!
I AGREE.
PLUS, I BET THIS DIDN'T QUITE GO WITH HER AESTHETIC, SO SHE WANTED TO COVER IT UP...
WHAT...IS THAT...!?

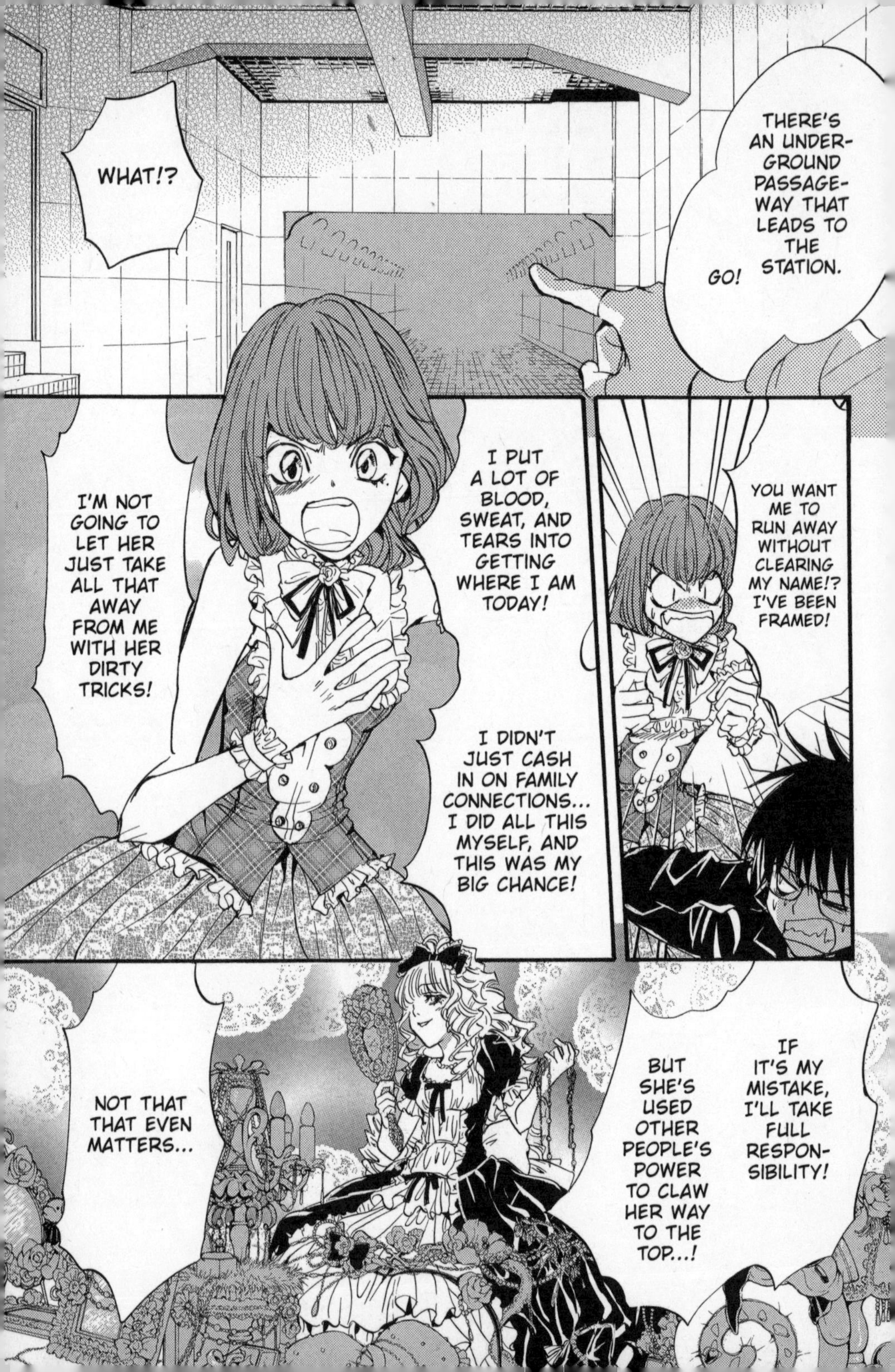
THERE'S AN UNDER-GROUND PASSAGE-WAY THAT LEADS TO THE STATION.
GO!
WHAT!?
YOU WANT ME TO RUN AWAY WITHOUT CLEARING MY NAME!? I'VE BEEN FRAMED!
I PUT A LOT OF BLOOD, SWEAT, AND TEARS INTO GETTING WHERE I AM TODAY!
I DIDN'T JUST CASH IN ON FAMILY CONNECTIONS... I DID ALL THIS MYSELF, AND THIS WAS MY BIG CHANCE!
I'M NOT GOING TO LET HER JUST TAKE ALL THAT AWAY FROM ME WITH HER DIRTY TRICKS!
IF IT'S MY MISTAKE, I'LL TAKE FULL RESPON-SIBILITY!
BUT SHE'S USED OTHER PEOPLE'S POWER TO CLAW HER WAY TO THE TOP...!
NOT THAT THAT EVEN MATTERS...

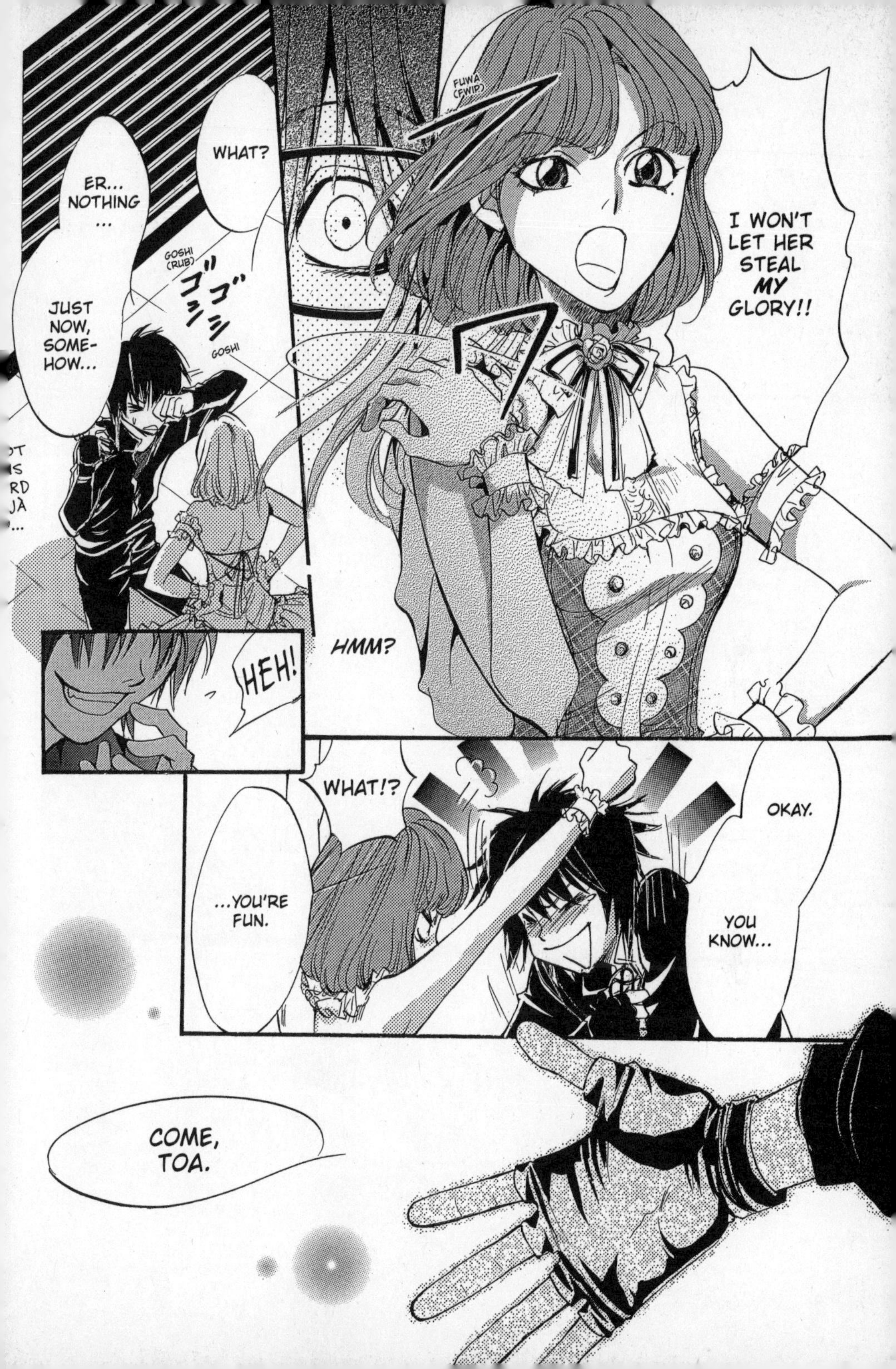
FUWA (FWIP)
I WON'T LET HER STEAL MY GLORY!!
WHAT?
ER... NOTHING...
GOSHI (RUB) GOSHI
JUST NOW, SOME-HOW...
HMM?
HEH!
OKAY.
YOU KNOW...
WHAT!?
...YOU'RE FUN.
COME, TOA.

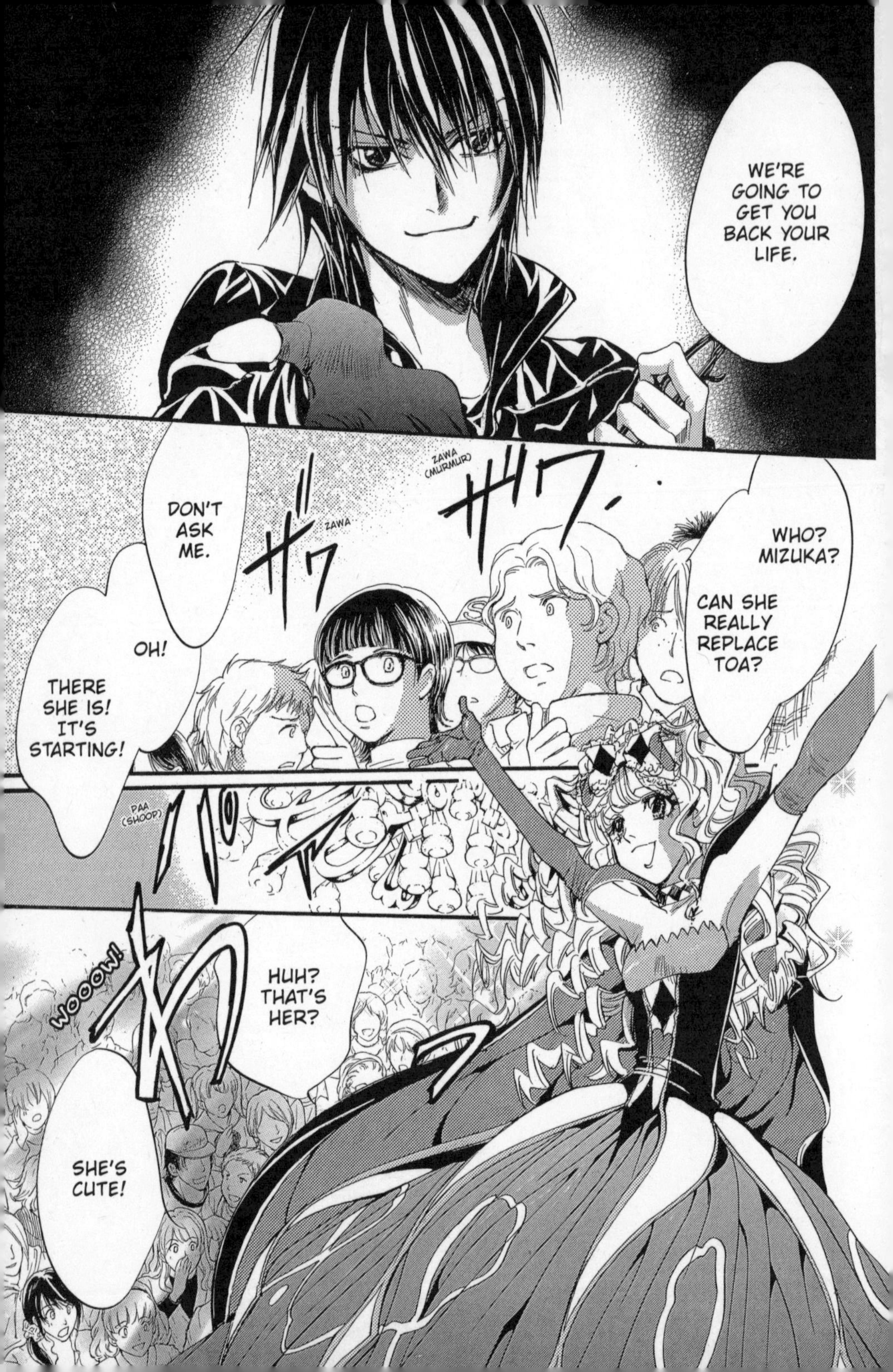
WE'RE GOING TO GET YOU BACK YOUR LIFE.
WHO? MIZUKA?
CAN SHE REALLY REPLACE TOA?
ZAWA (MURMUR)
ZAWA
DON'T ASK ME.
OH!
THERE SHE IS! IT'S STARTING!
PAA (SHOOP)
HUH? THAT'S HER?
WOOOOW!
SHE'S CUTE!

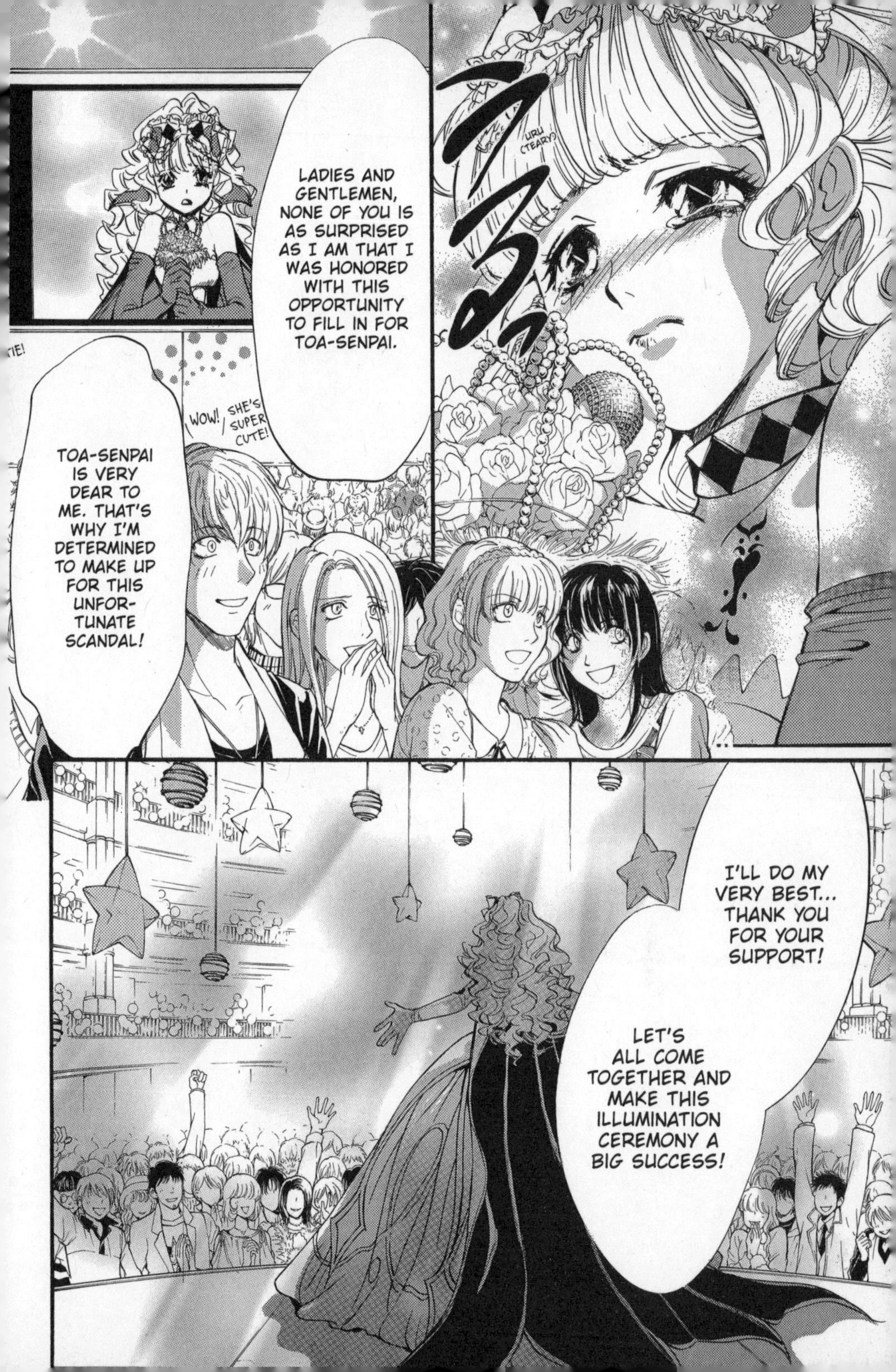
URU (TEARY)
LADIES AND GENTLEMEN, NONE OF YOU IS AS SURPRISED AS I AM THAT I WAS HONORED WITH THIS OPPORTUNITY TO FILL IN FOR TOA-SENPAI.
WOW!
SHE'S SUPER CUTE!
TOA-SENPAI IS VERY DEAR TO ME. THAT'S WHY I'M DETERMINED TO MAKE UP FOR THIS UNFOR-TUNATE SCANDAL!
I'LL DO MY VERY BEST... THANK YOU FOR YOUR SUPPORT!
LET'S ALL COME TOGETHER AND MAKE THIS ILLUMINATION CEREMONY A BIG SUCCESS!

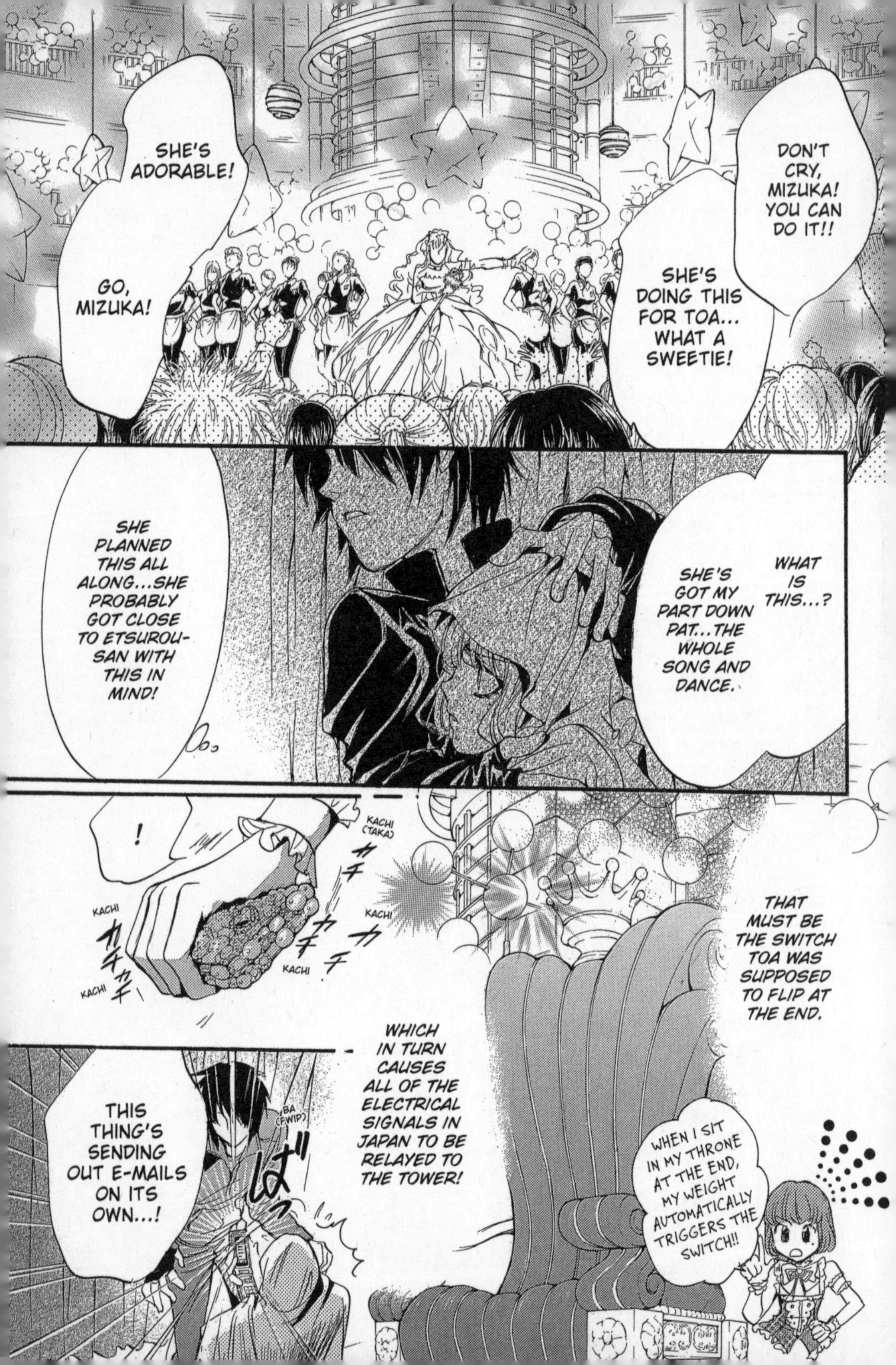

DON'T CRY, MIZUKA! YOU CAN DO IT!!
SHE'S DOING THIS FOR TOA... WHAT A SWEETIE!
SHE'S ADORABLE!
GO, MIZUKA!
WHAT IS THIS...?
SHE'S GOT MY PART DOWN PAT...THE WHOLE SONG AND DANCE.
SHE PLANNED THIS ALL ALONG...SHE PROBABLY GOT CLOSE TO ETSUROU-SAN WITH THIS IN MIND!
THAT MUST BE THE SWITCH TOA WAS SUPPOSED TO FLIP AT THE END.
WHEN I SIT IN MY THRONE AT THE END, MY WEIGHT AUTOMATICALLY TRIGGERS THE SWITCH!!
WHICH IN TURN CAUSES ALL OF THE ELECTRICAL SIGNALS IN JAPAN TO BE RELAYED TO THE TOWER!
KACHI (TAKA)
KACHI
KACHI
KACHI
KACHI
!
BA (FWIP)
THIS THING'S SENDING OUT E-MAILS ON ITS OWN...!

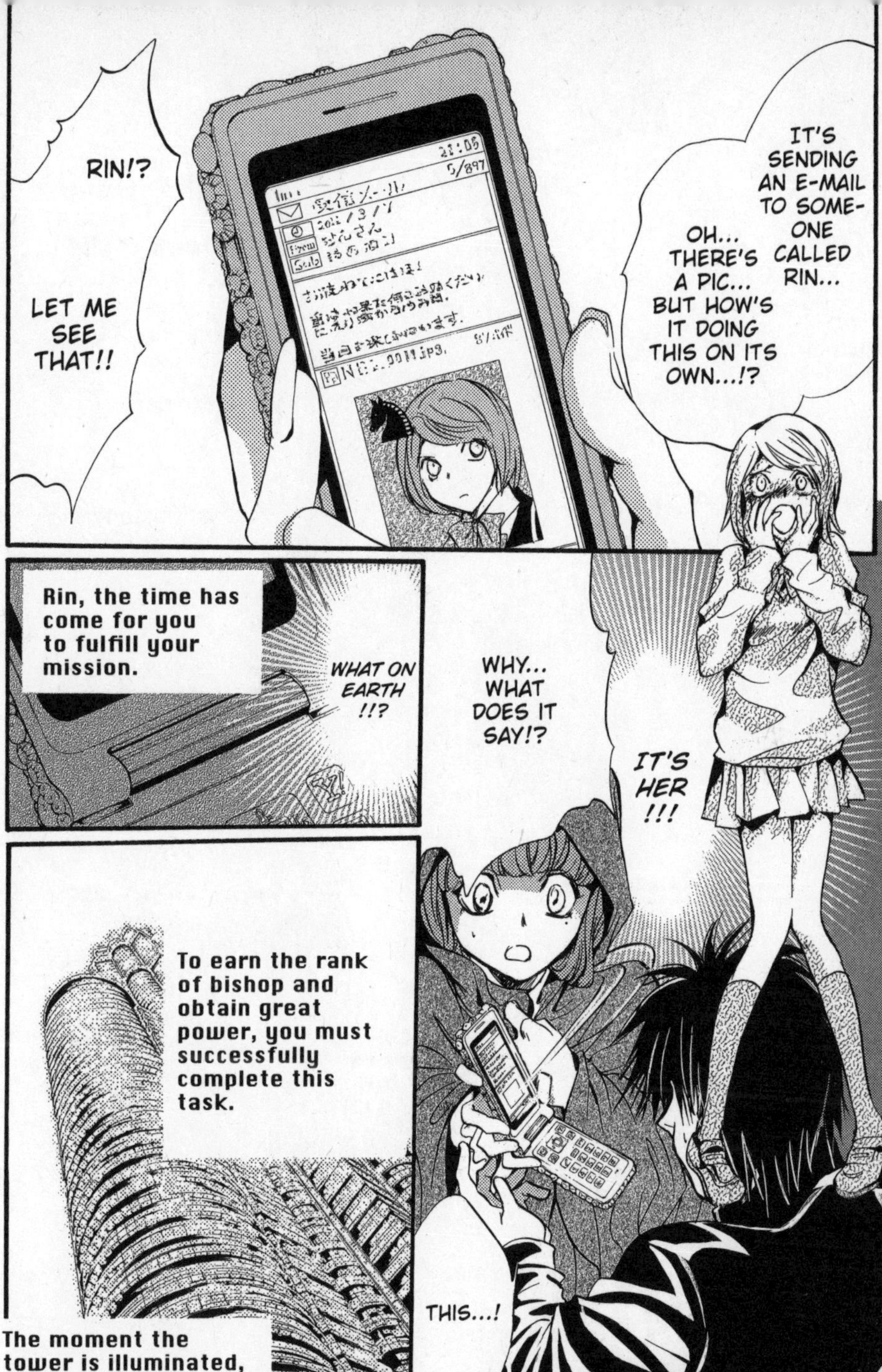
IT'S SENDING AN E-MAIL TO SOME-ONE CALLED RIN...
OH... THERE'S A PIC... BUT HOW'S IT DOING THIS ON ITS OWN...!?
RIN!?
LET ME SEE THAT!!
WHY... WHAT DOES IT SAY!?
IT'S HER!!!
THIS...!
Rin, the time has come for you to fulfill your mission.
WHAT ON EARTH!!?
To earn the rank of bishop and obtain great power, you must successfully complete this task.
The moment the tower is illuminated, the blood of the first living sacrifice...

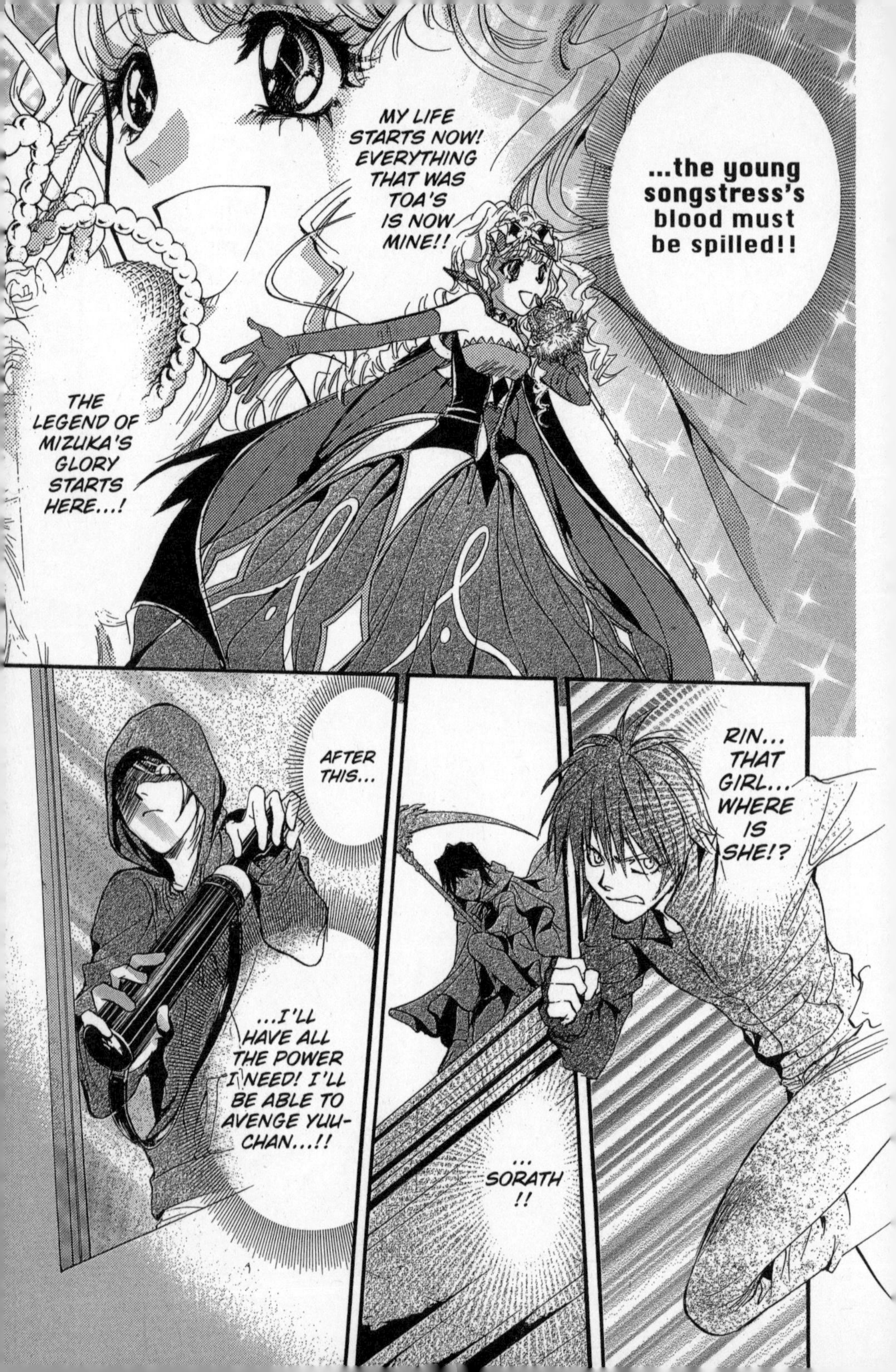
...the young songstress's blood must be spilled!!
MY LIFE STARTS NOW! EVERYTHING THAT WAS TOA'S IS NOW MINE!!
THE LEGEND OF MIZUKA'S GLORY STARTS HERE...!
RIN... THAT GIRL... WHERE IS SHE!?
...SORATH!!
AFTER THIS...
...I'LL HAVE ALL THE POWER I NEED! I'LL BE ABLE TO AVENGE YUU-CHAN...!!

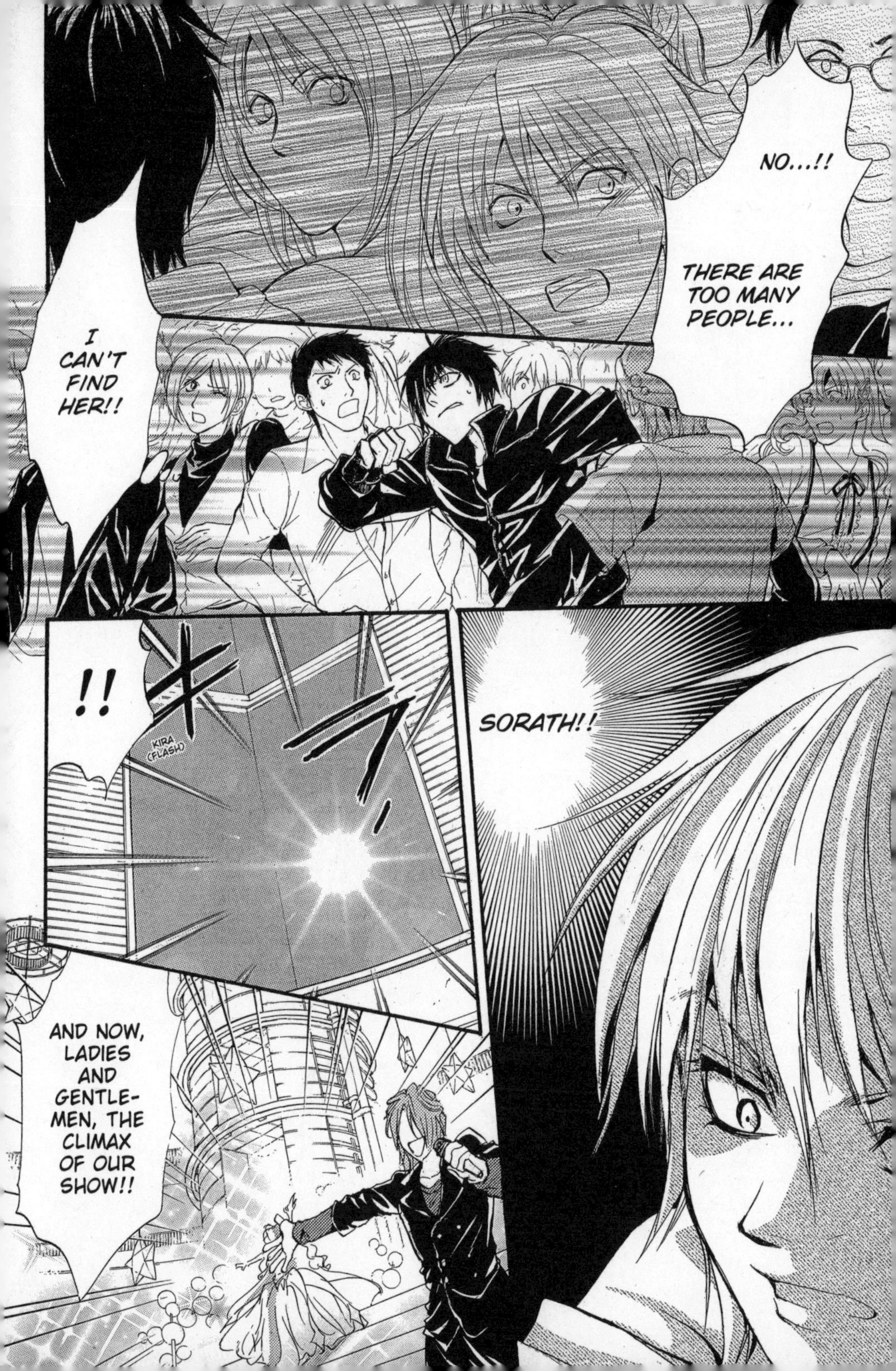
NO...!!
THERE ARE TOO MANY PEOPLE...
I CAN'T FIND HER!!
SORATH!!
!!
KIRA (FLASH)
AND NOW, LADIES AND GENTLE-MEN, THE CLIMAX OF OUR SHOW!!

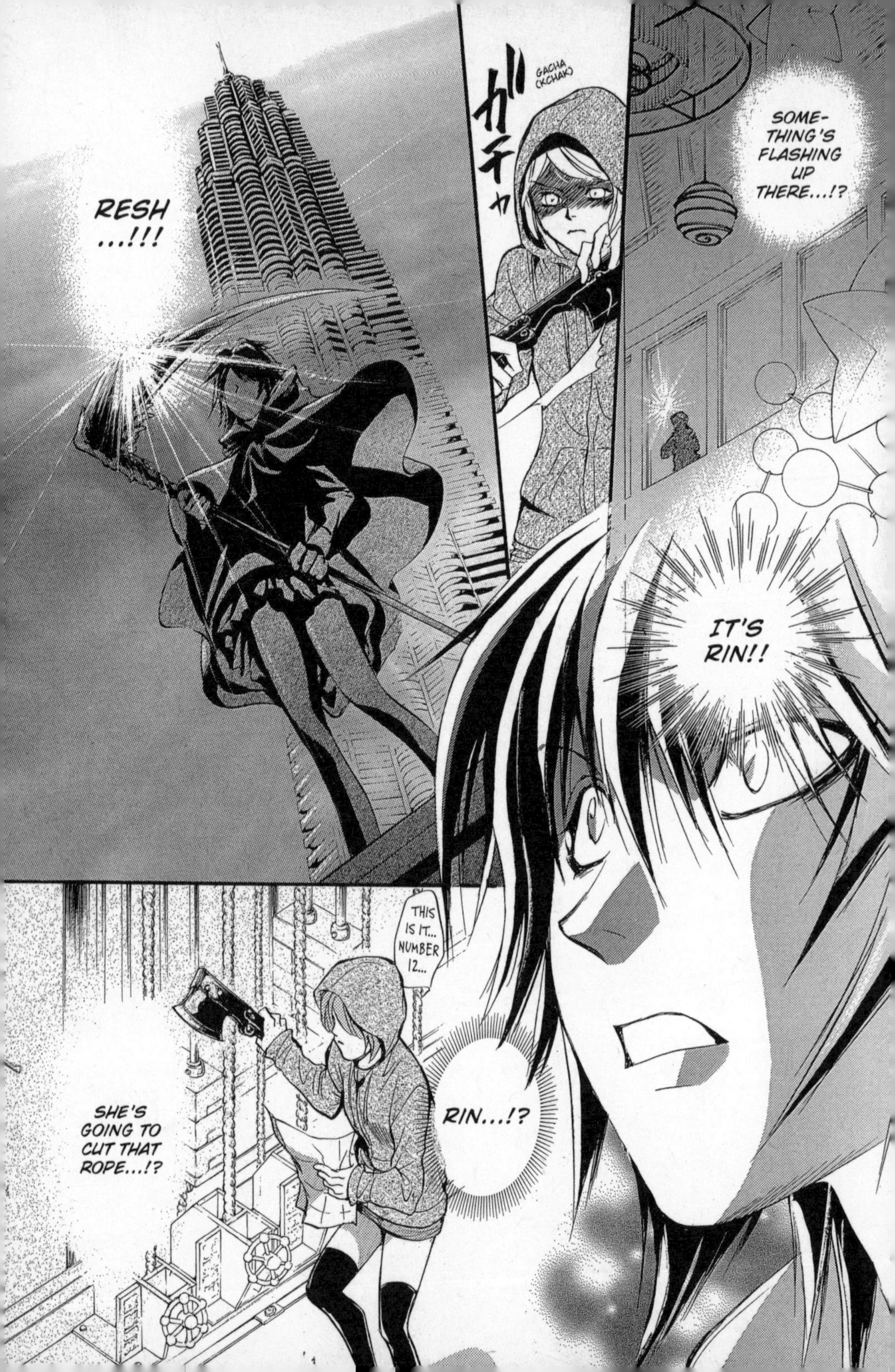
SOME-THING'S FLASHING UP THERE...!?
IT'S RIN!!
ガチャ
GACHA (KCHAK)
RESH ...!!!
RIN...!?
THIS IS IT... NUMBER 12...
SHE'S GOING TO CUT THAT ROPE...!?

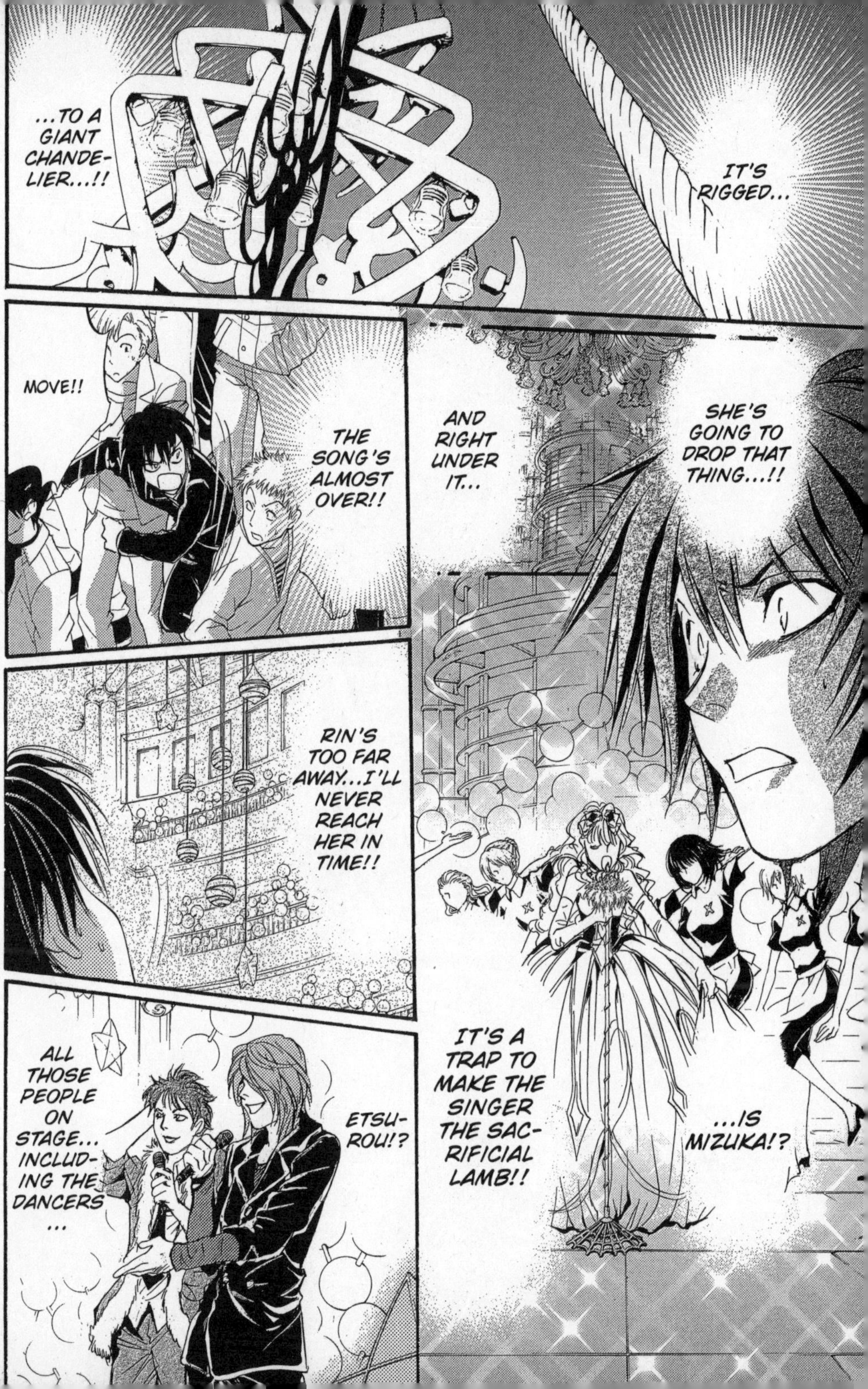
IT'S RIGGED...
...TO A GIANT CHANDELIER...!!
SHE'S GOING TO DROP THAT THING...!!
AND RIGHT UNDER IT...
...IS MIZUKA!?
IT'S A TRAP TO MAKE THE SINGER THE SACRIFICIAL LAMB!!
THE SONG'S ALMOST OVER!!
MOVE!!
RIN'S TOO FAR AWAY...I'LL NEVER REACH HER IN TIME!!
ETSUROU!?
ALL THOSE PEOPLE ON STAGE... INCLUDING THE DANCERS...

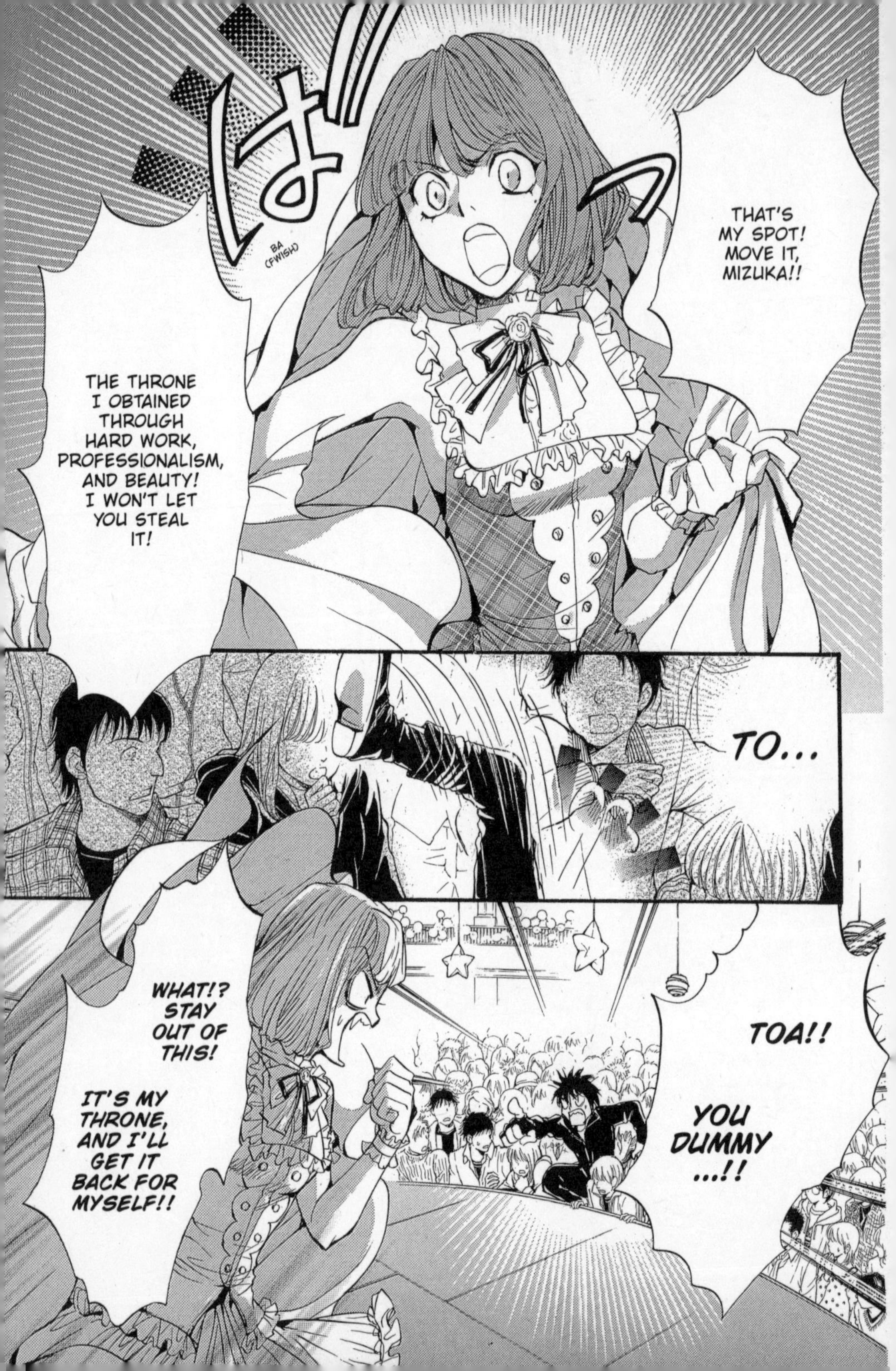
THAT'S MY SPOT! MOVE IT, MIZUKA!!
は
BA (FWISH)
THE THRONE I OBTAINED THROUGH HARD WORK, PROFESSIONALISM, AND BEAUTY! I WON'T LET YOU STEAL IT!
TO...
TOA!!
YOU DUMMY ...!!
WHAT!? STAY OUT OF THIS!
IT'S MY THRONE, AND I'LL GET IT BACK FOR MYSELF!!

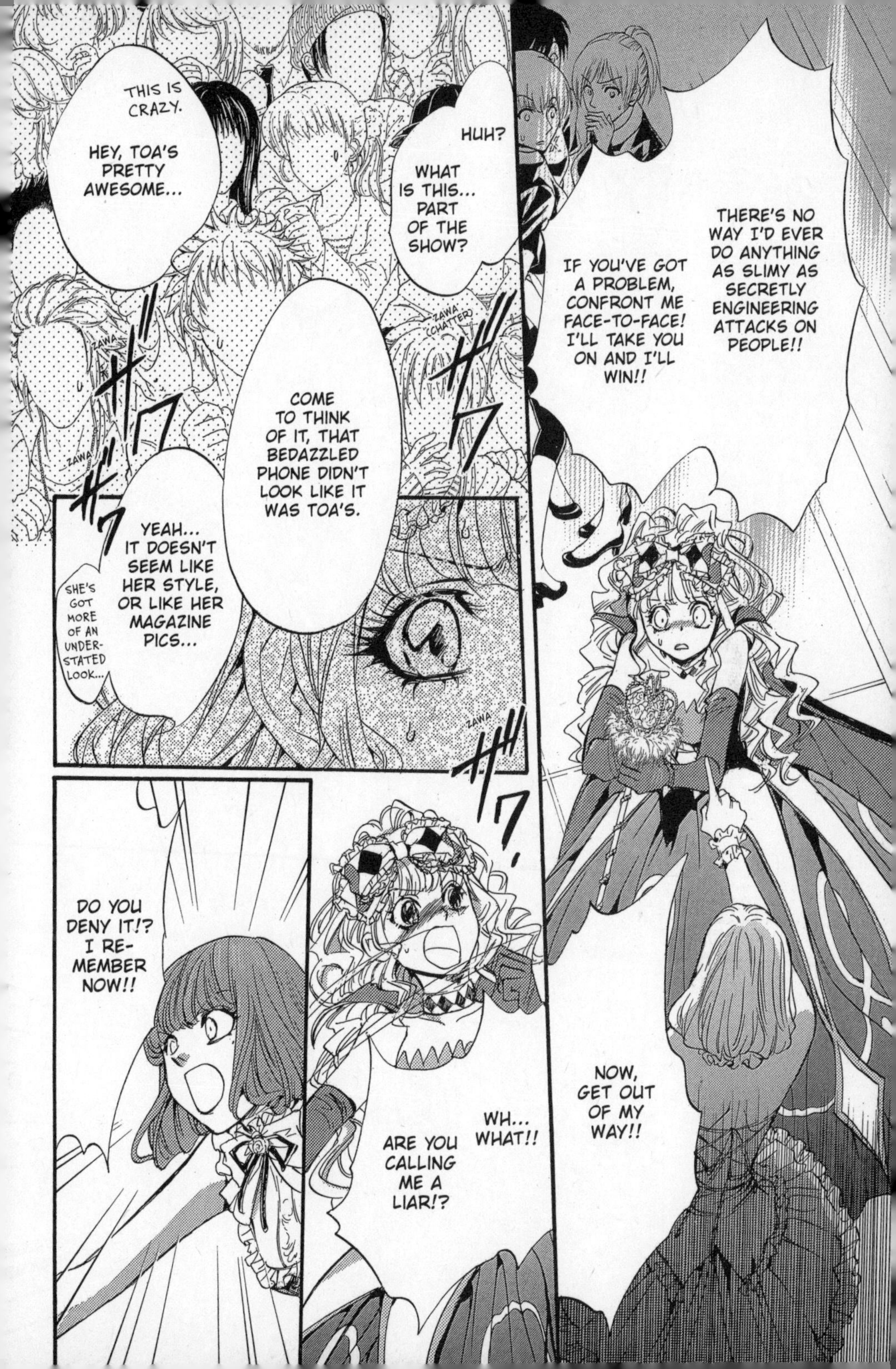

THERE'S NO WAY I'D EVER DO ANYTHING AS SLIMY AS SECRETLY ENGINEERING ATTACKS ON PEOPLE!!
IF YOU'VE GOT A PROBLEM, CONFRONT ME FACE-TO-FACE! I'LL TAKE YOU ON AND I'LL WIN!!
NOW, GET OUT OF MY WAY!!
HUH?
WHAT IS THIS... PART OF THE SHOW?
THIS IS CRAZY.
HEY, TOA'S PRETTY AWESOME...
ZAWA (CHATTER)
ZAWA
ZAWA
COME TO THINK OF IT, THAT BEDAZZLED PHONE DIDN'T LOOK LIKE IT WAS TOA'S.
YEAH... IT DOESN'T SEEM LIKE HER STYLE, OR LIKE HER MAGAZINE PICS...
SHE'S GOT MORE OF AN UNDER-STATED LOOK...
ZAWA
WH... WHAT!!
ARE YOU CALLING ME A LIAR!?
DO YOU DENY IT!? I RE-MEMBER NOW!!

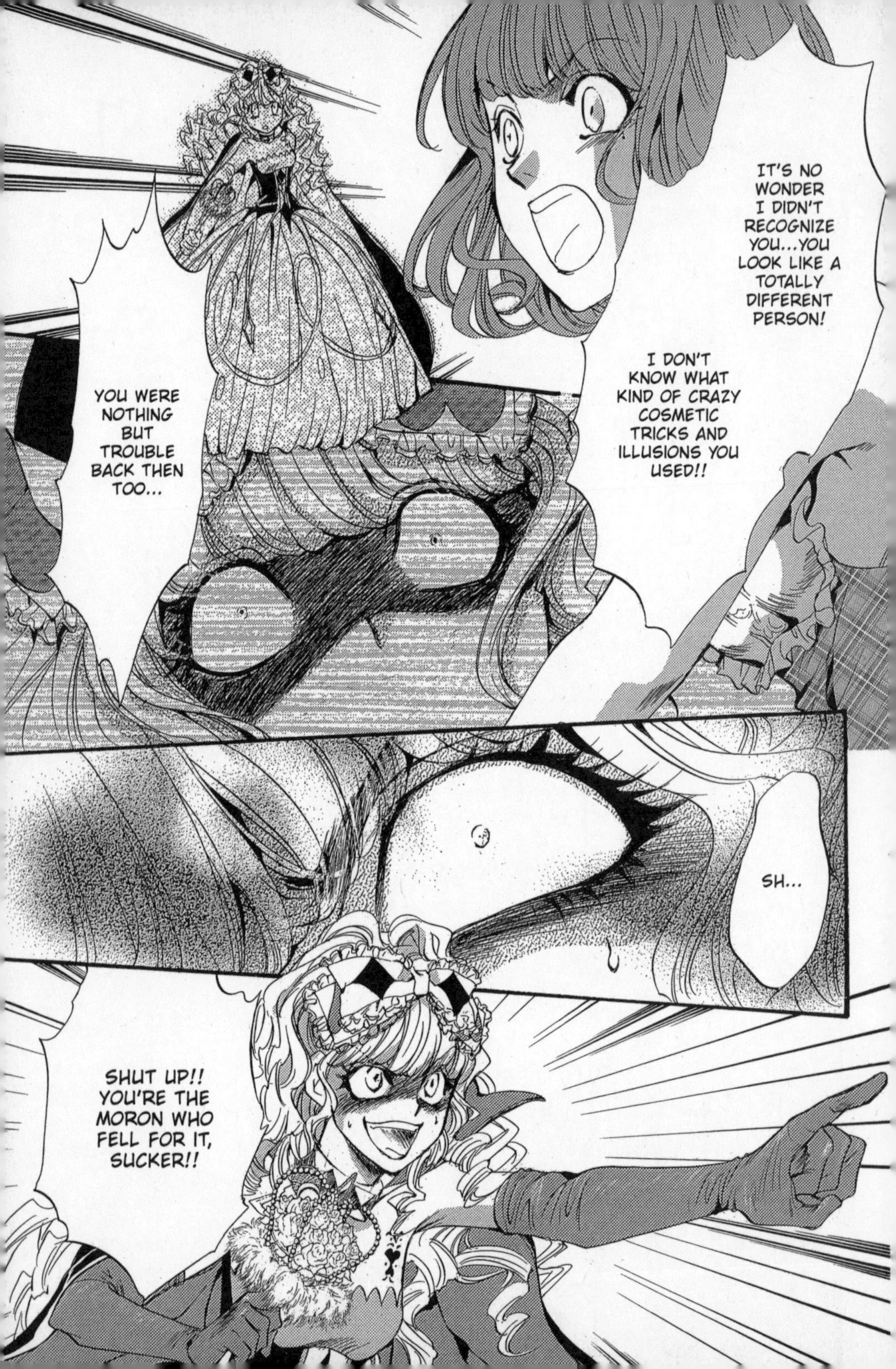
IT'S NO WONDER I DIDN'T RECOGNIZE YOU...YOU LOOK LIKE A TOTALLY DIFFERENT PERSON!
I DON'T KNOW WHAT KIND OF CRAZY COSMETIC TRICKS AND ILLUSIONS YOU USED!!
YOU WERE NOTHING BUT TROUBLE BACK THEN TOO...
SH...
SHUT UP!! YOU'RE THE MORON WHO FELL FOR IT, SUCKER!!

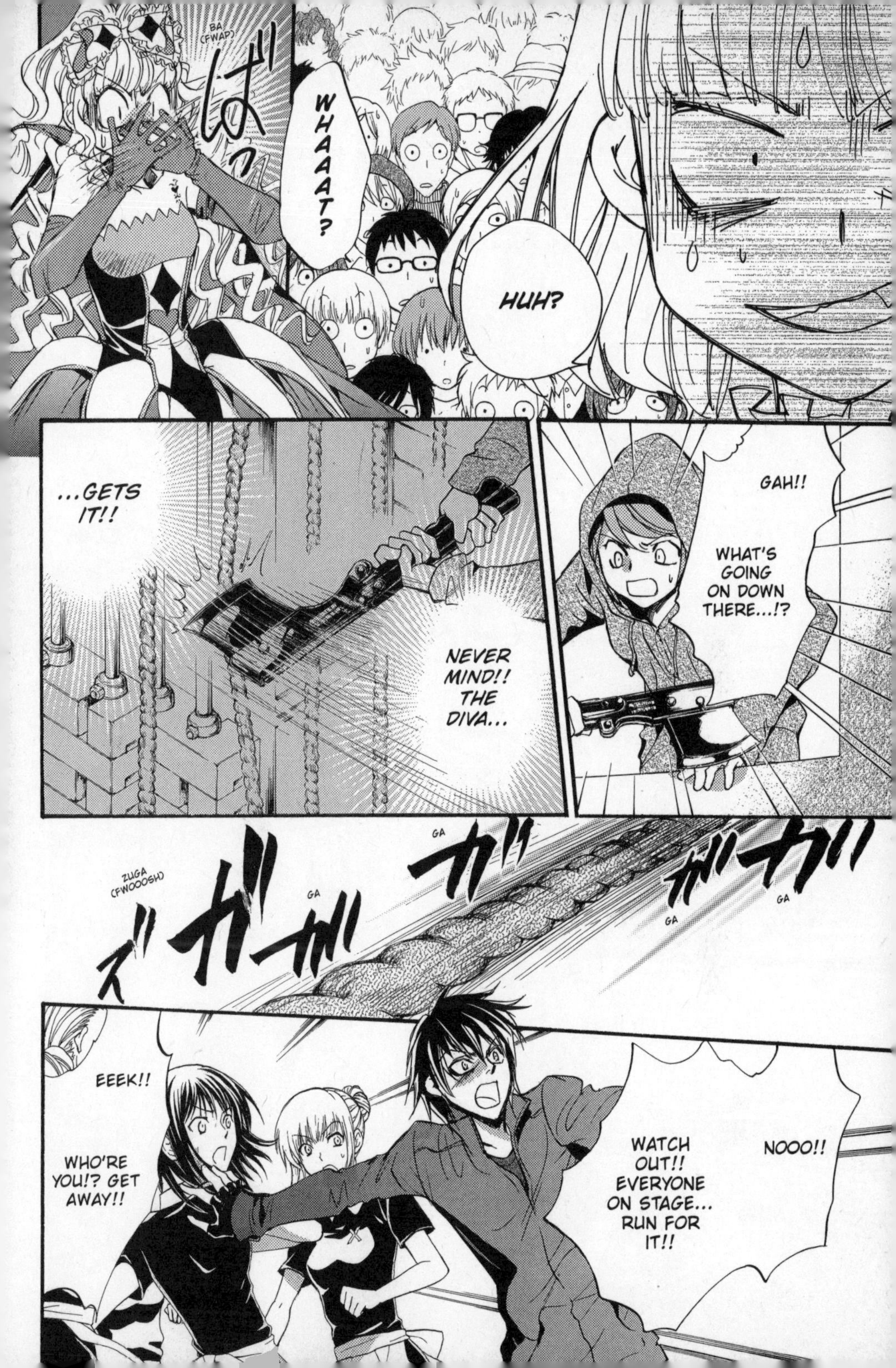
HUH?
WHAAAAT?
BA (FWAP)
GAH!!
WHAT'S GOING ON DOWN THERE...!?
NEVER MIND!! THE DIVA...
...GETS IT!!
GA
GA
GA
GA
ZUGA (FWOOOSH)
NOOO!!
WATCH OUT!! EVERYONE ON STAGE... RUN FOR IT!!
EEEK!!
WHO'RE YOU!? GET AWAY!!

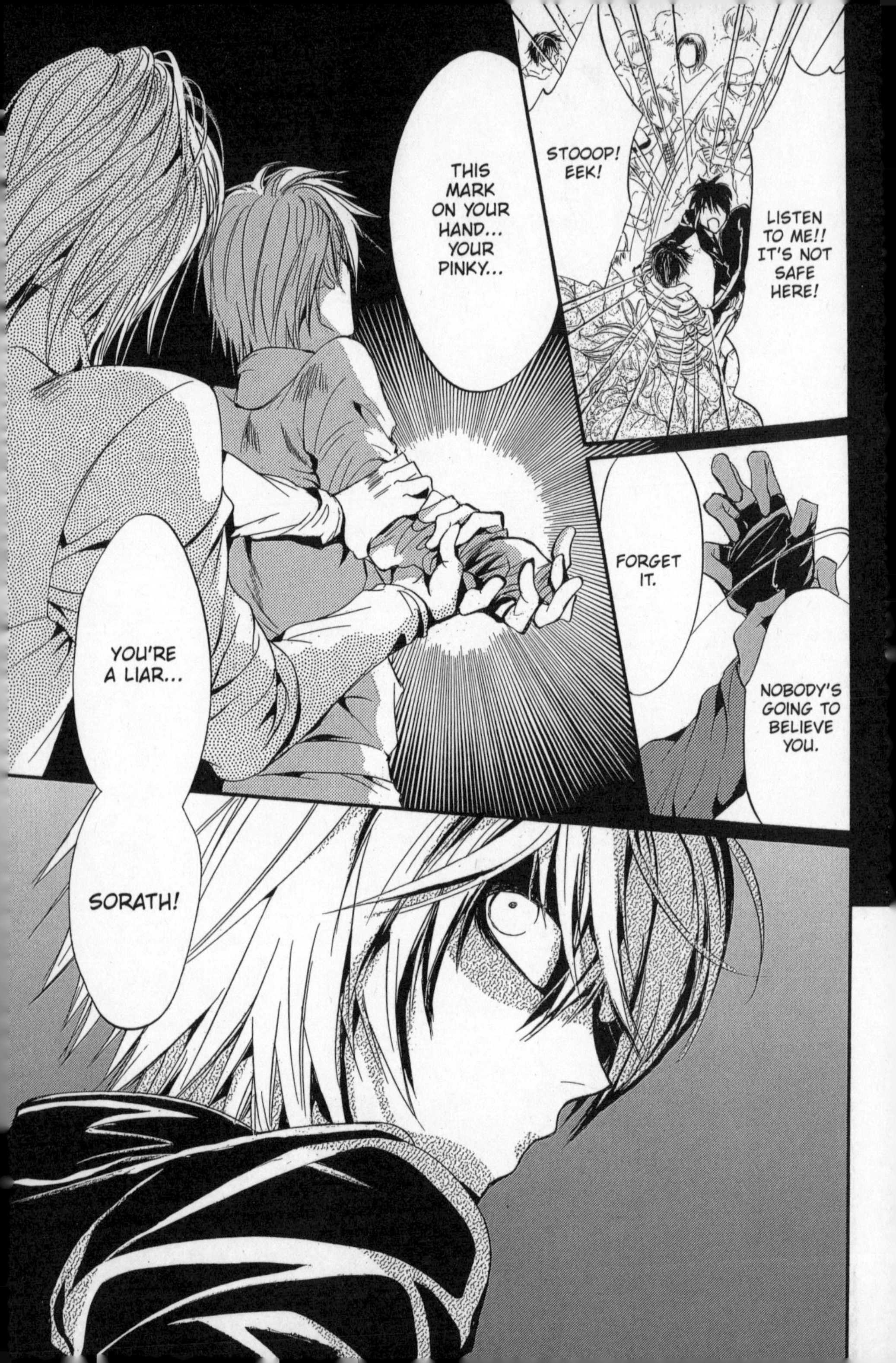

STOOOP! EEK!
LISTEN TO ME!! IT'S NOT SAFE HERE!
FORGET IT.
NOBODY'S GOING TO BELIEVE YOU.
THIS MARK ON YOUR HAND... YOUR PINKY...
YOU'RE A LIAR...
SORATH!

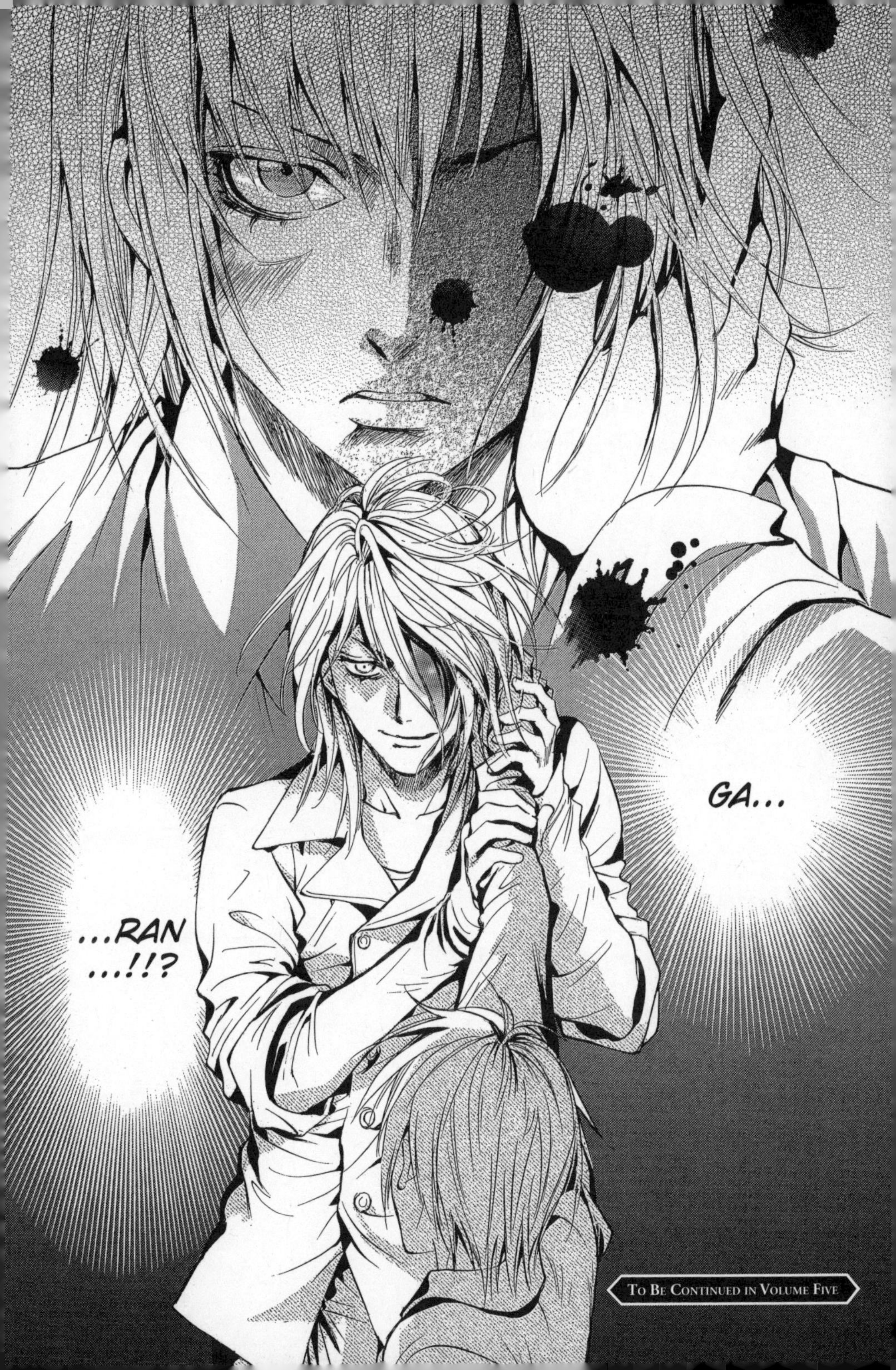
GA...
...RAN ...!!?
To Be Continued in Volume Five

Afterword

Glad to see you all again!
We're now in the fourth volume of *Demon from Afar*!
It's moving quickly...so please hang on tight and
don't fall off!

The story wound up revolving around Toa more than
expected, and she's become something of a heroine...
It occurs to me now that maybe I should've given her
a better name.

The character named Ai in volume three actually
should've been named Ran...the kanji for her name is
the Ran from Garan! So please fix it in your mind.

It won't be much longer until the story reaches its
climax...stay tuned!

Kaori Yuki

Official site: UnDER GARDEN
http://www.yukikaori.jp
Twitter:@angelaid

Translation Notes

COMMON HONORIFICS:

no honorific: Indicates familiarity or closeness; if used without permission or reason, addressing someone in this manner would constitute an insult.

-san: The Japanese equivalent of Mr./Mrs./Miss. If a situation calls for politeness, this is the fail-safe honorific.

-sama: Conveys great respect; may also indicate that the social status of the speaker is lower than that of the addressee.

-kun: Used most often when referring to boys, this indicates affection or familiarity. Occasionally used by older men among their peers, but it may also be used by anyone referring to a person of lower standing.

-chan: An affectionate honorific indicating familiarity used mostly in reference to girls; also used in reference to cute persons or animals of either gender.

-shi: An honorific used in formal writing and occasionally formal speech, often reserved for people known from academic journals, legal documents, and other formal publications.

In Volume 3, the character named Ran Uryuu was originally introduced as Ai Uryuu. By request of the author, the change was able to be implemented for the English editions of *Demon From Afar*.

PAGE 65
A *senpai* is someone senior to you at a school, job, or other group or institution. A *kouhai* is someone junior to you.

PAGE 76
UMA: Unidentified Mysterious Animal

DEMON
FROM
AFAR

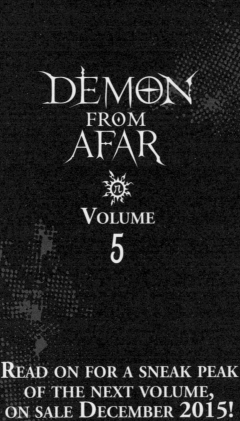

DEMON
FROM
AFAR

VOLUME
5

READ ON FOR A SNEAK PEAK
OF THE NEXT VOLUME,
ON SALE DECEMBER 2015!

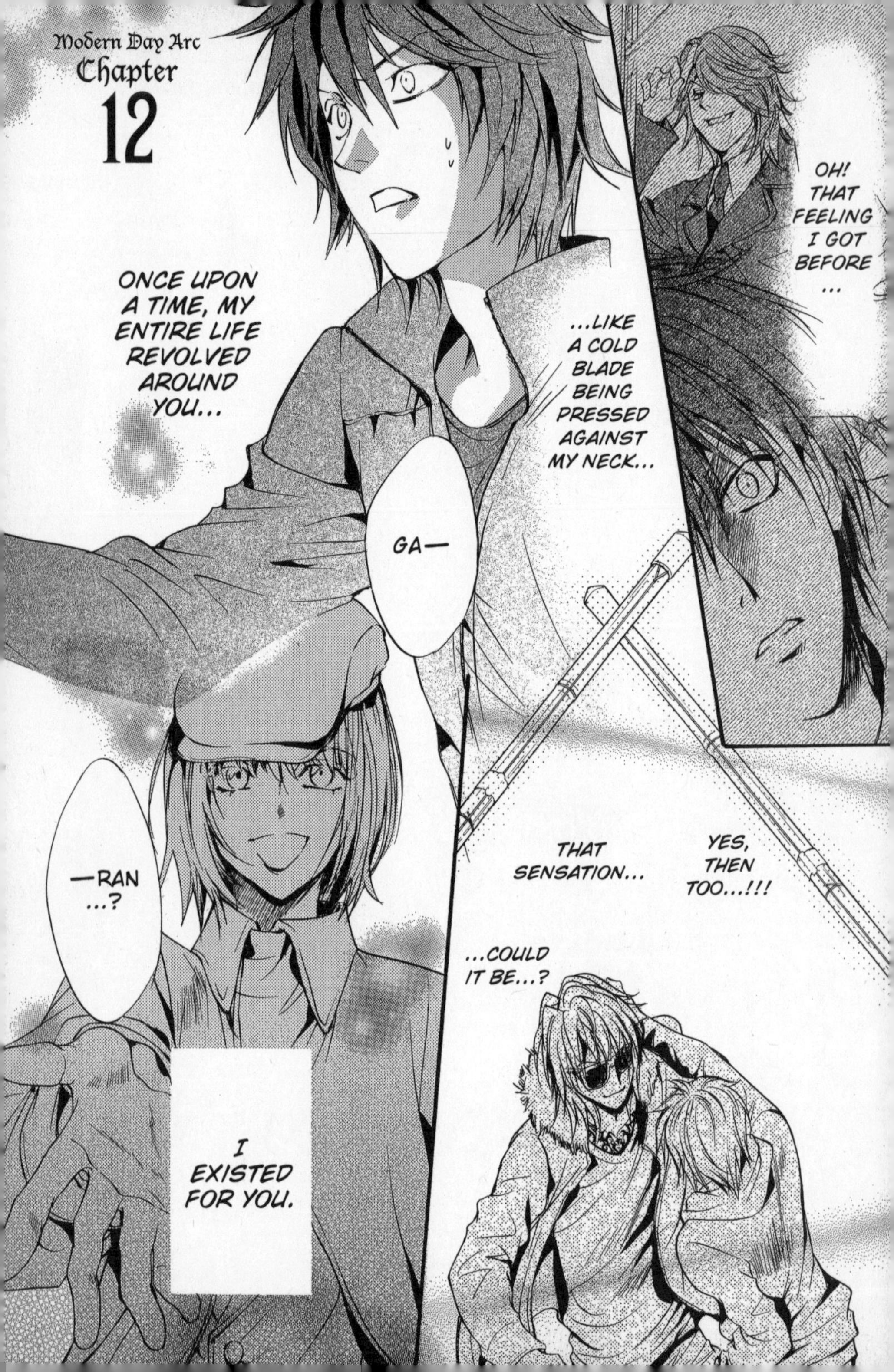
OH! THAT FEELING I GOT BEFORE ...
...LIKE A COLD BLADE BEING PRESSED AGAINST MY NECK...
YES, THEN TOO...!!!
THAT SENSATION...
...COULD IT BE...?
Modern Day Arc
Chapter
12
ONCE UPON A TIME, MY ENTIRE LIFE REVOLVED AROUND YOU...
GA—
—RAN ...?
I EXISTED FOR YOU.

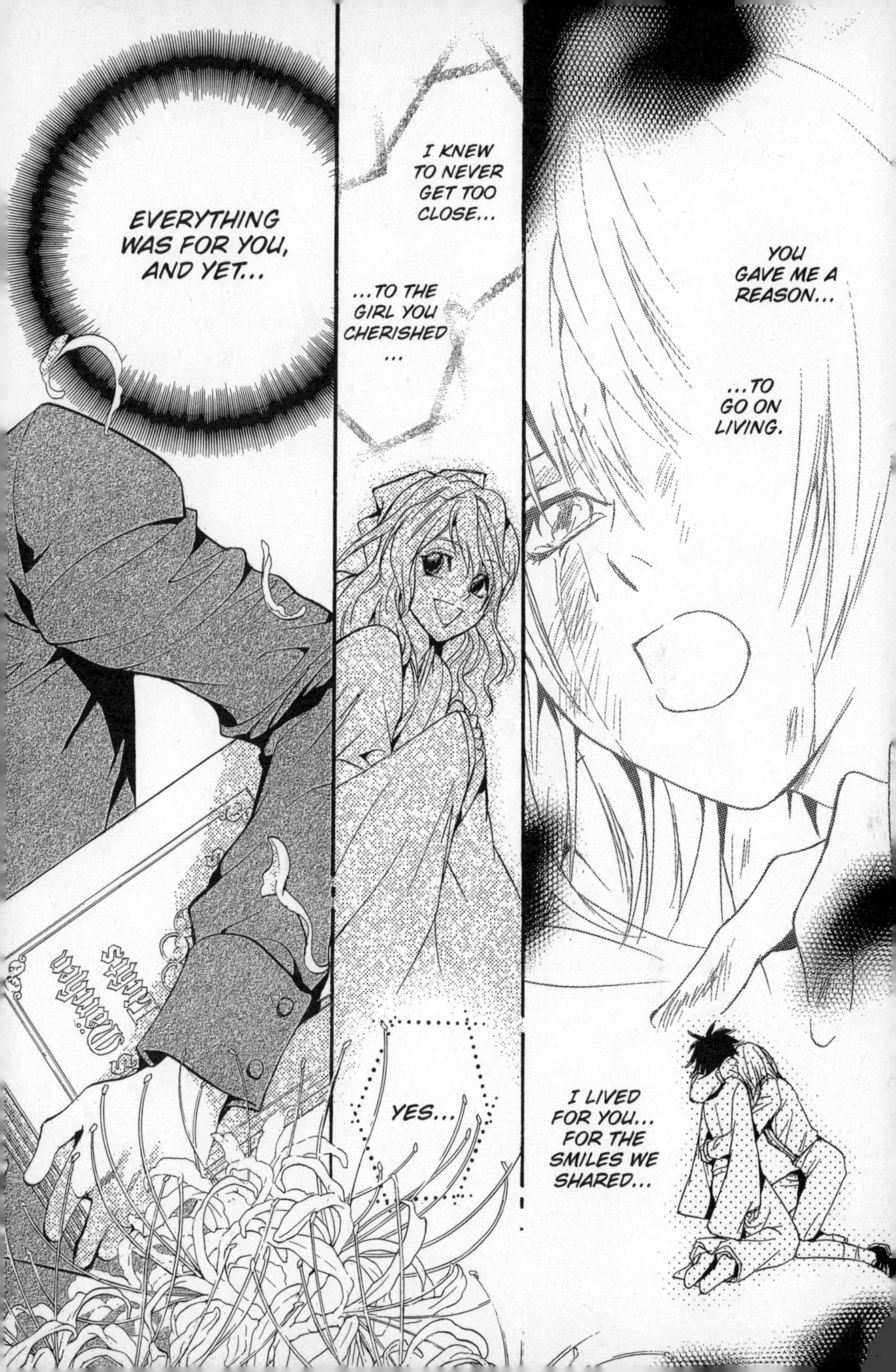
YOU GAVE ME A REASON...
...TO GO ON LIVING.
I LIVED FOR YOU... FOR THE SMILES WE SHARED...
I KNEW TO NEVER GET TOO CLOSE...
...TO THE GIRL YOU CHERISHED ...
YES...
EVERYTHING WAS FOR YOU, AND YET...

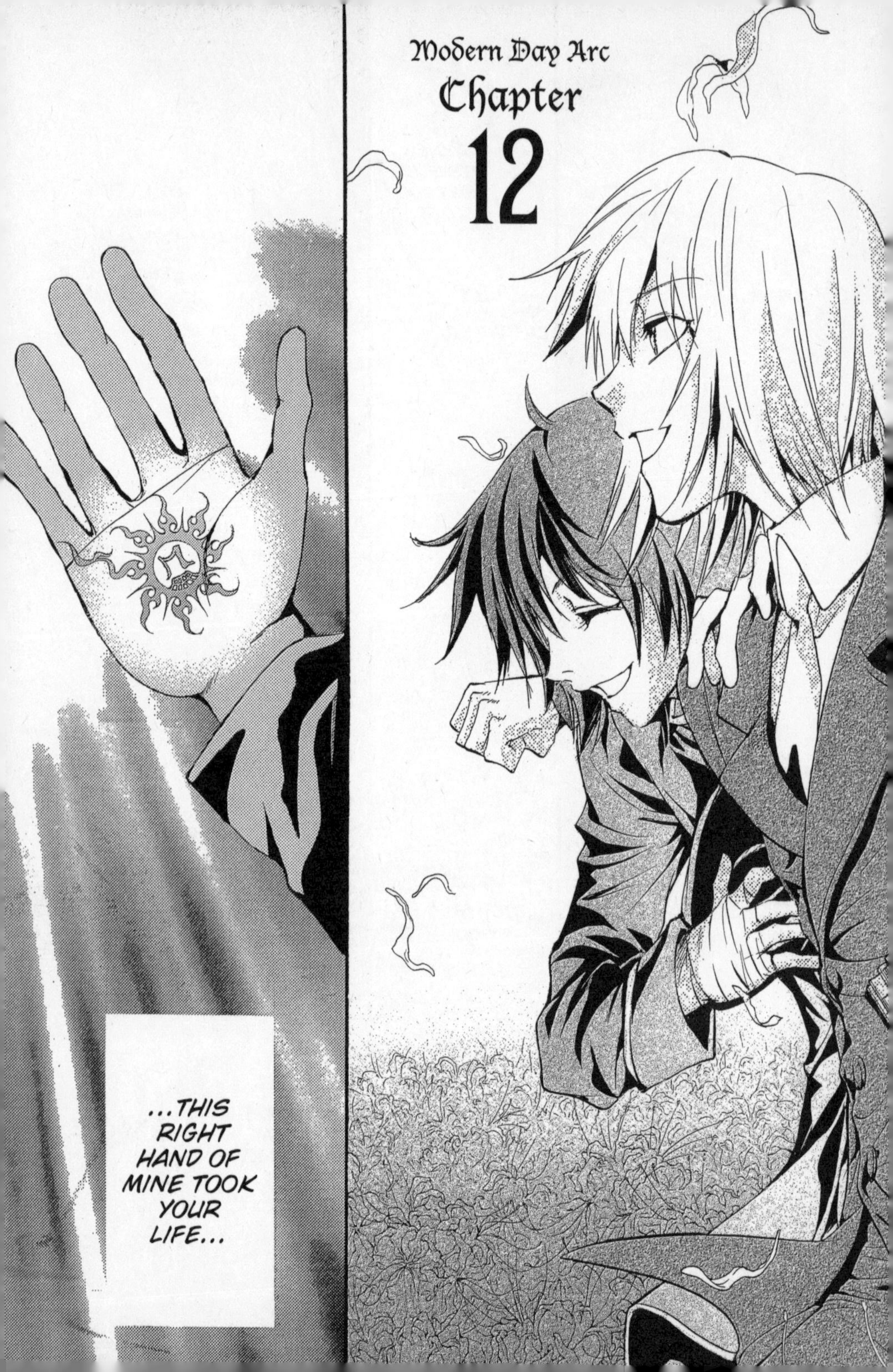
Modern Day Arc
Chapter
12
...THIS RIGHT HAND OF MINE TOOK YOUR LIFE...

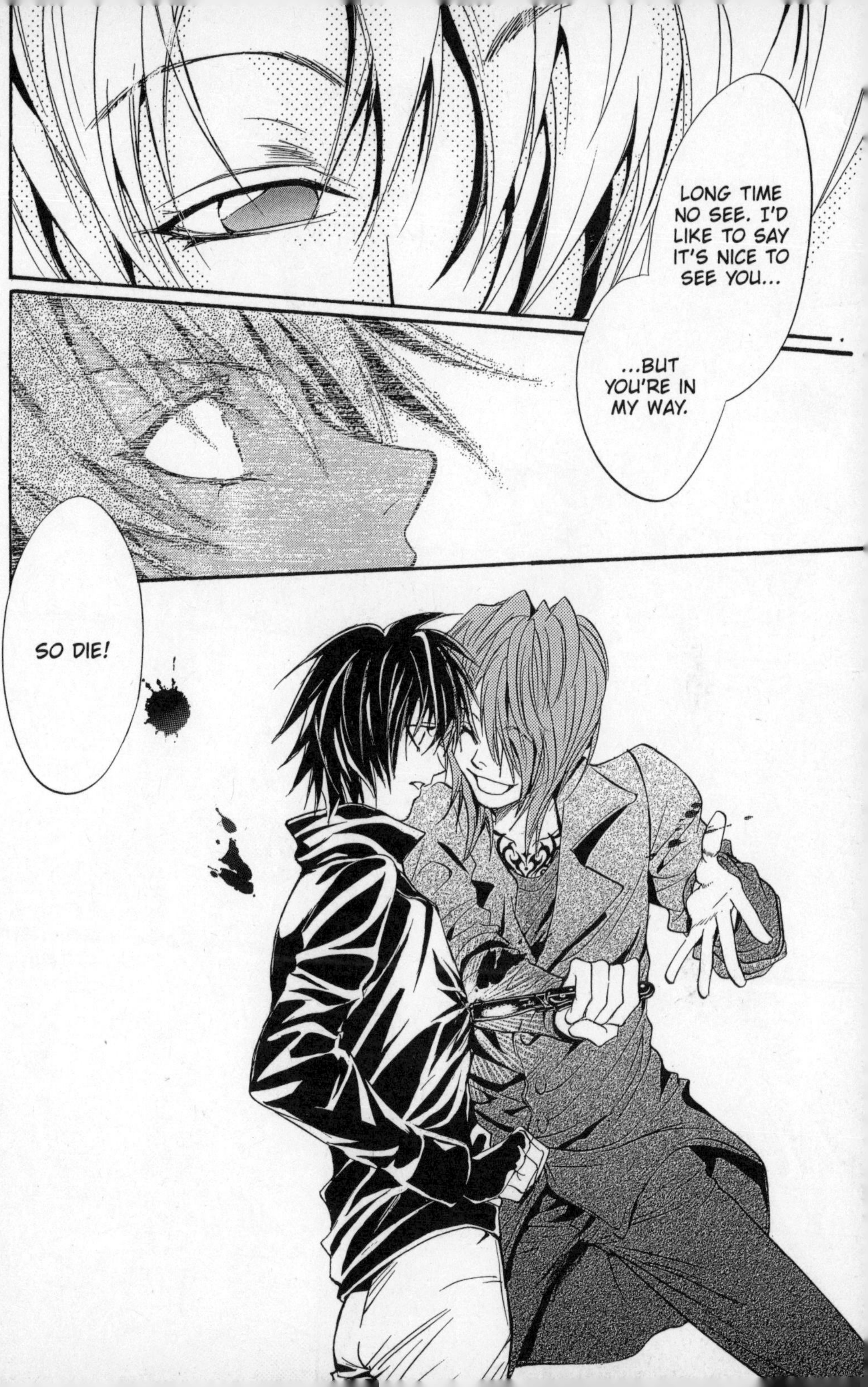
LONG TIME NO SEE. I'D LIKE TO SAY IT'S NICE TO SEE YOU...
...BUT YOU'RE IN MY WAY.
SO DIE!

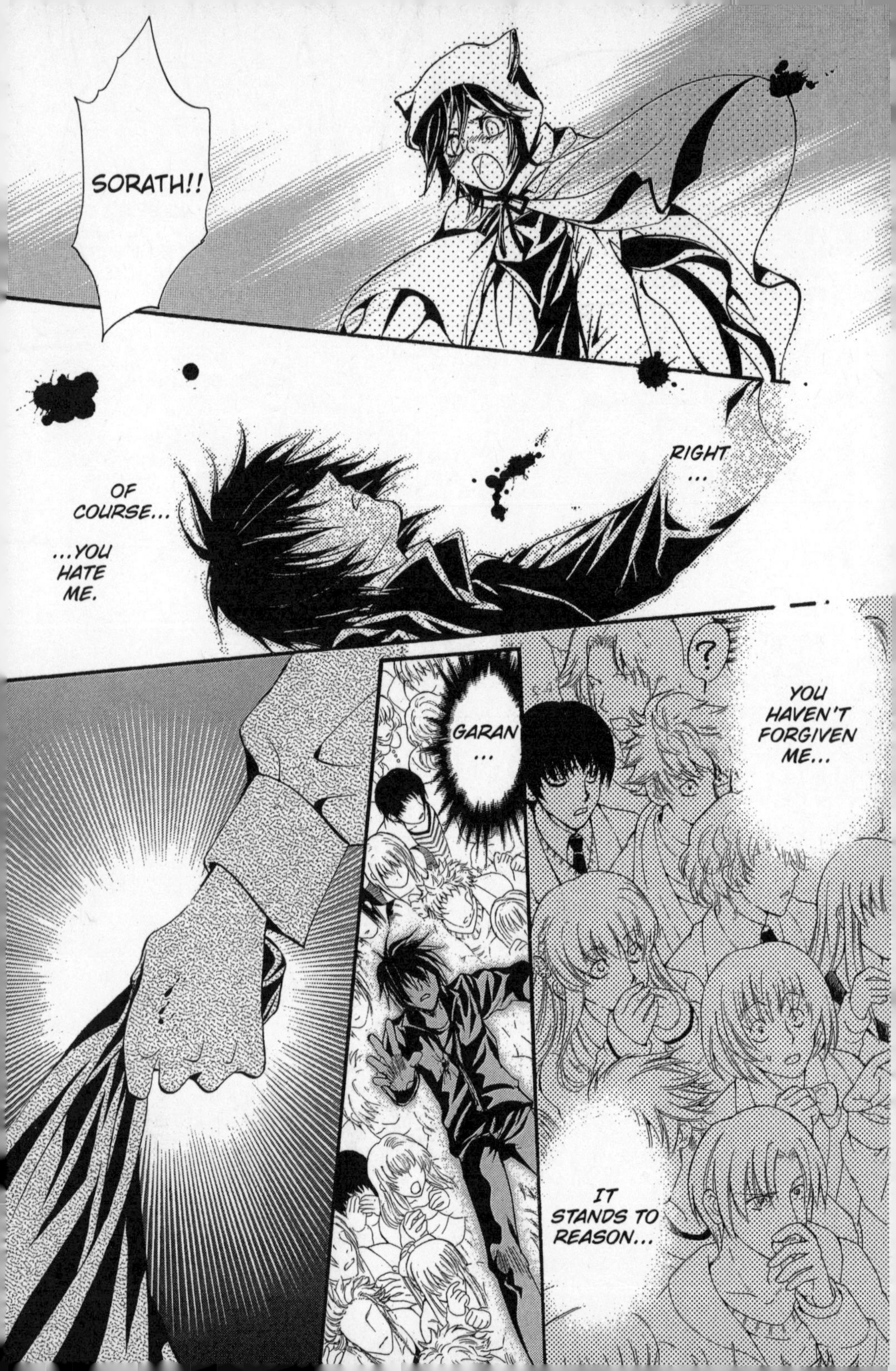
SORATH!!
RIGHT...
OF COURSE...
...YOU HATE ME.
?
YOU HAVEN'T FORGIVEN ME...
IT STANDS TO REASON...
GARAN...

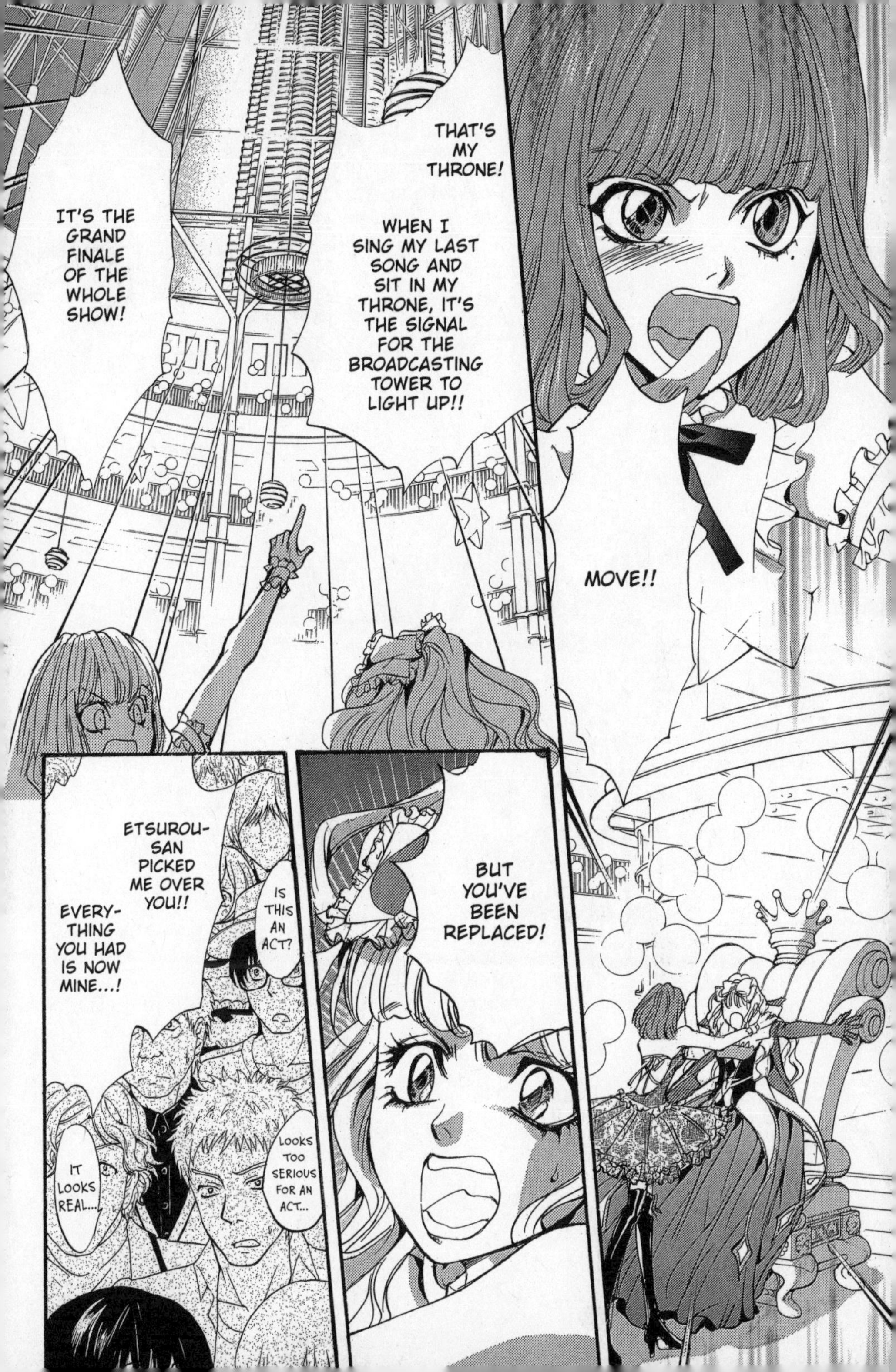
MOVE!!
THAT'S MY THRONE!
WHEN I SING MY LAST SONG AND SIT IN MY THRONE, IT'S THE SIGNAL FOR THE BROADCASTING TOWER TO LIGHT UP!!
IT'S THE GRAND FINALE OF THE WHOLE SHOW!
BUT YOU'VE BEEN REPLACED!
ETSUROU-SAN PICKED ME OVER YOU!!
IS THIS AN ACT?
EVERY-THING YOU HAD IS NOW MINE...!
LOOKS TOO SERIOUS FOR AN ACT...
IT LOOKS REAL...